T0284968

Things in Poems

EDITED BY JOSEF HRDLIČKA AND MARIANA MACHOVÁ

CHARLES UNIVERSITY
KAROLINUM PRESS 2022

Karolinum Press is a publishing department of Charles University
Ovocný trh 560/5, 116 36 Prague 1, Czech Republic
www.karolinum.cz
© Edited by Josef Hrdlička, Mariana Machová, 2022
Translation © Václav Z J Pinkava (texts by M. Collot, J. Hankiewicz, A. Hiltsch, J. Hrdlička,
J. Koblížková Wittlichová, K. Korchagin, P. Novotný, A. Stašková, J. Typlt, J. Vojvodík)

© Illustrations by Alois Nožička, 2022
© Cover illustration by Marie Blabolilová
Language supervision by Julia Bailey
Layout by Filip Blažek (designiq)
Set and printed in the Czech Republic by Karolinum Press
First English edition

A catalogue record for this book is available from the National Library of the Czech Republic.

This book is published as an output of the Charles University (Faculty of Arts) research programme
Progres Q12: Literature and Performativity.

This work was supported by the European Regional Development Fund project
"Creativity and Adaptability as Conditions of the Success of Europe in an Interrelated World"
(reg. no.: CZ.02.1.01/0.0/0.0/16_019/0000734).

ISBN 978-80-246-4939-9
ISBN 978-80-246-4940-5 (pdf)
ISBN 978-80-246-5030-2 (epub)
ISBN 978-80-246-5031-9 (mobi)

The original manuscript was reviewed by Michal Jareš, Institute of Czech Literature of the CAS,
and Záviš Šuman, Charles University, Prague.

Content

Introduction:
Things in Words[1]

JOSEF HRDLIČKA

The concept of the *Dinggedicht*, typically referred to in English as the "thing poem" or "object poem," was first brought into the debate about poetry by Kurt Oppert in the early twentieth century (Oppert 1926), as many of this book's authors remind us. In doing so, he managed to capture trends that went beyond the German-language poetry he was writing about, while also setting out a theme of some significance in modern poetry. Things – and let us note that, in a broader sense, the notion of a thing can encompass various entities, including living ones – have been appearing in poems since earliest times. At the very beginning of the Western poetic tradition as we know it today, we find the shield of Achilles, described in book 18 of Homer's *Iliad*, which Bill Brown (2015, 1) refers to as "Western literature's most magnificent object." Poets and dramatizers return to it again and again, and as Karel Thein points out in the opening chapter, for Homer this is certainly not just a simple description of an object, but a depiction creating an object through a process of *material imagination*. Homer's portrayal of the shield is a work of oral poetry, and in this respect, we may well draw a parallel between the workmanship of Hephaestus and that of the rhapsode, recounting the poem of the shield's creation to the audience. Unlike most subsequent objects in poetry, the shield of Achilles is primarily evoked through the medium of sound and the spoken word.

---

1   I have drawn a number of the ideas in this introduction from the PhD thesis being written by Jakub Hankiewicz and from our discussions about it, as well as conversations with other authors contributing to this book.

The somewhat later entry of the written word onto the ancient Greek stage brings a new element to the interplay of media and objects. In Greece, script was initially regarded in terms of voice. As E. Havelock (1977, 374–75) points out, the earliest preserved inscriptions, themselves found on objects, are formulated as the spoken words of the particular object that bears the writing – so that the mediating modality is not paper or papyrus, but the voice of the object. What we would today call the rhetorical trope (*prosopopoeia*) that lends voice to inanimate things, is, from the standpoint of an oral culture, much closer to our natural perception: writing is perceived as a spoken language, whose vehicle is the voice of a living being, not its material medium (clay tablets, stone, or papyrus). Many records of this form of expression have been documented in ancient inscriptions on earthenware and stones, often on tombstones, with the added complication that the writing here generally does not speak for the object, but is a would-be pronouncement by the deceased.

Thus, antiquity opens up a polymorphic media constellation, where we find poems that portray objects in different ways through verbal utterance (typically ekphrastic poems), objects that "speak," and in Hellenistic times also the first pictorial poems, which by their visual arrangement depict the object's shape. All three briefly outlined types of poetic treatments have their equivalents or continuations in modern and contemporary poetry. From the *technopaignia* of Simias of Rhodes (cf. Dencker 2011, 568–70), through Optatian's *carmina cancellata* (ibid., 623n)[2] and the medieval *carmina figurata*, through the baroque *Figurengedichte*, the lineage leads on to Apollinaire's calligrams and the visual poetry of the twentieth and twenty-first centuries.[3] Prosopopoeia appears as an element of the first type of poem and a similar, although more complicated, figure of animation of an object can have an unexpected effect, as in Rilke's poem "Archaïscher Torso Apollos" (The Archaic Torso of Apollo). In the twentieth century, an important role is played by the poetics of fictional epitaphs and inscriptions on stones, in the works of, among others, Edgar Lee Masters (*Spoonriver Anthology* 1915), or a few years earlier, in Victor Segalen's *Stèles* (1912), and later by, for example, Yves Bonnefoy in his collection entitled *Pierre écrite* (more loosely titled in English as *Words in Stone* [1965]). In his collection,

---

2   See Michael Squire's chapter on the topic.
3   See Dalia Satkauskytė's chapter on the role of visual poems in Lithuanian poetry of things and
       Julie Koblížková Wittlichová's chapter on things and thingness in the visual poetry of the twen-
       tieth and twenty-first centuries.

Segalen touches on an aspect also picked up by other poets in the early twentieth century. At the heart of his book are poems supposedly inscribed on stelae,
which, whilst not making a reference to these commemorative inscription-bear-
ing stones as such, do hint at their presence, as an imaginary framework. Yet
in his foreword, Segalen posits that these objects are both proffering their messages and defying to be read. He introduces to the very heart of the collection
a strange tension – between what is written and what lies beyond its reach:

> They disdain being read. They do not call for voice or music. They
> have contempt for the changing tones & syllables from the provinces
> that may happen to travesty them. They do not express; they mean;
> they are.
>
> (Segalen 2007, 61)

For the purposes of our endeavour, which includes reflecting on how things
speak in poems, it is not without interest that Segalen wrote *Stèles* while he was
in China, and devoted himself with great earnestness to the study of ancient
Chinese culture.

Pavel Novotný, in his chapter on modern poems, notes yet another approach
in analysing the media possibilities of an object poem, and shows how its theme
(a particular thing) can simultaneously be reflected in the structure of a poem,
as with Enzensberger, whose poem keeps balance between the expressed
content and the object, while the even more radical Artmann poem represents
more a "poem-object".

The central poet of Oppert's text is Rilke, and his collections *Neue Gedichte*
(New Poems; 1907) and *Der Neuen Gedichte anderer Teil* (New Poems: The
Other Part; 1908). Rilke produced both these collections at a time when philosophy and sociology were similarly inclined. At that time, Edmund Husserl
was putting forward his phenomenology programme, with his famous motto
about a return to the "things themselves," and the poetry of the era was turning
away from fast-fading Symbolism towards things in their own right. The poems
of Williams, and Pound's "imagist" thesis, according to which everything in the
poem is to serve the "treatment of the 'thing'" (Pound 1968, 3), are only a little
more recent. In his study on the "elusiveness of things" (2010),[4] William Waters

---

4   Its translation was published in the Czech version of this book.

shows how things in Rilke's works elude being directly grasped. The language of
the poem reveals its own materiality and does not allow us to perceive a thing
only as an illusion created by a poem. The reader is continually drawn into
a game between the presence of language and the presence of what the language
is evoking. This is quite different from the early Enlightenment-era poems of
Brockes, in which things serve their given purpose (to reveal God's creation)
and the thought-provoking language of the poem is intended to be lucid and
transparent.

Some of Rilke's work with language and the depiction of things foreshadows
elements of Baudelaire in his famous poem "Une Charogne" (A Carcass), which
Rilke credited with enabling the progression to factual testimony. "I could not
but think that without this poem, the whole trend toward 'telling it like it is,'
which we now presume to find in Cézanne, could not have started" ("Entwick-
lung zum sachlichen Sagen," "Letters on Cézanne," 19 October 1907, in Rilke
1996, 624). Baudelaire's poem seems at first glance to be an allegory in which
the woman addressee is, with apparent irony, likened to the cadaver she will
one day resemble. In several respects, Baudelaire upsets the convention of allegorical poems, which is found in pure form in his "L'Albatros" (The Albatross),
for example. The poem is not divided into two clear planes, but is presented
as a recollection of his encounter with a carcass, the narrative being more in
the past tense than the present, so characteristic of allegory; and, above all, the
depiction of the dead creature takes up the greater part of the poem, and in its
detail and suggestiveness breaks out of the figurative mould of allegory. Rilke
later consistently deconstructs the clear poetic figures and conventions of then
already waning Symbolism, and gives things (and beings) some basic autonomy in his poems – as if they were an other that a poem could touch upon but
never grasp. Here one might consider the similarity with Heidegger's distinction between an object (*Gegenstand*) and a thing (*Ding*), from his lecture "Das
Ding" (The Thing), in which a thing merely opens up more questions about its
"thingness" and eludes a whole gamut of simple answers. In *Der Ursprung des
Kunstwerkes* (The Origin of the Work of Art), Heidegger points out the thingness of a thing as seen through a work of art, using the well-known example of
Van Gogh's painting of shoes. As he puts it, the artwork reveals "what the equipment, the pair of peasant shoes, *is* in truth" (Heidegger 1993, 161). Yet it could be
said that Van Gogh's painting points out the difference between an object and
a thing, rather than revealing the thing as such. It presupposes a certain motion

of reflection, reminding us that the thing does not surrender itself to our grasp and stays hidden behind its object-based purpose and instrumentality.

In this book, we give some examples of the early poetics of things, when objects appear as stand-ins for something else, but at the same time keep their particular and detailed essence, their "thingness" – whether we look at the symbolic practices of Chinese poetry, based on the notion of a correspondence of all things as part of a universality unified by a shared order and vital energy; or the works of early German Enlightenment poet Barthold Heinrich Brockes. But even here we are not dealing with the purely functional use of objects. The earlier poets seem to get carried away with them, and their flourishes of description are foreshadowing how things will be breaking free of the figurative plane towards their autonomy, culminating with Baudelaire, Rilke, and others in European poetry. One stage in this movement is characterized by European Symbolism. Writers such as Jean Moréas, in his manifesto *Le Symbolisme* (Symbolism), follow up on the distinction between allegory and symbol that derives from Goethe and Romantic aesthetics (cf. Todorov 1985, 235–60). Seen from this perspective, in allegory the object stands for something else, while as a symbol it keeps its factual worth, even though in Symbolism it is the idea embodied in the symbol that prevails. One consequence of such a view is uncertainty about the significance of things, which an allegory can grasp unequivocally, as well as marking the beginnings of their elusive autonomy. It is well expressed by the characteristic inversion in the lines of Czech symbolist Otokar Březina, written in 1899: "Ve tmách symboly věcí / mlčenlivé" ("In the dark, symbols of things / silence-keeping" [Březina 1958, 179]). A quite blunt shift of emphasis from figurative meaning of the thing to the thing itself can be seen in the text of Ezra Pound (1917), which redirects Moréas' take on the symbol back to the thing:

> I believe that the proper and perfect symbol is the natural object, that if a man uses "symbols," he must so use them that their symbolic function does not obtrude; so that *a* sense, and the poetic quality of the passage, is not lost to those who do not understand the symbol as such, to whom, for instance, a hawk is a hawk.
>
> (Pound 1968, 9)

Pound's statement clearly reveals the fundamental contradiction of this distinction, in which the symbol, as a trope or poetic figure, stands contrary to the object as a thing in the world. A similar shift from Symbolism to the specificity of things – both from the point of view of tradition and in the intimate domain of, in this case, the kitchen – can be seen with Osip Mandelstam, whose work is discussed by Anne Hultsch.

Siding with things – if we can so name this motive force in the history of poetry, a move which took place sometime in the early twentieth century – means that things have definitely come out of the repertoire of tropes and figures, have ceased to be poetic instruments, and poems have turned attention to them in their own right. This step opens up a new horizon, in which things can continue to serve us, no longer as a poetic prop, but with the aim of their own depiction, and in relation to the human. Rilke's poetry is not here to illustrate a historical tipping point, but a distinguished example, akin to Heidegger's philosophy, which marks the ascent of the thing to autonomy – attained by virtue of its very elusiveness. The poetry which was to follow in the latter twentieth century seems to have been surveying this new field and asking how variously things could be approached. Somewhere on the border between such autonomy and utility stands a landmark Czech poem "Věci" (Things) by Jiří Wolker, from 1920. When we speak of things in Czech poetry, most Czech readers will be reminded of the opening line:

> Miluji věci, mlčenlivé soudruhy,
> protože všichni nakládají s nimi,
> jako by nežily,
> a ony zatím žijí a dívají se na nás
> jak věrní psi pohledy soustředěnými
> a trpí,
> že žádný člověk k nim nepromluví.
> Ostýchají se první dát do řeči,
> mlčí, čekají, mlčí
> a přeci
> tolik by chtěly trochu si porozprávět!
>
> Proto milují věci
> a také milují celý svět.

(Wolker 1953, 44)

> I love things, silent comrades,
> because everyone treats them
> as if they were not alive,
> and yet they do live and do watch us
> like faithful dogs do with attentive looks
> and suffer,
> because nobody talks to them.
> They're too timid to be the first to speak,
> they keep silent, waiting, silent
> and still
> they would so like to have a little chat!
>
> That's why I love things
> and love the whole world, too.

The consciously naively conceived poem has its subtlety, hidden even in the Czech word for comrade (*soudruh* – literally, fellow-companion). While it has a history linked with the communist movement, it has its rightful Czech etymology, in which the prefix *sou-* corresponds to the word meaning "together." Wolker, on the one hand, seemingly unjustifiably personifies things and puts them in the subordinate role of faithfully accompanying man; but on the other, he accurately describes the pitfalls of the relationship between people and Things, that voicelessness instead of language that would try to get a grasp on things. Moreover, he foreshadows the theme of the social life of things, which cannot be cut loose of human life in any way.

The long history of things in Western poetry could then be characterized as attempts at dialogue with things, the difficulty of which we are reminded by Wolker. Yet many subsequent poets were fully aware that personification is a dead end if we seek to touch the "secret" of things. Dialogue with things cannot take the form of a two-*person* conversation; rather it is a search for a form of speech that can "address" things in their autonomy and open up to their "response," which is unavoidably beyond verbal expression. Francis Ponge's objective lyricism, as written about by Michel Collot, can be understood precisely as such a ceaseless addressing of things. A particularly remarkable chapter here is on post-war Polish poetry, in which things have become a central theme. Poets such as Miron Białoszewski and Zbigniew Herbert, as Jakub Hankiewicz writes, were developing dialogic strategies from quite different sides, in order to get closer to things. We find another approach to entering into a dialogue with things in Jaromír Typlt's chapter on things in post-war Czech Surrealism. Leaving aside the surrealist conception of the object, which would merit its own treatise, in this chapter we see an unusual shift typical of late Surrealism in Czech poetry; Typlt characterizes it with the word "brazenness" – as though in these texts the things themselves were demanding to be heard and were actively breaking out of the confines of their graspable object purpose and relevance, as opposed to the person, who is merely passively reacting.

Many of the poems cited here focus on one or a very few specific things, and do not turn their attention to the "social life of things," written about by Arjun Appadurai and Bill Brown. Heidegger's concept of readiness-to-hand (*Zuhandensein*) well describes the fact that some things are within easy reach; but less well does it acknowledge just how fundamentally not only our hand, but indeed the entire human body is dependent on things. The human palm is open to things, and it is just when things are lacking that the social connection of man and things also becomes glaring. Poets like Günter Eich very accurately show this state of "material shortage" or need. Another oft concealed side of things arises in relation to architecture, which shapes our human space but at the same time has its object-minded side, as Josef Vojvodík shows by means of the poems of Czech poet Milada Součková, who lived in exile in America from 1948 onwards.

A late turn in this long "dialogue" with things is characterized by the term "hyperobject," coined by English philosopher Timothy Morton. This is taken up by Justin Quinn in a chapter devoted to Paul Muldoon's poems. Within the hyperobject concept, it is things that gain the upper hand in their own way, and a human being or the human body finds itself in a position where various aspects of objects beyond human graspability are revealed. This poetry shows a person's entanglement with things that subordinate his ostensibly central position. If we come back to our initial media-borne constellation of things in relation to language, the beginning of the poem by Slovak author Ivan Štrpka opens up a complex inversion where the writing speaks and a person is the object displayed, framing another object:

„Nevideli ste ma?" pýta sa nápis náhlivou detskou rukou sotva čitateľne načmáraný pod fotografiou vážne strateného dievčatka s akýmsi vážnym, neurčito odpudivým, nechutne premúdrelým zvieratkom v nešikovnom náručí.

(Štrpka 2016, 16)

"Have you seen me?" is the question posed by the inscription written in a hurried and barely legible child's scrawl under a photograph of a lost girl holding some kind of sombre, vaguely repulsive, objectionably smug-looking animal in her gawky embrace.

The Projected Heart: Ekphrasis, Material Imagination, and the Shield of Achilles

KAREL THEIN

In contrast to the narrow definition of *ekphrasis* as "the verbal representation of visual representation" (Heffernan 1993, 3);[1] the recent understanding of ekphrastic practice has moved, quite decisively, beyond a simple polarity of the verbal and the visual. As a result, ekphrastic creations appear to us as complex products of embodied imagination, which lends them an agency and animation. If these are culturally determined, they are also embedded in the reader's or listener's physical activity, which cannot be reduced to abstract meanings. To speak of ekphrastic life is therefore not just a metaphor, and if we cannot offer an exact definition of such a life, this uncertainty only echoes the equivocation of the term "life" in any context. In the following pages, I will assume that ekphrastic life is instantiated in what I call "material imagination." I do *not* use this term in Gaston Bachelard's sense of the allegedly original connection of imagination to the power of the four elements;[2] but rather to express the nexus of hands, heart, and voice, which all play a role in the birth of the paradigmatic

---

1   In what follows, the references are limited and incomplete, since I prefer to preserve, as much as possible, the format of a conference talk. For a sample of the enlarged field of ekphrastic cum art historical studies, see, e.g., Männlein-Robert 2007; Squire 2009; Elsner 2010; Morales 2011; Squire and Elsner 2016; Platt and Squire 2018.

2   Illustrative of this conception is Bachelard 2002. His chapter on "the dynamic lyricism of the blacksmith," which would seem close to our subject, deals only with modern texts and shifts the figure of Hephaestus-Vulcan to the background.

ekphrastic thing – the shield of Achilles forged by Hephaestus in Book 18 of Homer's *Iliad*.

Before addressing the circumstances of this shield's forging, and lacking the space to do justice to the long history of its interpretations, I take my first and direct cue from its recent revisionary reading in Bill Brown's book *Other Things*, whose opening sentence states that "Western literature's most magnificent object, Achilles' Shield, enacts a drama of animate matter" (Brown 2015, 1). I start with this quotation since Bill Brown's take on the shield of Achilles epitomizes the shift in emphasis towards the material aspects of ancient practices, which resist any clean-cut distinction between words, images, and things. Of these practices, there are innumerable examples, including those that engage the Homeric shield by engrafting it into other texts and visual artefacts.[3] In this large context, my necessarily modest aim is to demonstrate which qualities of the "original" shield of Achilles invite these treatments, which then become, in their turn, an integral part of its afterlife. I will elaborate upon the expression "a drama of animate matter" by focusing on the matter of the ekphrastic shield and in what sense this matter is animate. At the same time, I hope to indicate how this animation takes advantage of the ontological instability shared by artefacts and images.

Prior to turning to ancient texts, I wish to pause for a moment to consider the way in which Bill Brown brings out the animate character of the shield as created by Homer. Focusing on the life that awakens in the molded matter, he quotes a number of lines that explicitly describe how the crafted figures themselves take on the motions that originate in the god's manual labour. Lines 573 to 578 are an excellent example:

> The *artisan made next* a herd of longhorns,
> *fashioned in gold and tin*: away they shambled,
> lowing, from byre to pasture by a stream
> that sang in ripples, and by reeds a-sway.
> Four cowherds *all of gold* were plodding after
> With nine little dogs beside them.
>
> (*Iliad*, 18.573–78, trans. Robert Fitzgerald, Bill Brown's emphasis)

---

3 The most striking example is probably the shield of Achilles reincarnated on the Roman *Iliadic Tablets*. Regarding the latter, see Squire 2011.

The quotation of these lines immediately precedes the paragraph in which Bill Brown summarizes the task of taking the ekphrastic animation beyond a mere metaphor, and towards the more delicate but perhaps more original realm, where life meets artifice. Here is the paragraph in question:

> The poem repeatedly clarifies that Achilles' Shield is at once a static object and a living thing, just as it marks and celebrates the phantas-magoric oscillation among forms and materials: the furrowed earth behind the plowmen may be "black," but it is also "gold,/all gold – a wonder of the artist's craft" (18.631–33). Homer's distribution of vitality extends beyond the immortal and the mortal – to the arti-factual. This "wonder of the artist's craft" would seem to insist, then, on a kind of indeterminate ontology, in which the being of the object world cannot so readily be distinguished from the being of animals, say, or the being we call human being.
>
> (Brown 2015, 2)

Here we touch upon the question, debated already by ancient scholiasts, of where exactly the motion and sound take place: in the audience's mind or on the shield's surface?[4] This antithesis, however, is surmounted by the ekphrastic perspective, which relies on a sort of imaginative density, whose vitality embod-ies a perfect continuity between the described forging of the metal figures and the motion of imagining that espouses this forging. Hence the crucial insight: that "Homer's distribution of vitality" implies "a kind of indeterminate ontol-ogy." This insight leads to the suggestion that Homer is not aiming to under-mine the opposition between linguistic and pictorial media, but intends rather to destabilize "the opposition between the organic and inorganic, the vibrant and the inert" (ibid., 3). Here, we can safely assume that the quoted lines, and the whole shield of Achilles, undermine both of these oppositions; and that, in both cases, they rely on the least determinate and most ambivalent capacity of human mind, namely imagination. At this point a caveat is in order: I will use this term and talk about the corresponding capacity against the background of

---

4   On whether Hephaestus' figures, and not only those on the shield, can – and should – be taken as literally animate, see the texts quoted and commented upon in Cullhed 2014, 214–17. On the metals in the quoted lines, see Dubel 2006, 169–70, and also Becker 1995, 140–41.

how it was understood by the ancients. Naturally, there is no exact termino-
logical equivalent to "imagination" in ancient texts, and the variety of Greek
and Roman views on *phantasia* and related matters is astonishing; but there
certainly is a widely shared consensus that imagination, in all its forms, necessarily entails material processes. Even Aristotle, who is the only philosopher
before late antiquity who claims that thinking *as such* is not a material process
or a motion, repeatedly emphasizes that human beings cannot think without
the support of imagination or *phantasia*, which supplies our minds with enmat-
tered forms (see *De anima* 3.7, 431a14–17; or *De memoria* 1, 449b30–450a5).

I will therefore comfortably assume that imagination is a specific aspect of
the matter's animation that occurs in our bodies, and more exactly in our bloodstream, that brings mental images from our chest to our head. This understanding implies a question that may strike one as naive – but we must not forget
that we are chasing the "indeterminate ontology" of the shield of Achilles, and
there is no ontology without the issue of location. My leading question concerns therefore the location of imagination as an inherently animating activity
and, by extension, the location of animate mental images. The advantage of this
double question is that it leads directly to Homer's account of how the shield
of Achilles came to be. Obviously, this account offers no theory of imagination,
but it anticipates several theories of the classical and Hellenistic periods, by
placing the imagination's activity in the body's central area: the chest.

On this account, it is the region around the heart that is the seat of higher
vital functions, emotional and cognitive alike. Hence the view of imagination
that is implied already in Homer, no matter how rudimentary it may be compared to the whole range of the later philosophical texts about imagining and
its physiological basis.[5] The key point of this view is the difference between the
physiology of imagination and its *phenomenology*. If we naturally imagine that
we imagine things in our head, this is because the brain, which is the cooling
organ, makes our blood cooler, thinner, and hence more transparent than it is
in the rest of the body. Cooling the blood, the brain transforms the inside of
our head into a screen (an IMAX of sorts) where our imaginations achieve an
equilibrium of vividness and clarity that they could never have reached in the

---

5   The cardiocentric scheme of thinking and imagining was much alive throughout antiquity.
     Aristotle and the Stoics are its best-known proponents. In contrast, its later and most influen-
     tial critic is Galen. For an introduction to this issue, see Tieleman 1996, 38–65; Tieleman 2002;
     Rocca 2003, 31–47.

turbulent and overflowing area of their origin. Mental images and all articulate thought, including poetry, originate in and around the heart, where the
blood is too hot and thick to allow for clear and distinct representations – the
heart is where we feel emotional, not where we feel that we think and imagine
things clearly. This mismatch between the turbulent place where thinking and
imagining originate, and the clarity of *certain* thoughts and imaginations, is then
further reinforced by the fact that once we start to think and imagine things
clearly, we leave behind all evident connection to the *location* of our thoughts
and imaginations. In this situation, does it still make sense to enquire *where
exactly* the shield of Achilles is, as a thing described and imagined? Is there even
some "where," let alone some "exactly," to speak of?

Starting with this last sub-question, I would suggest that there is no "exact"
location of the things as imagined; but there is an ontologically grey yet phe-
nomenally vivid and overall vibrant area where the ekphrastic shield grounds
an ever-expanding variety of different life forms. And if the borders of this area
seem rather fuzzy, it is also because Homer enjoys playing with the ontological
ambiguity of his great ekphrastic creation. However, even Homer starts *from
where* the ekphrastic shield is imagined while it is being created: he starts from
the chest of the divine artificer, Hephaestus.

It sounds trivial to remark that the creation of the shield of Achilles is the
outcome of the visit that Thetis, the hero's divine mother, pays to Hephaestus,
from whom she demands new armour for her son. Yet, from the ekphrastic
point of view, the whole *mise-en-scène* of this visit is no less intriguing than the
shield that will be described as both locally and ontologically contiguous with
the god's previous creations, whose most striking feature consists, already, in
them being internally animate material artefacts. It was rightly suggested that
the artefacts Thetis encounters in the house of Hephaestus form a series, with
a gradually increasing complexity corresponding to the life forms involved.[6]
The first "wonder to look at" (θαῦμα ἰδέσθαι) that she observes are golden
self-moving tripods (18.372–81); and it is while describing the construction
of these automata that the poet first uses the formula, as articulated in Lattimore's modern translation, that the god is at work "in his craftsmanship and

---

6   See Francis 2009, 8, on tripods as "mechanical servants" that "give the audience a foretaste of an
       even more dramatic set of the god's creations." Francis grasps well the gradation, so to speak,
       from tripods to maidens, as well as the latter's more general ekphrastic importance (on which
       see also below).

his cunning." The original formula, used by Homer several times to describe the power of Hephaestus' art, is ἰδυίῃσι πραπίδεσσι – which literally means that the god is at work "with his visionary diaphragm." I borrow this great translation from the examination of this dative (locative or instrumental) by Françoise Frontisi, who offers a detailed overview of the poetic uses of *prapides*, a noun that designates a vital region of the chest, with an emphasis on the circulation of blood that is necessary for both the sensible and intellectual activity. It is a power of seeing, understanding, and imagining that is active in the lower chest and, in its location and function, seems to be very close to *phrenes*.[7] I will spare you the philological detail, but it is important to quote Frontisi's conclusion: "The chest of Hephaestus, sweating and puffing, is a vast image box [*une vaste boîte à images*], the seat of his creative inspiration, the organ of what will be, much later, the imagination" (Frontisi-Ducroux 2002, 479).

The god's visionary diaphragm will reappear in Homer's account once Hephaestus is ready to start his forging of the ekphrastic shield. In the meantime, we are given to understand that the god's power to create life extends beyond the tripods, whose only observable behaviour consists in local self-motion. The complexity of artificial life increases with the appearance of the god's two attendants:

> These are golden, and in appearance like living young women [ζωῇσι
> νεήνισιν εἰοικυῖαι].
> There is intelligence in their hearts [τῆς ἐν μὲν νόος ἐστὶ μετὰ φρεσίν]
>   and there is speech in them
> and strength, and from the immortal gods they have learned how to
>   do things [ἀθανάτων δὲ θεῶν ἄπο ἔργα ἴσασιν].
>
>   (*Iliad*, 18.418–20, trans. Lattimore)

——

7   See Frontisi-Ducroux 2002. In contrast to *phrenes*, *prapides* is only used in poetry; it may relate to the diaphragm etymologically: see Sullivan 1988, 179–80 and 283–84. On *prapides* as the central place of thought, see also Padel 1992, 19–20. The formula ἰδυίῃσι πραπίδεσσι occurs in the *Iliad* five times, always to paint Hephaestus in his role of the supreme designer and craftsman. Three of these occurrences focus on his double capacity as the architect but also the builder of the Olympian dwellings of the gods (including his own); the fourth connects to the self-moving tripods; and the fifth, as we shall see, is reserved for the making of the shield of Achilles.

These creatures complete the progression from the unfinished tripods to beings whose form is human and divine in equal measure, and whose life can hardly be described as only simulated. They *have* intelligence and speech, and thus the capacity for learning. In fact, they look like trial runs for the more famous Pandora, who will receive a full ekphrastic treatment from another poet, Hesiod. Intriguingly, their only difference from "living young women" is a material one: they are golden. The metallic *and* intelligent appearance of these maidens is important because it alerts us to the far-reaching possibilities of divine animation. In the same vein, but more generally, it reminds us of the amazing variety of the origins of human (and other) beings in ancient texts. That humans have always existed, that they evolved naturally as the universe was formed, and that they were formed in various places by various divinities are all equally valid options, sometimes found in one and the same author, or even in one and the same text. As a result, there is no definitive division between a natural life and an artificial life, since the latter can give birth to the former: their causal stories can not only meet, but literally interbreed.[8] Still, this does not mean that all life unfolds on the same plane – indeed, Homer maintains an uncertainty about the golden creatures who are "in appearance like living young women." Does this expression mean that they *look as if* they were alive, or that they *are* alive and, moreover, *looking like* young women? The difference would be crucial, if only we were able to draw a definite line between the two options.[9]

With this situation in mind, we can finally turn to the shield that the god will produce, again "with his visionary diaphragm" (18.482). It is precisely this *production* – as opposed to an observation – that has been at the centre of modern discussions of the shield since Lessing. Instead of repeating the latter's

---

8   The unnatural genealogies of humankind comprise not only technical artifice (in Hesiod and others), but also various couplings between the mortals and the immortals. This testifies to the remarkable indifference, in ancient texts, towards a unified account of human origin. Among the emblematic texts are Plato's *Critias*, where the Athenians are crafted by Athena and Hephaestus, whereas the inhabitants of Atlantis are sexually engendered by Poseidon (the Athenians are superior since craft, for Plato, always trumps sex); or the first book of Ovid's *Metamorphoses*, where we count no less than four different origins of the human race. For more on different forms of mostly artificial life, see also Mayor 2018.

9   In the same way, Pandora is both a likeness of a virgin and a real virgin. Also, her diadem is decorated with crafted beasts "similar to living animals endowed with voice" (ζωοῖσιν ἐοικότα φωνήεσσιν) (Hesiod, *Theogony*, 584; trans G. W. Most modified); these beasts are exactly like the creatures on the shield of Achilles. On these aspects of Pandora, see Platt 2011, 111–13.

comments, we can point out that Homer's repeated emphasis on the shield's ongoing creation ("he forged," "on it he wrought," "then he made") maintains the feel of contiguity with Hephaestus' "image box." It is thanks to this contiguity that the ekphrastic shield progressively acquires its "thingness" – an expression used by Bill Brown in order to explain that the sustained material vitality of the shield will always be in excess of the ready-made and perceptible "object-hood" (see Brown 2015, 5). In the case of the shield of Achilles, this excess is also encoded in the subtle yet persistent tension between the brilliantly vivid evocation of a number of details in every particular scene and a striking lack of determination of the overall arrangement of the scenes on the shield; after all, Homer even avoids specifying the latter's physical shape. This lack is not due to a simple omission: it follows from the impossibility to imagine one thing that would coherently enclose all smaller things *including ourselves* as both its parts and its external beholders. With some difficulty, one may construct such a "one thing" theoretically, but Homer is not after theoretical cosmology. The opening lines of the shield, which establish the cosmic coordinates for what follows, are therefore less a true image of the cosmos than the invitation to espouse the motion of the god's imagination:

> He made the earth upon it, and the sky, and the sea's water,
> and the tireless sun, and the moon waxing into her fullness,
> and on it all the constellations that festoon the heavens,
> the Pleiades and the Hyades and the strength of Orion
> and the Bear, whom men give also the name of the Wagon,
> who turns about in a fixed place and looks at Orion
> and she alone is never plunged in the wash of the Ocean.
>
> (*Iliad*, 18.483–89, trans. Lattimore)

These lines do the same job as the title sequences of some movies or TV series (the title sequence of *Game of Thrones* is one notable example providing an introduction equivalent to Homer's shield of Achilles, including the forge, metals, and cities). In contrast to what will follow, these lines leave aside the shield's materiality and create instead a three-dimensional structure, a celestial vault that is in motion and apparently described in several stages of its diurnal and annual rotation. It is not a static image or a diagram, but a planetarium, a mobile structure that teases the imagination by superposing the skies of different seasons. On a smaller scale, this tension will be re-enacted in every subsequent image on the shield, with its moving crowds, processions, armies, herds, and the repeated evocations of the slowly turning cycle of the seasons. These motions will be exercised by precise, internally animate figures, whose exact positions at any given moment it is nevertheless impossible to determine. Relying on language and voice as its equally material parts, this ekphrasis constantly reshuffles the products of our imagination, which starts to spontaneously move around the figures on the shield in much the same way as our blood flows through our chest, carrying around "our" mental images.

These observations presuppose that we can understand ekphrasis as activity and, in the case of the Homeric shield, as an internally animate re-enactment of this shield's generation – a re-enactment that exceeds the limits of simple visualizing: imagination is also about the creation of images that are naturally suffused with language and offer more than that which can be properly seen. Its permeability to words makes ekphrasis inherently dialogical, at least insofar as language and thought share some basic structure: that which ekphrasis makes us visualize is not simply given, but constantly negotiated and renegotiated. The main ekphrastic interest of the shield lies therefore in the excess of its vividness over its clarity – an excess that Homer keeps projecting into the matter that is being forged and progressively animated by Hephaestus. It is this vividness that carries on from one scene to the next: if there is an overall narration to be extracted from the shield, it is only the narration of its formation.

This last point qualifies – or at least complements – the influential interpretation of the shield as an image of the whole cosmos. This interpretation can be traced back to Heraclitus "the Allegorist," whose *Homeric Problems* start from the assumption that, in his fabrication of arms,

> Homer has included the origin of the universe in a grand creative idea. In forging the Shield of Achilles as an image of the revolution of the cosmos, he has shown by clear evidences how the universe originated, who is its creator, and how its different parts were formed and separated.
>
> (*Homeric Problems*, 43.1–2; Russell and Konstan 2005)[10]

---

10   I quote Heraclitus the Allegorist from Russell and Konstan 2005. I leave aside the (not entirely certain) allegorization of the shield of Achilles by Crates of Mallos. For more on the shield as a cosmic emblem, see Hardie 1985 and Hardie 1986, 340–42.

This also implies that line 485, about "all the constellations that festoon the heavens," carries a precise scientific meaning: "In this, Homer particularly teaches us that the universe (*kosmos*) is spherical. For just as a garland is a circular adornment (*kosmos*) of the head, so too the objects which girdle the vault of heaven, scattered all over its sphere, are plausibly called the garland of heaven" (ibid.).

A spherical universe would naturally map on a round shield so that the issue of the latter's shape is solved; but Heraclitus, who leads us away from the shield's materiality, does not proceed to enquire into the disposition of the shield's various parts. And indeed the spatial ordering of particular scenes *is* less important than the way each scene places us in the middle of an expanding event. The cosmic framework therefore does not play the role of some formal grid or box wherein the scenes on the shield would be simply contained. This is not to deny that the shield can be understood as what its modern readers will call "a total cosmic image" or "a cosmic icon."[11] However, the shield's cosmic dimension is clearly a background for a different kind of universality – one that relates to human actions and sufferings. The shield is not scientific, but eminently practical in building up an impressive inventory of not only human forms of life that appear everywhere, from peaceful vistas to war-torn landscapes. As this inventory stays on the universal level, without naming any particular city and its heroes (there is a comparison to Daedalus' labyrinth in Knossos, but it is just that: a comparison), it contains the seeds of various other – often politically charged – universes, of which a not negligible number will be realized by later ekphrastic practice, including other ekphrastic shields.

This kind of anonymous universality also implies two different instances of the *mise en abyme* (the shield's recursive effect): first in relation to the *Iliad* as a whole, and second in relation to the later accounts of ekphrasis in the rhetorical manuals or *Progymnasmata*. Concerning these explicit discussions of what ekphrasis is and what it is about, it is advisable to pay close attention to the broad range of objects recommended as suitable for vivid and evocative description. What is striking is that if we follow the list of topics established by Aelius Theon (in, probably, the first century CE), then all the elements of this list have their direct counterpart on the Homeric shield: the latter includes the ekphrases of

---

11   For "a total cosmic image," see Fletcher 2012, 215–17. The expression "cosmic icon" is from
      Philip Hardie's interpretation of the shield of Aeneas in Hardie 1986, 336–76.

persons (Ares and Athena), of events (war, peace, harvest), of places (cities, fields, waters, heavens) and times (the seasons). Besides, this mixed Homeric ekphrasis also contains a particular event of public legal dispute, one which makes sense, in advance, of rhetorical manuals such as Theon's own.[12] In all, if the Homeric shield is a materially embedded life, life imagined and produced by a god, it is also a blueprint for the *possible* worlds of human making – poetical *and* political. So, naturally, it did not escape the attention of Homer's interpreters that the very world of the *Iliad* can be understood, recursively, as a segment of the life suggested on the shield, regardless of the fact that the shield is produced within the *Iliad*.[13]

However, important as this recursion may be, it must not overshadow the life of the shield of Achilles beyond the literal limits of its original ekphrasis in Book 18. In time, this life unfolds in two different registers. On the one hand, the shield of Achilles becomes the blueprint for a series of other ekphrastic shields, including those that will fundamentally revise Homer's version. On the other hand, more rarely yet no less strikingly, the shield of Achilles will be re-described as a thing that possesses an inherent agency, irreducible to the motion of the figures on its surface. This too will happen in two entirely different ways. Homer himself will project the shield on the battlefield and emphasize its explosive impact. Much later, in contrast to this most public appearance, the shield will experience its own private drama and express its feelings in the voice of Hellenistic epigrams. These contrasting appearances of the shield instantiate perfectly the play of scale which is one of the motors of the ekphrastic tradition. Let me offer a brief glimpse of what happens in the poems in question.

In the *Iliad*, the shield acquires a power of its own, which almost resembles a sort of *impersonal* agency. In Book 18, Hephaestus produces the shield not as armour that would save Achilles' life, but as a wonder that will alleviate the hero's present sorrow: it will be a marvel admired by many men, says Hephaestus to Thetis, and we understand that the artificially created life is not only a summary of the partly natural and partly artificial human condition, but also a consolation. However, no one except, possibly, Achilles is described as

---

12   I cannot deal with this recursion in detail, but it should alert us to the complexity of the relation between rhetorical guides to ekphrasis and the broader (and older) poetic practice that we now design by this term. On Theon and *progymnasmata*, see, at least, Heath 2002/3; for the role of ekphrasis in *progymnasmata*, see Webb 2009.
13   An already classic example of this reading is Taplin 1980.

contemplating the shield or wondering about its execution and meaning. Achilles himself takes a long look at his new and "intricate" armour but, at 19.15–20, this only rekindles his anger, so that "his eyes glittered terribly under his lids, like sunflare" (19.17).[14] When the shield reappears later on in Book 19, it does so in full combat mode, where all detail disappears behind the shield's radiance. From being a cosmic icon, the shield is now transformed into a cosmic beacon, similar to the Moon or a burning fire. Hence the comparison of its effect to the light moving across open water (I will only quote the raising of the shield at 19.373–80, but the whole arming sequence is a perfect ekphrasis of action):

[Achilles] caught up the great shield, huge and heavy
next, and from it the light glimmered far, as from the moon.
And as when from across water a light shines to mariners
from a blazing fire, when the fire is burning high in the mountains
in a desolate steading, as the mariners are carried unwilling
by storm winds over the fish-swarming sea, far away from their loved
ones; so the light from the fair elaborate shield of Achilles
shot into the high air.

(Iliad, 19.373–80, trans. Lattimore)

While Achilles flies at the enemy, resplendent in his new armour, his starlike appearance also eclipses any particular design on the shield, which becomes one huge reflector, impossible to contemplate for those who face it.[15] On the battlefield, the shield therefore angers or terrifies. As a result, the only gaze that we are reasonably certain has contemplated the detailed finish of the shield's surface is that of Thetis, who was a witness to its fabrication (not incidentally, it

---

14   On this emotion, see Goldhill 2012, 102–3.

15   Cf. Frontisi-Ducroux 2002, 470: "Bien des éléments du texte contribuent ainsi à donner l'impression que cet ouvrage surhumain est quasi insupportable à la vision humaine, comme peut l'être le divin lui-même." Scully 2003, 29–47, reads the shield from precisely this perspective. Cf. also Goldhill 2012, 103, on the reaction to the shield of Achilles in the *Iliad*: "the pattern of focalisation excludes the heroic characters of the epic (unlike in Virgil). Neither Achilles, nor any other hero, looks at the imagery and seeks for or finds any meaning there. In Homer, ekphrasis is not a scene of recognition." Goldhill shows that many later (and learned) ekphrases will engage the issue of recognition with an eye on its inherent and often complex temporality.

is her gaze that takes the place of Hephaestus' projective imagination in Auden's modern version of the shield, where the Homeric rhythm of "then he made" gives way to the repetition of "she looked over his shoulder").

This situation makes us wonder about the complicity between the ekphrastic gaze and the divine gaze – a complicity that perfectly conforms to my previous suggestion that we are invited less to simulate an act of actual seeing than to imagine what the god imagines: there is more of an emulation than a simulation in such an imagining.[16] This emulation of the divine imagination by the ekphrastic imagination is what enables us to lend some degree of transparency to things whose creation retains some opacity, insofar as it surpasses the power of human craft. Hence the play with various *degrees* of transparency, and with transparency and opacity in general, that will be a favourite instrument of all ekphrasis.

At the same time, the *Iliad* itself opens the shield to a more troubled destiny. On the battlefield, this hand-held polymetallic entity with animated figures is not calmly scrutinized, but fiercely attacked. The second and much shorter Homeric chapter regarding the history of this shield is indeed, quite unexpectedly, about it being damaged. It is first attacked by Aeneas, who strikes "the terrible grim shield" and frightens Achilles by his mighty blow (20.259–63). Homer chooses these lines to say more about the body of the shield: in Book 18, we learned that the shield's body was composed of five folds made of bronze, tin, and gold, with added silver (18.474–81). Now, in Book 20, we are reassured that the divine gift will not break, since it has two folds of bronze on the outside and two of tin on the inside, and between them a single layer of gold. And it is precisely the layer of gold that holds fast against Aeneas' blow (20.266–72). Clearly, not to break is not the same as not to be damaged: again, at 21.165, the spear of Asteropaios also breaks through the two external layers and, once more, stops only when it hits the gold. Since ancient times, these verses have been found to

---

16   Cf. Lovatt 2013, 173–74, who points out the "association between the divine gaze and the ecphrastic gaze" and remarks, on the Vulcan-made shield of Aeneas, that "[t]he ecphrasis of the divine shield represents the ultimate god's-eye view of epic poetry." This perspective, connected as it is to Hephaestus' manual effort, is important since it precludes the ekphrastic imagination from turning into the "acentral imagining" that is "done from no-one's point of view" and is "likely to be purely visual." These expressions are from Wollheim 1986, 60. On central and "acentral" imagining, see, e.g., Giovannelli 2008.

be puzzling and often excised: not only because gold is not capable of assuming this impenetrable role, but also because, if we disregard this physical fact, the divine gift would be disconcertingly easy to ruin, at least in its carefully wrought external aspect.[17] In any case, the ekphrastic tradition will not take the blows of Aeneas and Asteropaios into account: the later variations on Homeric ekphrasis assume that the shield, as though a self-healing organism, survives and lives on in its restored original form.

As I have said already, this survival and afterlife are rich in ekphrastic options that enable the shield to travel around the ancient world. From among the relevant material, I will only evoke the version that gives the shield of Achilles the capacity to feel and express emotions. This account is realized in one of the three epigrams that are dedicated to the shield of Achilles and contained in Book 9 of the *Palatine Anthology*. More than tangential to the issue of ekphrasis, these epigrams and their editorial context are revelatory in terms of the shield's life, independent of its carefully wrought design. The three epigrams in question (9.115, 9.115b, 9.116) offer no description of the shield's surface, but instead relate its fortune after the *Iliad*. This starts with the quarrel over the arms of Achilles as reported at the beginning of the *Little Iliad*, when Odysseus, with the help of Athena, obtains the equipment to the detriment of Ajax. In the *Little Iliad*, Odysseus then departs for Scyros to meet Achilles' son Neoptolemus, whom he gives his father's armour before they both return to Troy.[18] In the epigrams, Odysseus' voyage to Scyros ends in a shipwreck; as a result, almost providentially, the shield of Achilles washes up on the shore of Salamis, at the tomb of Ajax, whose death followed from the unfair judgment.[19] Epigram 9.115 thus connects the shield to the concept of poetic justice:

---

17   See already Aristotle, *Poetics* 25, 1461a33–35. On the history of these doubts, see Edwards 1991,
      323. For a detailed ancient discussion, see Porphyry, *Homeric Questions on the Iliad*, Y 259–72;
      cf. also Cirio 1980–1981.
18   For the iconography of Odysseus giving the arms of Achilles to Neoptolemus, see the tondo of
      the Douris' red figure cup in the Kunsthistorisches Museum, Vienna (ca. 500–480 BCE). Typically, the design of the shield bears no likeness at all to the shield described by Homer.
19   The same story is reported in Pausanias 1.35.4: "About the judgment concerning the armour
      I heard a story of the Aeolians who afterwards settled at Ilium, to the effect that when Odysseus
      suffered shipwreck the armour was cast ashore near the grave of Ajax" (trans. W. H. S. Jones).

The shield of Achilles that had drunk the blood of Hector,
Was gained through the wrong judgment by the son of Laertes;
But when he suffered shipwreck the sea robbed him of it, and
    floated it ashore
By the tomb of Ajax, and not in Ithaca.

(Palatine Anthology, 9.115, trans. W. R. Paton modified)

The horizon of the injustice committed and rectified shows the shield as a triple survivor: both Achilles who bore it in battle and Hector whose blood the shield "had drunk" are dead, and so is Ajax, who should have inherited it. In the *Iliad*, the shield of Achilles is always expansive, whether as embracing the whole universe, or as emitting a blinding light on the battlefield. Here, in stark contrast to this glory, the shield is lonely and diminished, cast ashore in a landscape that suggests desolation.[20] Epigram 9.116 then zooms in on the shield itself:

The shield cries aloud and beats against the tomb,
Summoning you, its worthy bearer:
"Awake, son of Telamon, the shield of Achilles is yours."

(Palatine Anthology, 9.116, trans. W. R. Paton)

The connection to 9.115 is obvious: to say that the shield "had drunk the blood of Hector" is to personify it in a usual poetic manner; but the consumed blood also renders the shield alive and capable of speech (remember the *Odyssey* and the afterlife of souls in the underworld). The shield uses this capacity to lament its post-Iliadic fortune, and it does so in a way that is both genuinely funny and deeply sad. In this laconic tragicomedy, the most glorious ekphrastic object turns into an unseen castaway, one among the many speaking objects that inhabit the epigrammatic world, including other speaking shields.[21] A certain poetic equalization is at work here – all the more so because the shipwreck is another epigrammatic theme *par excellence*. Clearly, this very particular shield is still an *implied* ekphrastic object, but it is reimagined through the change of

---

20 Epigram 9.115b maintains the narrow perspective on the issue of justice, praising Poseidon, whose just action reversed the original judgment of the arms and brought the shield's glory to Salamis, to the tomb of Ajax.

21 See *Palatine Anthology* 6.124, 6.125, 6.127, 6.178, 6.264.

scale that throws it into an open maritime landscape: suddenly, the universal ekphrastic icon turns into an actor abandoned in the world at large.

As with all epigrams, what we appreciate is the art of achieving the greatest effect with the minimum words. Hence the importance of creating an atmosphere that surrounds what is said. Something similar is also true of ekphrasis, since the latter achieves its effect of palpability by suggesting sensible qualities that derive not only from linguistic meaning, but also from the materiality of the voice (or the writing) and from how we literally *feel* particular words. The quoted epigram relies on this palpability as it leads us from the large to the small, and offers its own concise description of an action.[22] Indirectly but logically, we are reminded that ekphrasis and epigram exploit the opposite sides of poetic closure: having originated in inscribed verse, the epigrammatic brevity implies a precise physical size of the object evoked; the ekphrastic instruction, on the other hand, can make any object expand in our imagination, regardless of its physical size. This polarity implies that these two different strategies converge through a shared interest in scale.[23]

There is a lot to be said regarding scale and animation, and also the imagination's own handling of scale as independent of the natural size of things (reading or hearing the shield of Achilles, we do not imagine the figures on it as corresponding to the size of an actual shield). As I am unable to develop this line of enquiry here, I would instead like to remark upon the agency of the shield in the quoted epigram, which is exemplary of a broad range of epigrams in which material things are animated by an inherent power of voice, which belongs as much to these things as to the poems that let them act upon us. This performative model is also assumed in the epic ekphrasis, whose performance by human voice takes on itself the voices of the animate matter of the shield. If it is true that "the voice is the site of perhaps the most radical of all subjective divisions – the division between meaning and materiality" (Silverman 1988, 44),[24] then

---

22   I cannot digress into the ekphrastic epigram and its inherently paradoxical nature. Squire 2010, 592n10, lists a number of important references, including Chinn 2005 and Prioux 2007. Vitry 1894 offers a still useful catalogue of ekphrastic epigrams.

23   On the "semantics of scale" in Hellenistic art and poetry, see Squire 2016b. My reading of the epigrams on the shield of Achilles is very close to Squire 2011, 335–36n78, which emphasizes how this shield, projected in the epigrammatic medium, "figures the ambiguous ontology of epigram between inscribed physical monument and anthologized literary fiction."

24   Quoted in Fredrick 1999, 70.

the poetic performance is a balancing act that strives to hold both sides of this division together,[25] with a special feeling for those moments where materiality prevails and thereby the possibilities of sense become all the richer – and more ambiguous as well.

In our case, these possibilities are enriched by the independence of the shield's own epigrammatic voice, which does not arise from any of the figures on the shield to whom Homer ascribes a voice in the *Iliad*. Here, the shield's animation is understood as inherent to the whole artefact as a single thing, which implies yet another instance of recursion or *mise en abyme* in relation to the "original" Homeric ekphrasis. Moreover, the shield expresses here its own view about who its rightful owner should have been, which is a remarkable instance of counterfactual imagination.[26] This further confirms that only *looking at* a silent shield would never tell us all there is to know about it. The epigram really suggests an agency that may go beyond the god's original design, and yet it still develops the implications of his animating craft that can make nature artificial and artifice natural.

The Greek and Roman ekphrastic tradition will take this agency in different directions, whether by elaborating new versions of the shield of Achilles (as Euripides, the author of *Ilias Latina*, Philostratus the Younger, or Quintus of Smyrna will do) or by creating new ekphrastic shields (those of Heracles, of Aeneas, of Theseus, or of Dionysus, among others). What these shields and many other ekphrastic creations share is the irreducibility of their animate and animating mode to something which would be alive in only a borrowed or metaphorical sense. The "kind of indeterminate ontology" with which we started will underlie this whole tradition where imagined figures become, quite literally, *matter* for further imaginations. As Michael Squire puts it, the ekphrastic tradition will work in the wake of the Homeric object that "slips *between* different ontological registers" and "is now raw matter, now worked image" (Squire 2011, 337). In this respect, I wanted to emphasize that this oscillation can only be efficient insofar as ekphrasis works its magic by relying on a real contiguity between the raw state of material imagination and its elaborate creations. The

---

25   Cf. Valéry 1960, 637, regarding poem as "hésitation prolongée entre le son et le sens."

26   Concerning the counterfactual imagination, see the epigram by Antipater of Sidon 7 GP (*Palatine Anthology* 7.146), where the personified Virtue sits at the tomb of Ajax and, mourning the outcome of the quarrel between Ajax and Odysseus over the arms of Achilles, imagines what the armour itself might say about it. See Harder 2007, 413–14.

great art historian Erwin Panofsky asserts, in a footnote to his interpretation of Disney cartoon animations, that to animate means to "endow lifeless things with life, or living things with a different kind of life" (Panofsky 1959, 23n1). In its original Homeric form and its long afterlife, the ekphrastic shield of Achilles fulfils both of these interpretations – reminding us that to limit life to only certain realms of being is not a natural but an artificial gesture.[27]

---

27   This chapter overlaps partly with some passages from Thein 2022. This work was supported by the European Regional Development Fund project "Creativity and Adaptability as Conditions of the Success of Europe in an Interrelated World" (reg. no.: CZ.02.1.01/0.0/0.0/16_019/0000734).

Navigating Poetry as Object and Object as Poetry: Optatian Porfyry and the Ancient History of *Dinggedichte*

MICHAEL SQUIRE

As critical term, *Dinggedicht* is an unabashedly modern invention. Coined by Kurt Oppert in 1926, and used to characterize work by the likes of Eduard Mörike, Conrad Ferdinand Meyer, and Rainer Maria Rilke (Oppert 1926), the phrase sought to diagnose a modernist turn in poetic form and voice – a new devotion to material objects, bound up with a new concern for the subjectivity of the speaking poet. Just as *Dinggedicht* is a recent denomination, applied to the work of relatively recent poets, it can be easy to assume that the term describes a modern literary phenomenon. Approached from the perspective of twenty-first-century "thing theory," *Dinggedichte* have even been associated with particular aspects of modern-day cultural life: a dissatisfaction, for example, with our day-to-day interactions with the world around us (in turn bound up with a late capitalist moment, or else with a changed ecological sensitivity); a new aesthetic or empirical awareness, premised on changed sorts of material or sensory engagement; an interest in redefining the relationships between human subjects and inanimate objects; and a new sense of the materiality of language – a self-conscious attentiveness to the physical objecthood, indeed the very "thingness," of poetic form.[1]

---

1   See in particular Brown 2001; further developed in, e.g., Brown 2015 and Stout 2018.

In rethinking this supposedly "modernist" diagnosis, the aim of my short contribution is to consider the phenomenon of *Dinggedichte* in longer historical perspective. Rather than focus on poets of the late nineteenth, twentieth, or twenty-first century, the chapter looks back to Greek and Roman antiquity. More specifically, it considers the work of one particular Latin poet, writing in the early fourth century AD: Publilius Optatianus Porfyrius – or "Optatian" for short.[2]

What we find in this late-antique case study, I propose, is a concern with manifesting – that is, with making literally present, as objective apparition on the page – the ideas, themes, and forms that are verbally represented through the written text. The results amount to "object poems" in a variety of senses. Sometimes Optatian's verses summon up the material form of the objects with which they engage: in three extant examples, the poet carefully varies the number of letters in each horizontal line, thereby turning the outer frame of the poem into an image – the schematic outline of an altar, water-organ, and set of pipes (see figs. 1–2).[3] At other times, objects are summoned up inside the field of verse. In these so-called *carmina cancellata* ("gridded poems"),[4] Optatian conceptualises his poetic artefact as a veritable mosaic of letters: the text emerges as a spatially arranged grid – a space for containing ornamental, mimetic, or alphabetic designs (see figs. 3–4, 7–8, and 12–13). As opposed to the calligrammatic

---

2 In what follows, I rely on Giovanni Polara's landmark edition (Polara 1973); I also refer to Polara's numbering of Optatian's poems ("*Carm.*"), as well as their internal *versus intexti* (delineated in Roman numerals). Optatian has still to receive an English translation. There are nonetheless a handful of other modern translations: Ernst (2012, 21–63) provides a text, German translation, and commentary of *Carm.* 1, 6, 10, 15, 21, and 25; Polara (2004; first published in 1976) provides a Latin text of the entire corpus, with facing Italian translation; finally, Bruhat (1999, 462–93) translates all but *Carm.* 22, 24, and 31 into French. A critical edition and German translation is being prepared by Johannes Wienand and John Noël Dillon for Mohr Siebeck's series *Studien und Texte zu Antike und Christentum.*

3 For an introductory discussion of *Carm.* 20, 26, and 27 (with further bibliography), see Squire 2017a, 36–40, along with, e.g., Kwapisz 2017 (revised as Kwapisz 2019, 89–111).

4 Although not directly attested, the term is taken from a reference in *Carm.* 21.i–ii: *mixta per amfractus diducunt carmina Musae, / seu cancellatos spatia in contraria exus* ("Muses disperse verses that are intermingled either with circuitous windings or else with gridded bends that proceed in the opposite track"; cf. Squire 2017b, 64–73). Sixteen such grid-poems have been ascribed to Optatian (*Carm.* 2–3, 5–10, 12, 14, 18–19, and 21–24), although the authenticity of two poems has been doubted (*Carm.* 22 and 24; cf. Squire and Whitton 2017, 86–91).

"images of verse" (*imagines metrorum*) that comprise the three extant figure-po-ems,[5] objects are here conjured up within the spatial span of the text. Once again, though, these creations also celebrate the very "thingness" of the poems that mediate them, emphasising the physicality of each constituent line, word, and letter:[6] while metamorphosing into a site of material manufacture, each literary creation is simultaneously presented as monumental object in its own written right.[7]

What, if anything, might this material contribute to our volume's wider-rang-ing investigation into *Dinggedichte*? In what follows, I suggest that Optatian's experiments with poetic and pictorial form have to be understood in the context of a particular cultural and intellectual historical moment, bound up not only with the politics of the early fourth century (and its Roman emperor, Constantine), but also with the rise of new Christian ways of viewing, under-standing, and representing the world. No less significantly, I suggest that these works deliver an object lesson in the history of "thing poetry" *tout court*. The very "antiquity" of Optatian's works, I propose, should give us pause to rethink the conceptual archaeology of this "modern" poetic, cultural, and intellec-tual historical category: as "thing poems" *avant la lettre*, as it were, Optatian's fourth-century works raise questions about the longer archaeology of a sup-posed twentieth-century literary and cultural phenomenon.[8]

*   *   *

5   Optatian uses the term in the context of his altar-poem, *Carm.* 26.23.

6   The classic discussion of "script" as language – and its independent relation to the structures of spoken convention – is Kristeva 1989, esp. 18–40; cf., for example, Derrida 1976, esp. 18 of the "aphoristic energy" of writing, which at once "communicates" and "supplements" language.

7   As such, Optatian's poems fit within much longer western – as indeed global – traditions of "figure" and "optical poetry." Of the many treatments, I have benefited in particular from Higgins 1987 (discussing Greek and Latin examples at 19–24 and 25–53 respectively, with ref-erence to Optatian on 25–28); Ernst 1991, 2012, and 2016; and Dencker 2011.

8   For insightful discussion here, see in particular Hernández Lobato 2017 on the parallels between twentieth-century conceptual art and Optatian's poetry; cf. Squire 2017b, 106–8.

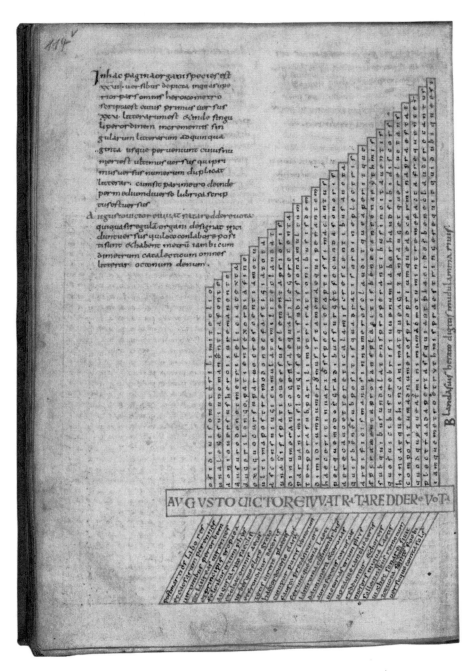

1. Optatian *Carm.* 20a and 20b, as presented in Codex Bernensis 212, folio 114v (Bern, Burgerbibliothek; labelled ms. **B** by Giovanni Polara); ninth century. © Burgerbibliothek Bern.

```
                    V I D E S V T A R A S T E M D I C A T A P Y T H I O
                    F A B R E P O L I T A V A T I S A R T E M V S I C A
        S I C P V L C H R A S A C R I S S I M A G E N S P H O E B O D E C E N S
        H I S A P T A T E M P L I S Q V I S L I T A N T V A T V M C H O R I
  5     T O T C O M P T A S E R T I S E T C A M E N A E F L O R I B V S
          H E L I C O N I I S L O C A N D A L V C I S C A R M I N V M
          N O N C A V T E D V R A M E P O L I V I T A R T I F E X
          E X C I S A N O N S V M R V P E M O N T I S A L B I D I
          L V N A E N I T E N T E N E C P A R I D E V E R T I C E
  10      N O N C A E S A D V R O N E C C O A C T A S P I C V L O
          A R T A R E P R I M O S E M I N E N T E S A N G V L O S
          E T M O X S E C V N D O S P R O P A G A R E L A T I V S
          E O S Q V E C A V T E S I N G V L O S S V B D V C E R E
          G R A D V M I N V T O P E R R E C V R V A S L I N E A S
  15      N O R M A T A V B I Q V E S I C D E I N D E R E G V L A
          V T O R A Q V A D R A E S I T R I G E N T E L I M I T E
          V E L I N D E A D I M V M F V S A R V R S V M L I N E A
          T E N D A T V R A R T E L A T I O R P E R O R D I N E M
          M E M E T R A P A N G V N T D E C A M E N A R V M M O D I S
  20    M V T A T O N V M Q V A M N V M E R O D V M T A X A T P E D V M
      Q V A E D O C T A S E R V A T D V M P R A E C E P T I S R E G V L A
    E L E M E N T A C R E S C V N T E T D E C R E S C V N T C A R M I N V M
    H A S P H O E B E S V P P L E X D A N S M E T R O R V M I M A G I N E S
    T E M P L I S C H O R I S Q V E L A E T V S I N T E R S I T S A C R I S

          5          10         15         20         25         30         35
```

2. Optatian *Carm.* 26; typesetting after Squire and Wienand (eds.) 2017: 49 (using the edition of Polara 1973).

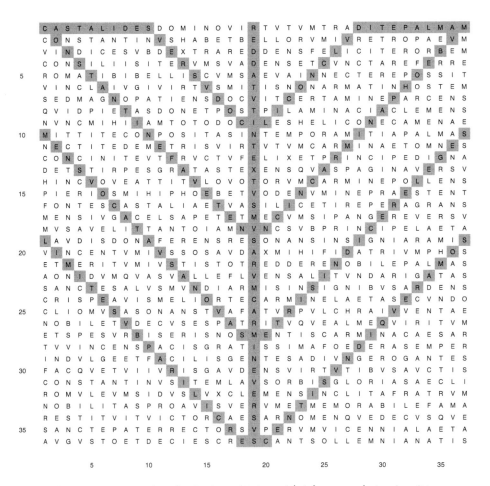

3. Optatian *Carm.* 9; typesetting after Squire and Wienand (eds.) 2017: 34 (using the edition of Polara 1973).

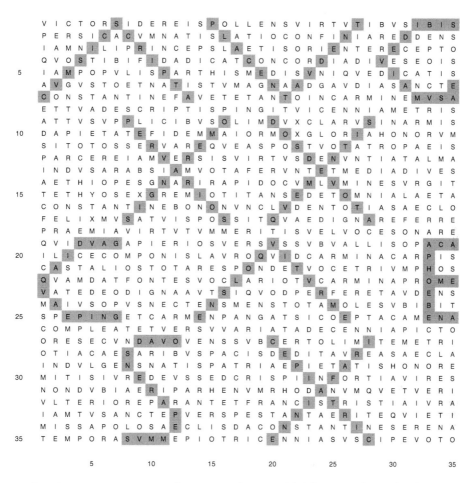

4. Optatian *Carm.* 5; typesetting after Squire and Wienand (eds.) 2017: 30 (using the edition of Polara 1973).

Let me begin by saying something about Optatian and his oeuvre. Despite a flurry of revisionist appraisals, especially over the last decade, Optatian has found little favour among traditional specialists of Greek and Latin literature.[9] The poet is the "author of hare-brained frivolities in verse," according to one typical assessment – trivialities which must leave the reader astonished "that a man wanted to squander his days in such laboriously contrived affectations (and pass them off as poetry), no less than that he should thereby have won approval from an emperor."[10] Other evaluations of the "unspeakable" Optatian have been no less disdainful.[11] "The text itself is devoid of all interest save its curiosity, paying witness to the decadence of an art and a culture," to cite the conclusion of another classicist;[12] indeed, these "ridiculous verses" have been deemed testimony to the "poet's futility," revealing how deeply "the corruption of triviality had eaten into poetry."[13] "Contrived," "tasteless," "decadent," "trifling," "risible," even downright "bad": that is the modern scholarly verdict on the poetry of Optatian, and it has prevailed, by and large, to the present day.

Earlier audiences reached a very different opinion.[14] True, at the beginning of the eighth century, St. Bede complained that Optatian was a "pagan" author – and duly deemed that his poems thus made for unsuitable monastic reading.[15] But few readers took heed of such proscriptions. From the distribution of manuscripts, and not least the large number of works written after Optatianic models, it is clear that Optatian was widely read and admired in the Carolingian period. This popularity seems to have peaked between the ninth and

---

9   For a historiographic review, including important revisionist contributions (beginning in particular with Levitan 1985), see Squire 2017b, esp. 84–86, along with Squire 2017a, 25–30. Smolak 1989 still provides a useful bibliographic guide to research carried out before the late 1980s. In the Czech Republic, some of the most important revisionist scholarship has been that of Marie Okáčová (e.g. Okáčová 2006 and 2007); cf. also Bažil 2017. A key contribution – published between the first airing of this paper in 2019 and its publication in English in 2022 – now comes in Körfer 2020.

10 Helm 1959, 1928 (my translation).

11 Cf. Courtney 1990, 5 – concluding that Optatian's poems are riddled with an "unending flow of tasteless platitudes and trifles," and hence "do not merit discussion."

12 Bardon 1957, 453 (my translation).

13 Raby 1957, 1:45.

14 On the western medieval reception of this poetry, the key contribution is Ernst 1991; more recent bibliography is surveyed in Squire 2017b, 73–84.

15 For the comments, see De arte metrica (Keil 1855–1880, 7:258.22–23).

tenth centuries: of the various writers who emulated Optatian's poetic-pictorial designs, few proved more influential than Hrabanus Maurus, whose anthology of poems "in praise of the holy cross" (*De laudibus sanctae crucis*) dates to the ninth century.[16]

If the work of Optatian has us look forward to issues of Carolingian and medieval reception, it also has us look backwards in time. To understand the genesis of this oeuvre means situating it against a longer tradition of poetry, literary criticism, and material culture, and in both the Greek and Roman worlds alike. One inspiration came in the so-called *technopaegnia* (literally, "games of skill") that seem to have originated in the early Hellenistic period.[17] Already by the third century BC, Greek epigrams were being written in such a way as to evoke the two-dimensional outline of particular object-forms: five such poems are preserved in the fifteenth book of the *Palatine Anthology*, attributed to Simmias (the "wings" of Eros, an axe, an egg), "Theocritus" (panpipes), and two subsequent imperial Greek imitators (the altars of Besantinus [fig. 5] and Dosiadas).[18] A little later, in first-century BC Republican Rome, a neoteric Latin poet by the name of Laevius is said to have penned a poem in the shape of a nightingale.[19]

Other parallels are preserved in the archaeological record.[20] Among the most sophisticated, in my view, are the so-called "Iliac tablets," or *Tabulae Iliacae* – specifically, seven such tablets that were engraved with "magic square" inscriptions on their reverse sides. On these tablets, dated to the late first century BC or early first century AD, cryptic textual messages were laid out in grid formation: starting from the middle letter and moving outwards to the extremities of each design, readers were invited to move across and along the engraved

---

16   For an edition, see Perrin 1997; cf. Ernst 1991, 222–332; Perrin 2009; Ernst 2012, 117–234, esp. 220–33.

17   For a detailed commentary on the six extant Greek picture-poems of the *Palatine Anthology* (*AP* 15:21–22, 24–27), see Kwapisz 2013, 59–190, along with the earlier work of Strodel 2002. There has been an explosion of scholarly interest over the last two decades: in addition to Squire 2011, esp. 231–35, and 2013b, 98–107, see, e.g., Guichard 2006; Männlein-Robert 2007, 140–54; Luz 2010, 327–53; Pappas 2013; and Kwapisz 2019.

18   On Optatian's knowing engagement with at least some of these poems, see Squire 2017a, 36–39 and Kwapisz 2017 (revised as Kwapisz 2019, 89–111).

19   On the *Pterygium Phoenicis*, see most recently Kwapisz 2019, 54–88 (with further bibliography); cf. Courtney 1993, 119, 136–37.

20   For an excellent overview, see Habinek 2009; cf. Squire 2011, 210–28.

material object, thereby piecing together the text from its repeated letters. The result was a message – stretched out in the shape of a square, polygon, or other representational form – that summarized the subjects depicted on the recto of each tablet. In some cases, the text even amounted to a line of verse: consider the drawing reproduced in fig. 6, for example, in which the text was written in the shape of an altar, furnishing a hexameter synopsis of what could be seen on the tablet's obverse side ("Achillean shield: Theodorean after Homer" [ἀσπὶς Ἀχιλλῆος Θεοδώρηος καθ᾿ Ὅμηρον]).[21]

Ὁλὸς οὔ με λιβρὸς ἱρῶν
Λιβάδεσσιν οἷα κάλχη
Ὑποφοινίηισι τέγγει·
Μαύλιες δ᾿ ὕπερθε πέτρης Ναξίης θοούμεναι
Παμάτων φείδοντο Πανός· οὐ στροβίλωι λιγνύι
Ἰξὸς εὐώδης μελαίνει τρεχνέων με Νυσίων.
Ἐς γὰρ βωμὸν ὁρῆις με μήτε γλούρου
Πλίνθοις μήτ᾿ Ἀλύβης παγέντα βώλοις,
Οὐδ᾿ ὃν Κυνθογενὴς ἔτευξε φύτλη
Λαβόντε μηκάδων κέρα,
Λισσαῖσιν ἀμφὶ δειράσιν
Ὅσσαι νέμονται Κυνθίαις,
Ἰσόρροπος πέλοιτό μοι·
Σὺν οὐρανοῦ γὰρ ἐκγόνοις
Εἰνάς μ᾿ ἔτευξε γηγενής,
Τάων ἀείζωιον τέχνην
Ἔνευσε πάλμυς ἀφθίτων.
Σὺ δ᾿, ὦ πιὼν κρήνηθεν, ἥν
Ἶνις κόλαψε Γοργόνος,
Θύοις τ᾿ ἐπισπένδοις τ᾿ ἐμοὶ
Ὑμηττιάδων πολὺ λαροτέρην
Σπονδὴν ἄδην. ἴθι δὴ θαρσέων
Ἐς ἐμὴν τεῦξιν· καθαρὸς γὰρ ἐγώ
Ἰὸν ἱέντων τεράων, οἷα κέκευθ᾿ ἐκεῖνος,
Ἀμφὶ Νέαις Θρηικίαις ὃν σχεδόθεν Μυρίνης
Σοί, Τριπάτωρ, πορφυρέου φὼρ ἀνέθηκε κριοῦ.

5. Altar of Besantinus (AP 15.25). Text and typesetting reproduced by kind permission of Christine Luz. The acrostich reads Ὀλύμπιε, πολλοῖς ἔτεσι θύσειας ('Olympian, may you sacrifice for many years').

---

21   Analysis and further bibliography can be found in Squire 2011, 197–246; cf. ibid. 303–70 and 393–95 on the "shield of Achilles" tablet (Rome: Musei Capitoloni, Sala delle Colombe, inv. 83a).

6. Reconstruction of the altar-shaped 'magic square' on the reverse of *Tabula Iliaca* 4N (Rome: Musei Capitoloni, Sala delle Colombe, inv. 83a). After Bienkowski 1891: Tav. V.

Optatian's own experiments with poetic form – his playful games with the materiality of writing, with probing the boundaries between words for reading and images for viewing – are in many ways the culmination of earlier Hellenistic and Roman precedents. As self-standing artefacts, these poems delight in their "graphic" verbal and visual qualities, while also developing a penchant for acrostichs (that is, verses that run horizontally down a manuscript, thus breaking the standard linear flow of text from horizontal left to right).[22] No less importantly, though, the poems likewise take on a knowing epigraphic quality, imitating the monumental backdrop of so much writing in the Roman Empire.[23] This inscriptional aspect is important: if Optatian summons up objects through his poems, he also inscribes those objects with honorific texts. The very act of composition consequently doubles up as an act of dedication – as though the resulting artefacts were in and of themselves inscribed votives, memorials, or offerings (most often, dedicated to the emperor himself).[24]

There is an overtly mathematical rationale at work here, too. Just as the poet's "organ," "altar," and "panpipes" are formed by varying the number of lettered alphabetic units in any given verse, so too are his grid-poems indebted to a numerical approach to language. We have already noted that, rather than exploit their outer frame, Optatian's *carmina cancellata* create a space for visual apparitions through the internal space of their grids. It is worth emphasizing, however, that those grids are once again derived from treating each line as a numerical unit of letters: on the one hand, Optatian breaks down each single verse not just to its metrical or word-based units, but to its constituent alphabetical letters, or *elementa*;[25] on the other, Optatian carefully controls the number of letters in each line, thereby providing an effective canvas for his

22   On the history of Greek and Roman acrostichs, see the surveys of, e.g., Luz 2010, esp. 1–77, and Squire 2011, 224–26 (both with references to the earlier bibliography).

23   For an excellent introduction, see now the essays in Petrovic, Petrovic, and Thomas 2018.

24   On the Roman "epigraphic habit," see Macmullen 1982; cf., e.g., Corbier 2006, esp. 9–128; Woolf 1996; Squire 2009, 146–49 (with further bibliography). Particularly relevant to Optatian's work are so-called *stoichêdon* inscriptions, in which letters were evenly distributed across the space of the epigraphic field. The "epigraphic" quality of these written texts – presumably laid out in "Roman square capital" script (so-called *capitalis quadrata*) – is also important: it bestows a certain monumental appearance, presenting the texts as "official" sorts of honorary imperial dedication (cf. Rühl 2006, 91).

25   For the term *elementa*, cf. *Carm.* 26.22 (*elementa crescunt et decrescunt carminum*). For discussion, cf. Squire 2017a, 91–93.

internal designs. By marking out individual units in different colours, or else using lines within the grid, the poet redeploys the letters between the background and foreground of his creations. In each case, those internal designs are integrated within the groundtext, while also adorning it with an external (one might say "parergonal," or indeed "paratextual") critical commentary.[26]

Optatian harnessed the designs of his *carmina cancellata* to various semantic ends.[27] Sometimes the patterns amount to geometric or floral ornaments (*Carm.* 2–3, 7, 12, 18, and 21–23), including lattice patterns and diamond formations. At other times, they furnish mimetic or schematic forms: depicted objects include a palm frond (*Carm.* 9 [see fig. 3]), a schematic drawing of an army in *quincunx* formation (*Carm.* 6), and a shield (*Carm.* 7). Then again, in further examples, the marked patterns yield still more letters (and by extension also Roman numerals), now arranged as gigantic graphic forms: whereas *Carm.* 5 reveals the letters *AVG. XX CAES. X* (celebrating the twentieth and tenth anniversaries of Constantine as "Augustus" and his sons as "Caesars" [see fig. 4]), for example, *Carm.* 23 can be understood to yield the letter "M" (emblazoning the initial of a certain "Marcus" addressed in the zig-zagging verse within).[28] Often these various rationales could be combined in one and the same poem, leaving it productively ambiguous as to how various sorts of apparition should be reconciled with one another.[29]

---

26 On Optatian's play with the "frames" of his poetry here, see the brief introduction of Squire 2017c (discussing *Carm.* 22, and with reference to Derrida 1978, 44–168); for "paratexts," see Genette 1997, esp. 1–15.

27 For the different rationales – "geometrische Gittergedichte," "literale *carmina cancellata*," and "gegenstandsmimetische Gittergedichte" – see Ernst 1991, 108–35; cf., e.g., Bruhat 1999, 134–70; Rühl 2006, 81–82; Squire 2017a, 40–45.

28 The initial M offers a cryptic clue to the message hidden inside it – namely, the poem's vocation to a certain "Marcus," disguised in the Latin characters of the *versus intextus*, which have to be transliterated into Greek (for the conceit, see below, pp. 51–70, on *Carm.* 19): Μάρκε, τε, ἢν ἄλοχον τὴν Ὑμνίδα Νεῖλος ἐλαύνει ("Marcus, Neilos is banging your wife Hymnis"). The Greek hexameter thus delivers on the hint that the reader will find hidden meaning in the poem (*haec occulta legens*, *Carm.* 23.3), no less than the promise that the "muse sounds to the Greeks" (*Musa sonat Graecis*, *Carm.* 23.10). For translation and brief discussion, see Squire 2011, 221–22.

29 *Carm.* 3 offers a particularly intriguing case study, tendering a promise not only that the artefact amounts to a sort of "portrait" (*uultus Augusti*), but also that it outstrips the paintings of Apelles (that is, antiquity's most famous painter). See Squire 2016a for discussion and bibliography.

What is so remarkable in all this is the poet's simultaneously deconstructive and reconstructive attitude to written language.[30] With each gridded poem, Optatian proceeds on the level of individual word, phrase, clause, and sentence, while also paying close attention to the metrical prescriptions. Ultimately, though, the essential unit of his works is the individual letter, itself recycled between groundtext, internal patterns, and the text contained within the design. As always, Optatian could look to contemporary visual culture for concrete parallels. For one thing, his works are formed after the manner of elaborate mosaics, each made up from the polychrome *tesserae* of individual alphabetical elements.[31] For another, these artefacts are spun like tapestries, literalizing a long-standing analogy between the weaving of poetry and the manufacture of textured fabric: the patterns embroidered within the grid consequently amount to a sort of cross-stitch – "interwoven verses" (*versus intexti*), as Optatian labelled them.[32]

That metaphor of weaving provided Optatian with a favourite figure for discussing his distinctive "new art."[33] Just as the *versus intexti* recycle lettered elements from the groundtext, so too is the fabric of his poems sewn from the appropriated textures of the literary past: it is "stitched" together from literary precedent – embroidered with words, phrases, and ideas drawn from a library of canonical texts. If the resulting poems might remind us of contemporary *centones* (poetic "patchworks" made up of isolated literary tidbits, drawn first and foremost from Virgil),[34] they also parallel artistic practices of spoliation: they form a literary counterpart to compound monuments, like the arch that Constantine erected in Rome in AD 315 and pieced together from the elemental *spolia* of multiple earlier imperial buildings.[35]

---

30   See in particular Squire 2017a, 82–97.

31   For the analogy, see also Bruhat 1999, 136–41 (with particular reference to the geometric shapes of *Carm.* 7, 12, 18, and 21–23). More generally on the parallels between late antique poetry and mosaics, see Roberts 1989, esp. 57, 70–73.

32   The term *intextus versus* is itself embroidered into the "interwoven verses" of the ninth poem (*Carm.* 9.v): cf. *Carm.* 21.16 (*texti ... versus*). On the metapoetic metaphor, see especially Bruhat 1999, 107–14; Scheidegger Lämmle 2015, 176–83; and Bazil 2017.

33   For a selective inventory of Optatian's many references to such "novelty," see Squire 2017a, 49n75.

34   Among the most important recent discussions of the Latin *cento* are McGill 2005; Bažil 2009; Hernández Lobato 2012, 262–317; and Pelttari 2014, 96–112. Cf. also Elsner 2017.

35   For comparison between the Arch of Constantine and Optatian's works, see Squire 2017a, 95–99, along with, e.g., Levitan 1985, 269; Elsner 2000, 175; and Rühl 2006, 91–92.

One obvious question to arise is about how Optatian presented his work to his original fourth-century readership. Extant manuscripts are much later in date, and the evidence that they provide is therefore limited.[36] That said, there is good reason to think that many of the extant poems attributed to Optatian once formed part of an anthology dispatched to Emperor Constantine: according to St. Jerome, the poet "was released from exile after sending a remarkable volume to Constantine" in AD 329 (*Porphyrius misso ad Constantinum insigni volumine exilio liberatur*).[37] In a poem that, so far as we can tell, was written to open such an anthology, Optatian paints a vivid picture of how his works appeared.[38] Before exile, we are told, the poet's works were *ostro tota nitens, argento auroque coruscis / scripta notis [...] / scriptoris bene compta manu* ("all shining in purple, written with letters that glitter in silver and gold [...] well adorned by the hand of the writer"; 1.3–5). The contrast with the later collection, written in exile, could not be starker: each page is *pallida nunc, atro chartam suffusa colore, / paupere vix minio carmina dissocians* ("now pale, with each leaf tinted in a black colour, scarcely distinguishing its poems with impoverished cinnabar"; 1.7–8).[39]

---

36 On the presentation of Optatian's works in extant manuscripts, see Squire 2017b, 73–74 (with further bibliography on manuscript traditions in n51: fundamental is the work of Giovanni Polara and Ulrich Ernst).

37 *Chron.* on AD 329, see Helm 1956, 232. On this evidence, and the whole question of the chronology of Optatian's work and exile, see Wienand 2017, with detailed overview of earlier bibliography.

38 On the poem and its Ovidian debts, see Bruhat 2017. Cf. Squire 2017a, 30–35 (with more detailed references).

39 Optatian frequently refers to the "painterly" and "colourful" qualities of his work: e.g. *Carm.* 3.15, 35, iii–iv; *Carm.* 4.7; *Carm.* 5.7–8, 25, 26, iii; *Carm.* 6.34; *Carm.* 7.7; *Carm.* 8.1–2; *Carm.* 10.9; *Carm.* 18.21; *Carm.* 19.20; *Carm.* 22.9, viii, xiii–xiv. He also sometimes talks of particular colours, including gold, silver, and purple (that is, colours associated with imperial majesty: cf. Rühl 2006, 97; Bruhat 2009, 103–4). Given his "Porphyrian" name, the "purple" (*purpureus*) references seem especially playful (*Carm.* 1.17; *Carm.* 20.13; *Carm.* 21.i; *Carm.* 28.9, 12): just as Optatian seems to have used gold script to literalize the figure of a Constantinian "golden age," we might think so too that a purple colour may have been used to pun upon the poet's name (nowhere more playfully than in the opening *versus intextus* of *Carm.* 21: *Publilius Optatianus Porfyrius haec lusi* ["I Publilius Optatianus Porfyrius have played these games"]).

7. Fictive reconstruction of Optatian *Carm.* 22, based on a folio of the ninth-century Codex Laureshamensis (Bukarest, Biblioteca naţională a României, Ms R II 1, folio 18v). After Squire and Wienand (eds.) 2017: plate 16.

Any attempt at reconstructing the original appearance of Optatian's poems must remain conjectural (see, for example, fig. 7).[40] That said, at least one aspect of Optatian's description in this opening poem deserves additional emphasis: for notice how Optatian talks of the individual "leaf" (*charta*) and "page" (*pagina*).[41] This language was well established, and my hypothesis is beyond empirical proof. But at work behind such talk, in my view, was a new conception of the material manuscript: we seem to be dealing not with an unfolding scroll, but with a bound codex, one in which each luxuriously adorned folio was carefully delineated from the one that precedes and follows it.[42] This new technology seems to have played a critical role in steering Optatian's experiments with poetic-pictorial form: the poet's newfound concern with the object-formations of his poetry, we might say, is itself premised on the objecthood of the mediating codex.

* * *

At this stage, in the second part of my chapter, I want to turn to a specific example of Optatian's lettered art: poem 19 (see fig. 8).[43] The poem consists of

---

40   Fig. 7 is a fictive reconstruction: the image shows a polychrome reconstruction of *Carm.* 22 (itself a poem of contested attribution), based on a folio of the ninth-century *Codex Lau-reshamensis* (Bucharest, Biblioteca naţională a României, Ms R II 1, folio 18v). Aspects of this reconstruction do nonetheless mirror one of the most lavish extant presentations of Hrabanus Maurus' ninth-century *De laudibus sanctae crucis*, which in turn emulated Optatian's designs (cf. above, n. 16): in a ninth-century manuscript housed in the Biblioteca Apostolica Vaticana (Codex Regiensis Latinus 124), Hrabanus Maurus' poems are written in gold and silver against a purple parchment, in a presentation which might itself reflect earlier (and now lost) manuscripts of Optatian.

41   For other references to the *pagina*, see *Carm.* 3.33, iv; *Carm.* 4.2, 9; *Carm.* 7.11; *Carm.* 8.i; *Carm.* 9.13; *Carm.* 19.4, 35. For *charta*, see *Carm.* 1.7. Cf. Ernst 2012, 59–60; Rühl 2006, 90–91; and Wienand 2012, 364–65.

42   On the rise of the codex form, see, e.g., Stanton 2004 and Schipke 2013, esp. 143–52; cf. Engels and Hofman 1997, 67–76. On the luxury codices of late antiquity, see Mazal 1999, 95–98 (mentioning Optatian on p. 96).

43   For more detailed discussions, see Squire 2015a, 104–21 (from which some of what follows is adapted, including the translation), with further bibliography listed at 106–7n40; cf. Squire 2017a, 72–74; Squire and Whitton 2017, 80–82. Important analyses include Bruhat 2008 (with discussion of parallels on Constantinian coinage), along with the discussions by, e.g., Lunn-Rockliffe 2017, esp. 445–52, and Hernández Lobato 2017, 487–88.

38 hexameter verses, each varying in horizontal length from between 35 and 38 letters. The poem was included in Welser's 1595 printed edition of Optatian's works, where *uersus intexti* were marked by hand (see fig. 9). But it is in fact known from just two extant manuscripts: in the first (Codex Parisinus 7806: thirteenth century), the text is presented in miniscule script, with the *versus intexti* written in a reddish orange, grouped together with additional lines (see fig. 10); in the second (Codex Augustaneus 9 Guelferbytanus, Wolfenbüttel: sixteenth century), the internal patterns are written in red and shaded in a golden yellowish tint (see fig. 11).[44]

As with all of Optatian's poems, the text can be read at face value. Before proceeding, I therefore present the groundtext in Latin, complete with my own attempted translation.[45]

> *Prodentur minio caelestia signa legenti.*
> *Constantine, decus mundi, lux aurea saecli,*
> *quis tua mixta canat mira pietate tropaea*
> *exultans, dux summe, nouis mea pagina uotis,*
> *aemula quam Clarii genitoris Calliopeae*   5
> *composuit tali nunc mens perfusa liquore?*
> *uersificas Helicon in gaudia proluat undas,*
> *clementique nouum numen de pectore uerset,*
> *namque ego magnanimi dicam numerosa canendo*
> *sceptra ducis. Gazzae nobis dat Graecia dona,*   10
> *saeclaque Blemmyico sociali limite firmas,*
> *Romula lux. condigna nouis florentia uotis*
> *uoto scripta cano. tali Mars cardine tecto*
> *iam bellis totum Myseum perplectere ciuem*
> *ut pateat Rubicon parili petit aethera iure.*   15
> *nunc felix proprios pakis me scrupea uisus*
> *iam stimulat signis exultans Musa notare,*
> *gaudia laetus nunc per me notat auia Phoebus;*
> *retito quoque texta nouo cane laurea plectro,*

---

44   See Polara 1973, 2:116–27; Pipitone 2012, 86–91, 93–94. Further information on *Codex Parisinus 7806* can be found at https://archivesetmanuscrits.bnf.fr/ark:/12148/cc67057f.

45   For two Italian translations, see Simonini and Gualdoni 1978, 61–62, and Polara 2004, 173–75. Bruhat 1999, 483–84 provides a translation into French.

arte notis picta felicia saecula plaudens.   20
sic aestus uates fido duce, Pythie, carpens
nunc tutus contemnat, summe, procax; ego uero
nunc mare Sigaeum ualeam bene frangere remo,
carbasa Noctiferum totum si scrupea tendo,
pulpita deportans. uisam contexere nauem   25
Musa sinit; coniuncta tuo spes inclita uoto.
mentem per tortum fessam non frangat hiulco
laus mea ficta pede stans magna mole docendi.
signa palam dicam laetissima flumine sancto,
mente bona; contemnat, summis cum sibi agonem   30
uotis post fractum Martem clementia reddet?
sic nobis lecto quo crescunt aurea saecla
mox Latio uincens iam bis uicennia reddes,
carmine quae pietas miro de nomine formet.
flore notans uotum uario dat pagina felix,   35
Augustae sobolis memorans insignia fata.
iudice te uel teste pio condigna parentis
iungentur titulis felicia facta nepotum.

The red cinnabar will reveal the heavenly signs to the reader. Constantine, glory of the world, golden light of the age, with what new vows might my exultant page, o greatest of leaders, sing of your trophies combined with wondrous piety – the page rivalling the Clarian father of Calliope, and that my mind has now composed, steeped in such a potion? Let Mount Helicon pour forth joyful, verse-giving waters; let it produce a new godhead, whirling it out from its merciful heart: for, singing in verse, I shall tell of the sceptres of the magnanimous general! Greece bestows on us the gifts of Gaza, and you, light of Romulus, make our age secure thanks to your allied frontier with the Blemmians! I sing of things in blossom – of things which are worthy of new vows, themselves written with a vow. Now that this region is defended (so that it is clear that the Roman Rubicon crushes all the citizens of Mysia in its war), Mars approaches heaven with the same right.

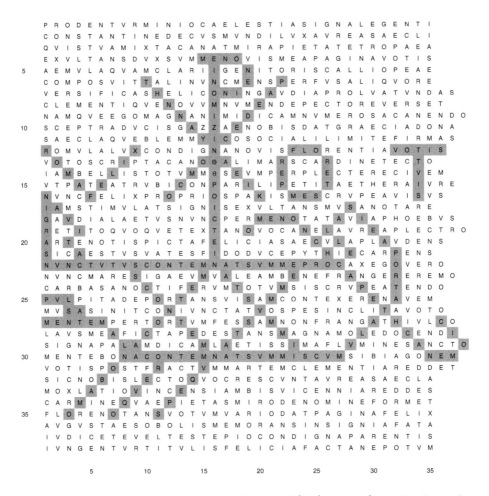

8. Optatian *Carm.* 19; typesetting after Squire and Wienand (eds.) 2017: 42 (using the edition of Polara 1973).10.

PRODENTVRMINIOCAELESTIASIGNALEGENTI
CONSTANTINEDECVSMVNDILLVXAVREASAECLI
QVISTVAMIXTACANATMIRAPIETATETROPAEA
EXVLTANSDVXSVM...NOVIS...PAGINAVOTIS
AEMVLAQVAMCLARI...ENITORISCALLIOPEAE
COMPOSVITVALINVCMENS...BREVISALIQVORE
VERSIFICASVELIC...GAVDIAPROLVATVNDAS
CLEMENTIQVEOVVMNVMDERECTOREVERSET
NAMQVEEGOMAGNANMILICAMNVMEROSACANENDO
SCEPTRADVCISGRATANOBISDATGRAECIADONA
SAECLAQVEBLEMMOSOCIALILIMITEFIRMAS
OMVLALVCONDIGANOVISELORENTIAVOTIS
VTOSCRIPTACANALIMASCADINETECTO
IARBELISTOTYMSVMPERPICTERECIVEM
VTPATEATRVBICONARLIETIAETHERAIVRE
VNCFELIXPROPRIISPACSELECRVPEAVISVS
MSTIMVLATSIGNISBXVLTANSMVSANOTARE
ARDIALABTVSNVNCPERMLATINIAPHOEBVS
ETITOQVOQVETEXANOVOCALEAVRAPLECTRO
ARTENOTISPICTABLICIASAEGVSAPLAVDENS
ICAESTVSVATISFIDODVGBPITHICARMENS
IVNCTVTVSCONTEMNATSVMMEPROGAXEGOVERO
NVNCMAREIGAEVVALEAMBENEFRANGEREREMO
CARBASANOGTIGERVMTOTVS1SCRVEATENDO
PITADEPORTANSVIACONTEXERENAVEM
MVSASINITCVNCTATOSPESINCLITAVOTO
PERTORVMFESANONFRANGATIVLCO
LAVSMEVFICTAPEDESIANSMAGNAMOEDOCENDI
SIGNAPALAMDICAVALAETISSVMAFLVMINESANCTO
MENTEBONACONTEMNATSVMMISCVMSIBIAGON
VOTISPOSTFRVCTVMMARTEMCLEMENTIAREDDET
SICNOBISLACTOQVOCRESCVNTAVREASAECLA
MOXLATIOVINCENSIAMBISVICENNIAREDDES
CARMINAQVAEFICTASMIRODENOMINEFORMET
FLORENTANVVOTVMVARIODATPAGINAFELIX
AVGVSTAESOBOLISMEMORANSINSIGNIAFATA
IVDICETEVELTESTEPIOCONDIGNAPARENTVR
IVNGENTVRTITVLISFELICIAFACTANEPOTVM

1. Trophaea. 2. Clavae. 3. Versa. 4. Lammeasila. 5. Flumina. 6. Vince--iam

C

9. Optatian *Carm.* 19, as presented in Welser 1595.

10. Optatian *Carm.* 19, as presented in Codex Parisinus 7806, folio 1v (Paris, Bibliothèque nationale de France; labelled **Q** by Giovanni Polara Giovanni Polara); thirteenth century. © Bibliothèque nationale de France, Paris.

4.

```
P R O D E N T V R M I N I O C O E L E S T I A S I G N A L E G E N T I
C O N S T A N T I N E D E C V S M V N D I L V X A V R E A S A E C L I
Q V I S T V A M I X T A C A N A T M I R A P I E T A T E T R O P H A E A
E X V L T A N S D V X S V M M E N O V I S M E A P A G I N A V O T I S
A E M V L A Q V A M C L A R A E G E N I T O R I S C A L L I O P E A E
C O M P O S V I T T A L I N V N C M E N S I E R F V S A L I Q V O R E
V E R S I F I C A S H E L I C O N I A G A V D I A P R O L V A T V N D A S
C L E M E N T I Q V E N O V V M N V M E N D E P E C T O R E V E R S O
N A M Q V E E G O M A G N A N I M I D I C A M N V M E R O S A C A N E N D
S C E P T R A D V C I S G A R Z A E N O B I S D A T G R A E C I A D O N A
S A E C L A Q V E B L E M M Y I C O S O C I A L I L I M I T E F I R M A S
R O M V L A L V X C O N D I G N A N O V I S F L O R E N T I A V O T I S
V O T O S C R I P T A C A N O A L I M A R S C A R D I N E T E C T O
I A M B E L L I S T O T V M M Y S E V M P E R P L E C T E R E C I V E M
V T P A T E A T R V B I C O N P A R Y L I P E T I T A E T H E R A I V R E
N V N C F E L I X P R O P R I O S P A C I S M E S C R V P E A V I S V S
I A M S T I M V L A T S I G N I S E X V L T A N S M V S A N O T A R E
G A V D I A L A E T V S N V N C P E R M E N O T A T A V I A P H O E B V S
R E T I T O Q V O Q V E T E X T A N O V O C A N E L A V R E A P L E C T R
A R T E N O T I S P I C T A F E L I C I A S A E C V L A P L A V D E N S
S I C A E S T V S V A T I S F I D O D V C E P I T H I E C A R M E N S
N V N C T V T V S C O N T E M N A T S V M M E P R O C A X E G O V E R O
N V N C M A R E S I G N E V M V A L E A M B E N E F R A N G E R E R E M O
C A R B A S A N O C T I G E R V M T O T V M S I S C R V P E A T E N D O
P V L P I T A D E P O R T A N S V I A M C O N T E X E R E N A V E M
M V S A S I N I T C O N I V N C T A T V O S P E S I N C L I T A V O T O
M E N T E M P E R T O R T V M F E S S A M N O N F R A N G A T H I V L C O
L A V S M E A F I C T A P E D E S T A N S M A G N A M O L E D O C E N D I
S I G N A P A L A M D I C A M L A E T I S S I M A F L V M I N A S A N C T
M E N T E B O N A C O N T E M N A T S V M M I S C V M S I B I A G O N E M
V O T I S P O S T F R V C T V M M A R T E M C L E M E N T I A R E D D E T
S I C N O B I S L E C T O Q V O C R E S C V N T A V R E A S A E C L A
M O X L A T I O V I N C E S E S I A M B I S V I C E N N I A R E D D E S
C A R M I N A Q V A E P I C T A S M I R O D E N O M I N E F O R M E T
F L O R E N O T A N S V O T V M V A R I O D A T P A G I N A F E L I X
A V G V S T A E S O B O L I S M E M O R A N S I N S I G N I A F A T A
I V D I C E T E V E L T E S T E P I O C O N D I G N A P A R E N T V R
I V N G E N T V R T I T V L I S F E L I C I A F A C T A N E P O T V M
```

11. Optatian *Carm.* 19, as presented in Codex Augustaneus 9 Guelferbytanus, folio 4r (Wolfenbüttel, Herzog August Bibliothek; labelled ms. **W** by Giovanni Polara); sixteenth century. © Herzog August Bibliothek, Wolfenbüttel.

At this stage my rugged Muse, blessed and exultant, incites me now to mark her own visions of peace with signs; Phoebus, in his rejoicing, now marks out through me a previously untrodden path of joy. Laurel, you too sing your weave with a newly netted plectrum, applauding a blessed age with an art painted in characters! With you as his faithful guide, Pythian Apollo, let the bard, as he makes his bold way through the waves, now defy them in safety, greatest one; but as for me, may I have the present strength successfully to break the Sigaean sea with my oar, if I strain my rugged sails the evening long, propelling my craft. The Muse allows me to weave a ship that she has made visible: my celebrated hope is made one with your vow. Let my crafted praise, resting on its great mass of metrical learning, not crush my mind with a gaping foot, weary as it is from its detours.

With good intention, and a sacred river of eloquence, I shall openly tell of the most joyful signs. Should his mercy make light of them when it competes with the greatest vows after war has been crushed? So you, since whose election our golden age is growing, will soon victoriously celebrate (now for the second time) the twenty years of your rule in Latium: let my piety give shape to those twenty years, in a poem on your wondrous name. The blessed page acts out its vow in its characters of floral polychrome, recording the remarkable destinies of the imperial progeny. The blessed deeds of your descendants will be worthy of you as judge or as pious witness, and will be joined to the titular triumphs of their ancestor!

As the poet makes clear, this is no ordinary text. Right from the outset – that is, from the opening word, *prodentur* – Optatian promises to make something literally manifest: "the red cinnabar *will reveal* the heavenly signs to the reader" – or more literally, given the passive verb, "the heavenly signs *will be revealed* to the reader through the red cinnabar" (*Prodentur minio caelestia signa legenti*).[46] The poem begins by establishing a tension between "showing" and "reading." As readers proceed with the text, moreover, they find the theme further drawn out and expanded. On the one hand, the poem alludes to its own writtenness (e.g. *scripta*, verse 13), with frequent additional references to "speaking" and

---

46   On the significance of the reference to *caelestia signa*, cf. below n. 74.

"singing" – that is, to the gesture of turning words back into sonic artefact (e.g. *canat*, verse 3; *dicam*, verse 9; *canendo*, verse 9; *cano*, verse 13; *cane*, verse 19; *dicam*, verse 29).[47] On the other, the text underscores its status as a visual as well as verbal entity: in talking about an "art painted in characters" (*arte notis picta*, verse 20), Optatian delights in the very ambiguity of his *ars*, at once referring to the literary and visual craftsmanship alike;[48] similarly, when he mentions "visions of peace" (*pakis... uisus*, verse 16), or for that matter a "ship made visible" (*uisam... nauem*, verse 25), the poet alludes to the material apparitions on the page.

Optatian's talk of moving between poetic and pictorial form – as indeed between written text and sonic artefact – has to be understood against a larger critical backdrop. One important context comes in established traditions of comparing painting with poetry, not least Simonides' famous analogy between poetry as "speaking painting" and painting as "silent poetry."[49] Another lies in rhetorical thinking about ekphrasis (literally, a descriptive "speaking out" in the context of a narrative speech or text).[50] By the time Optatian was writing, this phenomenon of ekphrasis had been the subject of numerous discussions – in extant Greek imperial *Progymnasmata* (essentially, schoolboy "textbooks" in rhetoric), as well as in Greek scholiastic commentaries on canonical literary texts.[51] According to the definition by Theon, itself repeated by the authors of other *Progymnasmata*, ekphrasis could be understood as "a descriptive speech

---

47 On the theme, cf. Squire 2016a, 200–1, along with, e.g., Squire 2017a, 44–45. Cf. more generally the scintillating studies of Boeder 1996 (on Latin and late antique materials) and Männlein-Robert (on the earlier Hellenistic prehistory).

48 For Optatian's talk of *ars*, cf. *Carm.* 3.30; *Carm.* 6.14; *Carm.* 7.19; *Carm.* 21.6, 9; *Carm.* 26.2, 18 (and cf. also *Epist. Con.* 10). For Optatian as *artifex*, cf. *Carm.* 26.7 and *Carm.* 20b.18.

49 Plut. *mor.* (*de glor. Ath.*) 346F (= Simon. frg. 190b Bergk): [...] ὁ Σιμωνίδης τὴν μὲν ζωγραφίαν ποίησιν σιωπῶσαν προσαγορεύει, τὴν δὲ ποίησιν ζωγραφίαν λαλοῦσαν ("Simonides informs that a picture is a silent poem, and a poem a speaking picture"). For discussion, cf., e.g., Sprigath 2004; for the way in which this Simonidean adage looks back to earlier traditions of Homeric ekphrasis, cf. Squire 2013a, esp. 161.

50 Greek and Latin ekphrasis has attracted a substantial bibliography over the last twenty years in particular. For some different orientations, cf. (along with Karel Thein's chapter in this volume) Elsner 2002; Zeitlin 2013; Squire 2015b.

51 The most important study of the *Progymnasmata* is Webb 2009 (complete with appendix of the most important passages on pp. 197–211); on the scholastic tradition, cf., e.g., Rispoli 1984; Meijering 1987, esp. 29–52; Manieri 1998, 179–92; and Squire 2018 (with further references).

which vividly (*enargôs*) brings about seeing through hearing" (ἔκφρασίς ἐστι λόγος περιηγηματικὸς ἐναργῶς ὑπ' ὄψιν ἄγων τὸ δηλούμενον).[52] In poem 19, as throughout the corpus, Optatian seems to have played upon the thinking. Here, after all, the notion of rhetorical *enargeia* ("vividness") is given material form, and verbal discourse really does metamorphose into visual spectacle on the page.[53] Where the *Progymnasmata* recurrently frame ekphrasis as an art of fiction – that is, of *almost* bringing about "seeing" through "hearing," so that audiences are *all but* transferred into spectators[54] – Optatian forges physical images out of his words: he bestows his lettered texts with a literal sort of iconicity.

There is much to say about the content of the nineteenth poem, as indeed about its historical and political backdrop.[55] We might note in passing, for example, that the text is oriented first and foremost around its praise for Emperor Constantine. Traditions of imperial panegyric loom large throughout the poem, which is explicitly oriented around "crafted praise" (*laus ... ficta*, verse 28).[56] Optatian begins with an encomium of Constantine's military feats, addressing the emperor directly (verses 2–15). After turning to celebrate the peace that the emperor has established, Optatian then charts a different course, reflecting on the craft of the poet (verses 16–28), before returning full circle to

---

52   Theon, *Prog.* 118.7 (= Patillon and Bolognesi 1997, 66), with discussion in Webb 2009, 51–55.

53   Like the trope of ekphrasis, the quality of *enargeia* has attracted a formidable bibliography. See, e.g., Sheppard 2014, 19–46; Webb 2016; Lausberg 1998, 359–66nn810–19 (collecting rhetorical sources on the related Latin quality of *evidentia*); cf. Squire and Elsner 2016, esp. 60–61, 68–69 (in the context of another work that plays knowingly with the notion of *enargeia*: the *Imagines* of the Elder Philostratus).

54   As Goldhill (2007, 3) nicely puts it, "rhetorical theory knows well that its descriptive power is a technique of illusion, semblance, of making to appear" (cf. Becker 1995, 28). For the relevant passages, see Hermog, *Prog.* 10.48 [= Rabe 1913, 23], Theon, *Prog.* 119 [= Patillon and Bolognesi 1997, 69] and Nikolaus, *Prog.* [= Felten 1913, 70]. "Even if the speech were ten thousand times vivid (*enargês*)," as John of Sardis later commented on a passage of Aphthonius' *Progymnasmata*, "it would be impossible to bring 'the thing shown' or ekphrasized itself 'before the eyes'" (κἂν γὰρ μυριάκις ἐναργὴς εἴη ὁ λόγος, ἀδύνατον αὐτὸ κατ' ὄψιν ἀγαγεῖν τὸ δηλούμενον ἤτοι ἐκφραζόμενον, Rabe 1928, 216).

55   The poem can be dated to around AD 326, not least on the grounds of its reference to Constantine's *vicennalia*: cf. Bruhat 1999, 500; Edwards 2005, 458–59; Wienand 2017 (on broader questions of chronology).

56   For a scintillating discussion of encomium in the work of Optatian, see Schierl and Scheidegger Lämmle; cf. more generally Wienand 2012, 355–420.

Constantine, the golden age of his reign, and the exploits of his sons (verses 29–38).[57]

But it is the apparitions summoned up in, by, and through the poem that I want to focus upon here. For whatever we make of the underlying hexameter groundtext, its constituent letters have been laid out so as to function in a pictorial way. If we look to the internal patterns of the text – if we view the poem rather than simply read it – we see the figurative profile of a ship, complete with a stern (at the right-hand side), prow (at the left), and ramming spike (lower left). Further details enhance the picture: at the aft of the vessel, for example, are a tiller and rudder; observe, too, how three sets of oars emerge from its hull. The schematic outline of a mast adorns the middle of the ship, in turn emblazoned with a chi-rho monogram: in the context of the mast, the motif doubles up in turn as a make-believe sail.

How might readers have approached this imagery? To read the Latin hexameter poem is to discover an array of possible semantic frameworks. On one level, the picture might be understood as alluding to Constantine's various naval victories (themselves evoked in verses 10–15).[58] At the same time, the figure also lends itself to more figurative interpretations: as a literal image of Optatian's desire to be shipped back to Rome from exile (developed in verses 22–26), for example; as a metapoetic image for the poet's own tricky navigations, steering his compositional way through metaphorical "waves" (cf. *liquore*, verse 6; *undas*, verse 7; *aestus*, verse 21), with a "rugged" Muse as guide (*scrupea ... Musa*, verses 16–17); and not least as an emblem for Constantine himself – the good "helmsman" who pilots the "ship of state" back to safety.[59]

The text of the poem offers readers different frameworks of interpretive navigation. Within the picture itself, moreover, we find additional letters that help to steer a response. For as audiences gaze upon this visual field, they find letters lurking within the picture (itself comprised from the alphabetic units of the

---

57   The encomiastic journey of the poem moves full-circle – from its vocative address of *Constantine* at the beginning of verse 2 to its mention of the crowning deeds of his *nepotum* at the end of the final line.

58   In this context, the reference in verses 35–36 to the "remarkable destinies of the imperial progeny recorded on the blessed page" (*pagina felix, / Augustae sobolis memorans insignia fata*) has been understood as an allusion to Constantine's naval victory over Licinius in AD 324, in which Crispus played a decisive role: cf., e.g., Barnes 1975, 82; Wienand 2012, 397–98.

59   Cf. Squire 2015a, 109–11, with further references.

hexameter poem). Most obvious are the characters *VOT*, sandwiched either side of the ship. The word is a common abbreviation, referring to the imperial *uota* mentioned in numerous verses (not least in the *uotis* hidden within the horizontal bar of the letter *T* itself): as verse 13 wittily puts it, vows have been, quite literally, "written with / by way of the 'vow'" (*uoto scripta*).[60] Still more intriguing are the letters concealed within the mimetic outline of the ship: criss-crossing the ship's hull are seen a pair of symmetrical characters, adding up to an *XX* formation. Although woven into the picture formed from Optatian's words, this detail can also be understood "alphabetically," albeit in a rather different sense from the *VOT* written/depicted above. These letters, after all, are imbued with a potential numerical significance, referring to the number 20 – and hence celebrating Constantine's *vicennalia* in AD 325–26 (as mentioned explicitly in verse 33). Once again, Optatian flags the conceit explicitly: as verse 34 puts it, the poem will give literal shape (*formet*) to the *uicennia* of Constantine's reign.

What is so staggering about all these figurative-alphabetical-numeric patterns is their capacity not only to be viewed, but also to be read.[61] In each case, the patterns in the poem mark out additional verbal messages for the reader. The simplest – and most prosaic – line is encoded within the letters *VOT*. We have to read in a variety of directions, of course – horizontally, vertically, diagonally, even around a never-ending ring (an appropriate subject for the words *floret semper*). Put the pieces together from left to right, though, and we end up with *Roma felix floret semper uotis tuis* ("blessed Rome will always flourish under your vows").

The letters that comprise the ship are still more impressive. In line with the image of the ship, readers can here embark upon a variety of different itineraries, even though not every journey will result in a sensical (still less a metrical) line. If we begin with the *N* which opens verse 16, one option is to navigate a reading that moves vertically down and then horizontally across the grid, proceeding from the top of the prow to the top of the stern. The result

---

60   For the argument that the letters instead amount to an abbreviation for *Victor Oceani Terraeque* ("a variant on the more common title 'Victor Terrae Marisque'"), or alternatively *Victor Orbis Terrarum*, see Edwards 2005, 459; Pipitone 2012, 91.

61   The *uersus intexti* (as well as the Greek elegiac couplet) that I discuss in the paragraphs that follow were already drawn out by extant (Carolingian?) scholiasts: cf. Polara 1973, 1:73; Pipitone 2012, 86–91.

is a hexameter, and one which overtly develops the naval theme: *nigras nunc tutus contemnat, summe, procellas* ("let him now defy the black storms in safety, o great one"). Another possible verse begins with the zigzagging word *nauita*. If a reader commences the hexameter with this dactyl (instead of the spondee *nigras*), it is possible to continue in the same direction, arriving at a related verse, and one which this time specifies its subject: *nauita nunc tutus contemnat, summe, procellas* ("let the sailor now defy the storms in safety, o great one").

A range of additional or alternative journeys are to be had. Consider a third option – namely, to begin a hexameter neither with *nigras*, nor with *nauita*, but instead with the word *tutus*, in verse 22. If readers allow themselves to take a diversion via either one of the criss-crossing symmetrical X letters, they end up once again at the ship's stern – and with a different corresponding verse (albeit one ending up with the same letter S in verse 17): *tutus contemnat summis cumulata tropaeis* ("let him defy in safety even that which is piled high with greatest trophies"). Alternatively, of course, we might begin lower down, with the make-believe ramming-spike at the ship's prow (verse 25). If readers trace a path up either one of the X letters, they once again trace a hexameter: *pulsa mente mala contemnat, summe, procellas* ("with ill intent cast aside, o great one, let him defy the storms").[62] At the same time, there is always the option of proceeding from the oars. From a semantic point of view, these figurative letters may at first look nonsensical (read the lines from left to right, for example, and we arrive at a puzzling OMABONOQUERNSPEQN).[63] But as audiences shove and heave in their efforts of viewing/reading, they eventually strike upon a hexameter: if the reader instead moves from right to left (crucially, thereby following the ship's own imagined course of motion) and from the extremities inwards, they find *spe quoque Roma bona contemnat, summe, procellas* ("with good faith, let Rome also defy the storms, o great one").

Whichever poetic-pictorial journey we choose, our response to this poetic object must navigate between different paths, as indeed between different representational registers. Optatian opens his poem by talking about "signs" (*signa*), returning to the same language in verses 17 and 29 (*signis; signa … laetissima*).[64]

---

62 With its talk to *pulsa mente*, the hexameter nicely aligns with the pictorial subject – the ramming spike of the ship...

63 My ideas about "nonsense" here have learned from Stewart 1978 in particular.

64 One might also note Optatian's reference to the *insignia fata* of Constantine's descendants (verse 36). Similar language recurs in numerous other poems: e.g. *Carm.* 4.1 (*uicennia signa*);

But these *signa* possess a knowing semiotic slipperiness. Just as the letters of Optatian's words do double duty as the tessellated units for his images, so too does the imagery, objectified on the page, slip back into the letters of language. The result is a knowing poetic-pictorial game, one that has the audience move between different modes of verbally interpreting the visual patterns on the one hand, and of visually interpreting the verbal language on the other.

It is from this perspective that we should approach what is perhaps the most extraordinary feat of all: the cryptographic chi-rho emblazoned at the upper centre of the grid. This is a signum redeployed in no fewer than three other poems attributed to Optatian, and in a range of different contexts.[65] In one example (poem 8 [fig. 12]), the emblem is surrounded by giant letters of the name *IESUS*, so as to spell out an explicitly "Christian" significance; in the second and third poems (poems 14 [fig. 13] and 24), the motif went without further embellishment.[66] In each of these other examples, the chi-rho stretches to occupy the full span of the poetic field. With poem 19, by contrast, the emblem is itself incorporated within the mimetic framework of the visualized object, forming part of the represented ship to which it is attached. The chi-rho thus takes on an iconic significance within the image – not just as recognizable insignia, but also as depicted mast and/or sail.

So what are audiences to make of the text within this literal-figurative pattern? To read the picture as Latin letters is to be faced with a semantic challenge: wherever we start and however we proceed, the visual pattern at first yields no sensible verbal message; there seems to be no rhyme or reason to the text. Try out an alternative poetic-pictorial strategy, however, and it is possible to see things quite differently. It might be remembered that, in linguistic terms, this monogram – sandwiched between the Latin letters *VOT* – refers to something encoded in Greek: it is an iconic fusion of two Greek *grammata*, the chi

---

Carm. 5.2 (*signare*); *Carm.* 6.34 (*signare*); *Carm.* 7.12 (*signatur*); *Carm.* 8.2 (*pia signa*), i (*salutari ... signo*); *Carm.* 16.29 (*signa*); *Carm.* 18.23 (*suis signis*); *Carm.* 24.35 (*aeturnum ... signum*). For discussion of these "dynamic signs," see Squire 2017a, 53–82.

65   For expanded discussions, see Squire and Whitton 2017 and Lunn-Rockliffe 2017.

66   Poems 14 and 24 nonetheless strike very different notes in their frame of (non-)Christian reference – so much so, indeed, that the authenticity of poem 24 has been doubted: see Squire and Whitton 2017, esp. 86–91.

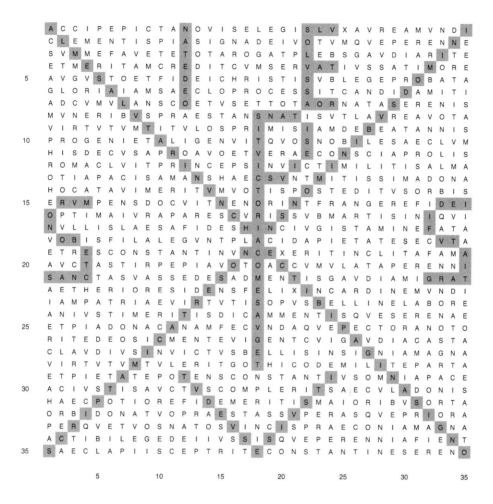

12. Optatian *Carm.* 8; typesetting after Squire and Wienand (eds.) 2017: 33 (using the edition of Polara 1973).

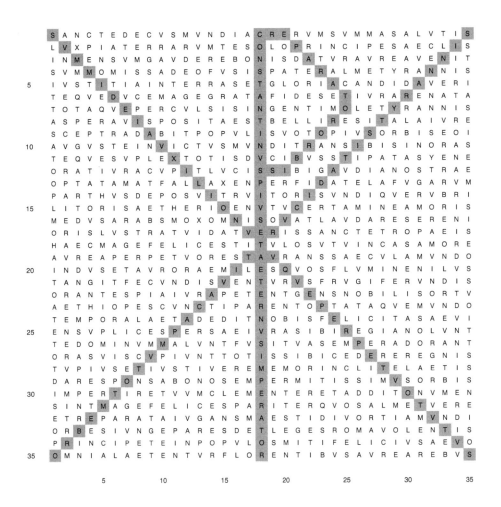

13. Optatian *Carm.* 14; typesetting after Squire and Wienand (eds.) 2017: 39 (using the edition of Polara 1973).

andthe rho.[67] What happens, then, if we try reading the constituent letters not in Latin, but as Greek text? Needless to say, the Latin letters have to be converted into their Greek visual "equivalents": A doubles up as alpha and delta, for example, C as sigma, H as eta, T as both theta and tau, P as rho.[68] Proceed with this conversion, however, and something miraculous happens.[69] Starting with the upper left-hand arm of the chi and moving downwards, then proceeding in the opposite direction with the parallel arm below, and finally looping the loop with the rho (subsequently proceeding down its "mast"), we arrive at a full hexameter and the first part of a pentameter. To complete the distich, audiences must turn to the tiller and rudder below, arriving at the following text:

THNNAYNAEIK – *OCMONCEDEAP* – *MENONEINIINOMIZINTYPOICTEIN* – *OMENONCHCAPETHCANEMOIC*
ΤΗΝΝΑΥΝΔΕΙΚ – ΟΣΜΟΝΣΕΔΕΑΡ – ΜΕΝΟΝΕΙΝΙΝΟΜΙΖΙΝΘΥΡΟΙΣΤΕΙΝ – ΟΜΕΝΟΝΣΗΣΑΡΕΤΗΣΑΝΕΜΟΙΣ

The result is a Greek elegiac couplet, created out of an object manifested in the Latin hexameter text. Crucially, the text also delivers a textual commentary on the scene that has been visualized on the page:

τὴν ναῦν δεῖ κόσμον, σὲ δὲ ἄρμενον εἰνὶ νομίζ<ε>ιν
θούροις τείνομενον σῆς ἀρετῆς ἀνέμοις.

One must think that the ship is the world, and that you are the hoisted rigging, tautened by the strong winds of your virtue.

Miraculously, translated from text to image and back again, and simultaneously converted from Latin hexameters to Greek elegiac couplet, these lines deliver a new instruction in how to view. The meaning of the image is said to lie in its symbolic or allegorical significance. Although the picture stands before us,

---

67 At the same time, the *chi* of the chi-rho recalls the shape of the double X formation that makes up the hull of the ship depicted below.

68 Similar oscillations from Latin to Greek are to be found in *Carm.* 16 and 23 (in those two poems, however, A must be understood as a Greek *lambda* in addition to serving as *alpha* and *delta*, while X must be understood as Greek *chi*): cf. Squire 2017b, 88–91.

69 To cite the (later Carolingian?) scholiast, the "obscurity" is thus "alleviated from the heart" (*in hac pagina a monogrammo Iesu oritur principium lectionis, ut pectore leuetur obscuritas*). On the scholia, cf. above, n. 61.

its cryptic text steers audiences in a more (or rather less?) figurative direction of interpretation: it is necessary, readers are now told, to "un-see" the picture, to "consider" (νομίζ<ε>ιν)[70] its imagery in an intellectual capacity.[71] Within the manufactured world of this poem-cum-picture, audiences are urged to envisage the cosmos as idea – to look not to sensory sight, but to the mind's eye of the imagination. In all this, the epigram enacts a kaleidoscopic twist in how we see: what things really are (εἰνί) is said to be at odds with how they objectively appear.

Such ontological games take shape against a larger sea of critical ideas – debates about the nature of representation, but also about the relation between sight and insight. But crucially, it seems to me, Christian perspectives could also come into play.[72] There is little in the Latin hexameter poem to prompt audiences to approach the artefact through a Christianizing lens: for all the nods to Mars, Apollo, and the Muses, Christ goes unmentioned in the poem, which addresses Constantine as the "glory of the world, golden light of the age" (*Constantine, decus mundi, lux aurea saecli*, 19.2). As so often with Optatian, however, first impressions can be deceptive. For those minded to see the motif in such terms, the ship had at least the potential to float a Judaeo-Christian significance: already by the early fourth century, we find the symbol of the ship being used in various Christian explicatory frameworks, and in Christian visual culture as a cryptic Christian emblem.[73]

Despite the lack of explicit reference, it is also possible to find hints of this Christian interpretative frame in the Latin hexameter poem. Consider, once

---

70   The spelling of νομίζειν as νομίζιν (with the final diphthong rendered as single *iota*) is in keeping with the word's spoken pronunciation in this period. For references, see Squire and Whitton 2017, 81n84.

71   On the Neoplatonic elements of Optatian's poetry in particular, see, e.g., Levitan 1985, esp. 263–66; Moreschini 2013, 597–617; Squire 2017a, 75–76; Habinek 2017.

72   As I have explored at greater length elsewhere (especially Squire 2017a, 61–74), the modern predisposition to read Optatian as *either* a "pagan" or "Christian" author is deeply problematic. In an explicit discussion of Optatian, Green (2010, 67) nicely anticipates the point: "in this period there was surely a high degree of fluidity, of uncertainty, and of intermediate positioning between the poles, which makes a simple division into sheep and goats quite unhelpful."

73   Already in the second century, Justin had noted a parallel between the cross and the mast of a ship (*Apol.* 1.55), just as Clement of Alexandria specified that the ship was an appropriate symbol for Christian seal rings (*Paed.* 3.11.59.2): cf., e.g., Bruun 1963, 129–30; Ernst 1991, 130–31; Spier 2007, 52nn310–15; Squire and Whitton 2017, 81–82; Lunn-Rockliffe 2017, 445–52.

again, the opening verse, with its reference to *caelestia signa* ("heavenly signs"). Not for nothing, I think, does this phrase reverberate with Lactantius' famous account of the Constantine's vision before the Battle of the Milvian Bridge in AD 312 – the divine instruction, experienced in the emperor's dream, that Constantine should inscribe a "heavenly sign" (*caeleste signum*), forged from the letters of Christ's name, onto the shields of his soldiers.[74] For those attuned to the rhetoric, these opening words could be understood to refer not just to the chi-rho, but also its potential to spell out a "Christian" message; given the letters *UOT*, sandwiched either side of the emblem, one might even be minded to conceptualize the work as a kind of prayer or *uota* – to rededicate it, as it were, to Christ. To approach the poem in such Christianizing terms is to raise further questions about the identity of the person addressed in the cryptic Greek text, signalled both through the second person (σέ) and the possessive adjective (σῆς ἀρετῆς). For is the addressee here to be understood as Constantine? Or might we be dealing with something wholly more heavenly – an unspoken Christian God, as made manifest through the chi-rho apparition? Ultimately, our poem leaves its figurations slipping and sliding between different frames of interpretive reference, just as it does between words and pictures, as indeed between Latin and Greek linguistic systems.

*   *   *

This has been a necessarily brief overview, centred around an introduction to Optatian's works on the one hand, and an examination of a single Optatianic poem on the other.

In what ways, though, might this material contribute to the larger themes of the present anthology? In my view, Optatian's importance lies in anticipating so many aspects of modern *Dinggedichte* – if not in the actual appearance of his compositions, then at least in the thinking that gave rise to them. Quite apart from his interest in manifesting, as opposed to simply representing, objects, Optatian was overtly sensitive to the physicality of his poetic compositions: written script is conceptualized as a self-standing, monumental entity – as

---

74 *De mort. pers.* 44.5, with discussion in Squire and Whitton 2017, esp. 74–77 (with further bibliography). We might compare Optatian's reference to the chi-rho as a *salutare signum* in the first *versus intextus* of *Carm.* 8, which resonates with Eusebius' recurrent description of the chi-rho as a "saving sign" (σωτήριον σημεῖον: *Vit. Con.* 1.28–32; *Hist. eccl.* 9.9.10–11; *Tric. Or.* 9–10).

multifaceted artefact, made up of elemental letters, that can be deconstructed and reconstructed at whim. The form of Optatian's poems, we have said, is bound up with the innovative technology of the codex, establishing the page as the appropriate unit of scrutiny. But such writerly experiments also stem from an acute awareness of the text as present material artefact – as entity to be experienced in its own fabricated right.

The point strikes me as an appropriate note on which to conclude. Throughout this chapter, one primary objective in introducing Optatian has been to encourage modernists to take a longer view of the *Dinggedicht* as cultural phenomenon. But a second and related purpose has been to showcase the sheer brilliance of Optatian's works: on the one hand, to demonstrate the conceptual, technical, and literary artistry of this material; on the other, to engage a scholarly readership that is used to dealing with wholly more modern poetic traditions. As poet and artist, Optatian has been distinctly ill served by those who specialize in ancient literature. Scholars of modern poetry, I suspect, will be much better attuned to the complexity of his oeuvre.

Beautiful Stones and Exotic Objects: The Symbolism of Things in Early Medieval China

ZORNICA KIRKOVÁ AND OLGA LOMOVÁ

Poems and Things in the Universe

In China a special kind of literature "about things" (*yong wu*) has been practised for many centuries in various genres. The earliest known examples date back to China's antiquity, to the second half of the Warring States period (475–221 BCE). Through the Han dynasty (202 BCE–220 CE) literature dedicated to "things" developed in the form of the *fu* genre – relatively longer prosimetric compositions with prominent narrative and descriptive dimensions. *Fu*, commonly translated into English as "rhapsodies," were usually composed and recited during various social occasions at the courts of the rulers.[1] This type of poetry flourished also during the following early medieval period, when shorter lyrical poems (*shi*) gradually started to marginalize the *fu* genre. The

---

1   The earliest known literary compositions named as *fu* and dealing with objects are in the form of versified riddles, included in *Xunzi*, a philosophical book dating from the third century BCE (Knoblock 1994). The early meaning of *fu* as a literary genre is not clear; it was applied to a variety of compositions and its original definition – "to recite without singing" – was concerned with the performative aspects and could apply to different genres.

emergence of new genres never obliterated the topic of things, which remained popular for many centuries and indeed millennia to come.

A "thing" (*wu*) in the Chinese case can be almost any object, man-made or natural, including stones, plants, animals, and insects, but also atmospheric phenomena, such as wind or snow. *Wu* was a category in traditional cosmology, which conceptualized the universe as consisting of heaven, earth, and "ten thousand things" (*wan wu*) – in other words, individual entities and phenomena of all kinds.[2] As expressed in the philosophy of change of the *Yijing* (Book of Changes), the universe is constantly "becoming" rather than "being," it is an organic, never-ending process, in which the interactions of heaven and earth generate the ten thousand things (*Chong kan Songben Zhouyi zhushu* 171.2; Legge 1963, 393). This means that no single unequivocal definition can exhaust the meaning of a certain "thing." Instead, each "thing" of the ancient and medieval Chinese universe is observed in the process of becoming and changing, and in its interactions with other things. As a result, the nature of a "thing," as described since late antiquity in the "encyclopaedias" (*leishu*),[3] is revealed within a broad network of qualities, manifestations, relations, and situations that endow it with complex and always contextualized meaning (Zheng Yuyu 2012, 245–48).

In traditional Chinese cosmology, the interconnection of "things" was conditioned by one single, unitary and universal substance, known as *qi* (a term translated as "breath," "pneuma," etc.), which provided the "material and energetic basis of things and their transformations." All entities – from inanimate objects to gods – exist only as a modality of *qi*, in different degree of condensation and movement: when *qi* coalesces, it brings things into existence and gives them shape, when things die or disintegrate, their *qi* disperses and passes into other forms. This never-ending, pulsating process of life and death is governed by a natural "order of things" which, according to ancient thought, structured both nature and culture, ordered material objects of the world as well as social norms and relations, and also determined human character. In this holistic universe, the informing inner order manifests itself in the external phenomena and

---

2   A human being may also be regarded as a *wu* – a special one, "the most highly endowed of all" (Legge 1960, 283).

3   There is no single authoritative source that provides a systematic description of the cosmological system of ancient China. For a survey of traditional cosmology and the *lei* categories, see Needham 1956, 216–303.

physical features, while outward qualities function as indicators of the under-lying natural principles. The very term that denotes the "order of things" – *li* (sometimes translated as "principle") – also captures the close interrelation of external properties with inner qualities. Its original meaning is "veins in jade," understood as a pattern visible on the surface of the precious stone which at the same time permeates its material substance and determines its inner structure. On an epistemological level, this concept means that one could grasp the inner order of the universe through careful observation and sensuous perception of outer phenomena. Analogically to this general understanding of the workings of the universe, anything perceived by the senses could be (perhaps even *should* be) read as a manifestation of the inherent "patterning," of the structure and substance of a thing, and possibly a key by which to arrive at a true understand-ing of the order of things (Cheng 1997, 57–58).

Rhetoric of Things

Rhapsodies *fu* developed a standard rhetorical treatment of things: they described faithfully and in detail the physical features of a certain thing, includ-ing a variety of sensory perceptions, and its possible manifestations and trans-formations. An essential part of this description was the origin of a thing – real or imagined, even mythical.[4] A "thing" depicted in this way is eventually endowed with human qualities as well, and the description becomes a reflec-tion (frequently an indirect one) on human character and social values. As a result, the description of a certain "thing," while true to life, may eventually embody the personal situation of the poet, his emotions, or demonstrate the values to which he subscribes. In other words, it may fulfil the dictum of the Great Preface to the *Shijing* (Book of Odes) of the Confucian canon: to "express the intent" (*yan zhi*) of the poet. One of the oldest "rhapsodies on things," which has set up a paradigmatic relationship between a thing (in this case, the orange tree) and a man of noble aspirations, is the "Ju song" (Ode to the Orange Tree), traditionally attributed to Qu Yuan (ca. 340–278 BCE). This poem depicts an

---

4   A good example available in English translation is "Qin fu" (Rhapsody on the Zither) by Ji Kang (223–262), in Knechtges 2014, 279–303.

orange tree, the "fairest of all God's trees," as firmly rooted in its home country, longing for its ruler to recognize its qualities and lamenting his neglect.[5]

During the early medieval period, impromptu composition of rhapsodies on things became a popular diversion during social gatherings at the prince's courts. The common practice was for the prince, as the host, to set up a theme – often, but not exclusively, an object present and visible to all. The prince would often compose the first poem and then ask his guests to provide compositions of their own. The guests, in their verses, responded to their companions and also tried to surpass them in poetic skill. Xie Huilian (407–433), in his "Rhapsody on Snow," depicted a fictious poetry contest at the court of Prince Xiao of Liang during the Western Han, providing a vivid account of a poetic exchange of this kind.[6]

In the highly competitive, prestige-oriented environment of the early medieval courts, poems improvised during social gatherings would routinely express, in an elegantly indirect way, loyalty and gratitude to the host, subtle flattery or wishes of happiness and success. Poetical meetings also provided an opportunity for self-promotion; a poet might use the occasion to exhibit his talent and erudition, and attract the attention of his patron by means of witty and sharp argumentation. Polemics with the other present poets could also occur, as part of a literary game in which the best and most original poem would be rewarded by the prince. The ready and witty display of poetic skill could even result in securing special favours from the prince, including promotion within the court hierarchy.[7]

Such poetry, being a form of social practice, commonly included references to specific personal experiences or topical allusions to events which were familiar to all companions. Sometimes a short prosaic preface to the poem summarizes the biographical and historical facts, but in many other instances the specific circumstances that provided inspiration are now unknown. Today, the reader of these poems, which originally responded to concrete events, stumbles across passages that are hard to understand outside the original context, and the full meaning of a medieval poem may elude our grasp.

---

5   For the topos of the orange tree in ancient and early medieval literature, see Lomová 2004.
6   For an annotated English translation, see Knechtges 2014, 21–31.
7   For a detailed analysis of poetry as part of the social life at the courts of Chinese rulers and nobility in early medieval China, see Blitstein 2015.

Symbolism of Things

The idea of the world as an interconnected and interacting continuum of "heaven, earth, and ten thousand things," which also includes human character and social norms, and where perceptible phenomena are understood as manifestations of universal inner principles, determines a specific mode of symbolism of "things." The symbolic meanings of a thing are generated through the evocative and exhaustive description of perceivable qualities and processes. The more truthful to reality a representation of a thing is, the more powerful its symbolism becomes. The symbolic meanings of a thing find expression in its external features and behaviour, and the main duty of a poet is to observe reality carefully and to record and decipher it correctly. Paraphrasing Kang-I Sun Chang's discussion of the much later genre of *ci* songs, symbolism in Chinese poetry about things operates on the principle of "associative representation," which unites a thing, through its material qualities, with the human situation and character it symbolizes (Sun Chang 1986, 358).

The association of things with human qualities is not simply a matter of mechanical selection of pre-existing, conventional symbols. Rather, the poet carefully observes an object in all its aspects, aiming to extract from its appearance and behaviour the inner qualities, the informing "pattern," that may also be generalized as applicable to the "pattern" of a human situation, character, or emotions. An example would be the resilience of bamboo as an embodiment of the firmness of character of a gentleman; or the gentle fragrance of otherwise inconspicuous flowers of certain orchids of the *Cymbidium* genus as equivalent to the unpretentious, charismatic virtue *de* of an upright man, who does not promote himself, yet naturally becomes known to others. Poetry on things typically comprises specific vocabulary of words with multiple meanings which denote both the physical properties of a thing as well as human values and qualities: for instance, *gao*, which means "tall" in the case of a tree, but also "noble" in the case of man. A special category among these are homonyms, which enable the poet to encompass in one word both the physical world and human character. That is to say, the symbolism of things in Chinese poetry results from the potentiality offered by physical, sensually perceptible features, and a poet actualizes certain symbolic meanings through his selection of particular attributes and careful choice of words. Despite certain tendency towards conventional symbolism, the inherent symbolic potential of a particular thing is generally realized in novel ways each time a creative poet writes about it.

Careful observation of the physical qualities of things was, however, only one part of the process by which a medieval poet learned about the world. Equally important were authoritative books of the past, which had previously mentioned and described a certain thing and anchored it in particular semantic contexts. For the early medieval period, these were typically the Confucian classics systematized in the second century BCE and thereafter studied and memorized by all educated men. Potentially, however, any other literary or philosophical text could become a source of "knowing" a thing. Highly respected ancient books were regarded not only as a wellspring of poetic motifs and refined literary works, but also as the starting point for all cognition. "Knowing" a thing was inseparable from remembering how the sages of the past had conceptualized and described it in their books. As a result, literary allusions endowed a thing with the meanings that had been potentially attached to it in the ancient classics. It may even happen that what seems to be a true-to-life depiction of a thing is in fact not the result of the poet's own keen observation, but an allusion to one of the Confucian classics, the *Erya* dictionary, the "encyclopaedia" *Lü shi chunqiu*, the book of the philosopher Zhuangzi, or others.

The importance of allusions in refined poetic style grew over time and became a precondition for a good poem. Around certain "things," there accumulated recurring motifs endowed with specific connotations, which were at the disposal of later poets. References to earlier texts provided, however, more than a shortcut to pre-existing meanings; once taken out of their original context, they could be reshaped and reinterpreted in a playful dialogue with the original source. Playfulness was an important feature of the "thing poems" of the early medieval period, appropriate for the informal poetry of social gatherings.

Reading such poems today is sometimes like deciphering a message concealed in ambivalent words and obscure textual references. This may feel burdensome, devoid of the true spirit of poetry. However, for medieval poets and their readers (and listeners as well, for the poems were customarily recited aloud), such expression was considered natural and did not pose an obstacle to comprehension. After all, this was the poetry of the educated elite, which shared profound knowledge of their literary heritage and an appreciation of erudition, originality, and subtle wit. A good poem about a thing would be more than a riddle with a straightforward solution; it would retain a level of ambivalence to be savoured and appreciated by the reader, who might join in with his own companion poem and offer a different perspective on the same thing. In the following part of this chapter, we will examine one specific case: poems about a bowl made of precious stone, presented to a powerful gentleman as a gift from a distant land.

The Precious Gift to Cao Cao

At the end of the Han dynasty the empire was engulfed in civil wars and political turmoil. The real political power was in the hands of several military strongmen, the most important of whom was Chancellor Cao Cao (155–220). He reunited Northern China and de facto demolished Han rule, laying the foundations for the new, albeit short-lived state of Wei (220–265). Cao Cao was not only a brilliant ruler, but also an accomplished poet and patron of writers. Most of the leading poets and scholars of the period took up residence in his capital at Yecheng and participated in the literary gatherings hosted by Cao Cao and his sons Cao Pi (187–226) – the future emperor of the Wei dynasty – and Cao Zhi (192–232), who was considered by his contemporaries to be the greatest poet of his time. It is under the patronage of the three Caos that the practice of improvising poetry on a shared topic during literary gatherings and banquets became established, and this set a precedent for later writers. Some of the group compositions of *fu* are short pieces written about precious and exotic objects presented as gifts to the Cao family. For instance, Cao Pi ordered members of his entourage to compose rhapsodies about jewelled bridles made from a carnelian that he had recently obtained; while another group of rhapsodies was written about the exotic rosemary that had been recently brought all the way from the Roman Empire to be planted into Cao Pi's garden.

Another rare treasure at the Cao court was a bowl made from a large ornamental stone called *juqu* (most probably agate), which had been presented to Cao Cao by Central Asian rulers.[8] Five rhapsodies about the precious bowl

---

8   The identification of *juqu* is uncertain. *Juqu* generally denotes the giant clamshell, *Tridacna gigas*, which was popular for making drinking vessels. Our translation is based on another possible meaning of the word *juqu* – a semi-precious stone with a prominent, mottled pattern.

are extant, though not all in their entirety.[9] They were composed by the fore-most poets and prominent figures of the day, and all five must have been pro-duced on the same occasion – a feast hosted by the future emperor Cao Pi that most likely took place in 216, the year that his father Cao Cao assumed the title "King of Wei."[10]

The material from which the bowl was carved – precious stone – possessed in itself rich potential for engendering symbolic meanings. By that time, a cluster of motifs and meanings had grown up in Chinese literature around the image of beautiful stone, commonly designated as *yu* (jade).[11] In classical texts, the physical properties and outward appearance of jade manifest the inner order of things also associated with moral qualities. Thus, in the *Li ji* (Book of Rites, 5th–1st centuries BCE), Confucius is recorded as saying that jade is valued not because of its rarity, but because it typifies the inner charismatic power *de* and all the fundamental virtues of a superior man:

> In the past gentlemen compared virtue to jade: It is soft, smooth, and glossy – like humaneness; fine, compact, and strong – like intelligence; angular, but not sharp and cutting – like righteousness; hanging down [in beads] as if it would fall to the ground – like [the humility of] propriety. When struck, yielding a note, clear and prolonged, yet ter-minating abruptly – like music; its flaws not concealing its beauty, nor its beauty concealing its flaws – like loyalty; with an internal radiance issuing from it on every side – like trustworthiness.
>
> (Sun Xidan and He Xiguang 2011, 61.1546–47; trans. Legge 1964, 2.464)

---

9   There might have been more rhapsodies composed on the same occasion which no longer survive. Two lines from another "Juqu wan fu" (Rhapsody on an Agate Bowl) by Chen Lin (d. 217) are extant (Fei Zhengang 1993, 708).

10 We deduce the date of the composition on the basis of additional historical information. The poems must have been written before 217, the year when three of the authors died, and before the winter of 216–217, when one of the writers, Wang Can, left with Cao Cao on a military campaign. Furthermore, the stone from which this bowl was made at the court could not have reached Cao Cao before 215, due to the disrupted contacts with Central Asia at the time. These were re-established only after mid-215, when Cao Cao pacified the western frontier regions.

11 The term *yu*, which is usually translated as "jade," more generally denotes any fine ornamental stone, including, for instance, marble. In addition, there exists an extensive vocabulary denot-ing various specific kinds of "jade," the precise identification of which is highly problematic.

The comparison of moral integrity of a refined man to beautiful stone also appears in the ancient *Book of Odes*, another important text of the Confucian canon. In a poem dated to the eighth or seventh century BCE, the poet compares his lord to cut and chiselled jade, among other things. The cutting and polishing of the beautiful stone here represents the process of the training and self-cultivation of a superior man.

> Look at that bay of the Qi River,
> Its green bamboos so delicately waving.
> Delicately fashioned is my lord,
> As jade cut, as jade filed,
> As jade chiselled, as jade polished.
> Oh, the grace, oh, the elegance!
> Oh, the lustre, oh, the light!
> Delicately fashioned is my lord,
> Never for a moment can I forget him.
>
> (Mao 55, 1st stanza; trans. Waley 1996, 46)

THE FIRST POEM

Qualities and symbolism associated in the classics with precious stone are central to the rhapsodies on the agate bowl ("Juqu wan fu" 車渠椀賦) composed at one of the feasts hosted by Cao Pi. On the occasion, the host passed among his guests a precious bowl that had been recently crafted from a stone presented as a tribute to the court of Cao Cao by a Central Asian (i.e. "Western") ruler. First, Cao Pi composed a short rhapsody in praise of the beautiful vessel and invited his guests to do the same. His poem commences with a short introduction about the origin of the stone, followed by a versified description of its extraordinary qualities:

車渠。玉屬也。多纖理縟文。生于西國。其俗寶之。小以繫頸。大以為器。

Juqu belongs to the jade category. It has many fine veins and elaborate patterns. It comes from the Western States, where it is a custom to treasure it. [People] tie small ones to the neck, and use large ones to make vessels.

惟二儀之普育	The Two Principles engender all,[12]
何萬物之殊形	but how differing are the forms of ten thousand things!
料珍怪之上美	I reckon the most beautiful of all rare marvels
無茲椀之獨靈	are not as uniquely numinous as this bowl.
苞華文之光麗	It enfolds the bright beauty of flowery patterns,
發符采而揚榮	shoots forth streaks and hues, brandishes blossoms.
理交錯以連屬	Its veins criss-cross and join together,
倡將離而復抃	they split and scatter, then merge again.
或若朝雲浮高山	Now like morning clouds that drift among high peaks,
忽倡飛鳥厲蒼天	then like a bird in flight, flitting across the cerulean sky.
夫其方者如矩	Their square shape matches the carpenter's square,
圓者如規	their roundness accords with the compass.
稠希不謬	They are dense or sparse without error,
洪纖有宜	[neither too] broad, [nor too] fine, in size just proper.

(Quan Sanguo wen, 4.1075)

This is a straightforward poem of praise – not so much of the vessel itself, but of the beautiful stone from which it is made. In the second couplet, Cao Pi points out its rarity and marvellous qualities, especially the divine potency of being "uniquely numinous" (*ling*). Then he evocatively depicts its colours and patterns. The poetic description endows the stone with qualities of growth and vitality, and renders its patterns as a dynamic nature scene where vegetation bursts forth, clouds drift, and birds fly. In the concluding two couplets, the imagery shifts from the vitality of nature to man-made instruments for measuring the world, which held a special place in Chinese mythology. The compass and the carpenter's square are attributes of the mythical first couple, Fu Xi and Nüwa. The two divinities not only measured and ordered the "round heaven" and the "square earth" with the help of these devices, but also established social

---

12   The Two Principles are heaven and earth.

institutions, government, and law and order. The square and compass are thus the very instruments by which civilization was created; even today, the expression "square and compass" (*guiju*) in the Chinese language denotes social norms and order.

While in the first part of the poem Cao Pi had related the stone to the larger domain of nature and the cosmos, at the conclusion he associates it with social structures. The beautiful stone, endowed with vitality and naturalness and simultaneously well-ordered, "square" and "round," "just proper" – that is to say, in accordance with the standards set up by the ancient sages – can be interpreted as a metaphor for the refined gentleman, who is both part of the cosmic natural order and conforms to the civilizing norms.

In their poetic responses to Cao Pi, the guests picked up and elaborated on the major motifs and images of the host's rhapsody, as required by the practice of group composition and as an expression of respect for the host. However, each of the poets manipulated the borrowed material and subtly changed its meaning in order to make his own point. Although the following four rhapsodies were all composed as variations on the same poem, they express different meanings, playing out the multiple symbolic potential of the same thing in a poetic dialogue that shows the originality of each poet.

THE SECOND POEM[13]

Cao Pi's younger brother Cao Zhi, considered the most accomplished poet of the period, further develops motifs from his brother's composition, trying to outdo him in evocative description and striking figures. He focuses on the lustre and the patterns of the stone, associating them with vegetation, birds, and celestial phenomena.

惟斯椀之所生	The place from which this bowl comes
于涼風之峻湄	is the steep slopes of Langfeng.[14]
采金光以定色	It draws from gold's brilliance to form its hues;

---

13   The sequence in which the poems are presented here is tentative; we have no information about the order in which they were originally composed.

14   Liangfeng (also Langfeng) is a peak of the mythical Mt. Kunlun in the West, connecting heaven and earth.

擬朝陽而發煇	it replicates the morning sun in emitting radiant light.
豐玄素之煒曄	It is replete with the dazzling glow of black and white;
帶朱榮之葳蕤	it is banded with the lush beauty of scarlet blossoms.
繙絲繪以肆采	Tangled threads and tassels, displayed and gathered;
藻繁布以相追	algal patterns intricately spread in mutual pursuit.
翩飄颻而浮景	They flitter and flutter like drifting shadows;
若驚鵠之雙飛	like startled cranes they fly in pairs.
隱神璞于西野	The divine, uncut stone laid hidden in the western wilds,
彌百葉而莫希	for a hundred ages it remained unknown.
于時乃有明篤神后	And then, there was a divine sovereign, generous and wise,
廣彼仁聲	who broadly spreads his beneficent name.
夷慕義而重使	Admiring his dedication to rightness, the foreign tribes sent an envoy
獻茲寶于斯庭	to present this treasure to our court.
命公輸使制匠	He commanded an artisan as great as Gongshu Ban[15]
窮妍麗之殊形	fully to bring out the beauty of its unusual form.
華色燦爛	Its flowery hues glitter and glisten,
文若點成	its patterns seem as if dotted on.
鬱蓊雲蒸	Dense and thick they swell like clouds;
蜿蜒龍征	twisting and twining, they course like dragons.
光如激電	Their brilliance is like flashing lightning;
影若浮星	their shadows are like drifting stars.
何神怪之巨偉	How great is this divine wonder!
信一覽而九驚	Truly, after a single glance one is thoroughly amazed!

---

15   A legendary craftsman.

雖離朱之聰目	Even someone with the acute vision of Li Zhu[16]
由炫燿而失精	would be dazed and dazzled and bereft of sight.
何明麗之可悅	How delightful its bright beauty!
起羣寶而特章	Surpassing all other treasures it alone is illustrious.
俟君子之閑宴	It attends our lord's grand feast,
酌甘醴于斯觴	he pours sweet wine from this goblet.
既娛情而可貴	It cheers the heart and is precious too;
故求御而不忘	thus it implores: "Use me, do not forget me!"

(*Quan Sanguo wen*, 14.1128; based on an unpublished translation by D. Knechtges, with slight alternations)

Cao Zhi here applies structure typical of many "thing poems." The poet narrates the "life story" of a certain thing – he first traces its origins in nature, then speaks about its discovery and crafting, and finally turns to its function in the human world. He starts with the pre-history of the bowl as an uncut stone, hidden in the western wilds, outside the civilized world. When the "divine sovereign," who is presumably his father Cao Cao, becomes renowned as a virtuous ruler, the barbarians submit to his moral authority and present the stone as a tribute to his court. There it is cut, so that its innate beauty can be fully manifested, and it is made into a useful utensil. The ending of this poem is typical of many "thing poems": the stone, now changed into an agate bowl, assumes the first-person voice to directly express its intent, in the same manner that the Great Preface speaks of the purpose of poetry – begging to be "used," in other words, to serve the sovereign.

On a symbolic level, the precious stone represents an unappreciated, raw talent living in obscurity; while its polishing represents the cultivation of a gentleman through which his abilities are fully realized and can be employed. The rhapsody can be read as a topical allegory, subtly interweaving several layers of meaning enhanced by the final personification. The beautiful stone represents gifted scholars who will fully realize their talents if they come to serve in the court of Cao Cao; while its crafting into a bowl signifies the court's beneficial, civilizing influence. Cao Zhi might allude to the fact that his father had succeeded in attracting truly exceptional men to his court, and thus implicitly

---

16   Li Zhu, also known as Li Lou, is a legendary paragon of keen sight.

compliments his companions present at the feast. He also uses the occasion to praise Cao Cao's discovery and appreciation of talented scholars – in the political ideology of the time, the ability to attract talented men into one's service was an important sign of the Mandate of Heaven and the legitimacy of a ruler. Thus, the poet may wish to flatter his father and ingratiate himself with him, especially if we assume that the precious object, which offers its service to the lord, might also be read as a self-presentation and expression of personal ambitions.

THE THIRD POEM

Only a fragment survives from the "Rhapsody on the Agate Bowl" by Xu Gan (170–217), in which the poet elaborates on the topic of social order from the conclusion of Cao Pi's rhapsody. Even though Xu Gan employs very similar vocabulary and images borrowed from Cao Pi, to the point of verbatim quotations, his message is significantly different. Unlike Cao Pi, he does not find the expression of the social order in the natural veining of the stone – that is, in one's spontaneous nature – but sees it as invested through crafting of the stone into a useful implement:

圓德應規	Its virtue of roundness corresponds to the compass,
巽從易安	compliant and docile, at ease and in comfort.
大小得宜	The size is proper,
容如可觀	the appearance is remarkable.
盛彼清醴	Filled with pure ale,
承呂彫盤	it is joined to a carved saucer.
因歡接口	On joyous occasions it touches the mouth,
媚于君顏	obtaining a favourable expression from our lord.

(*Quan Hou Han wen*, 93.975)

Through the image of the bowl carved in the shape of a cup with a saucer, which delights the eyes and serves during merry occasions, Xu Gan elucidates the relationship between the lord and his courtiers (or perhaps the patron Cao Pi and the gathered guests). Compliancy, docility, and relaxed ease are all qualities that a courtier should show towards his ruler. At the conclusion, the bowl is shown as being employed by the lord and favoured with his affection. Just like the bowl, the present scholars (or Xu Gan himself) are useful and bring delight through their talents, and are happy to receive the appreciation of their lord.

THE FOURTH POEM

Ying Yang (177–217), similarly to Cao Pi and Cao Zhi, depicts the origins and the features of the stone, and, yet again, articulates a very different message. He does not speak at all about the bowl, but focuses solely on the stone, emphasising even more its divine origins and extraordinary nature. He employs imagery and descriptions similar to those of Cao Pi and Cao Zhi, comparing the stone to clouds and dragons, and imbuing it with life and movement. In his rendering, the stone is truly divine: it originated from the Numinous Mound (the mythical Kunlun Mountain) and contains the most potent cosmic elements – the maximum solar energy, the auroras of the early dawn, the essences of heaven and earth. Further cosmological connotations are carried by specific vocabulary, such as "merging and generating" (*yinyun*), which points to the fertile mingling of heaven and earth (the "Two Principles" mentioned in Cao Pi's poem) at the inception of the cosmos, from which all beings are generated. The stone from which the agate bowl was crafted is thus imbued with the generating potency at the primordial origins of the universe.

惟茲椀之珍瑋	This bowl, precious and resplendent,
誕靈岳而奇生	hails from the Numinous Mount, miraculously born.
扇不周之芳烈	It was fanned by the balmy air of the Northwest,
浸瓊露以潤形	it seeped in rose-gem dew that moistened its form.
蔭碧條以納曜	Shadowed by jade branches, it drew in solar brightness,
吸朝霞而發榮	it breathed in dawn auroras and broke into bloom.
紛玄黃以彤裔	In a flurry, the black [heaven] and yellow [earth] swell and surge,
曄豹變而龍華	[like] leopard stripes shift and shimmer, [like] dragons iridescent.[17]
象蜿虹之輔體	A twisting rainbow glides along its body,
中含曜乎雲波	within it holds solar brightness, as if amidst clouds and waves,

---

17 The leopard stripes paraphrase a statement from the *Book of Changes* that compares the transformations of the superior man to this animal.

若其眾色鱗聚	manifold colours cluster like scales.
卓度詭常	Its outstanding manner surpasses all the common.
絪縕雜錯	Merging and generating, mixing and mingling,
乍圓乍方	now round, now square,
蔚術繁興	dense veins swell and spread,
散列成章	scattering, aligning, forming patterns.
揚丹流縹	Cinnabar raises, the silvery-grey flows,
碧玉飛黃	cyan jade flies into the yellow.
華氣承朗	Its flowery air is forever dazzling,
內外齊光	within, without – equally bright.

(Quan Hou Han wen, 42.700)

The most important shift of meaning compared to Cao Pi's introductory rhapsody comes with the description of the round and square veins of the stone. Although Ying Yang uses almost identical wording to Cao Pi, unlike him, he does not discern any order in the veining: the veins are in the process of constant change, they cannot be grasped – now round, now square, they scatter, they come together, all colours mingle helter-skelter. The depiction expresses not conformity to the civilizing norms, but radical nonconformity, corresponding to the natural order of things in constant flux. What Ying Yang presents through the image of the beautiful uncarved stone is a Daoist ideal of a human personality: the stone (or rather the man it represents) is imbued with primordial and elemental energies, he is untrammelled, spontaneous, and nonconforming. Like the stone not crafted into a vessel, he retains his naturalness and yet dazzles the company with his brilliance.

THE FIFTH POEM

The last author, Wang Can (177–217), commences his rhapsody with a description of the occasion: sitting in attendance at the feast, the gathered poets examine the precious bowl. He copiously quotes and paraphrases the rhapsodies of the other poets.

侍君子之宴坐	Sitting in attendance at the lord's feast,
覽車渠之妙珍	we peruse this marvellous agate treasure.
挺英才于山岳	It drew its supreme endowment from the mountains,

含陰陽之淑真	it contains the pure genuineness of Yin and Yang.
飛輕縹與浮白	The silvery-grey lightly flies, the white drifts along,
若驚風之飄雲	like clouds tossing in the whirlwind.
光清朗以內曜	Radiance, pure and lucent, flares from within,
澤溫潤而外津	a sheen, soft and smooth, bedews it from without.[18]
體貞剛而不撓	Its body is firm and true, cannot be bent,
理脩達而有文	its venation is refined, pervading deeply, above it makes patterns.
雜玄黃以為質	Mixed black and yellow make up its substance,
似乾坤之未分	resembling heaven and earth not yet divided.
兼五德之上美	It is accomplished with the supreme excellence of the Five Virtues;
超眾寶而絕倫	surpassing all treasures, it is beyond comparison.

(*Quan Hou Han wen*, 90.960)

This poem shares many images and vocabulary with the previous rhapsodies, but again there are important shifts of meaning. When describing the gloss of the stone in verse 8, Wang Can verbatim quotes the passage on jade from the *Book of Rites*, adduced above, in which the glossy lustre is associated with the Confucian virtue of humaneness. The following couplet uses vocabulary that describes both the thing and human virtues: a hard, unbending body refers both to the firmness of the stone as well as to the firmness of human character. The "venation" in the stone at the same time refers to the inner pattern or order of things, the informing principle, including the informing structure of human character. Patterns (*wen*) is another key term of Chinese philosophy – these are the patterns visible on the surface of a stone, which also denote "culture" or "civilization," including the patterning of the human character, achieved through cultivation. Through this vocabulary, the description applies both to the bowl and to human character – a man who is true and steadfast, with refined and thoroughgoing principles, possessing culture, and a bearer of civilization. Later, Wang Can picks up Ying Yang's cosmological motif of the stone as the essence of black heaven and yellow earth in their most potent, generative state

18   Cf. "It [the jade] is soft, smooth, and glossy – like humaneness," in the *Book of Rites* (Sun Xidan and He Xiguang 2011, 61.1546; trans. Legge 1964, 2.464)

of non-differentiation. However, he turns immediately to the "Five Virtues," to the norms of the civilized human society.

The ideal personality Wang Can presents balances between extremes: it achieves equilibrium between naturalness and conformity to social norms. It is this rare state of equilibrium between the two that makes the stone (or rather the human character it represents) so unique and precious. The social norms naturally complement the inherent spontaneity, without having to be "measured" or crafted by human hand.

The Precious Object in the Net of Personal Ambitions

The very fact that court poets wrote on the subject of a rare treasure that had been brought from far away to the court of Cao Cao carries political connotations connected with the ambitions of the Cao family on the one hand, and with the poets' pursuit of the patrons' favours and important positions on the other. There is a long tradition in China of writing panegyrics about rare and exotic items, such as stones, plants, and animals contained within imperial palaces and parks. Their presence at imperial courts symbolically expressed the power and authority of the ruler – power that extended to the furthest reaches of the known world. In this sense, the rhapsodies on the agate bowl, as well as other compositions about exotic items at the Cao court, should be considered paeans to the Cao family and its ascending political power.

The poetic depictions of the bowl, even more significantly, are rich in meanings that pertain to human moral qualities and their proper employment in the service of a ruler. The precious stone, from which a bowl had been cut, represented the men of talent whom the Cao family had gathered from every corner of the empire. The symbolism of the beautiful stone was employed in a similar way in the "Suizhi fu" (Rhapsody on Realizing My True Aim) by Liu Zhen (ca. 170–217), another talented man summoned by Cao Cao, who compared his patron's court to a numinous mountain, replete with noble trees and white jade (Yu Shaochu 1989, 7.196; English translation by Shih Hsiang-lin 2013, 74). These represented the courtiers, among whom Liu Zhen found comfort and wonder, and whose enlightened company broadened his mind. The rhapsodies on the agate bowl can be read as a discourse on the qualities these talented courtiers possess or should possess. In some of the rhapsodies, the envisioned features possibly refer to the qualities of the respective authors – thus the poems might have served as means of self-representation and subtle self-promotion – while in others they function as elegant flattery of companions.

Using the same system of allegorical associations, the poets manipulate it and ultimately articulate very differing opinions. Cao Pi and Xu Gan focus on the features and usage of the bowl and emphasize conformity to the Confucian norms. Cao Zhi, through narrating the "history of the stone," shifts the focus to the ruler's discovery of raw talents and their cultivation at court so that their potential can be realized and properly employed. Ying Yang sets himself apart from his companions and gives priority to nonconformity, spontaneity, and naturalness. Wang Can searches for a compromise between spontaneity and conformity in the idea that social norms are a continuation of the natural order.

Although the rhapsodies describe one single, concrete object, and borrow vocabulary from previous literature, they resonate with wider ideological issues at the end of Han rule. The collapse of the unified Han Empire shattered the confidence in the Confucian values that had provided the ideological basis of the Han state. This intellectual change brought novel interest in Daoist ideas of naturalness and spontaneity. The whole third century was marked by debates about conformity and naturalness and attempts to find a compromise between social engagement and Daoist detachment (Mather 1969) – a theme that underlies the poetic discourse on the agate bowl as well. In the context of the intellectual debates of the period, we can also read the five rhapsodies on an exquisite thing as one of the earliest recorded debates on this important topic in medieval Chinese philosophy.

The Poetics of Things in the Didactic Poetry of Early German Enlightenment: Barthold Heinrich Brockes

ALICE STAŠKOVÁ

To what extent can we speak of the didactic poem of early German Enlightenment as a "poem about things"? That is to say, in the sense given to the term *Dinggedicht* by authors of (classical) modern poetry, such as Rainer Maria Rilke, or the commentators Kurt Oppert, Emil Staiger, or Hugo Friedrich? Although the approach taken by these authors is itself open to question, several fundamental aspects find common ground. In the following, I will try to answer my opening question by example, focusing on the work of Barthold Heinrich Brockes, one of the most influential writers of early Enlightenment literature in Germany. In doing so, I will also focus on what makes Brockes' *Dinggedichte* particular and specific.

The argument of the following remarks is this: Brockes' early Enlightenment poems have three features in common with the modern concept of the poetry of things. Firstly, they are about a particular tangible thing-of-interest.[1] Following on, secondly, the poetic portrayal is not aiming to express some inner mood

---

1   Namely, that the item is in the first place an *object* rather than a *thing*, if we take into account the distinction proposed by Bill Brown (Brown 2001, 4–5). These items-of-interest gain value in Brockes' poems as "values, fetishes, idols, and totems" (ibid.) and thus become *things* only to the extent that they convey their purpose or, through their form, make God's Providence apparent to the senses, and thus represent it.

or momentary state of mind of the subject. The third common feature is that the transcendence to which these poems allude requires precisely that particular thing described in the poem. The specific nature of Brockes' factuality in this context combines three traditional ways of interpreting phenomena from the *Book of Nature* (*liber naturae*). The poems make use of the three-stage model of *intellectio–explicatio–applicatio*, as well as the older type of hermeneutic *alle-goresis*, and finally the newer type of hermeneutics, focused on the interpreta-tion of a word's literal or direct meaning or a phenomenon (*sola scriptura*). In the following pages, with regard to Brockes' "things", I shall first summarize the historical context to avoid inappropriate anachronisms. In the second part, I shall outline the philosophical background, known as physicotheology, from which the Brockes type of transcendence arises. The third part deals with an illustrative interpretation of two of Brockes' poems: his "Amarantus cristatus" and "Gläserne Kugel" (Glass Orb).

Things in Brockes' Poems

A native of Hamburg, Barthold Heinrich Brockes (1680–1747) portrayed mate-rial objects of various kinds in hundreds of didactic poems, published in 1721–1748 as part of the nine volumes of his *Irdisches Vergnuegen in Gott, bestehend in Physicalisch- und Moralischen Gedichten* (Earthly Pleasures in God, Consisting of Physical and Moral Poems). There are both natural objects (and phenomena), from insects to plants to celestial bodies, as well as things artificial or natural but adapted for human use, such as snuff, domestic animals, or pets – pugs in particular. The way Brockes brings things into play is consistent with the epistemology of that time. This, while experientially based, takes a distanced and unbiased view of things and phenomena and thus serves the purpose of rational understanding (cf. Neumann 2015, 11). Brockes' material poems are far from the later lyrical tradition of subjective mood, personal experience, and experiential tradition to the same extent as the *Dinggedichte* that Kurt Oppert – the author of the term – identified in 1926 as the "impersonal, epically objec-tive description of the extant" ("unpersönliche, episch-objektive Beschreibung eines Seienden"; Oppert 1926, 747–48). Unlike modern *Dinggedichte*, however, early Enlightenment poems are not autonomous in character. Their purpose is *prodesse* through *delectare* – that is, to bring benefit through delight, in a pleasant and easy way. As soon as the purpose is fulfilled and the benefit – knowledge, in this case – explicitly named in the text, the poem itself ceases to matter.[2] In other words, the created world is full of things that glorify their Creator, but the poem that delights us into that awareness is not one of those things. It remains a mere go-between, like speech, the purpose of which, according to the contemporary philosophy of language, is to convey a preceding idea (cf. Petrus 1997).

The useful knowledge conveyed by Brockes' poems is a recognition of the perfection of everything created and ruled by God: the poems are character-ized by theonomous, not autonomous, poetics. The theonomy of these texts is rooted in the period teachings of physicotheology, mediating knowledge in two ways: via imitation (mimesis) and reflection. A particular poem first uses various poetic means to highlight a particular thing, so it may be seen afresh, anew, as if for the first time, thus achieving a true picture of the thing depicted. This is followed by reflection, putting this knowledge in the context of the Cre-ation. The beautiful portrayal thus mediates the beauty of God's Creation in the original sense of the word "cosmos" – that is, as a perfect, orderly arrange-ment, its perfection manifested by its beauty. Whilst perfection can be appre-ciated with the mind, the beauty of Creation can be accessed by the senses. Unlike modern *Dinggedichte* or "thing poems," when the poem itself becomes "a new thing, unlike anything else in nature, a thing advanced and apart from it" (William Carlos Williams, cited in Müller 2007, 241),[3] the early Enlighten-ment poem is not self-sufficient, but merely serves to make evident the beauty of God's Creation.

Much as in the canonical poems about things by Rainer Maria Rilke, Brockes' presentation of a thing is explicitly identical with the presentation of the per-ception of the thing. Experiencing things here is not an internal experience, but remains determined by outward senses (vision, hearing, smell, etc.).[4]

---

2   Oppert briefly compares Brockes' poem "Der Wolf" to Rilke's poem "Der Panther," with regard to the teleological principle so essential for Brockes, but transient for Rilke (Oppert 1926, 758–59).

3   On the move from representation and portrayal of things in art towards art as a thing in Rilke's study on Rodin, cf. the commentary by Gerhard Neumann (Neumann 2001, 150–51).

4   By contrast with, e.g., Rilke's poem "Die Gazelle," in which the perceived and portrayed object is observed "with eyes closed," with an inner gaze (cf. Lamping 2003, 157).

The Presence of Things in the Service
of Physicotheology

The transcendental scope of knowledge in Brockes' poems is, as already suggested, based on the then current theory of physicotheology.[5] Prevalent in the first half of the eighteenth century, this doctrine is one of the possible solutions to the fundamental issue of German Enlightenment in particular, namely the problem of how to bring together rational knowledge on the one hand and faith in the Revelation on the other to create an organic whole. While movements such as Deism, Neology, or Pietism approach this problem from the perspectives of theology and practical philosophy – for example, in the debate over the original sin – physicotheology takes natural science as its starting point and overall inclination. In its applications, it serves to defend and promote the natural sciences. Physicotheology seeks to show that studious enquiry upon individual areas of nature represents (the only) proper use of God-given reason, in keeping with God's plan. This is readily evident from the title of one of the founding texts of physicotheology, written by John Ray in 1691: *The Wisdom of God Manifested in the Works of the Creation.* According to physicotheologists, the examination of mechanical processes does not contradict the orthodox conception of the Creator as the one who instigates the universe, but indeed makes it manifest. The progressive discovery of natural laws and the dissemination of corresponding knowledge, as dutifully demonstrated and undertaken by Brockes' poems, is the only worthy way to approach the Creation and divine omnipotence.

William Derham's treatises *Physico-Theology* (1713) and *Astro-Theology* (1715) were particularly popular in Germany.[6] The more accurate the examination and description of a given object, the more and better one can measure the grand scale and reach of God's plan:

---

5   At the very least, Brockes' poems about things rest on physicotheology. To what extent even those of Brockes' poems portraying motions or dynamic natural processes can be described as physicotheological (and in that sense, enlighteningly modern in their time) remains a subject for debate (cf. Günther 2016).

6   Both works were translated into German by the Hamburg philosopher, logician, and poet Johann Albert Fabricius. His translation of Derham's *Astrotheology* is dedicated to Brockes (cf. Derham 1728).

The *Creator* doubtless did not bestow so much Curiosity, and exquisite Workmanship and Skill upon his Creatures, to be looked upon
with a careless, uncurious Eye, especially to have them slighted or
condemned; but to be admired by the rational Part of the World, to
magnify his own Power, Wisdom and Goodness throughout all the
World, and the Ages thereof.

(Derham 1723, 427)

This justification for inquisitiveness or curiosity (*curiositas*, *Neugierde*), which,
until then, had been a reprimanded vice, is one of the important steps in the
development of the natural sciences, at least in the context of early German
Enlightenment. In terms of physicotheology, we can make distinctions, precisely with regard to Brockes' use of this doctrine, between two directions: the
rationalist interpretation, and the hermeneutic one that emphasizes its aesthetic
tendency, and thus builds on the notion that the Creation allows us to perceive
Providence and grasp it as evident through the senses.[7] Physicotheology soon
showed itself in a number of specific treatises, such as melittotheology (about
bees), acridotheology (dedicated to locusts), or brontotheology (about storms).
This list alone partly shows the side effect of the physicotheological justification for the natural sciences, such as the progressive elimination of prejudices
or misconceptions and traditional interpretations about various aspects of the
Creation (e.g., locusts).[8] Meanwhile, in the case of the physicotheological treatise on earthquakes (in reaction to the Lisbon earthquake of 1755), physicotheology finds itself in the service of theodicy (cf. foreword to Preu 1772).

The way Brockes presents earthly things and celestial bodies corresponds to
William Derham's intents and puts them into practice, primarily by describing
the object observed and then commenting and interpreting it from the point of
view of natural science. Sight becomes a privileged sense for knowledge acqui-
sition, and the inquisitive eye then serves as a metonymy of understanding
itself. The medium of a poem that follows Horace's principle *ut pictura poiesis*
seems to be particularly well-suited for the purposes of mediating science.

---

7   Cf. Günther 2016, 139–40, wherein referencing the treatise of Hans Graubner (1990, 118–19).
8   Cf. the subtitle of the treatise on locusts: *Acridotheology, or Historical and Theological Reflections
    on Locusts with Regard to Today's Locusts in Transylvania, Hungary, Poland, Silesia, and England,
    along with the Conjecture that the Selavas Eaten by the Israelites Twice in the Desert Were Neither
    Quails Nor Locusts, But Birds Called Seleucids* (Rathlefs 1748).

Two Brockes Odes: "Amarantus cristatus" and "Gläserne Kugel" (Glass Orb)

Amarantus cristatus

Noch kann man sonder Lust nicht sehn,
Wie sonderlich geformt, wie schön
Der purpurfarben' Amarant,
Der insgemein cristatus wird genannt.
5   Er hat fast keine Form; sein Blatt besteht aus Spitzen,
Die sonderbar vereint zusammen sitzen,
Und in sich selbst, aufs neue, Spitzen reich.
Der meisten Form jedoch ist einem Hahn-Kamm gleich;
Kein dunckel-rohter Sammt,
10 Ja fast kein feuriger Rubin,
Kann in so vollen Farben glühn,
Als diese Blum' in rohtem Glantze flammt.
Wenn ich nun die dem Hahn-Kamm gleiche Blume,
Mit aufmercksamen Augen, sehe;
15 So deucht mich, daß ein Hahn mit sanfter Stimme krähe,
Um aus dem Schlaf der Unempfindlichkeit,
Zu dessen Ehre, Preis und Ruhme,
Der alle Vollenkommenheit,
Der aller Dinge Schmuck und Pracht,
20 Blos durch ein Wort, hervorgebracht,
Mich zu erwecken,
Und seine Gegenwart in allen zu entdecken.

(Brockes 2016, 140)

One cannot look upon it without glee,
How beautifully shaped, how lovely
The purple amaranth is, widely named
As the cristatus, crest acclaimed.
5   It lacks firm shape; its leaf is of points comprised,
That oddly sit together cluster-wise,

Each of itself, in turn, spike-rich in form.
Its shape is most akin to a rooster comb;
No dark red velvet plain,
10 Scarce any ruby fiery is ever,
To glow with colours full enough to match
This bloom, with its red glaring flame.
When this rooster-comb-like flower
I see with my perceptive gaze;
15 A rooster seems a softer call to raise,
To rouse from sleep of apathy and scorn,
For all his honour, prize, and glory,
Who this perfection formed,
All things bejewelled and made splendid, fine,
20 With just one word inclined,
Awareness to me to bring,
To discover His presence in everything.

Gläserne Kugel

Auf einer Kugel, die von Glas, und auf gewisse Art vergüldet,
Sah ich die Vorwürff überall, Bewundrungs-würdig-klein gebildet,
Mit unverwendten Blicken, an. Unglaublich ist, wie klar, wie rein,
Wie nett und zierlich alle Cörper verkleinert und formiret seyn!

5 Indem ich es erstaunt betrachte, fällt mir nicht sonder Ursach bey,
Daß diese glatt' und runde Kugel ein Bild von einem Auge sey.
Der Unterschied steckt blos darin, daß von den Cörperlichen Dingen
Die Bilder auf der Kugel nur formirt, und gleichsam rückwerts
springen;
Da sie hingegen in das Auge, ja gäntzlich durch dasselbe dringen
10 Und auch die untre Ründe rühren, ja durch ein Nervgen weiter gehn;
Wodurch im menschlichen Gehirne, so dann Betrachtungen entstehn,
Wenn nur das Nervgen nicht verstopft. Weil sonst nicht mehr, als
Ochsen-Augen,
Der Menschen Augen was sie sehn, zu sehn und zu betrachten
taugen.

Wenn nun beym Sehen, ohne Dencken, die Menschen keine
Menschen seyn;
15 So fiel, so dir als mir zur Lehre, mir folgende Vermahnung ein:

Laß doch, bey aller Pracht der Wunder hier auf Erden,
Dein Auge, lieber Mensch, kein Ochsen-Auge werden!
Ach nein!
Laß es, zu GOttes Ruhm, ein Menschen-Auge seyn!
20 Eröfne die an ihm befindlichen Canäle,
Und laß die Pracht von den erschaffnen Dingen,
Durch sie, sich ins Gehirn, den Sitz der Seele,
Ja in die Seele selber dringen.

Laß durch Gewohnheit dir die Thüren nicht verriegeln,
25 Wodurch die Welt mit dir, du mit der Welt, vereint,
Durch die der GOttheit Glantz, als wie von hellen Spiegeln,
Aus seinen Wercken wiederscheint!

Wir sehen ja das eigentliche Licht,
Ohn einen Gegenschlag von festen Cörpern, nicht.
30 So kann man auch der GOttheit Lieb und Macht
Ohn seiner Creaturen Pracht
Unmöglich sehn, erkennen und verehren.
Die Creaturen sinds allein,
Die uns von seiner GOttheit Schein
35 Die herrliche Beschaffenheit erklären.

Drey Dinge braucht ein Thier zum Sehen: das Gesicht,
Der Cörper Vorwürff’, und das Licht.
Wer aber als ein Mensch will sehen, muß das Dencken
Annoch zu diesen dreyen lencken,
40 Und diese Seelen-Kraft noch zu den andern fügen;
Sonst hat der Mensch von allem, was auf Erden,
Kein’ eigentliche Lust, kein menschliches Vergnügen,
Und GOtt kann nicht gedanckt noch angebehtet werden.

(Brockes 2016, 203ff.)

Glass Orb

On an orb made of glass and artfully gilded overall,
I saw ascribed the surroundings, admirably rendered small,
With gaze transfixed on it, incredulous, how clear, how pure
How nice and dainty all the small-scale-formed bodies were!

5   As I observed it, quite awestruck, I had good reason to not deny
That this smooth and round orb bore likeness to the eye.
The only difference being that, while of corporeal things
The images on the orb are only shapes, and as such do backward spring;
Whereas, when in the eye, indeed quite through it they proceed
10 And touch the back wall, via a nerve they onward speed;
Whereby in the human brain, then to contemplations lead,
As long as the nerve's not blocked. Because, just like ox eyes, no more,
People can see and reflect on nothing beyond what they saw.
When seeing, yet unthinkingly, people aren't humankind;
15 So feeling, for you and me to learn, the following came to mind:

With all the splendour of miracles here on earth,
May your eye, dear mankind, not be just an oxen eye!
Oh no!
Let human eyes bear witness to God's glory, so!
20 Let channels made for access be wide opened whole,
Allow the splendour of all things created
Through them, into the brain, the seat of the soul,
Yes, right into the soul go permeating.

Do not let old habits shut the doors you have awaiting,
25 Through which the world and you, you and the world, are one,
By Divine radiance, as if from dazzling mirrors,
From His Works being shone!

Yet the light itself we cannot detect
Unless off tangible bodies it should reflect.
30 God's love and power too, being perceived the less
Without Creation in its wondrousness

Impossible is to see, to recognize, stand in awe.
Through his creatures alone we see it thus
His Godliness, thus apparent made to us
35   Making grand orderliness more than clear.

An animal needs three things, for to see: its face,
Physical bodies, and light upon their place.
But to see like a human being – thought
In addition to these three aspects must be brought,
40   And this soul-power to the rest must make connection;
Else for mankind, all the Earth has to give
Brings no true joy, no human satisfaction,
And God cannot be thanked, nor praise receive.

These two odes – among the shorter of Brockes' works – represent the two different types of representation of an object with physicotheological purpose. The formal, Horatian ode, favoured at the time, allows the free arrangement of both the actual representation (mimesis) and the reflection upon this representation. It makes possible varying lengths of stanzas and lines, as well as variations in types of rhyme (as opposed to baroque poetics). The varied length of the lines evokes a colloquial tone, close to prose.[9]

In the first part (lines 1–14), the poem "Amarantus cristatus" highlights the peculiar nature of this plant, which is beautiful, albeit seemingly almost without form. Most of the shapes that can be identified on this wonderfully purple flower resemble the comb of a rooster (the German name of the flower is "Hahnkamm" or "rooster comb"). In the second part (lines 15–23), the observing eye is replaced by the organ of thought, inspired by free association. The rooster comb brings in a soft crowing, which rouses our observer out of their apathy, turns their attention to the manifestations of God's presence in earthly phenomena, and exhorts them to glorify these wonders. In the first, mimetic

9   Here, it is worth reminding ourselves that (German) poetics right up to the end of the eighteenth century did not necessarily separate poetry from prose on the basis of the arrangement of the language in verse, but mainly by its aptness (*aptum*), that is, by the appropriate relationships between the subject of the text, the author's intent, the audience, and the way of representation – *aptum* (*Angemessenheit*) in this sense, as Johann Christoph Adelung put it, being "the truthfulness of the style" (Adelung 1974, 1:166).

part, the poetic representation of the flower is governed by the principle of metonymy. In the second, reflective part, there is a metaphorical substitution, whilst the steps taken to make the leap from the natural phenomenon to abstract meaning are not explicated or, rather, are omitted. The crowing most likely refers to the New Testament rooster and Peter's disowning of Jesus.

In the poem "Glass Orb," the first of the six stanzas renders the object – a gilded glass orb – present in such a way that it evokes admiration of how faithfully it depicts the surrounding objects. In the long second stanza, this is immediately followed by a double reflection on this phenomenon: the verb "betrachten" (line 5) here refers to reflection in the sense of contemplation of the seen (in this case, the sighted object is reflected).[10] This duality is functionally matched by the verb "staunen" ("to be in awe," "to wonder") – an allusion to the beginning of all philosophy (cf. Matuschek 1991). The sense of awe here takes the place of the prior wonder, "Bewundrung" (line 2), of the first stanza. Within the orb that so faithfully reflects its surroundings, the observer is awestruck to see (through analogy) the functioning of the human eye itself. There follows an introduction to the optics of an animal and, by extension, the human eye, from a neurological perspective. Metonymy once again facilitates the transition to the third stanza, dedicated to the moral application of this knowledge: speaking not of a general "Thier" ("animal") but of a bovine "Ochsen-Auge" ("oxen eye").

The watchful examination of the glass orb in the third stanza not only advises us about the natural laws of optics and the physiology of the eye, but turns our attention to the scandalous fact that, from a physiological point of view, a human is no different from an animal. The neurology of the eye then leads to the question of how a human being differs from a beast. This difference, according to the poem, lies precisely in the human ability of a further repeated reflection, as shown to us as early as in the second stanza: what is reflected in the eye is then reflected (unlike the observed orb) in the brain, which, in humans, unlike in beasts, is endowed by God with reason (here intended as the ability to think – "Dencken," line 14). The poem now develops both themes – reflection in the optical sense (on the glass sphere as a model of the eye) and reflection as consideration – and applies them to the tenets of practical philosophy. The poem makes an appeal to open one's eye to the perception of phenomena, thus allowing their reflection first in the brain, which judges them as wonderful, and then

---

10   Cf. Adelung's designation of the terms "betrachten" and "Die Reflexion" (Adelung 1811).

in the soul, which sees in their splendour a reflection of the perfection of God's Creation. The issue here is not the theory of knowledge, but practical philosophy, as signalled by the reference in the short fourth stanza to the force of habit ("Gewohnheit," line 24), a popular topic of moral philosophy of the period. The fifth and sixth stanzas first revisit the subject of physics (i.e., optics) and summarize the findings reached – that the ability to see is governed by three factors: sight, the presence of solid objects, and light. For a human being, another factor comes into play – that of thought ("Dencken") as an additional mental power. It is precisely the ability to think that allows a person – unlike a beast – to find rapture in what is beheld. This joy is then the immediate cause (*causa efficiens*) of giving thanks to and praising God. In contrast to the poem "Amarantus cristatus," which follows the aesthetic tradition of physicotheology and "takes a leap" from sensory perception by way of metaphor into the supersensory plane, the structure, arguments, and poetics of the "Glass Orb" are closer to the rationalist tendencies within physicotheology.

Let us return to our initial question: to what extent can Brockes' didactic poems about things stand comparison with modern-day *Dinggedichte*? Unlike modern "thing poems," Brockes' didactic poetry is not self-reflexive in the autonomous sense – not even where it makes a point of reflecting upon the very principle of reflection, as in the "Glass Orb." Rather, this poetry performs various hermeneutic operations on the object of inspection in order to grasp the dual purpose of the thing itself: its purposefulness in itself as a proof of the purposefulness of Creation. And it is in this originally hermeneutic focus of Brockes' albeit theonomic poetics about things that we find resonance with the aims of the *Dinggedichte* as per Mörike or Rilke: "the specific poetic purpose of being a poem about things," as Kurt Oppert puts it, is "interpretation [Deutung]" (Oppert 1926, 768).

In those of Brockes' poems discussed here, which hermeneutic operations are being applied to the *Book of Nature* specifically? At least three kinds of hermeneutics are in play. Within the progression of the poems themselves, we see the Enlightenment hermeneutic technique applying three degrees of understanding of the text (in our case, understanding a natural phenomenon): *intellectio, explicatio,* and *applicatio.*[11] The object of interest is first grasped and understood as

---

11   *Subtilitas intelligendi* focuses on the object and methodology of understanding, *subtilitas explicandi* on the way in which the acquired understanding can be conveyed to others (and thus

a phenomenon and its functioning: the observer performs *intellectio* – understanding itself. At the same time, the following text elucidates the functionality and effect of these phenomena to the audience, the reader, through conceptualization – *explicatio*. This is particularly evident in the "Glass Orb," making use of prevailing terminology used in physiology and optics. This is followed by a jump from natural philosophy to the field of ethics – *applicatio* – that is, application to the attitude and morality of the individual. It is in this application that these two of Brockes' poems make use of further hermeneutic interpretations, each different in turn. In the poem "Amarantus cristatus," Brockes turns to the (older) hermeneutic tradition of *allegoresis*. In order to interpret the particular shape of the flower for the furtherance of interest in Providence and Salvation, he departs from a literal interpretation – being here a botanical observation of the phenomenon – and links one part of the object to another ontological and epistemical category: from the shape of the foliage to Peter's disowning of the Saviour. In the "Glass Orb," we do not see the use of allegory, but, roughly speaking, a more modern type of hermeneutics, which follows the literal meaning of a word, or – in the case of didactic natural history poems – of a phenomenon, here specifically reflections. The poem finally returns to the optical principle of reflection and applies it to the then prevailing views of anthropology and theory of knowledge. In the phenomenon of reflection (reflection upon), two coexistent meanings are noted: the material-physical and the psychological.

Brockes' poems about things therefore use the poetic options available to promote the understanding of natural phenomena – namely, to reveal both the phenomenon itself and its provenance. This provenance is likewise the sole reason for and purpose of any given phenomenon: in other words, its ultimate conceivable *ratio sufficiens* – vested in God. In all of Brockes' poems, we thus witness a certain imbalance between the multiplicities and diversity of the phenomena portrayed on the one hand (typically forming the longer, first part of the poem) and the way these evoke the One and Only (Creator) on the other hand (typically the culmination of the poem). This technique was later to be critiqued by the Swiss theorists and poets Johann Jakob Breitinger and Johann Jakob Bodmer, as well as Gotthold Ephraim Lessing and others, and it can

---

about its interpretation in a narrow sense): cf. Ernesti 1761, 4–5. *Subtilitas applicandi*, which allows the transference of what has been grasped and understood and application thereof to individual spiritual and moral acts, is addressed and discussed in Germany largely in terms of pietistic hermeneutics (cf. Grondin 1996, 1368).

be said that this critical appraisal has continued until the formative conceptualization of modern *Dinggedichte*: for example, Oppert talks about Brockes'
"raw rupture" ("grober Zwiespalt") between the "physical" and the "moral" that
was surpassed only later by Conrad Ferdinand Meyer and Rainer Maria Rilke
(Oppert 1926, 767). Without exception, the various phenomena the respective poems focus on are progressively and almost mechanically related to one
sole principle: the perfection of God's Creation. Seen through the eyes of the
following generations, this can evoke a certain monotony, verging on mono-
mania. Judged in terms of the aesthetic theory of that time, however, the whole
of Brockes' cycle of *Earthly Pleasure in God* corresponds to the period ideal of
beauty. Beauty is defined as perfection which is perceptible by the senses and
causes pleasure, while at the same time perfection is defined as unity in diversity.[12] In this sense, Brockes' nine-volume cycle of poems performs mimesis on
its subject with fascinating consistency. It mimics and portrays the cosmos of
Creation as an infinite diversity, unified through its Revelation. As exemplified
by the triple reflection in the "Glass Orb" poem, Brockes' entire poetic *opus
summum* itself realizes the subject of its poetic exploration because it reiter-
ates the beauty of Creation as unity in diversity, arousing a sense of pleasure.
If we define the principle of literature or poetry as suggesting that a text is
poetic precisely when it is itself exemplary of what it is about, then this extensive collection of early Enlightenment poems is poetic indeed. This may explain
the fascination it continues to evoke, for instance, among modern authors with
a particular penchant for form, such as Peter Rühmkorf (Rühmkorf 1959) or
Arno Schmidt.[13] To be considered poetic in the *modern* sense – that is, if we
take the principle of autonomy as the defining feature of modern poetics –
we may judge Brockes' texts only contrary to their original intent – that is,

---

12   Cf. Christian Wolff's definition of beauty as finding delight in perfection (in the Leibniz tradi-
     tion) – "Hinc definiri potest Pulchritudo, quod sit rei aptitudo producendi in nobis voluptatem,
     vel, quod sit observabilitas perfectionis" (C. Wolff, *Psychologia empirica*, 1732, 421, § 545); and
     his definition of perfection – "consensus in varietate, seu plurium a se invicem differentium in
     uno" (C. Wolff, *Philosophia prima sive ontologia*, 1730, 390, § 503); both cited in Früchtl 2005, 378.
     Accordingly, in the eighteenth-century concepts of beauty determined by this view (Gottsched,
     Baumgarten, Sulzer, or Henry Home), the principle of *ratio sufficiens* in God the Creator gains
     importance compared to the ancient traditions.
13   Arno Schmidt dedicated one of his radio dialogues to Brockes: cf. Schmidt 2015 (in book form
     as part of the volume *Die Ritter vom Geist*, 1965).

neglecting their poetic foundation in theonomy, their foundation in God. Seen against the intents of their time, these texts can appear to be playful permutations of elements in a definitive, finite, and enclosed space. The only transcendence we might ascribe to these texts, in that case, would lie in the potential endlessness of this poetic play in itself.

Francis Ponge's Objective Lyricism

MICHEL COLLOT

Talking about lyricism when it comes to Francis Ponge may seem paradoxical: his best-known poetry collection, *Le Parti pris des choses* (Taking the Side
of Things)¹, from 1942, can be taken as a realization of the "objective poetry"
project, as first defined by Rimbaud in 1871. French poets like Jean-Marie
Gleize, who claim to be objectivists and reject any form of lyricism, still regard
it as paradigmatic, their role model.

Indeed, Ponge was sometimes critical of "lyrical vulgarity" (Ponge 2002, 66;
"Pour un Malherbe"), even making reference to "lyrical-romantic cancer"; but
he also claimed that his "critical moments" were at the same time his "lyrical
moments" (ibid., 170). When he collated a substantial body of his work into
four volumes, he called one of them *Lyres* and at the outset of the first volume
placed a poem of an undeniably lyrical tone, in remembrance of his father's
death (Ponge 1999, 447; "La Famille du sage," *Lyres*). Even the name *Taking the
Side of Things* is ambiguous: an *interest in respect of things* combines a quest for
"objective" poetry with a choice that is entirely subjective.

The role of the subject in Ponge's work is not to be underestimated, despite
such tendency in the objectivist or text-oriented reception that has long prevailed in criticism of Ponge. In a 1991 essay, I tried to assign Ponge a place
"between words and things" (Collot 1991). In order to stick to the theme of this
book, I will focus in my comments on the relationship between the subject and

---

1   This polysemic title can also be translated as "From the Side of Things"; published translations
     in English include "Taking the Side of Things" and "Siding with Things" (Ponge 1994).

the object and leave aside the "reporting on words," although that always goes hand in hand with "a passion for taking the side of things."

Allow me to express the hypothesis that, in Ponge's case, we are dealing with a form of lyricism, which I will call "objective," because it is focused on objects and rejects the subjectivity of a traditional lyricism, whilst not ruling out subjective expression. The idea of an objective lyricism can seem like a contradictory combination of two terms, if we subscribe to the general definition of the lyrical as an expression of personal feelings. So, before I get to Ponge's work, let me briefly discuss this concept and its history.

Towards an "Objective Lyricism"

The noun *lyrisme* (lyricism) seems to have appeared in French with Romanticism, sometime in the 1820s (see Maulpoix 2000, 25–42). At that same time, Hegel saw in lyrical poetry "the expression of subjectivity, as such [...] and not the expression of the external object," in contrast to epic poetry, which is taken to be "objective." According to Hegel, the lyrical poet creates an "enclosed subjective world," "a world closed within itself"; "external circumstances" are merely "a pretext for [...] expressing oneself and the state of one's soul" (Hegel 1979, 178, 184, 197). Romantic lyricism is too often interpreted as a pure and simple projection of the state of the soul onto the world. But it is also the work of giving voice to objects and events resonating in the poet's mind. Consider Lamartine, who defined the lyrical subject as "a sonorous instrument of sensations, feelings and thoughts," resulting from the "greater or lesser impact caused by external or internal things" (cited by Gleize 1983, 29–30).

The theory and practice of modern lyricism is characterized by a strong tendency to question the distinction between the subjective and the objective, between the internal and the external. Indeed, it had already been claimed by Baudelaire that "art in its modern sense" seeks to "create a suggestive charm comprising both the object and subject simultaneously, the artist's world, and the artist himself" (Baudelaire 1976, 598). His words are echoed in the work of Emil Staiger, who characterizes lyricism as an intertwining of inner and outer worlds, "if lyrical poetry is not objective, that is not yet reason enough to call it subjective [...] because 'internal' and 'external,' 'subjective' and 'objective' are not at all separate in lyrical poetry" (Staiger 1990, 49).

When Rimbaud dismissed his teacher Izambard's "subjective poetry," which he found "dry-as-dust," he condemned the "misunderstanding [...] of Ego," which reduces it to an identity closed in on itself and to inwardness. The "objective poetry" he pursued does not seek to remove the lyrical subject, but to redefine it and change it, through contact with words and things: "I is someone else." The poet is "around for the hatching of [his] thought" and becomes his own target, "he seeks his soul, inspects it, tests it, learns it." He cannot, however, reach into the heart unless it is reflected outside oneself, between "unheard and unnamed things" and "horizons" (Rimbaud 2003, 365–68).

Some of Rimbaud's *Illuminations* appear to evoke a world created from mere objects, called up by the most neutral and impersonal formulations. This is the case, for example, in the third part of "Enfance" (Childhood), with the well-known anaphora of the presentative "il y a" ("there's"), which spawned a plentiful succession in twentieth-century French poetry:

> Au bois il y a un oiseau, son chant vous arrête et vous fait rougir.
> Il y a une horloge qui ne sonne pas.
> Il y a une fondrière avec un nid de bêtes blanches.
> Il y a une cathédrale qui descend et un lac qui monte.
> Il y a une petite voiture abandonnée dans le taillis, ou qui descend le
> sentier en courant, enrubannée.
> Il y a une troupe de petits comédiens en costumes, aperçus sur la
> route à travers la lisière du bois.
> Il y a enfin, quand l'on a faim et soif, quelqu'un qui vous chasse.
>
> (Rimbaud 2009, 291)

> There's a bird in the woods, its song makes you stop and blush.
> There's a clock that never chimes.
> There's a hollow with a nest of white creatures.
> There's a cathedral that descends, and a lake that rises.
> There's a little carriage abandoned in the copse, or running down the
> lane, beribboned.
> There's a troupe of little players in costume, glimpsed on the road
> through the edge of the woods.
> There's someone, at last, when you're hungry and thirsty, who drives
> you away.
>
> (Rimbaud 2003–2008, 138)

This list of disparate objects, whose existence or presence the poem seems to be merely stating, touches on the poet more than we would have thought. Not only is it likely to be in part just a figment of his imagination, but it is also framed by a doubled appellation that indirectly includes him, in the pronoun "vous" ("you") or the general "on" ("one"), and which carries a great affective burden – as can be seen in the following section of the poem. Here, for the first time, we have the personal pronoun "je" ("I"), whose fourfold repetition recalls the foregoing repetition of "il y a." The poet lists various figures he identifies with – in particular, "the child left on the jetty washed to the open sea" ("l'enfant abandonné sur la jetée partie à la haute mer") and "the little farm-boy following the lane whose crest touches the sky" ("le petit valet, suivant l'allée dont le front touche le ciel") – and which resemble "a little carriage abandoned in the copse, or running down the lane." (Rimbaud 2003–2008, 140) Everything hints at the subject having identified his fate with the fate of the object, condemned to abandonment and wandering aimlessly, like himself. This means that seemingly the "most objective" kind of poetry can bring very intimate echoes and offer a depiction of the subject that, while fictional, still reveals a profound truth.

Mallarmé exacerbated the crisis of the lyrical, having "passed the initiative over to the words" and finalized the "elocutionary disappearance of the poet" (*la disparition élocutoire du poète*), and the murder of the thing. In fact, these radical formulations mask the complexity and subtlety of Mallarmé's reflection and practice. They avoid any reference to the person and life of the poet, but at the same time do not stop the expression of his experience and affectivity. This manifests itself in evoking things and creating a verbal object.

If poetry "expels into oblivion [...] the outlines" of the object and its material reality, it seeks to "reveal" not only its spiritual essence, "sweet idea," or "concept," but also its affective resonance. According to Mallarmé, the point is to "paint not the thing itself, but the effect it produces" (Mallarmé 1959, 137; letter to Cazalis, October 1864). As Käte Hamburger went on to write, lyrical poetry does not express "the object of experience, but the experience of the object" (Hamburger 1986, 243). "Destroyed" is the "claim [...] to instil into the fine paper of a book [...] a dense and deep forest of trees," but not "the dread of the forest or the mute thunder scattered among the leaves" (Mallarmé 1998, 210; "Crise de vers"). The point here is not about the external form of an object, but its inner reverberation, taken up by the poem's resonance. On the other hand, the expression of the subject is connected with the evocation of the object: we have to "gradually evoke the object in order to expose the state of the soul, or, conversely, to choose the object and reveal some corresponding state of the soul in it" (Mallarmé 2003, 700; "Sur l'évolution littéraire").

However, such internalization can lead to a denial of the exteriority and reality of the object. This idealism, characteristic of symbolism, was subsequently responded to in the early twentieth century by several poetic directions – notably Unanimism – which was subscribed to as late as 1920 by the initiators of the revue *Le Mouton Blanc*, the place where Francis Ponge was earning his literary spurs. Jules Romains characterized Unanimism as "objective lyricism," associated "with substances, events, visible shapes" (Romains 1983, 34; foreword from 1925). But, as Romains sees it, this lyricism still retains a "spiritual essence." A more radically "objective" format seems to be the "lyricism of matter" espoused by Marinetti, which seeks to explore and celebrate its own qualities. According to Marinetti, it is necessary to "replace the already exhausted psychology of man, with a lyrical obsession with matter"; and the poet should "avoid lending human feelings to objects." Energy, inseparably physical and affective, defined, not without humour, as "vapour-emotion" (*vapeur-émotion*), is meant to draw on their material qualities (Marinetti 1987, 20).

Taking the Side of Things

Ponge's taking the side of things resonates with Marinetti's approach, which takes issue with the subjectivity and spirituality of the traditional lyric, in terms of the heightened attention Ponge devotes to the most specific and often trivial aspects of things. Yet, as the title of Ponge's collection suggests, he does not shy away from making subjective choices and he is not anti-humanist: he expects the new perspective on things to restore human thought and sensitivity.

"Taking the side of things" was, for the young Ponge, a promising way out of the existential and intellectual crisis he went through after the death of his revered father – who played an important formative role in the early days of his literary career. At a time of such dire sadness, Ponge experienced what he called a "drama of expression"[2] – the inability to articulate his most intimate feelings in the language common to all: "Words are ready-made and express

---

2   Cf. Collot 1991, 22–45.

themselves. They do not express me" (Ponge 1999, 177). In 1943, Ponge was to mark out the connection between this personal trial and his passion for "siding with things":

> Historiquement, voici ce qui s'est passé dans mon esprit :
> 1. J'ai reconnu l'impossibilité de m'exprimer ;
> 2. Je me suis rabattu sur la tentative de description des choses.
>   (Ponge 1999, 206).

> From a historical point of view, here's what happened in my mind:
> 1. I acknowledged the impossibility of expressing myself;
> 2. I made do with attempting to describe things.

This choice of description in place of expression was far from a stopgap solution; looked at another way, it appears to be a true salve for the subject's identity crisis. In a poem dedicated to his father's memory, Ponge wrote: "Only a description will save my soul" (Paulhan and Ponge 1986, 115; "Le monument"). But how can salvation of the soul be achieved by describing things? By turning the poet away from his inner anguish, because describing turns his attention outwards and towards others. Ponge recalls that he attempted his first descriptions under the influence of "the rapture felt by an urban man faced with the indomitable otherness of nature" (Ponge 2002, 1189). For the poet, as well as for the artist, "everything begins with emotion" induced by contact with the "alien nature" of reality: "whatever the object is [...], encountering it evokes emotion: emotion formed by its beauty? Surely, but perhaps only by its otherness, its mystery" (ibid., 168). Poetic emotion is not an internal state, but a motive force taking the subject out of himself and opening him to the externality and otherness of things. That is why it is not expressed as an introspection or confession, but by way of description.

One has to "be forthright toward what moves us," and give the object its due – what Ponge calls its "distinctive quality" (Ponge 1997, 66). Paradoxically, then, it is emotion that evokes the drive for objectivity: we need to see things in themselves, for what they are, stripping them bare of the value judgements, meanings, and feelings that one constantly projects onto them, thereby overshadowing their own richness and diversity. When one pretends to be the yardstick by which all things are measured, one appropriates them and thus lessens them. Conversely, things "described from their own point of view" (Ponge 1999, 198) and on their own merits reveal "a million unknown qualities"; so instead of relating everything to oneself, you need to "move yourself toward things, and they will fill you with new impressions" (ibid., 202).

Thanks to this centrifugal motion, however, not only does the perception of an object change, but also the subject's own self, their affective life and concept of the world: "having his persona inundated with things" becomes an opportunity for enrichment; "a journey to the depths of things" gives the possibility to "open an inner trap door" (ibid., 203). Objects set the subject free of the limits of his "false persona," revealing new abilities he can make his own, by naming them:

> L'esprit, dont on peut dire qu'il s'abîme d'abord aux choses [...] dans leur contemplation, renaît, par la nomination de leurs qualités, telles que lorsqu'au lieu de lui, ce sont elles qui les proposent. [...]
> Alors, ô vertus, ô modèles possibles tout à coup, que je vais découvrir, où l'esprit tout nouvellement s'exerce et s'adore.
>
> (Ponge 1999, 197)

> The spirit, which can be said to immerse itself into things [...], into the contemplation of things, is restored by naming their qualities, not as they are proposed by the spirit, but by the things themselves. [...]
> Then, oh, the virtues, oh, the models suddenly availed that I discover, in which the wholly new spirit is self-exercised and self-adored.

As the lyricism of this *proema*[3] eloquently demonstrates, in describing things it is my *self* and its destiny that are at stake. And the stakes are not only intellectual, but also moral and affective. Things provide us with model "virtues," "manners of behaviour," and, through the "sensations they evoke in us," also evoke feelings (Ponge 1997, 67).

According to Ponge, this is not about a straightforward transfer to objects of affects that are usually reserved for people, but about specific mental states associated with certain states of things. In contact with one's peers, one can feel only a limited number of ever-identical emotions, which are those that give traditional lyricism its eternal common places (*loci communes*). Yet, thanks to the

---

3   Ponge's neologism "*proème*" combines poem (*poème*), prose, and the Latin *proemium*.

infinite variety of things, we have the possibility of getting to "know and experience" "millions of feelings [...] so different from the restricted catalogue of those
actually experienced by the most sensitive people" (Ponge 1999, 202). This res-
toration of affective life appears as one of the main aspirations of the poetry of
things in the essay "An Introduction to *Taking the Side of Things*," which Ponge
published only later:

> Les qualités que l'on découvre aux choses deviennent rapidement des
> arguments pour les sentiments de l'homme. Or nombreux sont les
> sentiments qui n'existent pas (socialement) faute d'arguments.
> D'où je raisonne que l'on pourrait faire une révolution dans les sen-
> timents de l'homme rien qu'en s'appliquant aux choses, qui diraient
> aussitôt beaucoup plus que ce que les hommes ont accoutumé de leur
> faire signifier.
> Ce serait là la source d'un grand nombre de sentiments inconnus
> encore. Lesquels vouloir dégager de l'intérieur de l'homme me paraît
> impossible.
>
> (Ponge 2002, 1033–34)

> The qualities we discover in things quickly become prompts for the
> feelings of men. For there are numerous feelings that do not exist
> (socially) without such prompts.
> Hence, I reason that one could make a revolution in the feelings of
> man just by inclining towards things, which will promptly disclose
> much more than the designations people usually give them.
> That would be the source of a great many previously unknown fee-
> lings. To hope to hew these out of men's hearts seems to me impossible.

Where Ponge gives preference to objects such as a pebble, seemingly the most
unlike ourselves, he is not seeking to present the image of a "world without
mankind," despite what Camus thought. He certainly does not wish to reject all
forms of humanism; on the contrary, he wants to expand and restore humanism.

> Ce galet [...] me fait éprouver un sentiment particulier, ou peut-être
> un complexe de sentiments particuliers. Il s'agit ici d'abord de m'en
> rendre compte. Ici l'on hausse les épaules et l'on dénie tout intérêt
> à ces exercices, car me dit-on, il n'y a rien là de l'homme. Et qu'y

aurait-il donc ? Mais c'est de l'homme inconnu jusqu'à présent de l'homme. [...] Il s'agit de l'homme de l'avenir.

(Ponge 1999, 526)

This pebble [...] lets me experience a particular feeling, or perhaps a complex of particular feelings. Firstly, it's about me becoming aware of them. Here comes a shrugging of shoulders and denial of any interest in such exercises, because, I'm told, there is nothing human about it. And what would there be, indeed? But this is about man as yet unchartered. [...] This is about the man of the future.

The relationship that Ponge sets between a new vision of things and the transformation of human behaviour and feelings entails something of a tendency in contemporary thinking to redefine consciousness not as an autonomous entity, but as "being in the world." Ponge's point is to "formulate anything according to ourselves; give our relationship with the world" (Ponge 2002, 43). In another essay, as an introduction to *Taking the Side of Things*, he admitted to "not trying [...] to know myself, unless it is also about things": "getting to know me and getting an idea of me will not be achieved except through my shell, my abode, my collections [...]. With the emphasis on how I see the world" (ibid., 1033).

This correlation between subject and object is somewhat reminiscent of Husserl's idea of intentionality, according to which every consciousness is a "consciousness of something": "Our soul is transitive. It needs an object that immediately touches it, as its direct supplement," Ponge writes (2002, 657).[4] The subject's affectivity is inseparable from the things that affect it, so it "has a chance to evoke its most extraordinary song when dealing far less of itself than with other things, when dealing much more with the world than with itself" (Ponge 1999, 130). Objective poetry is an indirect and paradoxical form of the lyrical: a lyricism that lets the "third person singular" speak.[5]

---

4   A similar notion seems to be at the cradle of the theory of an "objective correlative," as outlined by T. S. Eliot in his well-known essay "Hamlet and His Problems": "The only way of expressing emotion in the form of art is by finding an 'objective correlative'; in other words, a set of objects, a situation, a chain of events which shall be the formula of that particular emotion; such that when the external facts, which must terminate in sensory experience, are given, the emotion is immediately evoked" (Eliot 1998, 58).

5   This was the title of Ponge's "Tentative orale" lecture (Ponge 1999, 665).

This most intimate objectification also takes place when creating a verbal object. Ponge's tendency to regard and conceive of words as things, like "a concrete reality, containing the full evidence and substance [...] of the outside world" (Ponge and Sollers 1970, 169), was interpreted primarily from the perspective of mimologism (see Genette 1976). We cannot overlook the purely expressive sources of "these very special and strangely poignant objects, the signifying sounds that we are able to produce which also serve us for naming the objects of the world and expressing our intimate feelings" (Ponge 1999, 869).

As early as 1919, Ponge proved to be more sensitive to the material dimension of the phonic and graphic signifier that makes words into "mysterious objects," "perceptible by two senses," and wanted to "attend to the substance of words" and "to like them for themselves rather than for (their) meaning." But he also saw in them "a still store of emotional gestures" and called on them "to help mankind, who can no longer dance and no longer knows the secrets of gestures, and no longer has the courage or knowledge to be expressive directly through movement" (ibid., 176). Words treated as "substances" approach being things, but they are also carriers of emotions associated with the gestures of the body proclaiming them.

Contrary to the classical expression scheme, the expressiveness of words comes not from their transparency, but their obfuscation and opacity. Not only because they are brought closer by the materiality of things, but also because they protect them from the sway of meaning and spirit, thus making them carriers of affectivity, "matter-for-expression" (*matière-à-expressions*) (ibid., 539). "To delve into the dark foundation of things" (Ponge 1997, 102), "to plunge into the night of the logos" (*s'enfoncer dans la nuit du logos*) (Ponge 1999, 631) – these are two inseparable approaches of objective lyricism. For example, a fig "is clearly an object that we distinguish in the outside world – and it is a word [...] which evokes emotions, sensations, and associations of ideas" (Ponge 1988, 30): it is a small piece of "matter-emotion," to use the words of René Char.[6]

I would now like to give a few examples of this Ponge-practised objective lyricism and to show the internal tension it encompasses, as well as the evolution it had undergone during the poet's creative life.

The prevalent care for objectivity in *Taking the Side of Things* is manifested in particular by the very frequent use of impersonal utterance. Hence the high

---

6   I have used them myself in my essay *La Matière-émotion* (Collot 1995).

incidence of turns of phrase such as "il faut" ("it is necessary") or "il convient" ("it is appropriate"), the use of the presentative "c'est" ("that is"), or the infinitive as an impersonal mode. Ponge avoids the use of the personal pronoun "je" and prefers the more general "nous" ("we") or the French indeterminate pronoun "on"; at other times, all indications of personal utterance disappear. If the first-person singular does appear, its place is limited to a minimum, as in the case of "Pluie" (Rain), where it comes in only once at the beginning of the poem:

PLUIE

La pluie, dans la cour où je la regarde tomber, descend à des allures très diverses. Au centre c'est un fin rideau (ou réseau) discontinu, une chute implacable mais relativement lente de gouttes probablement assez légères, une précipitation sempiternelle sans vigueur, une fraction intense du météore pur. À peu de distance des murs de droite et de gauche tombent avec plus de bruit des gouttes plus lourdes, individuées. Ici elles semblent de la grosseur d'un grain de blé, là d'un pois, ailleurs presque d'une bille. Sur des tringles, sur les accoudoirs de la fenêtre la pluie court horizontalement tandis que sur la face inférieure des mêmes obstacles elle se suspend en berlingots convexes. Selon la surface entière d'un petit toit de zinc que le regard surplombe elle ruisselle en nappe très mince, moirée à cause de courants très variés par les imperceptibles ondulations et bosses de la couverture. De la gouttière attenante où elle coule avec la contention d'un ruisseau creux sans grande pente, elle choit tout à coup en un filet parfaitement vertical, assez grossièrement tressé, jusqu'au sol où elle se brise et rejaillit en aiguillettes brillantes.

Chacune de ses formes a une allure particulière ; il y répond un bruit particulier. Le tout vit avec intensité comme un mécanisme compliqué, aussi précis que hasardeux, comme une horlogerie dont le ressort est la pesanteur d'une masse donnée de vapeur en précipitation.

La sonnerie au sol des filets verticaux, le glou-glou des gouttières, les minuscules coups de gong se multiplient et résonnent à la fois en un concert sans monotonie, non sans délicatesse.

Lorsque le ressort s'est détendu, certains rouages quelque temps continuent à fonctionner, de plus en plus ralentis, puis toute la machinerie

s'arrête. Alors si le soleil reparaît tout s'efface bientôt, le brillant appa-
reil s'évapore : il a plu.

(Ponge 1999, 15–16)

RAIN

The rain, in the courtyard where I watch it fall, comes down with
very different cadences. In its midst is a thin, discontinuous curtain
(or network), a relentless but relatively slow fall of drops, apparently
quite light, a ceaseless, vapid precipitation, the intense fragment of
a pure meteor. Heavier, distinctive drops fall more loudly near the
walls on the right and left. Here they look the size of a grain of wheat,
there a pea, elsewhere almost a glass marble. On the ledges, on the
windowsill, the rain runs horizontally, while from below it clings to
the same obstacles, like bulging toffees. Across the entire surface of
the zinc canopy the gaze surveys, the rain streams like a very thin
tablecloth, moire-patterned by the various currents flowing over
the imperceptible ripples and bumps of the roof covering. From the
adjacent gutter, through which it flows with all determination down
a deep gulley without much slope, it suddenly falls in a perfectly vertical, rather coarsely spun thread to the ground, against which it shat-
ters, rebounding upwards in shimmering needles.
Each of the forms of rain has a special allure: this corresponds to its
own special sound. The entirety of it is intensively alive like a complicated mechanism, as precise as it is precarious, like a clockwork
whose spring is the gravity pull of a mass of condensing vapour.
The ringing on the ground of the vertical strands, the gurgling of
gutters, the tiny gong strikes multiply and resound together in concert,
without monotony, and not without charm.
Once the clock spring has wound down, some of the cogwheels continue to turn awhile, slowing more and more, until all the machinery
stops. With the sun appearing, soon no sign of anything remains, the
shimmering construction evaporates: it has rained.

This text, placed at the beginning of the collection, stands as a model of objective poetry, all the more so because the theme of rain is one of the most appropriate to express the relationship between mindscape and landscape. Let us

recall, in particular, Verlaine's famous poem "Ariettes oubliées" (Forgotten Songs): "Il pleure dans mon cœur / Comme il pleut sur la ville" ("it rains in my heart / as it rains over the town"). Ponge's attitude is the very opposite of such identification. He wants to avoid any predetermined judgement about the sight he is trying to describe, and does so in the most neutral way, thus also omitting the definite article in the title word "pluie." The role of the poet is limited to that of a mere witness, whose view is initially expressed in the first person ("I watch it"), and progressively becomes completely anonymous and impersonal ("the gaze surveys"). The writing tends towards a straightforward report delineated by the "gaze-as-it-is-spoken"; the poem reminds us of a record of scientific observation, resorting as it does to quite technical vocabulary in the present tense, covering the ongoing phases of the downpour. Rain, which is typically perceived rather indiscriminately, even vaguely, here becomes the subject of a very precise description and true analysis, which distinguishes the "very different cadences" and describes in detail even the smallest "distinctive drops." In contrast with the romantic and symbolic valorization of similarities, Ponge expresses a regard for differences: "what shapes me is actually the diversity of things," he declares (Ponge 1999, 517).

Yet this description, characterized by almost manic precision, cannot eliminate all traces of subjectivity. The poet's point of view discreetly emerges in value judgements, pejorative or meliorative turns of phrase: rain seems to be at times like a "*ceaseless, vapid precipitation*," sometimes as an "*intense* fragment of a *pure* meteor." Ponge is aware that maintaining perfect objectivity is difficult: "there is always some relationship to man," he acknowledges (ibid., 198). Similarly, it is not easy to avoid analogies: Ponge likens the raindrops to "a grain of wheat" or "a pea." These comparisons are meant to allow the reader to better imagine the object, but sometimes they bring an unnoticed anthropomorphism into the text, something principally excluded from the "side of things": natural phenomena are likened to human products, "glass marbles," or "toffees." We can even watch the flow of metaphors contiguously developing from one sentence to the next, such as the fabric metaphor: the image of a "curtain" is followed by the image of a "tablecloth," then a "thread," which splinters into "needles."

The textile metaphor has a clear correspondence to the text itself, which the poet is engaged in weaving, in the sense of a metapoetic function that draws together autoreference and reference and manifests itself especially at the end of the poem, likening the downpour to a "clockwork mechanism" and to a "concert, without monotony, and not without charm." Thus, the neutrality of the introductory report is increasingly replaced by aesthetically inclined judgment, whether negative or positive: the water thread is *rather coarsely spun* but "rebounding upwards in *shimmering* needles"; the mechanism is "*complicated*" and "*as precise as it is precarious.*" The vocabulary of meteorology and physics – the "gravity pull of a mass of condensing vapour" – is replaced by the vocabulary of ornament, craftsmanship, and art. The poem's conclusion coincides with the end of the downpour and seemingly only reports it, but the ambiguity of the (somewhat untranslatable) syntagma "il a plu" ("it has rained / it has pleased") allows the poet to simultaneously admit the pleasure he felt by observing and describing the phenomenon (it has rained, and how!).

Elsewhere in the collection, the poet's interventions are much more visible and the expression of his feelings more open. This is especially so in the poem dedicated to water, "De l'eau" (Of Water). In it, the self "je" is notably present, the description directed towards allegory, and physical inevitability abruptly denounced as a moral flaw:

> Plus bas que moi, toujours plus bas que moi se trouve l'eau. C'est toujours les yeux baissés que je la regarde. Comme le sol, comme une partie du sol, comme une modification du sol.
> Elle est blanche et brillante, informe et fraîche, passive et obstinée dans son seul vice : la pesanteur [...].
> À l'intérieur d'elle-même ce vice aussi joue : elle s'effondre sans cesse, renonce à chaque instant à toute forme, ne tend qu'à s'humilier [...].
>
> (Ponge 9, 31)

> Water is lower than I, always lower than I. I always look down upon it. Like the ground, like a stretch of ground, like a modification of the ground.
> It is white and sparkly, shapeless and fresh, malleable and obstinate in its only vice: gravity [...].
> This vice is also at play within it: it is eternally breaking down, renouncing form at every moment, inclined only to abase itself [...].

Because it tends to "obéir à la pesanteur" ("obeys gravity"), which casts it "toujours plus bas" ("always lower"), such personified water is suspected of being self-abasing and servile, like a "véritable esclave" ("true slave"), and the poet heaps his contempt upon her. While the rain has let him delight in its multitudinous forms, the liquid element as such, shapeless and uniform, is typical of everything that Ponge resents both aesthetically and morally:

> L'eau m'échappe... me file entre les doigts. Et encore! Ce n'est même pas si net [...] : il m'en reste aux mains des traces, des taches, relativement longues à sécher ou qu'il faut essuyer. Elle m'échappe et cependant me marque, sans que j'y puisse grand-chose.
> Idéologiquement c'est la même chose : elle m'échappe, échappe à toute définition, mais laisse dans mon esprit et sur ce papier des traces, des taches informes.
>
> (Ponge 1999, 32)

> Water escapes me ... slips through my fingers. And if only that! Nor is it so clean [...]: leaving on my hands traces, stains, which take a long time to dry or have to be wiped off. She eludes me, and yet leaves her mark on me without me being able to do anything about it.
> Ideas-wise it is the same: escaping me, escaping every definition, but leaving traces, shapeless stains on my spirit, and on this paper.

Ponge's practice of "gaze-as-it-is-spoken" cannot be confused with the practice of objectivism or with what was called the *École du regard* (School of Seeing) of the 1950s. Indeed, Alain Robbe-Grillet did not hesitate to blame Ponge for "the most overt psychological and moral anthropomorphism," making things into mere "mirrors" that "keep reflecting" a person's own image (Robbe-Grillet 1963, 62)

From *Rage for Expression* to *Objeu*

Even before the publication of *Taking the Side of Things,* Ponge was to question the approach that defined the entire collection. If we are to believe the text I cited above, which was written in 1941, Ponge intended the "description of things" as a salve for "the inability to express (himself)." In the end, however, he "arrived at the impossibility of expressing, but also of describing things" (Ponge 1999, 206–7).

In his works from the 1940s, Ponge seems to oscillate between the ideal of objectivity, which he knows to be impossible, and the need to express himself. This crisis is evident from a reading of the texts Ponge summarizes in the collection *La Rage de l'expression* (Rage for Expression), as well as from the very title of the collection. Ponge published a number of variations on poems that mostly remained unfinished, describing them as "failed descriptions." From this point on, he was intending to be "more a scientist than a poet" and embarking on "constant rectification of own expression" "toward the raw object" (ibid., 337). However, such clarity is opposed by the irreducible subjectivity contained in the author's point of view. For example, a mimosa becomes a "un sujet très difficile" ("very difficult topic") for Ponge, because this bush "a été l'une de (s) es adorations, de (s)es prédilections enfantines" ("was the object of his childhood awe and admiration", ibid., 366), and so he cannot prevent sensations and "emotions" with which he had "endeared it" from creeping into his pen: "Sur les ondes puissantes de son parfum je flottais, extasié" ("I floated in ecstasy on the potent waves of its fragrance"), he writes, quite characteristically. Although he then tries to purge his rendition of these overly personal memories, he is aware of the futility of the attempt:

> Tout ce préambule, qui pourrait encore longuement être poursuivi, devrait être intitulé : « Le mimosa et moi. » Mais c'est au mimosa lui-même – douce illusion ! – qu'il faut maintenant en venir ; si l'on veut, au mimosa sans moi…
>
> (Ponge 1999, 367)

> This whole preamble, which could be continued at length, should be called: "The mimosa and I." But it is the mimosa itself – sweet illusion! – we must return to now; if you like, to the mimosa without me…

As intolerable as the involvement of the self may seem, it comes into play already with the poet's choice of objects; hence, he considered calling his collection "sentiments choisis" ("selected feelings") or "objectifs intimes" ("intimate targets") (ibid., 433). When Ponge, an entrenched communist and future participant in the resistance movement, devotes all his attention for a whole month and all the paper at his disposal to trying to describe a small pine wood, this means, as he says, that he "comes back to it instinctively" ("y revient d'instinct"), as "au sujet qui (l')intéresse entièrement, qui accapare toute (s)a personnalité" ("a subject that fully interests and captivates his entire personality", ibid., 405).

And when, for several months, he relentlessly examines the "fleeting vision" of the sky in Provence, as captured in the window of a bus at a place called La Mounine, it must have evoked a profound emotion in him:

> Vers neuf heures du matin dans la campagne d'Aix, autorité terrible des ciels. Valeurs très foncées. Moins d'azur que de pétales de violettes bleues. Azur cendré. Impression tragique, quasi funèbre. Des urnes, des statues de bambini dans certains jardins ; des fontaines à masques et volutes à certains carrefours aggravent cette impression, la rendent plus pathétique encore. Il y a de muettes implorations au ciel de se montrer moins fermé, de lâcher quelques gouttes de pluie, dans les urnes par exemple. Aucune réponse. C'est magnifique.
>
> (Ibid., 412)

> Around nine in the morning in the countryside near Aix, the menacing authority of the heavens. Very dark hues. Less azure than on the petals of blue violets. Ashen azure. A mood quite tragic, even funereal. Urns, statues of cherubs in some gardens; fountains with masks and volutes at some crossroads, make this impression more acute, adding to its pathos. Mute imploring appeals to the sky to be less firmly closed, to release a few drops of rain, into the urns at least. No response. It is spectacular.

The never-ending attempts to describe this scene, in the most correct and accurate way, ultimately lead us to understanding why such a spectacle so impressed upon the poet's sensibilities that tears welled up in his eyes:

> Il s'agit de bien *décrire* ce ciel tel qu'il m'apparut et m'impressionna si profondément.
> De cette description, ou à la suite d'elle, surgira en termes simples *l'explication* de ma profonde émotion.
>
> (Ibid., 424)

> The point is to *describe* this sky well, how it appeared to me and so deeply impressed me.
> From this description, or as a result of it, will arise a simple *explanation* of my deep emotion.

Ponge will go on to seek an "explanation" for his emotion, of an aesthetic, political, moral, or scientific kind; yet the childhood memories, which he repeatedly recalls several times over, give a clue that is not devoid of more personal resonances. As time goes on, he is to become increasingly aware that it is not enough for the poet to "explain" a phenomenon such as this using external causes; he must also enquire about his inner response to it, to understand why he himself should be feeling involved. This at least is apparent from his 1954 note "À propos de l'art dit explicatif" (On So-called Explanatory Art):

> Je crois qu'on peut être explicatif, à condition que ce ne soit que *m'*explicatif ou *s'*explicatif, ou plutôt *self*splicatif, enfin qu'il ne s'agisse que de s'expliquer authentiquement les choses à soi-même [...] et seulement à soi-même.
>
> (Ponge 2002, 1018)

> I believe one can be explanatory, provided that it is no more than *myself*-explanatory or *oneself*-explanatory, or rather *self*-explanatory, in the end it is only a question of authentically explaining things to oneself [...] and only to oneself.

Poetic understanding, unlike science, is recognition and emergence jointly within the world and oneself: in the "laboratory of expression," the artist works just like a scientist "on the substance of raw matter," but also on the basis of "the emotions it brings, the desire it evokes" (ibid., 980). Taking the side of things as redefined in this way is also a way for the poet to "take his own side" (ibid., 1190): "respecting his first impression: what he receives from the objects of the world"; and yet "*face to face with the world* (given the emotions he receives from it) he expresses *the most personal of himself*" (ibid., 981).

Ponge's poetry of things continually seeks to combine the objective dimension with one's subjective components that transform the object, in the words of Braque, into the "object-emotion." Ponge achieves this only by mobilizing all his resources of language, and makes of his poem – to use the neologism that

Ponge created in 1954 – an *Objeu* (Ponge 1999, 776), namely a verbal object that combines the expression of the self "I" with the description of things.[7] Ponge's wordplay, in which he indulges with growing enthusiasm, is never gratuitous, since he finds such signifiers very significant-sounding:

> Il s'agit là d'objets très particuliers, particulièrement émouvants : puisqu'à chaque syllabe correspond un son, celui qui sort de la bouche ou de la gorge des hommes pour *exprimer* leurs sentiments intimes – et non seulement pour *nommer* les objets extérieurs.
>
> (Ibid., 647–48)

> These are very particular, particularly emotive objects: since each syllable has a corresponding sound, the sound that comes out of people's mouths or throats to *express* their intimate feelings – and not just to *name* external objects.

A little later, Ponge mentions *objoie*, a "bliss of expression," which lets "truth" rejoice "*jou(ir)*," lets the "object" jubilate "*jubil(er)*" when "it expresses its qualities," and lets "anyone understand their personal identity" and "signify themselves" (Ponge 2002, 416).

Taking the Side of Places

The increasingly overt expression of the emotions elicited by things adds a thoroughly lyrical tone to some of Ponge's writings. This is particularly so with texts about landscapes, which are by definition where one's viewpoint and the observed set of things come together. The sensation they evoke in oneself is not some vague state of mind, but a wholly physical reaction to making contact with the substance and fabric of the world: "Nothing compares to the colours of the Sahel region and the colours of the sea. There's something here akin to emotion, to skin, a very sentimental blush" (Ponge 1999, 554). This emotion

---

7 Translator's note: Ponge's neologism includes the French words *objet* (object), *je* (I), and *jeu* (game, or play).

comes not from the simple projection of inner feelings onto the outside world, but from the interaction between inside and outside.[8] The sentimentally moved (*e-moted*) poet steps out of himself and opens to the landscape, letting it deep into his inner self:

> Comment [...] rester insensible aux paysages ? [...] [I]ls produisent en moi la plus vive impression : morale et matérielle à la fois. Je n'y échappe pas. Je ne puis d'eux, non plus, rien laisser échapper. Ils me paraissent plus qu'intéressants. Ils s'engouffrent en moi, ils m'envahissent, ils m'occupent.
>
> (Ibid., 571)

> How is one to remain insensitive to landscapes? [...] [T]hey evoke in me the most vivacious impression: both moral and material at the same time. I can't escape from it. Neither can I let anything escape from them. I find it more than interesting. They engulf me, invade me, occupy me.

In his experiencing of the landscape, we see tested the poet's sense of belonging to the land, which he is celebrating in a text with almost religious expressiveness, though his piety is entirely pagan:

> Ce qui est tout à fait spontané chez l'homme, touchant la terre, c'est un affect immédiat de familiarité, de sympathie, voire de vénération quasi filiale.
> Parce qu'elle est la matière par excellence.
> Or, la vénération de la matière : quoi de plus digne de l'esprit ?
>
> (Ibid., 750)

> What comes quite spontaneously to a man in touch with earth is an immediate sense of intimacy, empathy, an almost filial reverence.
> For she is materiality par excellence.
> What else is more worthy of the spirit than to worship materiality?

---

8   See my essay *La Matière-émotion*, especially the passages devoted to *Taking the Side of Things* (Collot 1995, 45–50).

The sense of nature, expressed with great intensity in his "Le pré" (Meadow) rests on the belief that the creative and restorative ability of *poiesis* has the same dynamics as *physis*. The poet can respond to what the meadow offers him, because he is predisposed to do so by an affinity that makes human nature at one with the natural world:

> Que parfois la Nature, à notre réveil, nous propose
> Ce à quoi justement nous étions disposés,
> La louange aussitôt s'enfle dans notre gorge.
>   Nous croyons être au paradis.
>
>   Voilà comme il en fut du pré que je veux dire,
>   Qui fera mon propos d'aujourd'hui.
> [...]
>
> Parfois donc – ou mettons aussi bien par endroits –
> Parfois, notre nature –
> J'entends dire, d'un mot, la Nature sur notre planète
> Et ce que, chaque jour, à notre réveil, nous sommes –
> Parfois, notre nature nous a préparé(s) (à) un pré.

(Ponge 2002, 340)

> That Nature, as we wake, sometimes offers us
> Just what we're disposed to be doing,
> Immediately fills our throats with praise.
>   We believe ourselves to be in paradise.
>
>   So it was with the meadow I wish to speak of,
>   Which is to be my theme today.
> [...]
>
> So sometimes – or let us say in some places –
> Sometimes, our nature –
> I mean, in one word, Nature on our planet
> And that which, every day, when we wake up, are we –
> Sometimes, our nature has a meadow prepared for us / has us prepared
>   for a meadow.

The conclusion of the poem, with all the weight of testament, definitively seals this unification with nature and signs the page and the landscape with the name of the author as well as the names of the objects he identifies with, and which are seeming co-signatories of his text:

Messieurs les typographes,
Placez donc ici, je vous prie, le trait final.

Puis, dessous, sans le moindre interligne, couchez mon nom,
Pris dans le bas-de-casse, naturellement,
    Sauf les initiales, bien sûr,
    Puisque ce sont aussi celles
    Du Fenouil et de la Prêle
    Qui demain croîtront dessus.
      Francis Ponge.

(Ponge 2002, 344)

Gentlemen typographers,
Do please, insert here the last break.

Then below, without the slightest gap, put down my name,
In lowercase letters, naturally,
    Except for the initials, of course,
    For they are also the initials
    Of Fennel and Parsley,
    Which will grow atop, tomorrow.
      Francis Ponge

Conclusion

To end with, I would like to briefly revisit some of the forms that nowadays typify this examination of objective lyricism, of which – in my view – Ponge's work is an exemplary manifestation. Objectivists and fans of the literal some-times let some lyrical tones escape into their texts. According to Ponge, whom they often invoke, these are inevitable because "it is enough to *name* anything" "for the whole person to be *expressed*" (Ponge 1999, 648). This is, of course, in direct contradiction of their ideal of objectivity and/or literalism.

For many contemporary French poets, lyricism is a contaminant, a dangerous substance to be handled with caution; they are meant to use, as needed, an "objectivist cleanser,"[9] or to resort to the instruments provided by the "toolbox" of a textualist "Meccano" (Espitallier 2000, 15). In the first issue of their *Revue de littérature générale*, Olivier Cadiot and Pierre Alferi attempted to dismantle the gearing of "lyrical mechanics," in order to show everyone how possible it is to produce emotion without some "state of the soul," based on a few simple, skilfully applied procedures. They sought to rely on "spheres of sensations – thoughts – forms [...] or small sensory – affective – language clusters" (Cadiot and Alferi 1995a, 5–6); but by christening them "Unidentifiable *Verbal* Objects" (*Objets verbaux non-identifiés*; OVNI), they emphasized their language component and very quickly went back to the method known throughout the twentieth century, which essentially comprises working with collage and rewriting snippets of prior texts. It is up to the reader to judge whether these constructionist games do give rise to emotions. This remains uncertain – and the authors themselves admit as much, when, in the second issue of the magazine, they incline much more towards the orthodoxy of literalism:

> Vous avez peut-être eu entre les mains un volume intitulé « La mécanique lyrique ». Vous avez vu la mécanique, mais où était le lyrisme ? [...] Dans ce titre, « lyrique » désignait l'énergie même de cette mécanique littéraire qui change les formes en contenus et vice-versa. [...] Peut-être faut-il renoncer à appeler « lyrique » cette énergie.
>
> (Cadiot and Alferi 1995b, n.p.)

> You may have had in your hands the issue called "La mécanique lyrique" [Lyrical Mechanics]. You saw the mechanics, but where was the lyricism? [...] In this title, "lyrical" denotes the very energy of such literary mechanics, which changes form into content and vice versa. [...] Perhaps we should renounce calling this energy "lyrical."

---

9   Quote in reference to Emmanuel Hocquard (Manno and Garron 2017, 716).

More interesting, from my point of view, is the concept or practice of "objective singing" (*chant objectif*), which Philippe Beck tries to define and perform. By doing so, he contributes to the rehabilitation of the long-forgotten musical component of lyricism. The instrument he uses, in order to rule out any form of emotional outpouring, is the *lyre dure* ("hard lyre"; see Beck 2009), just as Ponge preferred his *corde la plus tendue* ("musical string as taut as can be"; Ponge 2002, 186). Such singing does not try to enchant the reader nor make the world magical again, but pits them against the objects, facts, and gestures of everyday life, and the fundamentals of human existence. It comes from the heart, but it is located in the heart of the world we share, in its harsh reality, there to be embraced: the lyre is hard, because life is brutal. The narrator does not close himself up in an inner world nor offers any easy way out: "in singing / the narrator knows the world" (Beck 2007, 15–16).

This openness to the world represents one pronounced tendency of contemporary lyricism, which differentiates it from subjectivism and the idealism of a certain lyrical tradition, still present among those who subscribe to the "new lyricism." I myself have often invoked this openness and tried to show it in my poems, especially in the recently published collection entitled – with a nod to Ponge – *Taking the Side of Places* (Collot 2018). And that is all I am going to say, because to go on would lack due objectivity...

In Mandelstam's Kitchen

ANNE HULTSCH

In the poems of the Russian Acmeist poet Osip Emilyevich Mandelstam (1891–1938), countless things or objects appear or are present in many different ways. Not always is this about *Dinggedichte*, "poems about things" in the narrower sense, as defined by Kurt Oppert in his 1926 article. In the following considerations, I focus on a small subset of Mandelstam's objects of interest: on everyday things, specifically kitchen items. They are fascinating in how they pop up in different textual forms and adopt different functions. Yet the kitchen in the title of this paper is also meant in the figurative sense: as the poet's workshop, his poetology, or culturology. Before I turn to Mandelstam himself, let me briefly mention the Russian poetic movement of Acmeism, which emerged in Russian literature as a descendant of Symbolism and the antithesis of Futurism.

Manifestos

In 1913, two manifestos of Acmeism were published in the originally symbolist-leaning magazine *Apollon*: one by Nikolai Gumilev ("Наследие символизма и акмеизм" [Acmeism and the Heritage of Symbolism]); the other by Sergei Gorodetsky ("Некоторые течения в современной русской поэзии" [Some Currents in Contemporary Russian Poetry]). A third manifesto, by Mandelstam ("Утро акмеизма" [The Morning of Acmeism]), was rejected by Gumilev and Gorodetsky, according to Mandelstam's wife, Nadezhda. It was published only in 1919 in the Voronezh magazine *Sirena* (Mandelstam 1972, 47) – virtually after Acmeism had ended. Despite this disagreement (or clash of egos?), all three authors devoted themselves to things in their own right.

Gumilev justifies his move away from Symbolism thus:

Романский дух слишком любит стихию света, разделяющего предметы, четко вырисовывающего линию; эта же символическая слиянность всех образов и вещей, изменчивость их облика, могла родиться только в туманной мгле германских лесов.

(Gumilev 1913, 42)

The Romanic spirit loves too much the element of light, separating objects, clearly delineating them; while the symbolic fusion of all images and things, the variability of their appearance, could only be born in the dark misty gloom of Germanic forests.

He goes on to state "все явления братья" ("all phenomena are brothers"; ibid., 44). Gumilev requires "a greater balance of power and more accurate knowledge of the relationship between the subject and the object than was common in Symbolism" (большего равновесия сил и более точного знания отношений между субъектом и объектом, чем то было в символизме; ibid., 42).

Gorodetsky combines this plea for independence and clarity of contours of three-dimensional objects with a credo to this world:

Борьба между акмеизмом и символизмом, если это борьба, а не занятие покинутой крепости, есть, прежде всего, борьба за этот мир, звучащий, красочный, имеющий формы, вес и время, за нашу планету Землю.

Символизм, в конце концов, заполнив мир «соответствиями», обратил его в фантом, важный лишь постольку, поскольку он сквозит и просвечивает иными мирами, и умалил его высокую самоценность. У акмеистов роза опять стала хороша сама по себе, своими лепестками, запахом и цветом, а не своими мыслимыми подобиями с мистической любовью или чем-нибудь еще. [...] После всяких «неприятий» мир безповоротно принят акмеизмом, во всей совокупности красот и безобразий.

(Gorodetsky 1913, 48)

The struggle between Acmeism and Symbolism, if indeed it is a struggle and not the seizing of an abandoned stronghold, is primarily a struggle for this world, full of sound, colour and form, weight and time, so as to capture our planet Earth.

Symbolism, by filling the world with "correspondences," turned it into a kind of phantom, significant only insofar as it transluces and lights up other worlds, and greatly diminished its substantial inherent worth. For the Acmeists, the rose is again beautiful in itself, with its petals, scent and colour, and not for its conceivable kinship to mystical love or anything else. [...] Coming after all its "rejection," the world is unequivocally accepted by Acmeism, in all its beauty and ugliness.

"The Morning of Acmeism" is not only a manifesto of Acmeism; it can also be read as a personal manifesto of Mandelstam's entire work. Like his colleagues, Mandelstam demands we return to the specific and earthly, to the three-dimensional object. He writes: "Любите существование вещи больше самой вещи и свое бытие больше самих себя – вот высшая заповедь акмеизма" ("Love the existence of a thing more than the thing itself, and your being more than yourself – this is the highest commandment of Acmeism"; Mandelstam 2017b, 23). Apollonian lucidity here stands in opposition to the Dionysian principle of Symbolism. Starting with his first collection of poems, Mandelstam himself implements the principle of identity, which he expresses using the simple formula "A = A", and refers to it as the "прекрасная поэтическая тема" ("beautiful poetic theme") suffered by Symbolism (ibid.). According to Annette Werberger (2005, 67): "Das akmeistische Programm der Dinglichkeit ist somit Gegenprogramm zur Entdinglichung und völligen Vergeistigung der Welt im Symbolismus" ("the Acmeistic programme of materiality can be considered the counter-programme of the desecration and complete spiritualization of the world in Symbolism"). To the extent that Mandelstam considers poetry to be a craft, his poems are examples of thorough craftsmanship.

The *Камень* (Stone) Collection

Speaking of poems about things in the narrower sense (*Dinggedichte*), every-one will surely recall Mandelstam's poems about architecture, such as "Notre Dame" (Notre Dame), "Айя-София" (Aya Sofia), and "Адмиралтейство" (Admiralty), from his first poetry collection *Камень* (Stone; 1913). I leave these aside here, since my focus is the kitchen.

Interestingly, in one early poem from 1909, "Есть целомудренные чары" (There Are Chaste Charms), Mandelstam already expresses his departure from the Symbolist approach to the world, and writes about a carefully tidied niche, where the Penates, the protective gods of the home, are stood. The poem closes with:

> Иных богов не надо славить:
> Они как равные с тобой,
> И, осторожною рукой,
> Позволено их переставить.

(Mandelstam 2017a, 31)

> To celebrate other gods there is no need:
> As your equals they do seem
> And, by careful hand, with due esteem,
> To reposition them you may proceed.

The Penates are things and have their place above the stove.[1] The Penates that Mandelstam writes about are small, fragile statuettes; they can be taken in one's hand and moved. They can thus be treated very intimately, they are tan-gible. This is emphasized by the rhyming couplet "славить" – "переставить" ("to celebrate" – "to reposition"). Careful repositioning thus becomes a cel-ebration of the domestic gods, since, after all, finding a more suitable place means caring.

----

1   They are considered "покровители домашнего очага" – patrons of the hearth, literally a stove, a fireplace, and by extension the whole house/home, protected by its patron, protector, guardian spirit.

One of the possible sources of inspiration for Mandelstam was probably the well-known poem by Konstantin Batyushkov (1787–1855) "Мои пенаты. Послание к Жуковскому и Вяземскому" (My Penates: A Letter to Zhukovsky and Vyazemsky), written in 1811–1812 (Batyushkov 1964, 134–41).[2] This verse was also written in iambs,[3] whereby Batyushkov imitates the rhythm of an intimate, friendly conversation (Fridman 1964, 288) with his literary companions (Simonek 1992, 87). Mandelstam adopts the insubstantial but homely and accommodating atmosphere of Batyushkov's poem. While Batyushkov addresses the Penates, Mandelstam writes about them; although paradoxically they are heard through their silence, as he writes in the third person. To paraphrase Omry Ronen: "Mandelstam directly identifies his Penates with the poets of the past" (Ronen 1983, XIV). From this point of view, the repositioning and rearrangement of the domestic gods has a poetic-programmatic character. His literary predecessors are present (because they are not his contemporaries, unlike Batyushkov), and provide a certain poetic creative power, having their place in his new work. Yet this place is not definitive – once and for all; it can change, and the predecessors/poets themselves can no longer have anything to say about that. The rightful place of poetry, or of the domestic gods, is in the kitchen, above a warm stove, on the stage set of everyday life.

Essays

In the early 1920s (after his early manifesto "The Morning of Acmeism"), Mandelstam began to write his key poetological essays. To account for the apparent contradictions in them, particularly with regard to "the word" not being a thing, Annette Werberger draws attention to time constraints. If the beginning of Acmeism was marked by a departure from Symbolism, its follow-up issue was to distinguish itself from the doctrines of so-called Socialist Realism; but, above all, Mandelstam "wendet sich immer gegen die Verkürzung und

---

2   There are other connections, to Pushkin's poem "Городок" (The Town), Nikolay Yazykov's "Моё уединение" (My Accord; cf. Ronen 1983, XIV), and Fyodor Tyutchev's "Певучесть есть в морских волнах" (In Ocean Waves There's Melody; cf. Segal 1993, 372).

3   Mandelstam diverges from Batyushkov in that instead of iambic trimeter he uses iambic tetrameter, also favoured by Pushkin.

Einengung des Wortes zum reinen Signifikanten oder Signifikat" ("always turns against the reduction and restriction of the word to being purely the signifier or the signified", Werberger 2005, 15).

In the essay "Слово и культура" (Word and Culture; 1921), Mandelstam refers to poetry metaphorically as "плуг, взрывающий время так, что глубинные слои времени, его чернозем, оказываются сверху" ("a plough that upturns time so profoundly that the deep layering of time, its black loam, turns uppermost"; Mandelstam 2017b, 44). The repositioning of the Penates here becomes a transposition from horizontality to verticality: poetry cuts deep into time and everything worthwhile is brought from the lower layers to the surface. The soil is made ready to receive new seed. Mandelstam continues:

> Не требуйте от поэзии сугубой вещности, конкретности, материальности. [...] К чему обязательно осязать перстами? А главное, зачем отождествлять слово с вещью, с травою, с предметом, который оно обозначает? Разве вещь хозяин слова? Слово – Психея. Живое слово не обозначает предметы, а свободно выбирает, как бы для жилья, ту или иную предметную значимость, вещность, милое тело. И вокруг вещи слово блуждает свободно, как душа вокруг брошенного, но незабытого тела.
>
> (Ibid., 46)

> Do not demand from poetry some divine substance, concreteness, materiality. [...] Why should you touch it with your fingers? And most importantly, why identify a word with the thing, with the grass, with the object it denotes? Does the thing command the word? The word is the Psyche – the soul. The living word does not denote objects, but freely chooses for its abode some or other significant aspect of the object, or some being, perhaps even a favoured body. And the word circles freely around the thing itself, like a soul around an abandoned but unforgotten body.

Only through the word do things come back to life and acquire their spirit. Things simply are: they can be used and can always be assigned a new purpose. They thus differ from the emotions or visions that are central to Symbolism. A word can be loosely assigned to one object or another – such is the poet's scope; for, as Mandelstam writes a year later (1922), in the essay "О природе слова" (About the Nature of the Word):

> Русский номинализм, то есть представление о реальности слова как такового, животворит дух нашего языка и связывает его с эллинской филологической культурой не этимологически и не литературно, а через принцип внутренней свободы, одинаково присущей им обоим.
>
> (Mandelstam 2017b, 59)

Russian nominalism, i.e., the idea of the reality of the word, as such, gives life to the spirit of our language and connects it with Hellenic philological culture, not in the etymological or literary sense, but through the principle of inner freedom that is equally inherent in both of them.

Mandelstam's plea is driven by an innermost, home-grown Hellenism:

> Эллинизм – это печной горшок, ухват, крынка с молоком, это домашняя утварь, посуда, все окружение тела; эллинизм – это тепло очага, ощущаемое как священное, всякая собственность, приобщающая часть внешнего мира к человеку, всякая одежда, возлагаемая на плечи любым и с тем же самым чувством священной дрожи [...]. Эллинизм – это сознательное окружение человека утварью вместо безразличных предметов, превращение этих предметов в утварь, очеловечение окружающего мира, согревание его тончайшим телеологическим теплом.
>
> (Mandelstam 2017b, 64)

Hellenism is a stove pot, a poker, a jug of milk, household utensils, dishes, all one's bodily surroundings; Hellenism is the warmth of the hearth, felt as sacred, all the possessions linking one with the outside world, all the garments laid on the shoulders of a loved one with the same feeling of sacred trembling: [...] Hellenism is one's conscious gathering-in of useful rather than indifferent objects, the transformation of these objects into tools, one's humanization of the surrounding world, imbuing it with the subtlest teleological warmth.

Mandelstam takes a deeply philological view. He considers objects in their particular meanings, the clear naming of the world of things that one is faced with and enveloped by.[4] Including the Penates in the everyday life of the household is part of this approach. The sacral does not remain outside the need for an internal, homely Hellenism, but is to be incorporated into the secularized everyday. In his essay "Пшеница человеческая" (Human Wheat; 1922), Mandelstam uses the metaphor of the "universal hearth," benefitting from utensils collected over millennia (Mandelstam 2017b, 72).

In his essays, Mandelstam addresses (1) continuity, (2) universality, (3) freedom of speech, and (4) the transformation of meaningless objects into significant tools[5] – all this under the banner of everyday life, homeliness, and warmth.

Poems for Children

Homeliness and warmth also play an important role in Mandelstam's books for children: *Примус* (Primus; 1925) and *Кухня* (Kitchen; 1926). These poems were created as jocular verse (according to Nadezhda Mandelstam 2014, 841), and not originally intended for children. From the very beginning of his poetry career, Mandelstam valued childishness, and even the joy of childish naivety, more than maturely sombre Symbolism. Whenever he uses words like "playful," "frail," or "childish," they always have a positive connotation (Dutli 2004, 202–3), as was also seen in the example of the Penates, which in his opinion are not short of grandeur and are worthy of inspiring poetry.

Children's books fill a five-year period in Mandelstam's work, during which time he did not write any other poems. From 1923, he was banned from publishing poetry, and had to earn a living by translating and, indeed, writing children's books. At that time, the Mandelstams moved to Leningrad, to an apartment where they could enjoy their kitchen and their household (Mandelstam 2014,

---

4   Cf. his critique of Martin Luther: "Лютер был уже плохой филолог, потому что, вместо аргумента, он запустил в черта чернильницей" ("Luther was already a bad philologist because instead of an argument he launched an inkwell at the devil"; Mandelstam 2017b, 62).

5   The tool will be "at once a utensil and an artifact, a means and a (self)purpose" – "the tool is always – in the act of being fashioned – also making itself" (Hansen-Löve 2008, 301).

842). Mandelstam was always particularly attracted to kitchens, his favourite place in an apartment: "Sometimes I go and work in the well-lit servant quarters – because I am much taken with the kitchen and the serving maids," he writes in a letter to his wife, dated 18 February 1926 (Mandelstam 2011, 415).

In the first of the books, the primus stove (kerosene cooker), a clothes iron, various water jugs and containers, a sugar cone, a telephone, a lightbulb, and other items are among the important objects.[6] The theme of the poems is therefore to note prosaic subjects. Things are personified, as is often the case in children's books. This is, of course, directly at odds with the doctrine published by Lenin's widow Nadezhda Krupskaya, whom Mandelstam parodied in his short text "Детские писательницы" (Children's Authoresses), where he clearly rejects the notion of children's literature being made into a tool and a vassal of the class struggle (Mandelstam 2011, 315–16). Everyday objects have their dignity, their own value, which is too valuable for life to thrust other meanings upon them. They are to be treated lovingly and sensibly, like the Penates. The primus stove needs to be cared for in order for it to work, as do glasses so they don't break...

– В самоваре, и в стакане,
И в кувшине, и в графине
Вся вода из крана.
Не разбей стакана.

– А водопровод
    Где
        воду
            берет?

(Mandelstam 1925, [6])

---

6   The objects are also drawn here to their proper scale – their due size. It is the illustrations (by Mstislav Dobuzhinsky) that turn these poems into texts seemingly for children. Alexei Panfilov, in his very interesting study, points to their distinctly political implications, quite alien to any literature for children, which are indeed stressed by the graphic design (Panfilov 2002). Thus, there is more to the book than meets the eye. Mandelstam responded to Viktor Shklovsky's suggestion that he should make some money writing scripts with the parodic "Я пишу сценарий" (I Write a Script). In the text, he writes: "Things should play. Primus can be monumental. For example: primus seen in close-up. Child gone to hell. It all begins with a crooked primus needle (detail). The needle also in close-up" (Mandelstam 2011, 232).

– In the samovar, and in the drinking glass,
In the jug, and in the carafe is
Water from the tap there.
Don't break the glassware.

– And the water supply, mind,
Where does it
                    Water
                        Find?

The final riddle is, of course, addressed to children. It is characteristically highlighting what is not visible in the kitchen, and yet is there. In our context, however, it is more noteworthy that the poems remind children to take care of things and, indeed, to be careful with them, because they serve a need. Things that emit heat and light play a special role in these poems:

Принесли дрова на кухню,
Как вязанка на пол бухнет,

Как рассыплется она –
И береза и сосна, –

Чтобы жарко было в кухне,
Чтоб плита была красна.

(Mandelstam 1925, [10])

They brought firewood into the kitchen,
the bundle thumps onto the floor,

how will it unentwine –
the birch and the pine –

for heat in the kitchen,
for the hotplate red to shine.

For the fire to burn well, different types of wood are needed. The motion and sound of the bundle falling turns into something that we can see and feel. The stressed syllables in words related to heat – "дрова" ("wood"), "вязанка" ("bundle"), "сосна" ("pine"), "жарко" ("heat"), "плита" ("hotplate"), "красна" ("red") – resonate breathily with the "a" (*aah*) vowel throughout. The whole poem concludes with an open cadence on the "a". The red heat persists. This ending has been planned ahead, because "красна" is not a rhyme with its preceding above line, but with both endwords of the previous pair.

Also in the short story "Египетская марка" (The Egyptian Stamp; 1928), the opening passage reads: "Но как оторваться от тебя, милый Египет вещей?" ("Oh, how to tear oneself away from you, dear Egypt of things?"; Mandelstam 2017b, 230).[7] The magic of everyday things is developed using the very example of a log:

> Он любил дровяные склады и дрова. Зимой сухое полено должно быть звонким, легким и пустым. А береза – с лимон-но-желтой древесиной. На вес – не тяжелее мерзлой рыбы. Он ощущал полено, как живое, в руке.
> С детства он прикреплялся душой ко всему ненужному [...].
>
> (Ibid., 234)

He loved lumber yards and firewood. In the winter, dry logs should be sonorous, light, and hollow. And birch – with lemon-yellow wood. By weight – no heavier than a frozen fish. He weighed up the log as if it were alive in his hand.
From childhood, he had been drawn to everything unnecessary [...].

---

7   He recommends "a glass of boiled water" as a family coat of arms: "Семья моя, я предлагаю тебе герб: стакан с кипяченой водой. В резиновом привкусе петербургской отварной воды я пью неудавшееся домашнее бессмертие" ("My family, I offer you a coat of arms: a glass of boiled water. I drink my failed ancestral immortality in the rubbery taste of boiled St. Petersburg water"; Mandelstam 2017b, 230). In the lamp shop, for the first time in his life, the protagonist has a sense of a "forest of things," and the primus stove also makes a reappearance: "Керосинка была раньше примуса" ("The kerosene lamp came before the primus stove"; Mandelstam 2017b, 251, 245).

The sound, colour, and weight of the log are crucial to make it burn well. Warmth is also necessary, so one can read:

Всякая вещь мне кажется книгой. Где различие между книгой и вещью? [...]
Всё трудней перелистывать страницы мерзлой книги, переплетенной в топоры при свете газовых фонарей.
Вы, дровяные склады – черные библиотеки города, – мы еще почитаем, поглядим.

(Ibid., 252)

Each and every thing seems like a book to me. Where is the difference between a book and a thing? [...]
It is becoming more and more difficult to turn the pages of a frozen book bound into tabars, by the light of gas lamps.
You lumber yards – black libraries of the city –
we'll read you yet, we'll take a good look.

Things cannot only be grasped, but also read; they carry their stories within them.

In his *Primus* collection, Mandelstam utilizes things to paint a very homely, family setting. What made it provocative was the fact that, at this time, industrial-scale kitchens were being created – factory-kitchen canteens for feeding the masses, concerned only with sustenance and time-saving, in a chilled, impersonal atmosphere. The tools in them were national property. A private kitchen, let alone a kitchen in which one could feel comfortable, was to have no place in the de-individualized society of the new age (cf. Shteyner 2002, 202–3). Mandelstam's approach to the respective items sustains a normality that was slowly but surely ceasing to be normal.

A similar principle is followed in a second children's book, *Kitchen*, which was Mandelstam's joint favourite, along with *Primus* (Mandelstam 2014, 841). So many pots, casseroles, pans, in which either something is being prepared on a warm stove or made ready for it![8] Here, the kitchen is once again a place of warmth and safety:

---

8   This time, the illustrator was Vladimir Izenberg.

Гудит и пляшет розовый
Сухой огонь березовый
   На кухне! На кухне!
[...]

Горят огни янтарные,
Сияют, как пожарные,
   Кастрюли! Кастрюли!

(Mandelstam 1926, [1–2])

Whistling and dancing a rosy
Dry birch fire, cosy,
   In the kitchen! In the kitchen!
[...]

Burning amber fires,
Aglow, like firefighters,
   Casseroles! Casseroles!

The various colours of the fire, which imbue everything in the kitchen with their light, evoke a joyful expectation of food.

The way Mandelstam's children's books turn their attention to three-dimensional things corresponds to both the poetics of Acmeism and the entire body of his lyrical, essayistic, and epic work. These things are not present here for the sake of children, but the lyrics, originally written as joke poems, also work as children's poems because they are so rich in everyday things that they lend themselves to excellent illustration.[9]

---

9   In addition to the poems about architecture, they are also poems about things, in Oppert's sense. The name itself points out the thing-of-interest, which is placed right before our eyes (cf. Oppert 1926, 775).

The *Полночь в Москве* (Midnight in Moscow) Collection

There is another particularly hard-hitting poem in which Mandelstam reintroduces the primus stove. Here, the homely atmosphere of the kitchen is disturbed by a feeling of transience: the speaker is in transit, not knowing where to turn, looking for shelter, and not wanting to be found.[10]

> Мы с тобой на кухне посидим,
> Сладко пахнет белый керосин;
>
> Острый нож да хлеба каравай...
> Хочешь, примус туго накачай,
>
> А не то веревок собери –
> Завязать корзину до зари,
>
> Чтобы нам уехать на вокзал,
> Где бы нас никто не отыскал.

(Mandelstam 2017a, 132)

> In the kitchen we'll sit with you for a bit
> The white kerosene is smelling sweet;
>
> A sharp knife with which to slice the bread...
> Pump the primus stove, do, if you would,
>
> Or quickly get together strings for ties –
> To fasten the basket before sunrise
>
> We need to leave, to the train station to get,
> Where not to be found out by anyone yet.

---

10   A literal translation of this poem: "We with you in the kitchen will sit awhile / Sweetly smells the white kerosene / A sharp knife the bread to slice... / If you want, pump the primus, / Or else gather some string – / To tie-up the basket before dawn / We ought to head off for the station, / Where nobody would discover us."

There is no metaphor here, just the sensory appreciation of things, suggestive of a brief interlude at a time of existential threat. The loss of one's home at the conclusion of the poem is the antithesis of the homely atmosphere of the opening lines (cf. Dutli 1986, 255–56), itself expressed by the chance to get the primus stove working. The sense of smell is brought into play by the sweet smell of kerosene. In the two books for children, olfactory sensations played no part whatsoever. Mandelstam clearly considered the sense of smell less important than auditory or visual sensations, by which things are better able to be captured concretely.

In one of Mandelstam's last poems, "Где я? Что со мной дурного?" (Where Am I? What's Wrong with Me?...) – which was published in the 1936 collection *Воронежские тетради* (Voronezh Notebooks) – the teapot becomes a nocturnal partner in a soliloquy in a cold, silent city (Mandelstam 2017a, 189). Only the teapot gives ultimate assurance that the speaker is not alone in the world.

The three-dimensional and tangible always comes up in the poems, instead of anything vague and indeterminate – even in the case of abstract qualities, such as time, catching its tail when the kitchen clock is being wound ("Полночь в Москве. Роскошно буддийское лето" ["Midnight in Moscow. A delectable Buddhist summer"; Mandelstam 2017a, 140]). Glass, which was mentioned before to children as something that should not be broken, comes back again in a 1932 poem dedicated to Batyushkov. Mandelstam now explicitly refers to Batyushkov and reaffirms his own culturalism:

> Вечные сны, как образчики крови,
> Переливай из стакана в стакан...
>
> (Mandelstam 2017a, 153)

> Eternal dreams, like sampled vials of blood,
> Are pouring back and forth from glass to glass...

The transference from one glass to another, even if it is a metaphorical glass, portrays the continuity of culture. It is symptomatic, that the givers of the image are, once again, drinking glasses – that is, everyday objects. The outer form of the glass can change, but it always adopts and contains elements of previous glass things. To keep the universality, glass has to be handled with care; as we know from the poem for children, because there is something out there with which it can be filled. Cultural continuity, respect for one's predecessors, does not mean becoming frozen in time and stuck with old forms, but implies an intimate and personal treatment of their work. They can be treated like the Penates. Taking an everyday object as a metaphor reminds us that culture is seen as a part of everyday life, of the same cultural homeliness that Mandelstam described in his essays.

Conclusion

I consider the case of Osip Mandelstam illustrative of how putting things at the centre of poems does not automatically imply impersonality.[11] Kitchen utensils are of the utmost emotional importance to him; hence, he makes them the focus of seemingly impersonal poems. In taking his stand against Symbolism, Mandelstam connects things with feelings – not the base ones, but those that are divine.

In the poems examined, the most salient fact is that the things of interest are typically kitchen items that give heat and thus bring about a sense of homeliness, which Mandelstam tries to extend metaphorically to the entirety of European culture: the primus stove, the teapot, the samovar, the hearth.

Let me finish with a short excerpt from the poem "Еще далеко мне" (I am still far), dating to 1931:

> Когда подумаешь, чем связан с миром,
> То сам себе не веришь: ерунда!
>
> (Mandelstam 2017a, 143)

> When you think how you connect with the world,
> You won't believe yourself: what junk![12]

These small, insignificant, perhaps even meaningless things ("ерунда" means "junk" or "clutter") do become quite momentous if they show a connection to the world. Metonymically, they stand for people, situations, experiences – as when the poets of the past were embodied in the Penates.

---

11   Oppert uses the term impersonality several times in his treatise (Oppert 1926, 747, 751), as does Müller (1974, 158, 165).

12   "If you think, you'd not believe yourself, / What ties you to the world is rubbish" (trans. Bernard Mears).

Two Polish Poems about Things

JAKUB HANKIEWICZ

Questions such as "What *is* a thing?" and "What is its essence?" are primarily a topic for philosophy. Plato thought about such questions when he spoke of ideas,[1] followed by others down the philosophical passages of time, through to the phenomenologists (see Husserl's motto of going back to the "things themselves") and Martin Heidegger, who first deals with them in his *Sein und Zeit* (Being and Time), and subsequently in "Was ist Metaphysik?" (What Is Metaphysics?), or *Der Ursprung des Kunstwerkes* (The Origin of the Work of Art).

But what can poets say about a thing and its nature? Does poetry allow for them to reveal something yet inaccessible to philosophers? How do the ways and means by which poetry approaches a thing differ from the tools with which philosophy seeks to grasp it? This chapter sets out to show a possible path towards some answers, taking two poems by way of example. Their authors are leading lights in the main currents of Polish post-war lyricism: Zbigniew Herbert is traditionally assigned to the neoclassical line;[2] while Miron Białoszewski is the most notable contemporary constructivist, representing the neo-avant-garde.

---

1   Cf. Plato, *Sophist*, 253d.
2   We mention this categorization here in the full knowledge of the (often debated) issues with it. The most significant doubts raised about Herbert as a neoclassicist came from Stanisław Barańczak, in his landmark monograph *Uciekinier z Utopia* (Fugitive from Utopia). Barańczak argues that "Herbert does indeed often hark back to the cultural paradigms of ancient epochs, but he always does so from a position of contemporary empiricist" (Barańczak 1994, 24). According to Barańczak, Herbert's poetry goes against "the understanding of classicism as erudite and abstract *poetry of culture* or as the case for a harmonious and unconflicted vision of the world" (ibid., 29). In this chapter, we need not dwell on the precise naming of the movement (sometimes also referred to as the "Miłosz current") to which Herbert belongs, but on how it contrasts with the one to which the second of our poets, Miron Białoszewski, belongs (likewise known as the "Przyboś current").

Literary history pits both streams against each other, yet many aspects link them together. One of them is an interest in the thing as such,[3] and – in certain aspects, as we will attempt to show – also in how it is perceived. Let us start with a poem by Miron Białoszewski. It dates from his debut work of 1956 and gave its name to the entire collection: *Obroty rzeczy* (Revolutions of Things):

O obrotach rzeczy

A one krążą

I krążą.

Przebijają nas mgławicami.

Spróbuj schwycić
     ciało niebieskie
     któreś z tych
     zwanych „pod ręką"...

A czyj język
     najadł się całym smakiem
     Mlecznej Kropli przedmiotu?

A kto wymyślił,
     że gwiazdy głupsze
     krążą dokoła mądrzejszych?

A kto wymyślił
     gwiazdy głupsze?

(Białoszewski 2016, 58)

---

3   The authors we are choosing to follow here also share this with other poets of the post-war generation, such as Tadeusz Różewicz and Wisława Szymborska.

On the Revolutions of Things

And they are circulating

and orbiting.

They permeate us with nebulae.

Try to capture
    a celestial body
    one of those
    as they say "at hand"...

And whose tongue
    has sated hunger with all the flavours
    of the Milky drops of a thing?

And who dreamt up the idea
    that stupider stars
    orbit around the smarter ones?

And who dreamt up the idea
of stupider stars?

The name of the poem refers to the writing of Białoszewski's compatriot Nicolaus Copernicus, *On the Revolutions of the Celestial Spheres* (the Latin original being *De revolutionibus orbium coelestium*). Copernicus' work deals with the structure of the universe, and caused a shift in mankind's perception of it: hence the so-called "Copernican Revolution." Białoszewski's chosen title focuses our attention on a much more compact space – our immediate surroundings: he speaks not of celestial bodies beyond our reach, but about the kinds of things, objects that we interact with daily. Although Białoszewski makes his poem touch on the "Copernican Revolution" with considerable irony, he also offers us the certain "shift" or "revolution" alluded to by the original Latin title of Copernicus' work.

When writing about Białoszewski, Polish literary critic Jerzy Kwiatkowski supports his approach with the following quote from René Marilla Albérès, to show that one of the potential aims of art is to provoke a certain type of revolution, and thus topple established notions:

> The poet is thus someone who looks for meaning; someone who is not content with that sense, which [...] is given to things, people, and the world by life experience. The poet gives them a different meaning, or at least arouses a feeling of wonder. [...]
> The hallmark of today's artist is precisely how their art acts as an antidote to everyday experience. [...]
> Art has had to become surprising and shocking. It knocks us off-balance, embarrasses us, because its goal is to incite mistrust of our everyday ways of seeing.
>
> (Kwiatkowski 1964, 163)

In evoking "mistrust of our everyday ways of seeing" things, in "arousing a sense of wonder" about the humdrum, therein is the nub of the "Copernican Revolution" to which the title of Białoszewski's poem refers.

The revolution takes place at several levels in the poem, and this chapter focuses only on one aspect of it. In his poem, Białoszewski shows, among other things, how things that we understand as close to us, "at hand," are actually eluding us. "Try to capture" one of them, the poet exhorts us – you won't succeed. This is not just a statement. Białoszewski makes use of a specific poetic facility, using words with multiple meanings, to illustrate how ungraspable things can be. Almost all nouns in the poem have multiple meanings. These indicate the polymorphism of objects around us, and thus form one interpretive approach to the poem. I will try to illustrate Białoszewski's particular treatment of multi-faceted words on three examples.

Such polysemy begins with the hard-to-translate title of the poem. The word "obrót" combines three meanings. The first is the aforementioned meaning of "obrót" as a revolution. The second is "obróts," as "orbits" (the revolutions of celestial bodies). We can paraphrase the third meaning of "obrót" as a "turnaround"; deriving from the affinity of the word with "obrócić" – to "turn around" or "turn over." The meaning of "obrót" as a revolution we discussed above. The other two go hand in hand in the poem, and relate to the poet's analogy between things and celestial bodies. This meanders throughout the poem and starts with placing things in the "celestial spheres" of Copernicus' work (see above). In the opening lines, they are then credited with the ability to "circulate" and "orbit."

Here, the second meaning of the Polish "obrót" appears. The ancient controversy between heliocentrism and geocentrism is then evoked by the last-listed
meaning of the word: "obrót" as a "spin" or "turnaround": turning something
leads to seeing the given object from another side, in another way. The hinted at
connection between the second and third listed meanings now becomes apparent: if things are constantly orbiting, our every sighting is a view from a slightly
different angle. We therefore never look at anything quite the same way. Therein
lies the "revolution" that Białoszewski offers us: while in everyday functioning
we approach objects as something immobile and constant, the poem suggests
that things always appear a little differently to us each time we look at them.

The idea is developed by the multiple meanings of "celestial bodies." We are
supposed to try to capture a celestial body. This, however, proves impossible,
because the bodies "circulate and orbit," and therefore elude us. The subsequent lines suggest what makes things so hard to grasp: "And whose tongue /
has sated hunger with all the flavours / of the Milky drops of a thing." One can
never be completely finished with getting to know an object: the object always
inevitably hides more than is apparent to us at any given time.

Objects are all around us in our immediate surroundings; we look at them or
use them daily. Yet we cannot claim to know them *entirely*. We become aware of
this when we focus our attention on them. To illustrate, let us consider how this
experience was described by the French philosopher Roger-Pol Droit when
he resolved to try to "draw nearer to things" (cf. Droit 2005, 12). After a few
months of "drawing nearer," he writes:

> Before I began the journey, if I am not mistaken, no object excited
> my particular surprise, every thing I encountered was effortlessly
> labelled and assimilated. They were all in order, all in their proper
> places. [...] As I gradually began to look at things differently – these
> things so close to hand, so easy to pick up or merely to brush lightly
> against, ever present, always within reach – these hitherto ordi-
> nary objects began to distance themselves steadily, so as often to
> seem unreachable and ultimately impenetrable. [...] Even the simp-
> lest of things, the most reassuring, [now] reveal an untamed depth,
> inhuman, inexpressible.
>
> (Ibid., 183–84)

Białoszewski does not just make a mention of this depth when he disputes that anyone could have "sated hunger with all the flavours / of the Milky drops of a thing," but uses the polysemic expression "ciało niebieskie" to illustrate it by linguistic means. In Polish, "ciało niebieskie" can mean both a "celestial body" as well as a "blue body." The phrase thus evades having a clear, unequivocal definition, just as things are beyond one objective cognisance or explanation.

The last polysemic keyword along our chapter's train of thought is "język." In Polish, this word has two meanings. Białoszewski uses it primarily in the meaning of "tongue" – that is, the bodily organ of taste. However, noting the purposiveness with which Białoszewski uses words in his writing, we also may read "język" in its second meaning: that is, "language." Thus, while the poem asks the question, "whose tongue" has been sated "with all the flavours of the [object]," it is at the same time asking who talks about the object, and how. First and foremost, it is philosophy that has, from its beginnings, addressed the object as an issue (see above). Yet there is another way of dealing with the matter, through poetic language. It differs from philosophical language: it has different means, different objectives, and therefore points out different aspects of the thing.

To analyse philosophical language would take us beyond the scope of this chapter. To keep things simple, let us briefly cover some characteristics of the traditional and rational Aristotelian line of philosophy, as generally understood. In *Úvod do současné filosofie* (Introduction to Contemporary Philosophy), Miroslav Petříček characterizes philosophy as a way of thinking, which holds "the view that thinking, if left to itself, is able to self-sufficiently and solely through logical operations deductively develop a cognitive system (comprising in systematic arrangement along the lines of mathematical construction the principles of everything extant), to coincide with what exists in real life" (Petříček 1997, 13–14). In philosophy, "various systems compete" (ibid., 15). Philosophy "proceeds by means of general concepts" (ibid., 85), and is thus "traditionally associated with the abstract, the general, the universal" (ibid.). Philosophical language in the Platonic-Aristotelian sense is a language that defines, categorizes, proves. Plato says that the task of dialectics is "the division of things by classes and the avoidance of the belief that the same class is another, or another the same" (Plato 1921, 401; *Sophist*, 253d). Aristotle, in turn, shows how akin the tools of rhetoric and dialectics are, arguing that both disciplines use for evidence that which is "true and irrefutable" (Aristotle, *Rhetoric* I, 2, 1357b17).

Philosophical language traditionally creates definitions, "generic concepts," and "systems of thought." Białoszewski shows that poetic language gives a thing the chance to elude any definition or inclusion in any system: the thing that is being perceived can at any moment appear in a new context and acquire new meaning; each percept of a thing is a view of it from a certain limited perspective which cannot be considered absolute, since things "circulate and orbit," and are thus always showing themselves to us anew. It is essential that Białoszewski does not use assertions to illustrate his approach, but rather the linguistic means of poetry: he uses polysemic words that can be interpreted in multiple ways, thereby demonstrating how things elude our efforts to grasp them in their entirety.

Contrasting Białoszewski's poem with the Aristotelian current of philosophy that creates "generic concepts" and "systems of thought" reveals that it is the handling of polysemy that distinguishes the way the poet speaks about things from the way traditional philosophy speaks about them. Not only does Aristotle establish the "rationalist" school of philosophy (cf. Petříček 1997, 13), but he argues against any reasoning that differs fundamentally from his. Such was the pre-Socratic philosophy, especially that of Heraclitus, a thinker highly thought of by the author of the second poem analysed in this chapter. "Aristotle mentions Heraclitus in his *Rhetoric* only when he wants to set an example of how not to write" (Kratochvíl 2006, 23), explains Zdeněk Kratochvíl, describing what it is about Heraclitus that bothers authors like Aristotle. An example is the fact that Heraclitus' text

[...] is marked by an abundance of semantic connections, intricately anchored in the chiastic structure of his statements, as well as numerous other syntactic means, and yet differing from the conceptual divisions, definitions, and one-dimensional chained conclusions that these writers take for granted. These are not syllogisms, it is a matter for serious reading, not a computer manual. Aristotle, however, thought he had come up with the only possible way of thinking properly (A 7/2):
"Yet we had declared that it was impossible for something to be and not to be at the same time. We showed this as the most certain of all the principles [...] It's simply ignorant: Not knowing what to seek and what not to seek to interpret."
He [Aristotle] is irritated by proclaiming opposites simultaneously.

(Kratochvíl 2006, 23–24)

As already seen from the short introductory characterization of Zbigniew Herbert, the poet resented abstract and purely logical reasoning (commensurate with the Platonic-Aristotelian current in philosophy). As a philosophy student at the University of Toruń, he confided in his teacher, Henryk Elzenberg, that he found pre-Socratic philosophy much more to his liking. Józef Maria Ruszar adds:

> It is no coincidence that writing to Elzenberg he tells of his love for most of the pre-Socratics, since, as he put it in his letter to the Master, at their time "concepts were only germinating out of things." If we are to translate that poetic image into the language of discourse, then it must be said that the poet finds Post-Socratic rationalism suspicious. Herbert builds on the earlier period of Greek reasoning, because he is more attuned to the nascent logos arising completely out of intuition and imagination.
>
> (Ruszar 2012, 162–63)

Herbert not only subscribes to the Pre-Socratics in his letter to his "guru," but also follows up on their formal methods; often the very ones for which Heraclitus was reproached by Aristotle. The aforementioned Zdeněk Kratochvíl, in his book on Heraclitus, describes the rhetoric of this great pre-Socratic philosopher and sets out his linguistic tools, the major ones being deployed in the introduction of Herbert's poem "Studium przedmiotu" (A Study of the Object) from the eponymous collection:

Studium przedmiotu

1
najpiękniejszy jest przedmiot
którego nie ma

nie służy do noszenia wody
ani do przechowania prochów bohatera

nie tuliła go Antygona
nie utopił się w nim szczur

nie posiada otworu
całe jest otwarte

widziane
z wszystkich stron
to znaczy zaledwie
przeczute

włosy
wszystkich jego linii
łączą się
w jeden strumień światła

ani
oślepienie
ani
śmierć
nie wydrze przedmiotu
którego nie ma
(Herbert 2011, 281–82)

A Study of the Object

1.
the most beautiful is the object
which is not

not used for carrying water
nor to keep the mortal remains of a hero

not caressed by Antigone
in which no rat has drowned

which has no opening
being all open

being seen
from all sides
that is being scarcely
supposed

the strands
of all its lines
combine together
into a single stream of light

nor
blindness
nor
death
will tear out the object
which is not

The first of these characteristics was already described by Aristotle in the passage cited above: he complains that although it is impossible for "something to be and not to be at the same time," in Heraclitus these "same-breath opposites" (Kratochvíl 2006, 62) can be found. A similarly constructed contradiction also opens Herbert's poem: "the most beautiful is the object / which is not."

Furthermore, Aristotle criticizes Heraclitus' sentence structure: "to parse Heraclitus' sentences is a difficult task, for it is often unclear whether something relates to what follows or to what precedes" (Kratochvíl 2006, 63). Kratochvíl calls this feature "the ambivalent relationship of the middle constituent" (ibid.). The opening two lines of "A Study of the Object" can also be read in two ways, depending on how we associate the word "object." Either it can be a claim that the most beautiful of all is an object that is not; or that, of all things, the most beautiful is the one that is not.

Another characteristic of Heraclitus' rhetoric is reflected in the first two lines of "A Study of the Object": the feature that Kratochvíl called the "promise of definition."[4] Kratochvíl explains it as follows:

---

4   The word "definition" should be taken with caution here, because a definition, as we understand it, is a concept more recent than Heraclitus' statements.

Some of the statements [by Heraclitus] begin with such a declaration of some basic expression that we would almost be expecting its definition to follow. Instead, Heraclitus will, of course, offer us a list of contradictions, an ambivalence or talk of changes over time.

(Kratochvíl 2006, 62)

For Herbert, the promise of definition is enhanced by the line break. After the first line – "the most beautiful is the thing" – we do not get the expected definition of the most beautiful thing, but an antithesis in the second line: "which is not."

"The most common syntactic figure of Heraclitus' speech" (Kratochvíl 2006, 60) is the chiasmus. In "A Study of the Object," Herbert uses chiasmatic relationships between parts of speech in lines 3–6. Line 3 is related to line 6, and line 4 to line 5. The relationships are best revealed by pair of lines being broken down into separate lines:

Water links "not [being] used for carrying water" and "in which no rat has drowned"; while the remains of the hero are linked with Antigone, who in Sophocles' tragedy buried her brother's body, despite it being forbidden. For Heraclitus, the chiasmus carries meaning and "particularly interesting [...] chiasmi happen when they contain side-by-side contradictions" (Kratochvíl 2006, 61). The writer Jerzy Zawieyski suggests such a contradiction in Herbert. In his considerations of another famous Herbert poem, "Tren Fortynbrasa" (Elegy of Fortinbras; also from the collection A Study of the Object), he puts up against one another the essence of Antigones and Hamlets – which consists of honouring principles and unwritten laws – versus Creont and Fortinbras – whose bywords are the "brud życia,"[5] sordid everyday life, as symbolized by the rat in "A Study of the Object."

---

5   Cf. Franaszek 2018, 409.

In arguably the most famous interpretation of "A Study of the Object," the poet Jarosław Marek Rymkiewicz attributes to each line a symbolic value: line 3 symbolizes usefulness, line 4 beauty, line 4 and 5 the past, and line 6 ugliness (cf. Rymkiewicz 1970, 50). He noted the link between lines 4 and 5, and described both as bearing the meaning of "the past, history," but he did not dwell on the mutual chiasmatic relationships of the other lines. Had he done so, he would have associated the beauty of the fourth line to the past of lines 4 and 5, and ugliness to the utility of lines 3 and 6. The symbolic meanings described by Rymkiewicz then correspond to Zawieyski's categories, building on them. Standing against one another is beauty, associated with the past, and the dross and ugliness of practical life, the actual present.

This is a dichotomy typical of Herbert. In his poetry we find that the ideal and the pure is often related to a legendary or ancient past. Apollo of the angels can serve as an example. Yet Herbert presents all things ideal and clean as rather cold and lifeless, and therefore inhuman. For an emblematic example we can turn to the aforementioned god, as portrayed in the poem "Apollo i Marsjasz" (Apollo and Marsyas; cf. Herbert 2011, 247–24962). Conversely, Herbert also writes about the earthly everyday. This is often connected with anguish – whether it be the suffering of Marsyas or the suffering experienced by Herbert's peers in communist Poland. In the cited monograph, Stanisław Barańczak shows how the author's position is ambivalent in the whole of Herbert's work; the poet does not stand on either side, whilst "both sides [...] in Herbert's poetry are in a state of dynamic equilibrium, with neither one of the opposing values reigning supreme, or one proving to be unconditionally above the other" (Barańczak 1994, 124).

In his monograph, Barańczak conducts a detailed analysis of "both sides" (cf. Barańczak 1994, 55–123). For our reading of "A Study of the Object", it seems crucial that, whilst in Herbert's work overall the clash between the two sides creates "tensions that are particularly relevant to this poetry" (ibid., 124), in this poem, both sides are negated: the most beautiful object *is not*, does *not* serve, does *not* have.

In conclusion, let us remind ourselves of one more feature of Heraclitus' rhetoric: "Heraclitus' chiastic structures are quite often preceded by a kind of 'heading'" (Kratochvíl 2006, 61). In Herbert's case, the heading consists of the first two lines: "the most beautiful is the object / which is not." The subsequent negation of the two contradictory values expressed by the chiasmus, which are crucial for Herbert's work, shows that the most beautiful object belongs to neither of them. The negation of these two poles demarcating the oscillations of the poet throughout his work exemplifies the writer's self-irony. After all, the topic is "the most beautiful object," which can also mean an ideal work of art.

As was the case with Białoszewski, where we could not "capture" an object because it was always able to elude us with its circling, Herbert leaves his most beautiful object open, indeterminate. He does not place it into the world of the ideal, nor does he restrict it to the purely utilitarian; the object is neither entirely specific nor abstract. In the seventh line it is described as "being all open."

This chapter set out to indicate possible answers to the question of what the poet's language tools enable him to say about the nature of an object. In the case of Polish post-war lyricism, exemplified here by two authors representing the two main currents in contemporary poetry, it is precisely the noting of the object's complete openness. A single word brings a multitude of meanings into the poem and opens up a host of readings. In this respect, Białoszewski finds a parallel between the word and the object. Just as a word has multiple meanings, an object can always be perceived in a different context and in a different set of connections, and therefore can be seen differently every time. For Białoszewski, the polysemic nature of the object is not an abstract artistic manifesto, but the everyday reality of war-torn Warsaw. This is displayed not only by a number of the poems from his first collections (most notably the poem "Sprawdzone sobą" [Personally Verified] from the collection *Rachunek zachciankowy* [A Calculus of Whims]), but also by Białoszewski's theatrical practice. The props of the renowned Tarczyńska Theatre, which Białoszewski founded with Ludwig Hering and Ludmila Murawska, were often repurposed items of everyday use, so that in the theatre's opening performance a chair became first a Greek amphitheatre and later a musical instrument.

Similarly, Herbert arrives at his object's openness through his language. Through its ability to readily negate everything he has said, to tear down everything he has constructed with the single word "not." If Aristotle is looking for "irrefutable" evidence (see above), then Herbert shows that there is no such characteristic in language. Language can negate everything, and Herbert self-ironically shows this by negating the two poles determining (to paraphrase Barańczak) the "dynamic equilibrium" of his own poetry. Aristotle parenthesized Heraclitus' "simultaneous expression of opposites", declaring it "ignorant." Herbert adopts the linguistic methods of Heraclitus that were criticized by Aristotle, and uses them to show what Aristotle's syllogisms fail to encompass.

Indeed, if language allows for "simultaneous expression of opposites," does that not say something important about the reality described by that language? Herbert is most certainly far from glorifying abstract negation. This is evidenced, *inter alia*, by the exchange of letters relating to "A Study of the Object" between Herbert and Czesław Miłosz (cf. Franaszek 2018, 816–17). To call an existing statement into question is to open up a new perspective on reality; it is an opportunity, or rather an invitation, to listen to things in a new way.

"Time's Seconds Prominent Arise / Trembling in the Façade": A Look Back at Roman Architecture. "Il Gesù" by Milada Součková

JOSEF VOJVODÍK

"Love the existence of a thing more than
the thing itself
and your being more than yourself..."

Osip Mandelstam, "The Morning
of Acmeism" (1913)

In her collection *Sešity Josephiny Rykrové* (The Notebooks of Josefína Rykrová),
Milada Součková (1899–1983) included, as Notebook 3, the section "Roman
Vedutas," inspired by her visits to Rome and Italy in April 1960 and March
1976. For Součková, the poetic topography of the Italian capital – with which
she had already engaged in her *Alla Romana* collection, inspired by her first
Roman sojourn – is much like her poetic topography of Prague, with scope for
recollection. To Součková, architecture and architectural monuments, some of
the prime themes of her Roman poems, represent being inherently in a world of
culture, and, equally, in the culture of remembrance. The poetological starting
point of these works is an immediate, sensory, quite material contact with the

architecture and atmosphere of the city. By linking architectural monuments and plants – in other words, by analogizing the aesthetics of architectural proportions with the aesthetics of plants, nature, and art, by cross-fertilizing the *semiosphere* of culture and the *biosphere* of plants[1] – Součková follows Goethe's analogization of plant morphology and architecture,[2] as well as the poetics of "expressive architecture" from the opening lines of *Römische Elegien* (Roman Elegies). The first line of Goethe's cycle evokes the call to the Muse in the opening line of Homer's *Odyssey*:

> Saget, Steine, mir an, o sprecht, ihr hohen Paläste!
> Straßen, redet ein Wort! Genius, regst du dich nicht?
> Ja, es ist alles beseelt in deinen heiligen Mauern,
> Ewige Roma…
>
> (Goethe 2007, 157)

> Stones, tell me, oh, do speak, you lofty palaces!
> Streets, say a word! Genie, will you remain mute?
> Yes, in your sacred walls all is imbued with a soul,
> Eternal Rome…

Architecture speaks its own language, which has its order and "grammar." In his rapture at Palladio, Goethe likens his construction skills to the poetic arts (Jeziorkowski 2002, 32). In his letter to his friend, the Swiss painter Heinrich Meyer (December 1795), Goethe writes: "The more we study Palladio, the more unbelievable seems the genius, mastery, richness, versatility, and grace of this man"

---

1   Yuri M. Lotman (1990a, 287–305) distinguishes between the semiosphere and the biosphere. The biosphere is a universally interconnected system of all organisms in their particular conditions and adapted to their surroundings, i.e., the continuum of life around the entire world. As a parallel to the biosphere, Lotman posits a semiosphere, comprising various symbolic complexes, as a human cultural work, formed by a diversity of languages and symbols, i.e., a semiotic continuum of symbolic and sign-representative systems.

2   In Italy, Goethe considered the "primal plant" (*Urpflanze*), from which, he theorized, all other plants had metamorphosed. The poet also applied this theory to the world of animals and to mankind. Goethe's elegy *Metamorphose der Pflanzen* (Metamorphosis of Plants) of June 1798 relates this theory in its poetic quintessence, as developed in Goethe's first natural-history, botanical treatise, *Versuch die Metamorphose der Pflanzen zu erklären* (1790). As an elegy, the *Metamorphosis of Plants* relates to the *Roman Elegies* (1795).

(Goethe 2013, 213). Another connection between Součková and the poet of the *Roman Elegies* comes from their botanical studies. Součková completed her studies at the Charles University Science Faculty in 1923, with the dissertation "O duševním životě rostlin" (On the Mental Life of Plants). The regenerative, resonant power of Italy, metamorphosing into poetry and images, is a theme to which Součková returns time and again, with explicit references to Goethe. As we read in his *Italienische Reise* (Italian Journey), Goethe does not appreciate the "things of this world" anywhere so much as in Rome. For Goethe, Rome is not only a paradigmatic cultural space, but also the locus of world and human history. In the first part of his *Italian Journey*, Goethe writes of Rome: "Much as I got along with natural history, I did here, too, because this is a place connecting with the whole history of the world, and I count my alternate birthday, a true rebirth, from the day I entered Rome."[3] This "rebirth" also applies in a special sense to Rome, and the poetry of Milada Součková, inspired by Rome and Italy.

Words are the building blocks of poetic architecture – a strategy that is semantically constitutive for the poetic meaning and the cultural model of the Russian Acmeistic poets (but also for Rilke), most importantly for Osip Mandelstam's image of the Gothic cathedral. As Renate Lachmann has shown, stone and architecture represent in this cultural model a dynamic and permanent storehouse of time and cultural heritage – cultural experiences stratified atop one another. Part of this concept of text is intertextualism, working with quotations and allusions, a multilayered and multilingual, syncretic coding of text. This creates a peculiar "fiction of time," which Lachmann characterizes as the "temporal solidarity of imported textual characters," through which we can roll back the text's lost time (Lachmann 1990, 370–71). For Mandelstam, a true poet is an architect, a builder, participating with their words in the architecture of culture; but not in terms of constructivist mechanics, but as creator who combines the realms of an inorganic material – stone – with that of nature, growth, ripening. In the programme-manifesto of "Утро акмеизма" (The Morning of Acmeism; 1919), Mandelstam writes:

---

3   "Wie mir's in der Naturgeschichte erging, geht es auch hier, denn an diesen Ort knüpft sich die ganze Geschichte der Welt an, und ich zähle einen zweiten Geburtstag, eine wahre Wiedergeburt, von dem Tage, da ich Rom betrat" (Goethe 2002, 147).

Acmeism is for the one who – inspired by the spirit of building – does not small-mindedly refuse his own ponderousness, but joyfully accepts it to awaken and use the power architectonically dormant within it. The builder says: I build – therefore I am in the right. [...] In the builder's hands the stone block is transformed into a substance, and none is called upon to be a builder for whom a stonemason's chisel pounding the stone does not sound like a metaphysical proof. [...] As though the stone started to yearn for another form of being. Once it has discovered the secret power of dynamism within, it seems to desire to become a part of a "cross vault" so as to enjoy happy interaction with its peers. [...] We can only build in the name of spaciousness, since that is a prerequisite of any construction. The architect must therefore be a person staid and steady, which makes the Symbolists bad builders. To build is to confront emptiness, to hypnotize space.

(Mandelstam 2010, 22–26)

In Mandelstam's poetics, the word-stone is a building block with its inner dynamic that the architect-sculptor-poet with his "masonry chisel" can form, thus awakening it to a new life. He transforms the inorganic into the organic, turning the word-stone into "another form of being." This is, for Mandelstam, the paradigm of this universalist cultural model and a "new organic understanding" of Gothic art.[4] Not in the sense of a cultural-historical and artistic-historical epoch, of course; but as a transepochal, spiritual-cultural phenomenon that Mandelstam connects – in his essay "Гуманизм и современность" (Humanism and the Present; 1923) – not with utopian projects (the way that the futuristic and constructivist avant-garde did at the time),[5] but quite to the contrary, with cosy domesticity, with the domain of privacy and practical handicraft.

---

4   Mandelstam's Gothic is discussed by Aage A. Hansen-Löve (1999, 80–106).
5   The period after the First World War brought a great revival of interest in the Middle Ages – indeed, a fascination with the medieval period as an epoch of great syntheses and orderliness. Published as early as 1919, a few months after the end of the war, came the famous work of Dutch cultural historian Johan Huizinga, Herfsttijd der middeleeuwen (The Autumn of the Middle Ages), concerning the lifestyle and spiritual formats of the fourteenth and fifteenth centuries in France and the Netherlands. In 1922, philosophy student Paul Ludwig Landsberg (1901–1944), a disciple of Max Scheler and Edmund Husserl, published Die Welt des Mittelalters

These are qualities that Součková also points out in baroque culture. In her last book, *Baroque in Bohemia,* she also deals with folk handicraft art, glass painting, embroidery, gingerbread moulds, baroque garden architecture, legends, everyday life, and so on. For Milada Součková, the baroque represents the qualities that Mandelstam associates with his own peculiar understanding of the Gothic. Indeed, it is the Church of Il Gesù that presents, as Alois Riegl and Max Dvořák have shown, a symbiosis of the "neo-Roman style" of the late sixteenth century with Gothic tendencies:

> As in the old Christian and Gothic art, in other words, in times when new universal ideas are coming to the fore in architecture, we see a frenzy of construction, the leading proponents of which, in Rome, were Carlo Maderno, Martino Longhi, Domenico and Giovanni Fontana, alongside Giacoma della Porto. [...] It is not hard to cite Spanish, Belgian, and Southern German examples, in which there is a striking conformity with local Gothic traditions, interestingly enough, but also quite understandably, since there was certainly a contrast with the Renaissance, but no contradiction between the Gothic and the neo-Roman styles. The tendencies of this style align easily with the tendencies of Nordic Gothic, which greatly influenced

---

und wir (The World of the Middle Ages as It Relates to Ourselves), which concedes a fascination for the idea of a statehood based on higher social strata of "estates." Young Landsberg sees in the horrors of the First World War, and the post-war wave of European revolutions and chaos, an attempt to fragment the world and revolt against order: "Every breaking of the order (*ordo*) is primarily about abandoning Man's place in it."

In contrast to the Bolshevik revolutions, which deny anarchism and individualism, Landsberg posits a "conservative revolution, a revolution of the eternal," capable of turning a worn-out "order" that has ossified into a "habit" (*Gewohnheit*) – which leads to anarchy – into a new order that would be a "form of life" for mankind (Landsberg 1922, 112–114). At about that time, Karel Teige wrote in his piece "Nové umění proletářské" (New Proletarian Art; 1922) about Gothic cathedrals as a model for the future architecture of a new society, seeing the Gothic in a way directly contradicting Mandelstam's approach: the Gothic as a utopian prequel to the folk art of prospective socialist society: "In socialist society, just as in the Gothic, there will be no difference between the governing art form and the undercurrent of primary production. Folk proletarian art will attain the might that created the Gothic cathedrals" (Teige 1966, 61). Walter Gropius started out by considering the term "Bauhütte" (a medieval building foundry) for the Bauhaus.

the architectural character of the entire Nordic baroque, with its high
façades, towers, and interior spaces.

(Dvořák 1936, 139–40)

What unites the poetics of Osip Mandelstam and Milada Součková above all is
their perception of heritage, cultural memory, and reminiscence as a dialogue
with culture and with the past, which through the poem becomes a part of the
experienced present. This dialogue also establishes specific intertextual strategies for both Mandelstam and Součková. This makes for a text that is conceptu-
ally broad and all-embracing, based – as Renate Lachmann shows in Mandelstam's Acmeistic poetry – on the overlaying of references to reality and of textual
references, "because it is the texts by others that refer to 'reality' and act as the
language of Acmeistic texts. The overlaying of textual references to reality with
the reality of the textual reference, the overlaying of natural language with the
language of culture leads to an intensification of the 'secondary modelling' function of the text thus conceived" (Lachmann 1990, 359). The Acmeistic poems –
and likewise the poems of Milada Součková – are characterized by their heterogeneity, in which there is the "idea of textual co-presence" but also the breaking
down of the particular text: in the sense that, by referencing imported texts, it
transcends its boundaries and "opens out into the text of culture, into a mac-
rotext" (ibid., 359). A transgressive and heterogeneous text creates a "complex
dynamic time structure," in which the time frames of imported texts and of
the given text are engaged in a "forward-flowing duration," as they interweave
through the writing process (ibid., 360). "Reminiscent writing" and participating in "cultural remembrance" creates a text formed as though by the layering of
time strata, constructing an achronistic, ateleological image of history, in which
the past is understood as emerging, referencing forward to the future.

The poem "Il Gesù" (about 1976) – inspired by the first Jesuit church in
Rome, built between 1575 and 1584 to designs by Giacomo Barozzi da Vignola
and Giacomo della Porta – occupies a unique position in the poetic semantics
and architectonics of Milada Součková's memory. It is a specific structure, but
it acquires – as a materialized reminder of a particular work of sacral architecture in a particular place – a dimension of aesthetic fiction through its transformation into poetic text. Il Gesù is, for Součková, a meeting place between
poetological and cultural-historical concepts, semantic, cultural, and artistic-historical and aesthetic-theological references, sacral and profane, the past
and the present, the sphere of inorganic artefacts and the vegetative sphere of

plants and fruits. At the same time, the poem evokes – by mentioning Charles Square – the Prague counterpart to the Roman Il Gesù: the Jesuit Church of St. Ignatius, built between 1665 and 1678 to plans by the Bavaria- and Bohemia-based Italian architect Carlo Lurago. Rome and Prague, recollection and fiction, the concurrency of poetic practice, cultural history, artistic history, and aesthetic-religious references, permeate each other in the poem, mirror each other, and co-create its textual and metatextual plane.

Il Gesù

Obklopen domy
v Římě, v Praze, ulicemi
provoz řinčí podle zdí
vysoko okna s mříží
5   omítkou domy splývají
ne snad že by neomšely
schody z žuly zastaví
zrak i kroky v průčelí
Il Gesù
10   s dvířky pro denní úpění
kovové květy zasvítí
v ornátu každou chvíli
na světě slouží mši
Beata morte hodinky
15   pro hospodyně, penzisty.
Z nádoby mračno trhovkyni
chrstlo vodu v zeleniny
v zlato tvarů v průčelí,
v piazze dei fiori e legumi
15   levné artičoky handlují
dva, o anemonky, zevlují
čas jako každý utrácí
snad také pršelo i jindy
dávno, v průčelí na ulici
20   omítky světlo stíny kreslí
hnědnou vlhkem, skoro zelení
zlátnou svitem v letním dni

(na Karlově náměstí)
u zdi, výš, okna, mřížoví
30 dole bez rozdílu věku
na chodníku muži, ženy
z všedních zoufalství, radostí
vteřiny času vystoupí
zachvějí se v průčelí
35 v šeru svítí kovy (anemonky)

(Součková 2009: 93–94).

Il Gesù

By houses surrounded quite
in Rome, in Prague, by streets
traffic jangling past walls
high-up windows with a grille
5   plasterwise houses blending in
not that they'd not be fading still
The granite stairs arresting hold
the gaze and pace at the façade bold
Il Gesù
10   with little doors for daily wails
metal flowers light up glint
in the chasuble every now and then
serving Mass in the world
Beata morte Liturgy of the Hours
15   for housewives and for pensioners.
From a bowl the cloud made fall
water spewed at the vegetable stall
in the gold of facets in the façade,
in the piazza dei fiori e legumi
15   they're haggling for cheap artichokes
two, dawdling at anemones,
spending time just like everyone
perhaps it's rained at other times
long ago, in the street-side façade

20 the plasterworks light shadow drawn
   browning with moisture, almost green
   sun-gilded on a summer's day
   (on Charles Square)
   by the wall, higher, windows, grilles
30 beneath of ages one and all
   on the sidewalk men and women
   from their everyday despairs, joys
   time's seconds prominent arise
   trembling in the façade
35 in the gloom (anemone) metals glow

Architecture, *Kunst-Ding,* and *Dinggedicht*

In his seminal treatise "Das Dinggedicht" (1926), Kurt Oppert writes about architecture in poems as "things of architecture" (*Dinge der Architektur*), their meaning determined by purpose and function. An architectural work is a specifically created "artistic thing" (*Kunst-Ding*) that combines functional, constructive, and artistic elements (Oppert 1926, 770). This combination is the basis not only of architecture's specific aesthetic effect, but also of the aesthetic experience associated with sensory perception, in which touch, hearing, and sense of smell are also involved, in addition to vision. August Schmarsow described this experience of architecture, in his inaugural professorial lecture at the University of Leipzig (1893), as being the co-author of our spatial sensibility and a polyaesthetic experience. Schmarsow's anthropologically based concept of architecture was a pioneering one, in that it placed emphasis on one's bodily adaptation to and experience of architectural space. His approach foreshadowed certain motifs in Edmund Husserl's treatment of the phenomenology of space and Maurice Merleau-Ponty's phenomenology of perception. Schmarsow showed that the bodily axes govern a person's idea of three-dimensional space, and he countered the bias towards visual perception with the tactile and proprioceptive senses. For Schmarsow, architecture was always the result of an aesthetic fashioning of form, as a "shaper of space" (*Raumgestalterin*), closely related to sensory experience. It is "a creation by man for man, the creative will of a subject permeated by bodily form and inner space itself" (Schmarsow 1914, 74).

Sacral architecture, be it a temple or a church, is architecture of representation (of a heavenly citadel), and of self-representation with a particular cultic function, as the house where a community of believers gathers to celebrate the sacrament. At the same time, however, precisely because of its ritually performative aspect of celebration, sacral architecture is mankind's public place and space, the intersection of the sacred and the profane, of spirit and nature, of transcendence and everyday life. According to Karsten Harries, this is the essence not only of sacral architecture, but of architecture itself: in his words, its ethical function. At the conclusion of his book *The Ethical Function of Architecture* (1998), Harries writes:

> There is a continuing need for the creation of festal places on the ground of everyday dwellings, places where individuals come together and affirm themselves as members of the community, as they join in public reenactments of the essential: celebrations of those central aspects of our lives that maintain and give meaning to existence. The highest function of architecture remains what it has always been: to invite such festivals.
>
> (Harries 1998, 365)

But there is still another significant moment that makes it possible to perceive a church as (perhaps above all) the due place of man – and, of course, of God – the boundary and relationship between space outside and within. One is always standing at the frontier between the finality and infinity of being, as Georg Simmel put it in his famous 1909 essay "Brücke und Tür" (Bridge and Door): "Man is a boundless yet borderline being" (Simmel 2001, 60). It is mankind's fate to unite and divide, as Simmel writes, but also to put up boundaries while having the freedom to cross such borders. Such a boundary is typified by a door, since "a door expresses decisively how separating and connecting are only two sides of the same act. [...] By being the juncture between space and man and defining all that is beyond him, the door brings into question the distinction between inside and outside." Through the door,

> [...] the bounded and unbounded meet, but not in the lifeless geometric form of a mere dividing wall, but as an opportunity for mutual

interchange. [...] Closing off one's home with a door is [for a person]
to set apart a piece of the natural continuum of being. But just as a shapeless border acquires a shape, its boundedness obtains its meaning
and its dignity only through the demonstrable mobility of the door:
the possibility of stepping out from that limitation to freedom at any
time.

(Ibid., 57–58, 61)

Being a poet in exile, Milada Součková is most eminently a poet of this frontier experience. The tension and dynamism between the without and within,
distance and proximity, home and exile, Prague and Rome, and Prague and
Boston, is a cardinal element of her poetry. The fifth volume of Součková's collection *The Notebooks of Josefína Rykrová* bears the name "Interiéry a exteriéry"
(Interiors and Exteriors). Roman Jakobson described this correlation of distance and proximity, division and connection in the poems of Součková at the
end of his afterword to the *Notebooks*: "The entire collection is an emotional
drama of small events, words relentlessly focused on the inner continuity of
relations between the narrower and the wider, the incidental and the historical, the earthly and the astronomical dimensions of space and time" (Jakobson
1993, 115). Out of the crossing of borders, the frontline experience of exile and
insurmountable distance, are born a pioneering aesthetic experience and value
transformed into poetic form. This tradition of exile poetry, beginning with
Ovid's *Tristia*, is one that Součková explicitly follows. In her first collection
written in exile, *Gradus ad parnassum* (1957), she included a section entitled
"Ex Ponto," which opens by citing from the first page of Ovid's eponymous
elegy.

Georg Simmel is also worth noting in connection with Součková's Roman
poems, as the author of the essay "Rom: Eine ästhetische Analyse" (Rome:
An Aesthetic Analysis), published in May 1898 in the Vienna daily *Die Zeit*.
Simmel gives us a "portrait" of the city, whilst not focusing his attention on
specific monuments and places. He is more drawn to the phenomenon of
"unity in diversity" and "the soul of the city": "What is quite incomparable
about one's impression of Rome is that the separate epochs, styles, historical
figures, life stories that have left their mark here are as distant from each other
as anywhere in the world, and yet united in a unity, alignment and belonging
like nowhere else in the world" (Simmel 1898, 138). This is also "why Rome
so indelibly leaves its mark on one's memory." According to Simmel, the unity

and "co-belonging" of the individual elements find their reflection in the holistic mood of the viewer. Simmel opens his "aesthetic analysis" of Rome by defining beauty, which acts upon us in that its "forms and elements," which might at first seem indifferent and far from things of beauty, acquire their aesthetic value only when they combine in their "formative togetherness" (*formendes Zusammensein*), which overrules all the idiosyncrasies (ibid., 137). According to Simmel, the special power and allure of the eternal city also lies in conveying the impression that all disharmonies between the various partially viewable components and elements of the image of the world here merge into an organic whole: antiquity and the present, old and new structures, and so on. But there is another essential motive force here. The transcendent power Rome exerts is not just a gift, but also a challenge to the perceiver: "The unity into which the elements of Rome fuse lies not in themselves alone, but in the perceiving [cognisant] spirit. For [this unity] seems to happen only in certain culture, under certain conditions of mood and of education. Yet this does not diminish its significance at all, for the autonomy it demands is indeed Rome's most precious gift. Only the most lively, albeit unconscious activity of the spirit is able to bring together infinitely differentiated elements into the unity that lies within it as a potentiality, not yet as a reality" (ibid., 139). If we do not feel overpowered by Rome, but instead find that in this place our personal flourishing has reached its peak, this amounts to "a reflection of the tremendously stimulated action of one's inner self" (ibid., 139). The organic metaphors and notion of unity harken back to Goethe, to whom Simmel also subscribes; but he brings these closer to his own philosophy of life.

Milada Součková also composes her poems using pieces, fragments, things, distant "epochs, styles, historical figures, life stories that have left their mark here," as Simmel writes, turning them into new entities, or, perhaps more accurately, formations. The metaphorical transference from the domain of nature to the sphere of art and culture is one of her poetological stratagems. The principle of metamorphosis was something Goethe took forward as a universal aesthetic principle. To him, the laws of nature were the antithesis of the randomness and arbitrariness of human history (Bubner 1993, 135–45). In Goethe's theory of metamorphosis, every individual item (in nature) is immediately alive in itself and potentially contains the whole (Troll 1956, 64–76). For Součková, the principle of metamorphosis is a creative principle, in the sense that it, so to speak, condenses a multitude of experience – literary, artistic, cultural, but also botanical and, last but not least, living – into a specific form, where each separate thing is the starting point of new associations.[6] The poem "Metamorphosis," from her collection entitled *Případ poezie* (The Case of Poetry; 1971), conjoins with the legend of the nymph Daphne, turned into a laurel tree, as the legend goes, and rendered by Ovid in the first book of his *Metamorphoses*. Yet the inception of Součková's poem is the name of the decorative bush *Daphne mezereum* (spurge laurel), whose rich red fruits are highly poisonous. We are at the same time faced with the *metamorphosis* of one artistic medium into another: a poetic text into the famous sculpture of Apollo and Daphne by Gian Lorenzo Bernini (from 1622–1625), in Rome's Galleria Borghese.

"By houses surrounded quite / in Rome, in Prague...": Chiesa del Santissimo Nome di Gesù

The Church of Il Gesù was built as a purposive and representative work of Counter-Reformation art. In his university lectures on the origins of baroque art in Rome (*Die Entstehung der Barockkunst in Rom*; 1898–1899), Alois Riegl observes that "if one was ever to talk of works of art as representatives of the anti-Reformation spirit, of Jesuit artistic works, the façade of the first Jesuit church in Rome is one such" (Riegl 1923, 112). Riegl considers the façade of Il Gesù – the work of Michelangelo's perhaps most successful disciple-architect, Giacomo della Porta, dating from 1575 – to be one of the most important chapters in art history, as it is the "Catholic church façade of the new era" (ibid., 107). Likewise, in the poem by Milada Součková it is one of the main architectural

---

6   Součková's interest in the Biedermeier movement is characteristic: in Biedermeier, art is an important link between man and nature, as a medium of cultivation and uplifting of the spirit. The principle of revival and regeneration is constitutive to the spiritual atmosphere of that time, be it religious or social regeneration, related to the idea of community as an organic corpus. The cyclical conception of time as eternal returning, conceiving of human existence as part of the organic cycle of waxing and waning, everyday life with its festivals within the immutable rhythm of vegetative nature underlies Biedermeier culture and its value system (Heselhaus 1951, 54–81). Goethe's botanical and morphological studies, his idea of metamorphosis (rejuvenation, in Faust), had a big influence. Součková also took note of the text of the Czech national anthem, which she interpreted as a *locus amoenus*, a rendition of the idyllic space of an "Earthly Paradise" (Součková 1980, 26–32).

motifs (the "façade"), which is repeated as a refrain in the poem four times: "the gaze and pace at the façade bold" (line 8); "in the gold of facets in the façade" (line 18); "long ago, in the street-side façade" (line 24); "trembling in the façade" (line 34). What makes it so significant? The poem also makes explicitly thematic the correlation and contrast between the outside and inside of the church, between the spiritual and the mundane: "from their everyday despairs, joys / time's seconds prominently rise" (lines 32–33).

Contrasting with its refined and intricately composed façade – which is also intended to impress, with all the diversity of the individual construction elements of the church unified into one impressive image – we find an otherwise inconspicuous, modest exterior to the church, just as meek and mundane as the neighbouring houses. This contrast is also the starting premise of the poem: "By houses surrounded quite / in Rome, in Prague, by streets / traffic jangling past walls / high-up windows with a grille / plasterwise houses blending in" (lines 1–5). Max Dvořák begins his lecture about Il Gesù by noting the special location of this first Jesuit church:

> The choice of site alone, the relationship of the building to the street is quite noteworthy. At the height of the Renaissance, a monumental building would have of necessity dominated its surroundings [...]. By contrast, the new Jesuit church was built along a street, and its side aligned with it: a brick wall with no ornaments, as though it were merely there to mark the boundary between the profane and the sacred world. The artistic decoration of the exterior is confined to the façade [...].
>
> (Dvořák 1936, 118)

But it is precisely on this boundary between the profane and the sacral, Rome and Prague, above and below, one second and eternity, that the core meaning of the whole poem crystallizes. Doors – for Georg Simmel, paradigmatic of borders, of openness and closure, partition and connection – are also characterized by the Il Gesù of Milada Součková: "Il Gesù / with little doors for daily wails" (line 10). But not only the door – the window is another topos of transition: "high-up windows with a grille" (line 4); "by the wall, higher, windows, grilles" (line 29). The church becomes the subject of poetic reflection and "beholding": "The granite stairs arresting hold / the gaze and pace" (lines 7–8) – from the outside, "from below" on the street, "by houses surrounded quite [...] by streets / traffic jangling past walls" (lines 1–3). The church is part of the everyday, mundane life of the big city, as represented in the poem by the fruit and vegetables market, the figures of housekeepers, stallholders, pensioners, men and women on the sidewalk: "From a bowl the cloud made fall / water spewed at the vegetable stall" (lines 16–17), "in the piazza dei fiori e legumi / they're haggling for cheap artichokes" (lines 19–20).[7] This connection – architecture and art permeated with the mundane reality of urban life, but also the interplay of architecture with the landscape – this fundamental theme of Milada Součková's poems, inspired by Rome and Italy, has its origins in Italy itself, in the union of man and the landscape, colours and light, life and art. Součková gives poetic expression to that which makes Italy incomparable: a unique continuity from the simplest way of life to the most lofty artistic, cultural, spiritual manifestations, as indeed most prominently present in Italian architecture. In his book *Erinnerungen an italienische Architektur* (Memories of Italian Architecture; 1946), which remained unfinished, Theodore Hetzer describes this relationship of Italians to architecture and art; for it is since the Renaissance at least that an Italian, as Hetzer shows, makes an intimate connection between their living space and his or her self, life, and existence. Since the Renaissance, architecture has come to express this personal relationship, to every single person who, as an individual, becomes its progenitor:

The physically precise yet relaxed gestures of an Italian are a prerequisite for the kind of art in which man plays the central role, and the art form reflects brightly onto ordinary life. [...] Although an Italian living in his city is scarcely aware of this artistic aspect, even more so nowadays, when everyday life in Italy, as elsewhere, has almost nothing to do with art, the vista is even today nevertheless more artistic and beautiful, and the external framework established

---

7   A passion for the exterior, everyday reality of the city, comprising fragments of recorded life events, brings together the poetics of *The Notebooks of Josefína Rykrová* and those of the Group 42 poets, as well as the poetics of Anglo-American poets, such as Eliot, Auden – and in the poem "Via Sistia" from "Notebook 3," even a glimpse of Ferlinghetti. Součková remained in written contact with the theorist of Group 42, Jindřich Chalupecký, for the rest of her life. Regarding the correspondence between Součková and Chalupecký, see Aleš Haman (2001, 104–8) and Milan David (2001, 109–11).

by artistically vibrant epochs still has the power to attract modern-day man, transforming him and making inherent abilities more immediate.

(Hetzer 1990, 403–4)

It is striking that Milada Součková's poem does not convey the artistic and aesthetic effect of the Church of Il Gesù as a whole, as applies to all her Roman and "Italian" poems themed around architectural works. In her poem she makes no mention of the monumental nave of the church, or of the space beneath the dome that dominates the entire interior, nor of the impressive frescoes and decoration. The church is evoked through its respective architectural elements, ornaments, details: the façade, windows, doors, stairs, plaster, metal flowers, metals, gold. The Church of Il Gesù is evoked by what might be called the "poetics of shadow-projection," in the sense of Husserl's concept of *Abschattung* ("shadowing" or "adumbration").[8] Josef Hrdlička writes, in his interpretation of Součková's poetry, about her "passionate phenomenologizing observation" (Hrdlička 2017, 110). According to Husserl's shadowing theory, objects can only be perceived one-sidedly – even those we fantasize; never from all sides. We see a certain thing, more precisely every thing or object of the real world, just *so*, although it could always be seen and perceived differently. However, each act of perception transcends itself and refers "overreachingly" to a new act of perception, as "the shadowed given," whose given side refers us to another, further, unseen, sensorically ungiven one (Husserl 1966, 5).

---

8   Husserl returns to the concept of "shadowing" in his lectures in various contexts, first appearing in lectures (from 1907) on the phenomenology of space and the perception of things in space, which were published under the title *Ding und Raum* in the XVI volume of the Husserliana (1973). This term originally refers to the perception of light and shadow (playing with shadows, as in a silhouette theatre). That's why Husserl thinks about "shadowing" when he talks about the differences in how things are revealed under different lighting. In his lectures on things and space, he cites as an example the "shadowing of yellow" (*Abschattung des Gelb*) on a "uniformly coloured sphere" (Husserl 1973, 4470). Yet "shadowing" is also taken to mean a transformation of the perceived object's movement when the object or the perceiver's orientation or position changes. Husserl also uses the term "shadowing" for phenomena that belong to the area of sensory perception, but cannot be perceived in the ordinary sensory manner, such as the recalling of a tone just heard but that has already faded (Sommer 1996, 271–85). The term *Abschattung* is dealt with by Eckhard Lobsien in his phenomenologically based literary theory book *Schematisierte Ansichten. Literaturtheorie mit Husserl, Ingarden, Blumenberg* (Lobsien 2012, 46–52, 133–38).

It is as though, in the poem, the architecture of Il Gesù was always only hinted at in a particular detail only to some degree – as the playing of light and shadow, which the poet-subject observes from a distance: "in the street-side façade / the plasterworks light shadow drawn / browning with moisture, almost green / sun-gilded on a summer's day" (lines 24–27). Il Gesù is evoked in the poem through these shadows: revealed and also overshadowed. The colourful and luminescent qualities – *browning, greening, sun-gilding* – change with time and memory, as if they were the "foreshadow" of a monumental and magnificent whole, as represented by this church in Rome. But this shadow of the whole turns our attention to individual objects and their details, and at the same time it is as though the whole, the work of art as such, its *essentia*, were radiating from the depths to the surface of those individual objects such as the gold-glinting "metal flowers" which have their counterpart in the "organic" flowers (anemones), plants, vegetables, and fruits which are "haggled for" in the "piazza dei fiori" (line 19). The image of light radiating from the gloom also brings the poem to its conclusion: "in the gloom (anemone) metals glow."

The parallels of artistic objects, architectural elements, fruits, and plants can be read as an aesthetic, poetic reflection of the relationship between art and life, the regenerative power of art and artistic creation. In the poem "San Paolo fuori le Mura," which Součková included in the section "Roman Vedutas" in *The Notebooks of Josefína Rykrová*, and which is inspired by the famous Papal Basilica, we find the motif of the regenerative and metamorphic power of art, of the word, and of the plant domain, expressed even more explicitly: „Z břečťanu narcis vyrazí / bledý, z pochvy zeleni [...] / vyrostly zdi, kostely / střídali se architekti [...] / vznosně stavbu rozehráli / v barokní litanii [...]" ("From ivy a daffodil emerges / pale, out of a sheath of green [...] / walls and churches have grown up / architects taking turns [...] / aloft resounded the edifice / in a Baroque litany [...].")

Theodore Hetzer writes in his *Memories of Italian Architecture*:

> The Italian is a visionary, an amazingly swift and acute observer [...] instantly transforming the seen into gesture and sound, into sculpture and music. Thus, the foreigner is *nolens volens* unwittingly drawn into the typical behaviour of Italians: by not standing in the thick of Italian life, but by observing it from a distance, he can see it depicted.
>
> (Hetzer 1990, 377)

This observation can be related to Součková's Italian-inspired poems, her distanced vision of Italian cities and Italian architecture, transformed into vedutas.

What does Rome's Il Gesù have in common with Prague? It is the aforementioned baroque Jesuit Church of St. Ignatius, as evoked in the poem by the mention of its location of Charles Square. At the same time, the Roman Il Gesù evokes the Church of Our Lady Victorious beneath Petřín, in which the Child of Prague is to be seen and where Milada Součková was baptized. Il Gesù in Rome and the Church of St. Ignatius in Prague are both architectural monuments connected in one poem by the "associative power of memory," as Součková calls this *ars combinatorium*, which is the strategy of her *ars memoriae*, which serves as an afterword to "Vlastní životopis Josefíny Rykrové" (The Autobiography of Josefína Rykrová). They are part of her "inner life story" and a part of the cultural memory in which she is participating as a poetess. This applies to most of the poems in *The Notebooks of Josefína Rykrová* and the entire poetic collection *Alla Romana*. But in the poems inspired by sacral architecture, participation in cultural memory takes on a special role. The poems "Il Gesù" and "San Paolo fuori le Mura" – between which Součková inserted the poem "Via Sistina," in the "Roman Vedutas" section – are related. They relate firstly through art history: in the aforementioned treatise on the Church of Il Gesù, Max Dvořák recalls that the architecture of this church departed significantly from the Renaissance ideal of a sacred building and followed on from the Italian architecture of the early Middle Ages and even early Christianity. This is the type of sacral architecture, Dvořák says, that is exemplified by San Paolo fuori le Mura. The two poems are also connected by the parallelization of architecture as an artefact and of botany: the parallel of *Naturwerk* and *Kunstwerk*, to use the concepts of Alois Riegl from his 1901 study of the same name. In the poem "San Paolo fuori le Mura," the theme of organic plant growth and art-historical development is introduced through explicit and cryptic references to the relationship with the "word," in both the poetological and theological senses. Hence, the theme of metamorphosis and regeneration in these and other poems by Součková, connected with sacral architecture, also has theological connotations related to baptism as a symbolic rebirth: a theme to which Součková returns in several poems, as well as in "The Autobiography of Josefína Rykrová."

Rome in "Poussin Blue" and Poussin in the Poems of Milada Součková

In her two poems from the section "Římské procházky" (Roman Walks) from the *Alla Romana* collection – "Torquato Tasso" and "At Via Appia" – we find references to the "French Roman" Nicolas Poussin (1594–1665). The painter spent some thirty years of his life in Rome after arriving in the "eternal city" as a thirty-year-old in the spring of 1624. It was not just in Rome and through Rome that Poussin's art acquired the "*charisma* of his personal greatness" (Badt 1969, 95), but also through relentless effort, as Kurt Badt writes, and its characteristic unity of "supreme reality and supreme humanity." Indeed, Poussin's art has the kind of merit that ranks him alongside Vélazquez, Hals, Rubens, and Rembrandt as the greatest painters of the high baroque. Poussin's art is poetry expressed through the medium of art, the essence of which is, on the one hand, making apparent "the existentiality of Greco-Roman religious content, especially of the *existence of the Gods*" (ibid., 25), as well as a balanced unity in portraying the spirit and nature as "equally developing forces" (ibid.). Stemming from his distinctive, unifying view of nature and the spirit came Poussin's take on antiquity and mythology, with the life of the figures in their landscape founded – as Badt points out – on his admiration for the natural. Unlike the ecstasy of the high baroque soul, the world of Poussin's paintings is imbued with a spirituality of fulfilment, which connects Poussin in a unique way with the spiritual world of antiquity. In this context, Badt quotes religionist and classical philologist Walter F. Otto: "Where there is spirit, we find the realm of clarity and form. It is not so much about the transcendental and the supernatural as, far more often, being linked by an inseparable bond with nature. Nature and the spirit live within themselves and for themselves" (Otto 1934, 205). This creative grasp and reshaping of the legacy of antiquity, which also made its way into Poussin's biblical scenes, could only have come to Poussin in Rome: through his readings of Latin authors, as well as the surrounding ancient Roman monuments and works of art. That is why a man of faith finds in Poussin a specific relationship with God (Badt 1969, 97–99). This concept was also conveyed by Poussin's antiquity, *genus Romanum*, and his knowledge of the Roman environment and culture: "He was beholden to the Romans for the idea of man as far removed from God, but deeply religious, yet no longer able in this duality of destiny to be manifestly natural and spontaneous in form and being. He is *characterized* and thus becomes, in Western imagination, the archetype for human character as a quality" (ibid., 440). As "inventions," Poussin's paintings are "a thing of faith, which they reaffirm and annunciate," and in their artistic perfection they worship Divinity, as Badt observes (ibid., 451).

Inextricably linked with Rome is the architecture of Poussin's paintings: the monumental architecture of Rome corresponds to Poussin's idea of a monumental human existence: "His Roman citizen is a being who, with the ever-growing intensity of his life, claims the space around him, which he then fills with great, sweeping, all-encompassing gestures. He is the being of an independent architectural structure in accord with Roman architectural features, the kind of art in which the Romans were truly creative, he is 'transfigured'; as an artistic 'figure,' he is in his element when emphasizing architectural construction and its relations with other figures of the painting and the picture as a whole, right up to an unremittingly insistent detailing of the architectural parts of a strictly rhythmic composition derived from its form-featuring respects" (ibid., 457).

In seventeenth-century art, as Theodor Hetzer points out, architecture is a dominant force. The most striking feature of Italian architecture is its naturalness, its "earthiness," which it then transcends with architectural order. One element that is preserved even in the most sumptuous and demanding buildings is the simple cubic form. There is thus not much difference between the sacral and the profane in Italian architecture (Hetzer 1990, 24–25). In Italy, painting and architecture also coexist in unique harmony: "Everything built here is for the sake of *man*, for his sensory and spiritual needs, his physical and mental existence. Sculpture and painting themselves reach out to humanity" (ibid., 418).

Poussin's art features in two contexts in Milada Součková's *Alla Romana* poems. In the poem "Torquato Tasso," it is the biographical context of the author-poet of *La Gerusalemme liberata* (Jerusalem Delivered). Tasso's lines relating the love of Erminia, Princess of Antioch, for the Christian knight and warrior Tancred (*La Gerusalemme liberata* XIX, 103–14) had inspired Poussin to paint *Tancred et Erminia* (Tancred and Erminia; two versions from the 1630s are now held in Birmingham, UK and St. Petersburg, Russia). Inevitably, by its very name, Součková's poem at the same time evokes Goethe's eponymous drama *Tasso* (1789–1790), as well as Rome itself, where the Italian poet died in April 1595 at the Monastery of Sant'Onofrio at the foot of the Gianicolo Hill, and where he has a commemorative plaque on the Rampa della Quercia, under the torso of an ancient oak, propped up by an iron structure; a tree under whose crown the poet sought shade:

Na Rampa della Quercia duby
živoří, v železech, s podpěrami
ne snad, že hynulo by básnictví
leč ztratily se sličné Múzy.
Ó zlatý věk pastýřské idyly!
(Součková 1999: 212)

On Rampa della Quercia the oaks
eke out their life, in irons, with supports
not to say that poetry would be dying
but the fair Muses have indeed been lost.
O golden age of idyll pastoral!

But the Goethe intertextual horizon of Součková's poem also evokes the German writer's own reception of Poussin, whose paintings – as well as those by Poussin's Rome-based compatriot, Claude Lorrain – Goethe knew and admired. Goethe wrote about coming across Poussin's and Lorrain's works as a watershed experience that enabled him to understand the "inner truth" of external nature (Moses 2006, 29–43).

The poem works up an intricate intratextual isotopy, centred around reflection on the fates of poetry and the poet in modern times. This is projected onto an intertextually invested foil, featuring the fate of the biographical Torquato Tasso; Goethe's drama (Goethe visited the Monastery of Sant'Onofrio on 2 February 1787); an evocation of a metaphorical poet-as-a-bee from Horace's *Ode*; and François-René de Chateaubriand's recollection of Sant'Onofrio from his *Mémoires d'outre-tombe* (Memoirs from Beyond the Grave; 1848–1850) – the particular passage engraved on the memorial plaque erected (in 1948), together with a commemorative plaque to Goethe, on the wall of the monastery garden.[9] A quote from this passage – "À Saint Onuphre – Rome entière sous mes yeux"

---

9   "Si j'ai le bonheur de finir mes jours ici, je me suis arrangé pour avoir à Saint-Onuphre un réduit joignant la chambre où Le Tasse expira... Dans un des plus beaux sites de la Terre, parmi les orangers et les chênes-verts, Rome entière sous mes yeux, chaque matin, en me mettant à l'ouvrage, entre le lit de mort et la tombe du poète, j'invoquerai le génie de la gloire et du malheur."

("To Saint Onuphrius – All of Rome before my eyes ") – was chosen by Součk-ová as the motto of her poem. However, it is the topos itself, Gianicolo, and last but not least Poussin, who are significantly a part of the poem's intended missive. The network of cultural references, quotes, paraphrases, and relations between the characters of the poem is linked together not least by the fact that it was Chateaubriand who, in 1828, during his time as ambassador in Rome, had a tombstone made for Poussin. On this – under the painter's bust – is carved a motif from Poussin's famous painting *Et in Arcadia ego* (1638–1639). Součk-ová is connected with Chateaubriand not only by her experience of exile, but also by how the author of *Génie du christianisme* (The Genius of Christianity) resided in Prague while on diplomatic service.

[...]

Ó zlatý věk pastýřské idyly!
ne snad že náš již nedá mléko, strdí
že člověk dobývá je v potu tváři
leč básník ztratil svoje vavříny
svěží, jak je Múzy zapomněly
v loži, se svítáním odběhly.

V šumu vodotrysku, acquatici
mostricciuoli dovádějí
své nesmrtelné drama hrají
bez Goetha, bez Génia křesťanství.
Torquato Tasso, Múz tiburských med
a mantovských vlil mu do šalmaje,
pro fide čitelné, vavřín svěží,
ve vzduchu šumí v Poussinově modři
nad Římem, svatému Onufriovi
(Součková 1999: 212)

[...]

O golden age of idyll pastoral!
Not that ours will give no more milk, or honey
That man attains them by his brow's own sweat

But the poet has lost his laurels
fresh, as the Muses have forgot them
in the bed, having run off at dawn.

In the fountain's murmur the aquatici
mostricciuoli are frolicking
play out their immortal drama
without Goethe, without the Genius of Christendom.
Torquato Tasso poured honey of Tiburtine
and Mantovani Muses into his shawm
for fide readable, and laurel fresh,
the air murmurs, full of Poussin blue.
over Rome, for Saint Onuphrius

The evocation of the mythical world – and this applies more or less to most "Roman" and ancient-culture-inspired poems by Součková – only amplifies an awareness of an unreachably distant mythical horizon: the "golden age of idyll pastoral" is a mythical/aesthetic fiction, dreamt up by Goethe's Tasso. The Princess (Leonore d'Este) says at the play's opening: "Wir können unser seyn und stundenlang / Uns in die goldne Zeit der Dichter träumen" ("We can be our own while for hours / dream ourselves into the poets golden age"; lines 22–23). And just like the irretrievably lost mythical past is "immersed" in "Poussin blue" *as* an aesthetic fiction, transformed into a subtle, sublime, intangible sensory essence, into the spuming murmur of the water in the baroque Fontana Paola and the whispering cypresses on Gianicolo: "the air is spuming, full of Poussin blue." It is no accident that this line is repeated twice as the poem's refrain.

The second poem, "At Via Appia," is dedicated to "the shepherd Hermas." This dedication relates to an old Christian volume by the author called Hermas (according to some sources, the brother of Pope Pius I) from the mid-second century BCE (between 140–145). The volume comprises five visions, twelve commandments, and ten parables, and its main theme is spiritual revival, exhortations to a moral life, and repentance through frugality:

Cypřiše jak u Poussina
i hodina pastorální
stádo ovcí štětcem Angeliky
šňůra barevného prádla

na dvorku mezi chlévy
kmen révy zakrslý
u zdi v cypřišové aleji.

Hleď, tak bychom byli žili
bídou, dětmi požehnáni
s koněm, je napůl slepý
vyjel bys na trh zrána,
akvadukt v azurném nebi
moruše jak u Poussina,
hleď, tvé ruce – fialy
hebké, to že by bylo štěstí?
Pastýři dobrý, chvíli zmatený
setkáním s Múzou v Campagni
nad prázdnými mauzolei
stromoví jak u Poussina
pod zakrslým kmenem révy
stolek, sklenky octa–vína
v záhonu kvetou noční fialy

(Součková 1999: 223–224)

Cypresses like Poussin's
and a pastoral hour
a herd of sheep by Angelika's brush
a colourful washing line
in a backyard between the byres
a scragged stunted vine
by the wall in the cypress avenue.

Behold, how we'd have lived
with penury and children blessed
with a horse, who is half blind
you'd go to the market in the morning,
an aqueduct in an azure sky
mulberries like Poussin's,
behold, your hands – as violets

so soft, would that be fortunate?
Good shepherd, briefly muddled up
having met the Muse in Campagni
above the empty mausoleums
tree rows like Poussin's
under the scraggy grapevine trunk
a table, glasses of wine-vinegar
in the flowerbed night violets bloom

The poetic retort to the early Christian commandment of "the shepherd of Hermas" ("would that be fortunate? / Good shepherd, briefly muddled up") is based on the parallel developings of the poetological and of the cultural- or art-historical concept. The ascetic "shepherd of Hermas" is projected on the foil of the Arcadian, pastoral "simple life" of baroque-classicist landscape paintings by Nicolas Poussin, Claude Lorrain, and Goethe's confidante, the Swiss-Austrian painter Angelika Kauffmann. Just like the Czech poet Součková in the mid-1960s, all these artists were foreigners in Rome, where they also found their final resting place. Poussin's tombstone – the cenotaph built by Chateaubriand – is in the Church of San Lorenzo in Lucina, where Josef Mysliveček is also buried and where we also find a chapel dedicated to St. John of Nepomuk. Lorrain is buried in the Church of Santissima Trinità dei Monti, above the Spanish Steps, and Kauffmann in the Church of Sant'Andrea delle Fratte, with its beautiful bell tower by Francesco Borromini.

The poetic fiction that, with its title and dedication to "the shepherd of Hermas," harkens back to *arkhé*, to the ancient Rome of Via Appia, and to the origins of Christianity, is at the same time an evocation of Poussin and his landscapes. At the close of the poem, the poetic fiction is immersed, like a *tableau vivant*, in "Poussin blue," in painterly fiction – similarly to the poem "Torquato Tasso." It is as if the whole poem were a poetic ekphrasis of a Poussin landscape. The second stanza also begins with the invitation to "Behold." Who speaks the poem? Who is it that asks, "would that be fortunate?" The name Angelika evokes – as it does in other poems of the *Alla Romana* cycle and the "Roman Vedutas" from *The Notebooks of Josefína Rykrová* – the friendship between Goethe and Angelika Kaufmann, who was hailed as the "Tenth Muse of Rome," and reminds us of the mutual inspiration felt between painting and poetry (Poussin is, after all, the author of the painting *L'Inspiration du poète* [The Inspiration of the Poet; ca. 1630]). In Rome, Kaufmann lived in a sumptuous house on Via Sistina, which was soon to become a renowned meeting place for foreign artists and art lovers. Součková placed the poem "Via Sistina" between her poems "Il Gesù" and "San Paolo fuori le Mura," and the section "Roman Vedutas" concludes with the poem "Angelika Kauffmann."

In Součková's poems, it is as though this relationship between the poet (Goethe) and the painter (Kauffmann) were overturned; as if the poetic self were turning back to its artistic, painterly counterpart – not forgetting that Součková's husband, Zdeněk Rykr, was a painter. *The Notebooks of Josefína Rykrová* could *also* be read as a continuation of this fictional dialogue.

In Součková's Roman poems, Poussin is a *Roman* painter, whose work combines mythical ancient gods with Christianity, spirit with nature, nature with culture, with the culture of people and gods, people and heroes of ancient myths: a symbiosis that is closely linked with Součková's poetry. All the closer in how Poussin handles this symbiosis, in a style that Kurt Badt calls "poetic":

> Arching over Poussin's work we see, together with the "divina signa decoris" (*Aeneis V*), the exceptional brilliance of poetry, an extraordinary form of painterly declamation, which does not exhaust its artistic means in the very subjects of its rendition, in the events depicted, in expression, in mood, but presents them forth as uncommonly perceptible. This *lustre* of Poussin's works is a peculiar form of transformation of things, as per Goethe's dictum: "By the transposition of individual events pure prose becomes poetic."
>
> (Badt 1969, 25)

According to Badt, the poetic power of Poussin's art is also reflected in the painter's strong architectural sensibility, with which he created his sacral compositions. Badt characterizes Poussin's art as "the quintessential imagery of man" (ibid., 21).

Architecture, Time, and "Protention Culture"

In "Il Gesù," Součková follows the ancient tradition, updated during the Renaissance, of the analogy between the places of memory (*loci*) and the images of memory (*imagines*). In this tradition, the architecture of the city – specific houses, palaces, churches, parks, fountains, streets, and the like – act as the mnemonic tools of memory's spatial domain. As Renate Lachmann shows, the given city acquires its own fictional dimension to become a place of memory, in which are deposited images (*imagines*) of culture, experience, and history that act merely as a likeness, a *simulacrum*, as a "backdrop to the theatre of memory" (Lachmann 1990, 42).

The poems of Milada Součková are not only about the texts of the past, but are also about the culture of earlier epochs and the experience of encountering that past culture, imprinted in memory and revived with every recollection. In Součková's poems, recollection has a projective character, just as culture has its regenerative character. Each memory from which a new text is born creates another new layer, akin to a palimpsest. This palimpsest-like property is also present in Součková's poems when it comes to places and their architecture: the image of Rome and Il Gesù is "translucently backlit" by Prague and the Jesuit Church of St. Ignatius on Charles Square, just as the architectural concept of Il Gesù is a "palimpsest" through which the idea of ancient Christian and Gothic architecture can be made out, of the type exemplified by the Basilica of San Paolo fuori le Mura – a point made by both Riegl and Dvořák. The city is like a Freudian "Wunderblock", into which the monuments are embedded as into wax. Through its aesthetic rendition in a literary text, the particular architecture becomes „readable" again as an imagined architecture transformed into poetic images. "Roman Vedutas" – the title of the section in which Součková included the poem "Il Gesù" – literally means "images of the city."

The syncretism and heterogeneity of the text reflect its heterotopy (Rome, Prague) and its heterochrony, between the present moment and eternity. The semantics of time give structure to the entire poem: "in the chasuble every now and then / serving Mass in the world / Beata morte Liturgy of the Hours" (lines 12–14); "spending time just like everyone / perhaps it's rained at other times / long ago" (lines 23–24); "time's seconds prominent arise" (line 33). Flashes of remembrance radiate out of words as things, like the glints of gold in the façade of Il Gesù, radiating from the past and "in the gloom (anemone) metals glow." Fleeting moments, "seconds," stand out from the stream of time, as something unrepeatable in its sensory aesthetic delight, something that glints, glows, and disappears. And at the same time, something substantially timeless that penetrates consciousness has to come into existence. Yet, the heterogeneity of the text of the poem, its heterotopy, and the polarity of the moment and eternity are syncretized and synchronized in the poem in a semantic unity – just as the façade of Il Gesù creates an intricately composed unity of various building elements. The synchronizing and transformative element is *the word* and its open semantic potential: in the poem "San Paolo fuori le Mura," this potency of the word is expressed in the lines „Z aramejské řeči slova přeložena / z řečtiny do češtiny / v listech Šavla, Pavla / agape, svatá láska / překládá bible Kralická" ("From the Aramaic language words translated / from Greek to Czech / in the pages of Saul, of Paul / Agape, divine love / translated by the Bible of Kralice"; Součková 1993, 87–88). *Translatio* as the power and potency of speech, words, and poetry. This *translatio* corresponds in the poem with the regenerative, ever-expanding power of the biosphere and of culture, analogous to the concept of *rinascimento*.

It is therefore not only the transitivity between the artefact – the work of art – and the biomorphic plant-sphere, between rational construction and natural growth, between arising and demise, epochs and styles, the ancient past and the present; but also the transitivity and transfer and, indeed, transgression between languages. Transitive ("From the Aramaic language words translated / from Greek to Czech") and transgressive ("v Praze, v Tarsu, v Cilicii" ["in Prague, in Tarsus, in Cilicia"]), the power of the creative word, its transformation – a word that became flesh, that materialized into architecture, into the San Paolo fuori le Mura, second only to St. Peter's as the largest temple of medieval Western Christianity. But also, the word "Thaletovo, Pythagorovo, Herakleitovo" ("of Thales, Pythagoras, Heraclitus"; Součková 1998, 194). The words, addressed as "jste stvořila tento svět" ("you, who created this world"; ibid.), represented by the logos-imbued cosmos, taking effect in all things and people, is one of the main themes not only of Součková's poetry, but also of her prose[10]: from *První písmena* (First Letters), through *Mluvící pásmo* (Talking Zone), to her last poems. In the *Talking Zone*, which arose under dramatic circumstances in the second half of 1939, we read the lines:

Rychle ke mně má slova!
Ó slova, vy jste vytvořila tento svět!
na počátku bylo slovo.
Dříve než biblické slovo bylo logos
[...]

---

10   As described in the treatise of Zuzana Stolz-Hladká (2001, 22–33).

Ó slova, tvořící svět naší sféry, přistupte ke mně!
Stvořte novou víru, nové symboly, ó slova, stvořte nový svět!
ó slovo, stvoř nové zákony,
ó slovo, stvoř nové filozofy,
ó slovo, stvoř nová města,
ó slovo, stvoř novou pravdu,
ó slovo, stvoř nové lidi!

(Součková 1998: 194–195)[11]

Come to me quick my words!
Oh words, you, who created this world!
In the beginning was the word.
Before the Biblical word was the logos
[...]
Oh words, forming the world of our sphere, come to me!
Create a new faith, new symbols, oh words, create a new world!
Oh word, make new laws,
Oh word, create new philosophers,
Oh word, create new cities,
Oh word, create new truth,
Oh word, create new people!

Only where artistic creation draws from it, writes Hedwig Conrad-Martius, from the essence of the logos, can there be a transposition from nothing (*ex nihilo*) into being. A productive person is able to create, and even more so, is able to make the dizzying descent into nothingness, to bring forth from its nadir to the surface what is supposed to be realized through the creation of forms (Conrad-Martius 1939, 813–15).

---

11   The world, as Hedwig Conrad-Martius writes, is "not in itself far removed from the logos, but exactly the opposite: *it is nothing but the logos incarnate*. [...] *And yet the essence of God seems as though spilled out over the world*. And yet the divine logos is mirrored in the world. Even in its present disfigured form! [...] It is not that the divine logos itself, which is like the fruit of labour akin to its father, is spilled out over the creator's world or has even come to exist within it, but the meaningful content of that logos, its essence deep within the divine Spirit. [...] Thus is the world, due to its being, out of nothing, given its content, derived from God. [...] God is the creator of the world and *its* spiritual father" (Conrad-Martius 1939, 826).

In the poem "Il Gesù," the word is the name itself, which gave the title to the poem, and to which the first Jesuit church is dedicated: *Chiesa del Santissimo Nome di Gesù*. This name is also a symbol and metonymy of the Christian religion and the Church, the seat and centre of which is Rome, which in the poems of Součková also creates a universalist framework for the perception of the history of culture and art. The Catholic Church and its liturgy have, in "Il Gesù," this universalist synchronizing element: "in the chasuble every now and then / serving Mass in the world" (lines 12–13). Being the first Jesuit church, Il Gesù is an architectural realization of this universalist idea. As Max Dvořák writes in his lecture on Il Gesù: "All Catholic Christendom was to be merged into a spiritual unity once again. [...] [I]n this building, a certain transformation of artistic intentions was expressed for the future, of those intentions that were of decisive importance for the spirit of Baroque art" (Dvořák 1936, 139).

In "The Autobiography of Josefína Rykrová", Součková writes: "I have none of what are called 'emotional' memories, relationships, just the knowledge that events and relationships are once and for all an immutable part of life. People on the street [...]." These "people on the street" – "on the sidewalk men and women / from their everyday despairs, joys / time's seconds prominent arise," as we read in "Il Gesù" (lines 30–33) – spend their time; for them the Mass is served "every now and then", they pray the "Liturgy of the Hours" (*horarium*) "for housewives and for pensioners" (line 15). People spend their time – their "alloted span" – which is, in the face of the absolute and the long "timespan of the world," only brief: "death" – "*Beata morte*" – makes an appearance in Součková's poem as a discreet *memento*. These moments of the "allotted time span of life" are rare, as Hans Blumenberg points out in his book *Lebenszeit und Weltzeit* (Lifetime and Worldtime). Here, too, *memoria* has irreplaceable meaning: according to Blumenberg, it neutralizes the antagonism between the "timespan of life" and the "timespan of the world" by smudging the edges of a "lifespan" and letting the bygone, the disappeared, live on, as if it were "even now here."

Memoria is, as Blumenberg perspicaciously puts it, the basis of a "culture of protention," of recollection that anticipates the future:

> What might be called a "culture" of protention: duty that is owed to the past enters as a *memoria*, as "history" back to prehistory and archaeology, as a learned and teachable form into the culture of those surviving after. It thus becomes a "culture" of protention.
>
> (Blumenberg 2001, 303)

Milada Součková's poetry also participates in this "protention culture." Her poems, inspired by Rome and Italy, by Roman and Italian architecture and art, are a remarkable example of this. In the poem "Il Gesù," it is as though glimpses of the "timespan of life" of men and women on the sidewalk, of their "everyday despairs, joys," were tremblingly reflected, and for a moment shining onto the façade of Il Gesù, itself built in praise of the most holy name, and thus of the absolute, of God. But one also needs "respite from the absolute" (*Entlastung vom Absoluten*), as Hans Blumenberg's phenomenology of time has been pointedly characterized by Odo Marquard (1998, XVII–XXV).[12]

Nowhere so apparent is this connection of spirit and matter, the intermingling of the physical and the atmospheric, the experience of architectural form as spiritual force but in an intimate connection with man, as it is in Italy, in its architecture, its art – as Theodore Hetzer showed in his lectures on Italian architecture of the fifteenth and sixteenth centuries:

> The Italian is, as they say, anthropocentric, to this day. He feels good in the world, he looks upon it with a kind charming naivety as his domain, sees everything in terms of human affairs. [...] Hence his only faint interest in nature, where it does not relate to man, [hence] his revulsion toward lack of culture and form, toward absolutism in philosophy and religion, the system. [...] This anthropocentric attitude also determines Italian architecture, both secular and profane, as much as it possibly can. Italians have been building churches to glorify God and the city ever since the thirteenth century.
>
> (Hetzer 1990, 26–27)

---

12   "[...] the basic idea of Hans Blumenberg's philosophy seemed to me as offering some respite from the absolute. People cannot endure the absolute – as a reality and as God – they seek to get some distance from Him; and their life pensum – culture – is a work-in-progress on this distance, which is ever at the same time abating simplicity with diversity: a respite from that absolute that we cannot endure for its indivisible power, and which we can only bear by distancing ourselves from that power by a plurality of forms of good behaviour, by the 'proclamation of pluralism' as Eckhard Nordhofen called it" (Marquard 1998, XX).

As for the monumentality of Palladian architecture, Hetzer says: "Palladio is all about celebration, while both gentle and humanist. Humanism first and foremost" (ibid.). This is true not only of Italian architecture, but also of the poetry of Milada Součková.

Let us pause to consider briefly the relationship between architecture, the architectural work, and things. It is certainly possible to talk about a work of architecture as a specifically created thing, perceivable in space and time; to speak in terms of an "artistic thing" (*Kunst-Ding*) about, say, a temple, which, as already mentioned here, has its aesthetic as well as its cultish function. Rilke gave some thought to the "artistic thing" – influenced as he was by Rodin's sculptural art and, a little later, by Cézanne's idea of "realization" – as being the equivalent of the "thing poem" (*Dinggedicht*) and vice versa. According to Rilke, a poem as a "thing" must exist in the outside world in its own right, as a completed, self-standing work. The most important elements that underpin the "thingness" of a poem are – in Rilke's approach – its structure and form, but also its rhyme, its sound connections (the relationship between its sonorousness and meaning) in the overall "architecture" of the poem. Among his *Neue Gedichte* (New Poems; 1907), it is the sonnet that offers such form. As early as in *Das Stunden-Buch* (The Book of Hours; 1905), Rilke included the poem "Ich finde Dich in allen diesen Dingen" (I Find You in All These Things; 1899): "Ich finde Dich in allen diesen Dingen / denen ich gut und wie ein Bruder bin" ("I find you in all these things / to which I'm kind and brotherly"). The poet is the "good brother" of things. One has to bring things to life – that is one of the main ideas of Rilke's essay on Rodin's work: the creation, realization of things – giving things their reality – from their substance and origin: "How are things related to us at all? What is their story?" (Rilke 1965, 209).

At the same time as Rilke, the philosopher Wilhelm Schapp – who in 1910 defended his dissertation *Beiträge zur Phänomenologie der Wahrnehmung* (Contributions to the Phenomenology of Perception) with Edmund Husserl – was asking himself the same question. It seems, writes Schapp,

> [...] as if each and every thing has its own story, and as if this story had left traces within it. [...] Each thing shows, in its always chancy creation, what it has already been through, and thus its own story, its idiosyncrasy, how it has come through its fated course.
>
> (Schapp 1925, 114)

Schapp returned to the philosophy of stories in the early 1950s, when he published the book *In Geschichten verstrickt: Zum Sein von Mensch und Ding* (Entangled in Stories: On the Being of Man and Object; 1953). In Schapp's reasoning, stories take precedence over the surrounding, external world; for that is merely a derivative of stories and the place "where we should look for reality or the last semblance of reality" and that would be "entanglement in stories." This means that Schapp is considering, on the one hand, the world of stories, and, on the other hand, the objective external world of experienced reality. The objectivity of the outside world, as based on sensory perception, is called into question by Schapp, since the sphere of original contact with a given thing is a story. Schapp also deals with the analysis of the way things *appear to be* and how they are – what he terms *Wozudinge* – that is, man-made things, artefacts with a specific purpose. In this respect, *Wozudinge* differ from natural objects (such as a tree branch). Schapp bases this first on the "wozu" ("what for"), which does not here refer to purpose and efficaciousness, but to the right and proper basis of the thing, to the context in which the thing is in its place: "a cup, a table, a chair, a house, a temple, a street, railtracks" (Schapp 1976, 11). We never find before us any absolutely isolated thing, but always one that has *its own* individual story, having been made under particular circumstances by particular people, and thus becoming a part of the story of humanity. The essence of *Wozudinge* is how they arise and appear, along with some story and in a story. By its creation, each *Wozuding* also references its creator or maker: man, his own entanglement in stories. This is not about any *status of a thing*, it is about the "what for" of the thing, how it is "entangled" in stories. According to Schapp, each *Wozuding* can only appear in *its own* story.

It could be said that the world of things in Milada Součková's poems is, in a specific sense, the world of their stories and relationships with people, with the world of plants, of space and time, as Roman Jakobson described in the aforementioned afterword to the first (exile) edition of *The Notebooks of Josefína Rykrová*. Such hings include Rome's churches, palaces, villas, or monuments, which Součková presents in her poems. They have not only their stories, but also their unmistakable sensorial atmosphere, which the poems evoke. In the essay "Rom" (Rome; 1946), Marie Louise Kaschnitz describes this unique character of the Italian capital as a city of "speaking stones," palaces, and buildings, as Rome was apostrophized by Goethe in the opening lines of his *Roman Elegies*. Kaschnitz writes: "Whoever *contemplates* Rome, sees and feels the building materials, the black lava stone of the old streets and the Cyclops masonry of the castle buildings, the clean, porous stone of ancient city buildings, golden travertine and the red porphyry" (Kaschnitz 1989, 449).

Each of the Roman buildings we encounter in Součková's poems has not only its own individual story, but also its own atmosphere, which allows the particular building as a hing – like Schapp's *Wozuding* – to "ecstatically" overstep its demarcated boundaries and again become a thing of aesthetic experience. The ecstasy of time in "Il Gesù" is quite as much the ecstasy of the "thing"[13] itself: "time's seconds prominent arise / trembling in the façade / in the gloom (anemone) metals glow."[14]

---

13   The "Ecstasy of Things" (*Ekstase der Dinge*) is a term coined by Gernot Böhme in his aesthetic – or, more precisely, aisthetic – theory. It is a mode of sensory perception and of experiencing things. Their shapes, colour, lustre, aroma, etc. do not, as sensory qualities, remain constrained to the thing itself, they do not remain "locked within" its boundaries, but expand into the surroundings, creating or co-creating an ambient *atmosphere*. "Ecstasy" is seen by Böhme as (resorptional or dispersive) quality and modus, by which things come to be sensed by us in varying intensities, not only apparently, but conspicuously: colours, light, lustre, sound, etc. Especially in contemporary architecture theory, Böhme's aesthetic is rather well received (Böhme 2001, 131–44). See, e.g., Zumthor 2006.

14   This work was supported by the European Regional Development Fund project "Creativity and Adaptability as Conditions of the Success of Europe in an Interrelated World" (reg. no.: C Z.02.1.01/0.0/0.0/16_019/0000734).

The Poem as a Rotary Object: On Texts by H. M. Enzensberger and H. C. Artmann

PAVEL NOVOTNÝ

Modern literary texts are characterized by how they view language more or less reflexively, namely as the target of critique or exploration, often as a field for open play. Romanticism brought with it a tendency to treat language as material for poetic experiment (cf. Novalis and Schlegel's *Fragments*),[1] and, at the end of the nineteenth century (notably so with Mallarmé), this tendency came to life again and more clearly. In the twentieth century, this reflexive approach to language went deeper and became more radical, varied – most notably in Dadaism, later in concrete poetry. Of course, the degree of radicalism, that is of the shift towards the concretness of the linguistic sign, can vary: from a critical stance towards language in the sense of a linguistic crisis (Rilke, Hoffmannsthal); through various caligrammatic, typographical, or phonetic games; to a seemingly dry, mathematical, combinatorial structure. Any such form of estrangement of language should not ultimately restrict, but rather extend, the creative possibilities, or variables, that poetry can work with – for example,

---

1   For example, Silvio Vietta recalls that in Romanticism there is a certain "step towards knowledge" (*Erkenntnisschritt*), when poetry acquires a linguistically reflexive dimension (cf. Vietta 1992, 158).

Gerhard Rühm, one of the most radical language experimenters, speaks of *erweiterte Poetik* ("poetics extended"; Rühm 2008).

The expansion of poetic scope need not be taken merely as a crossing over into different media domains (e.g., typeface–imagery, writing–sound),[2] but also as a link between modern, linguistically reflexive creative techniques and the very nature of poetry. Modern literary texts are perhaps at their most impressive when by freeing themselves from conventional practices they paradoxically return to ancient traditions; when they are evidently not incompatible with them, but on the contrary, confirm them through the critical arc and develop them further. The poem can, through its own body, form, and material, demonstrate and produce the contents it delivers, and make the most of the traditional connection between content and form.

The aim of this chapter is to show such a close connection, focusing on two selected poems by H. M. Enzensberger and H. C. Artmann, linked by the principle of permutation, even rotation. Before we take a closer look at these texts, let us recall that the dynamic (such as a rotary one, indeed) arrangement of a text is typical of concrete, particularly visual, poetry, with examples of rotational dynamics aplenty: from Franz Mon's "rotor" (Gomringer 1992, 106); through André Thomkins' letter dial (ibid., 137); Tim Ulrich's "stets," where stasis turns to motion, or his magical spiral (*image-magic*) (ibid., 143); all the way to Kriwet's text discs (*Rundscheiben*; Kriwet 2011, 137–41). In addition to such visual poems, there are equally modern texts that take rotation (or other dynamic processes) as their theme, using the conventional horizontal axis of the lines, and which straddle tradition and the linguistically reflexive approach to varying extents. By moving continuously between the two poles, they have the benefit of an extremely broad spectrum of expression and interpretation. At the same time, they fulfil the essence of *Dinggedicht* in quite an innovative way: "Such a poem creates its content, that sequence of moods, directly from a productive moment, it *does not indicate* some certain state, but at the same time *is* the process itself" (Oppert 1926, 727). It is just this method of representation, or, more precisely, its latter variation, to which we will turn our attention in the following pages.

---

2   See, for example, the highly regarded anthology *Slovo, písmo, akce, hlas* (Word, Font, Action, Voice), edited by Josef Hiršal and Bohumila Grögerová (1967).

The famous wordsmith Hans Magnus Enzensberger (born 1929) is often referred to as a *poeta doctus*, and also as an author who creates what has been called "antipoetry" (cf. Rey 1978, 147–62, 308–21). His poetic work – although it does not restrict itself to the realms of concrete poetry – does, at first glance, smash traditional notions of lyricism: it is often completely dry, verging on documentary, prosaically factual. This is very much the case in his well-known poem "Leuchtfeuer" (Lighthouse), which speaks of a lighthouse seemingly simply and matter-of-factly. Yet the subject is projected directly into the structure of the poem, and thus a typical poem-object comes into being, as can be found, *inter alia*, in the case of C. F. Meyer (exemplified by the poem "Der römische Brunnen" [The Roman Fountain]) or R. M. Rilke (e.g., his poem "Das Karussel" [The Merry-Go-Round]).[3] In principle, like both these poets, Enzensberger balances between the content and the text-object itself: the poem speaks about a lighthouse, it describes it, and at the same time articulates itself as a lighthouse – and thus *is* one:

Leuchtfeuer

I.
Dieses Feuer beweist nichts,
es leuchtet, bedeutet:
dort ist ein Feuer.
Kennung: alle dreißig Sekunden
drei Blitze weiß. Funkfeuer:
automatisch, Kennung SR.
Nebelhorn, elektronisch gesteuert:
alle neunzig Sekunden ein Stoß.

---

3   With these two authors, we find the poem resonating with the object it portrays not only by its content, but also by its structural arrangement. In C. F. Meyer's well-known poem, lines flow into the lines that follow, mimicking the water flowing between the bowls of the Roman fountain. Rilke's "Merry-Go-Round" not only creates a certain permutating rotation of the text, but ingeniously works with the gradual blurring of the contours and colours of objects moving through time and the course of life.

II.
Fünfzig Meter hoch über dem Meer
das Insektenauge,
so groß wie ein Mensch:
Fresnel-Linsen und Prismen,
vier Millionen Hefnerkerzen,
zwanzig Seemeilen Sicht,
auch bei Dunst.

III.
Dieser Turm aus Eisen ist rot
und weiß, und rot.
Diese Schäre ist leer.
Nur für Feuermeister und Lotsen
drei Häuser, drei Schuppen aus Holz,
weiß, und rot, und weiß. Post
einmal im Monat, im Luv
ein geborstener Wacholder,
verkrüppelte Stachelbeerstauden.

IV.
Weiter bedeutet es nichts.
Weiter verheißt es nichts.
Keine Lösungen, keine Erlösung.
Das Feuer dort leuchtet,
ist nichts als ein Feuer,
bedeutet: dort ist ein Feuer
dort ist der Ort wo das Feuer ist,
dort wo das Feuer ist ist der Ort.
(Enzensberger 1986, 59–60)

Lighthouse

I.
This beacon flare proves nothing,
it glares, it blares:
there is a flare.

A signal: every thirty seconds
three flashes of white. A radio beacon:
automatic, an SR signal.
A foghorn, electronically controlled:
every ninety seconds a blast.

II.
Fifty metres high above the sea
an insect eye
as big as a person:
Fresnel lenses and prisms,
four million Hefner candles,
twenty nautical miles visibility,
even in fog.

III.
This iron tower is red,
and white, and red.
This skerry is desolate.
Just for keepers and steersmen,
three wooden huts,
white, and red, and white. Post
once a month, windward
withered juniper,
stunted gooseberry bushes.

IV.
Beyond than it means nothing.
Beyond that it portends nothing.
No solution, no absolution.
The flare there glaring,
is nothing but a flare,
meaning: there is a flare,
there is the place where the flare is,
there where the flare is is the place.

In terms of technique and form, this text turns, permutes around its own axis, seemingly about nothing but the beacon light as such and its technical infrastructure: "This beacon flare proves nothing, / it glares, it blares: / there is a flare." This rotating signal, as Enzensberger writes, reveals nothing and offers no great prize, no great comfort ("This skerry is desolate"), presenting itself as an extremely inhospitable venue, an ascetically cold structure or construction, offering only direction.

The lighthouse is a solid, bright, and very noisy landmark, a "fire" visible from all directions – "twenty nautical miles visibility, / even in fog"; or indeed, "there is the place where the flare is, / there where the flare is is the place." With respect to sensory perception, the text seems visual, speaking out from a barren or desolate expanse of paper, visible and readable, providing clear information. At the same time, however, it also has its auditory, sonic aspect, just like the lighthouse, which in addition to optical signals also sends acoustic signals: "A foghorn, electronically controlled: / every ninety seconds a blast." The poem presents itself here as something opto-phonetic,[4] essentially a sensory device, something that can be seen and heard, which illuminates the darkness and pierces the wastes, or indeed, the fog. The word "Nebelhorn," or indeed Nebel, fits this scheme of things exactly: read backwards, it spells "Leben" – life. (This dichotomy is also, incidentally, to be seen with, for example, the concretist Konrad Beyer, the Czech poet Ivan Wernisch, and not forgetting some common sayings.)

With his seemingly completely dry, apoetic description, Enzensberger synthesizes and textually "spreads out the scroll" of an ancient symbol or metaphor. If his lighthouse stands as the embodiment of light and sound, then we can understand such a motif as directly linked with literary, religious, and philosophical traditions. After all, it is the idea of the word as a light that illuminates or fills the void, that brings life, just as a song or singing makes life manifest, that forms the very basis of poetry and the perception of language. This metaphor of light stretches in various forms: from the mythical Orpheus through the Bible, the Romantic mysticism of the poetic word to Symbolism, and, in various other forms, beyond. Enzensberger, however, gets to such an image in

---

4   Klaus Peter Dencker uses the term "optophonetics" (Optophonetik) when referring to visual poetry. He uses this term for texts that simulate acoustic processes in their visual form. See, for example, F. T. Marinetti's visual creations (e.g., Hultberg 1993, 9n; cf. Denker 2011, 45).

a completely dry, rational, and quite documentary way, and it is this tension between apparent apoetism and its clear poetic legacy that makes the poem straddle the space between literary tradition and the experimental practices of the literary neo-avant-garde.

While Enzensberger takes a measured and critical approach to purely concretist practices,[5] the founding member of the legendary Wiener Group, the Austrian author H. C. Artmann, is one of the authors who were at the very birth of radical poetic practices of post-war literature; but, at the same time, he is not to be boxed in by any attempt at labelling. This elemental and hard-to-classify wordsmith has been described as the most versatile and original German-writing poet since 1945.[6] This "language juggler" (used in a positive sense) graduated in comparative linguistics and mastered several languages, including some Czech.[7] In his writings, he often involved foreign-language dictionaries and grammars, creating texts that could be called linguistic and literary contaminations. His poem "tom du tümmel" (1955) represents one specific spatial object – and let us leave aside, for now, exactly which:[8]

tom du tümmel

tom
tom tom tümmel
tom du tom und tom
o tom du

---

5   See in particular his essay "Die Aporien der Avantgarde" (The Aporias of the Avant-Garde; cf.
     Enzensberger 1962).

6   See the foreword of the book *The Best of H. C. Artmann* (Artmann 1970, 2). The interpretation of
     Artmann we publish here is partly based on more freely conceived essays – Novotný 2016a and
     Novotný 2016b – in which I considered the possibilities of translating Artmann's poem into Czech.

7   This is how the Czech poet Josef Hiršal speaks of Artmann's linguistic sensibility: "We were
     sitting together over some drink, when Artmann, having until then spoken only in German,
     turned to me with a question in pure Prague Czech: – "Co to piješ?" (What's that you're drink-
     ing?) – Nobody would have asked it like that, without an intimate knowledge of Czech. Any for-
     eigner would have asked: "Co piješ?" "What are you drinking" (Grögerová and Hiršal 2007, 786).

8   Artmann's poem is untranslatable in all respects, due to its close ties to German speech sounds,
     so a translation has to look for alternative phonetic solutions: "ben / ben ben bynner / ben you
     ben and ben / o ben you / leather hooded / ben you / ben ben / you ben ben / skyward ben / drag
     ben drag turn / your hoods ben / ben you bynner / turn you / cannon bynner / ben you / ben."

lederne cappen
tom du
tom tom
du tom tom
am himmel tom
dreh tom dreh dreh
deine cappen tom
tom du tümmel
dreh du
canonen tümmel
tom du
tom

(Artmann 1985, 102)

Artmann also plays with his approach to words, songs, or poems, like light and life; but he does so very much more radically than Enzensberger. He literally upturns the traditional idea, giving it a distinctly cynical character. The articulation component plays a distinctive role in his poem; the text is clearly meant to be read aloud and is very close to the Dadaist *Lautgedicht* ("sound poem").

At first glance, Artmann's poem seems very minimalist. It has a distinctly meagre vocabulary, revolves around word variations, and at first it seems to be going nowhere developmentally. Here, someone is addressing some Tom, with the familiar appellative "du" ("you"), and we read that Tom is a "tümmel" – not a proper word in German, which we can perceive as garbled or a contamination of sorts, quite typical for Artmann's work.[9] The term "tümmel" can thus allude to "Lümmel" ("a lout"), or it can be understood as the mumbled word "Tummel" ("tumult") or "tummeln" ("romping about"). Both are very well-suited to the poem: from the point of view of phonetic interplay, Tom can't be just some "Lümmel," but truly *Tom-Tümmel*, perhaps even a little "tölpel" – a dolt, clod, or oaf. The word "tümmel" here acts as a kind of polysemic hub that draws in and concentrates the whole poem dynamic around one single utterance; it

---

9   In this context, we can mention not only Artmann's well-known dialect poems, but also, for example, the remarkable language mix "Die Fahrt zur Insel Nantucket" (Cruise to Nantucket Island), which mixes elements from old and new German with Dutch and English, to the limits of Dadaist Lautgedicht language abstraction. See Rühm 1985, 85–88.

connects "Tom the lout" with his surroundings, with the swarming objects that tumultuously whirl around him, apparently in the sky: "am himmel."[10]

Note that this poem – like the vast majority of Wiener Group texts – is written in lower case; so the expression "tom" is not only a name, but also a sound, an interjection. This sidestepping of parts of speech again corresponds to the overall nature of Artmann's text. The whirring of the whole poem is alliteratively hectic, yapping; the first four lines literally shake with the explosive *t*, and the rhythmically repetitive terms "tom" and "tümmel"; indeed, we may argue that the poem thus mimics the actual explosive rhythm and sound of gunfire: "tom / tom / tümmel / tom du tom und tom / o tom du" (noting that German pronunciation has a breathed *p*, *t*, and *k*, so the plosive consonants have significantly greater dynamic force than in Czech, for instance). The notion that the poem mimics gunfire in its construction can incidentally be supported by the link of the name "tom" with the English designation "tommy gun"; Tom, who is being addressed here (or, possibly, who is talking to himself), thus functionally and nominally becomes one with the weapon, synonymous with it, a human being who is, at the same time, the very antithesis of humanity – a deadly inhumane automaton: a firearm. If we interpret the poem as Tom's soliloquy, then we can view such a deviation from the lyrical self, from the first-person singular to the second-, as a distancing from oneself, the murderous reduction of oneself to a mere puppet, or even a machine.[11]

Who is this Tom, exactly? Is he a soldier? A criminal? A sports rifleman? Reading on, we find: "lederne cappen" – that is, "leather hoods" (in the modern spelling: "kappen"), probably aviator caps. They are followed again by an explosive series of "tom-toms," followed by further information that the objects on

---

10   A similar polysemy can be found in, say, the work of Konrad Bayer, Artmann's fellow creative writer from the Wiener Gruppe, and one with whom Artmann often collaborated. Bayer's poem "franz war" (see Rühm 1985, 139) breaks not only the divisions between parts of speech, but also between languages: the word "war" can be understood as the past tense of the verb "sein" (i.e., "franz was"), but also as the English term "war." The title itself thus captures cause and effect in one go: Franz (Ferdinand) *was*, so he is no longer; this fact directly overlaps with the outbreak of the (First World) War, or, as Bayer writes, "wirrwarr."

11   Ernst Jünger speaks of just such a transformation of the human being into a military automaton in his study on "combat as a subjective experience" (*Der Kampf als inneres Erlebnis*; Jünger 1926, 97), reflecting on his experiences of the First World War. The Germanist Manfred Schneider later identified this phenomenon as one of the basic elements of the creation of terror and horror (see Schneider 1999, 237–49).

which Tom is to focus his attention are located "am himmel" – in the sky, above, seemingly a swarm of moving targets: fighter planes. The phrase "canonen tümmel" may refer to something like a cluster, a swarm of cannons, but at the same time it can also be perceived as a vocal barking: "cannons, you oaf," or "cannons, you lout." The term can also be understood as the unfolded composite "Kanonentümmel," the vocative of something like "you machine-gunning dunderhead." The instructions given to Tom continue, the poem literally "turning" to its finale: "dreh tom dreh dreh" can express movement in the aerial gun turret, but also the linguistically reflexive dimension of the poem, namely the swirling progression of the text.

The text is thus in itself a kind of military object, a thing. This poem-object, or *Dinggedicht*, is a turning cabin, growling in all directions with the gunfire of barking sounds and syllables. By contrast, we have the long and clenched "dreh," which expresses the sound that comes with the grating and creaking as the gun turret rotates, at the same time a kind of deadly Poe-style cawing, the creaking of a ghostly aircraft wreck. Perhaps this too explains the older spelling of the word "cappen," since even such a minor detail can induce a certain dustiness from beyond the grave, the timeless danse macabre of wartime corpses. The image then twists directly to the motive of the cannons and finally to the fragmentary "tom du/tom," a kind of severed abrupt ending, seemingly suggesting sudden and rapid death; and at the same time the whole poem, which begins and ends with the word "tom," comes full circle. With this final explosion, Artmann's text produces something akin to Ernst Jandl's famous poem "schtzngrmm," where the final *t*, as the last of a long series of shots, interrupts the flow of text – and let us not overlook that, typographically, this grapheme resembles a cross. In a broader context, we might put it like this: this lethal and definitive "tom" marks Tom's end, and with it the Orphic articulation of life. What follows is a grave silence, or, indeed, the wasteland of a plain, white page.

So far, we have only briefly mentioned how the text deals with its "imparted information." The author distils the content of the poem down to the minimum necessary; "tom" is no specific soldier, nor is it certain that he is a soldier at all. "Tom" is first and foremost a word form; we are obliged to grasp its function, to play out its role ourselves. In any case, we are faced with starting from a precisely dosed modicum of information to compose an image of circling fighter planes with pilots in leather aviator caps, as well as having to animate the entire rotary mechanics of the poem, its gun turret self. In other words, we have to extricate the thing or object from the poem through our own reading, to complete the picture ourselves. The invocation of our imagination lies primarily in the poem's soundscape, with its consonant specifics to guide us. The author does not explain anything, but only gently toys with the phonetic components, constructing out of them a delicate and enclosed mechanism, with not an iota of excess. The absence of any superfluous information, in an image that clearly stands out in relief, turns Artmann's seemingly simple and inconspicuous text into poetry of the highest merit. In the field of minimalist linguistic testimony, the author unleashes a refined play on conjoined form and content. The words create a very plastic and dynamic image of dread, sound-based, thus perfect for live rendition.

When Hans Magnus Enzensberger wrote his excellent poem "Lighthouse," he let his poem rotate verbally too, turning its own variations on itself, but yet retaining the essence of the *word* as something reviving, something that comes with a glow radiant of civilization and life – "Lighthouse" essentially reaffirms the ancient principle of a song or poem, as a modern ode to poetry itself. Artmann's poem brings us quite an opposing and consistently cynical approach: its visual and sonic whirr is a fiery dance of death, the futile struggle for life in the midst of all-pervasive destruction and chaos. Here, the *word* is no longer the embodiment of life or inception, but portrays total destruction, wartime apocalypse. This destruction, despite the very minimal textual space it occupies, is of a universal, all-embracing kind: it goes in both centrifugal and centripetal directions, both outward and inward, up and down.

The aim of this short study was to outline how a *Dinggedicht* or poem-object can function in its intrinsic – and, in this case, rotary or permutative – dynamics. It cannot be argued that Enzensberger – let alone Artmann – created his poem in the spirit of the *Dinggedicht* of the nineteenth and early twentieth centuries. Logically enough, their arsenal of creative possibilities was different and, in many ways, wider than that of prior generations of poets. The spectrum of their scope was widened not only by their experience of the most radical creative practices, which boil the *word* down to mere material; but also with the shared experience of the technicist twentieth century and its murderous machinery of war. What makes both poets remarkable in the context of modern post-war literature is that the radical practices of the neo-avant-garde can be quite organically interlinked with classical literary references; in that they take the very myth of words and songs for their theme, and thus reaffirm the existence and meaning of poetry.

Words Turned into Objects: Things in Visual Poetry

JULIE KOBLÍŽKOVÁ WITTLICHOVÁ

In this chapter, we shall deal with various ways of representing things in poems that come under the term "visual poetry": poems that depict the subject not only by means of language, but also through visual means. Depicting a thing through text has, generally speaking, very much to do with describing it. The question arises: how to present to the reader something that is found in a world that lies outside the poem's text itself, no matter whether fictional or real. Classical ekphrasis relies on the power of rhetoric: to describe something is to pronounce "a speech which leads one around bringing the subject matter vividly before the eyes" (Webb 1999, 7). Yet modern poetry has relinquished most of the classical rhetorical tools of the trade, or at least exposed them, overtly and ironically. It has no desire to bring things out for the reader – for example, by the rendering of its storyline, or by describing the feelings that contact with something evokes in the poem's author; and indeed shies away from invoking multi-word, colourful descriptions that would cocoon the given thing in fine yarns spun of poetic language. At the heart of Imagism – striving for "direct treatment of the 'thing'" and preferring "presentation" to "description," as Ezra Pound later put it (Pound 1918) – lies the idea of an ideal description of a thing that would present it to the reader as it really is, or as it seems to be at the given moment.

One of the poets whose work brings together these modernist tenets with the illusiveness of classical ekphrasis is William Carlos Williams. His poem "Nantucket" (1934) describes an as-yet unoccupied hotel room, in which ordinary, impersonal accessories, of the kind one normally overlooks, await the arrival of a prospective guest.

Nantucket

Flowers through the window
lavender and yellow

changed by white curtains –
Smell of cleanliness –

Sunshine of late afternoon –
On the glass tray

a glass pitcher, the tumbler
turned down, by which

a key is lying – And the
immaculate white bed

(Williams 1986, 372)

In this poem we are faced with an ordinary list of objects, seemingly without the cause of relating to some story or some other human interest. The language of the "Nantucket" poem is almost sterile, without any metaphors and other rhetorical figures. The lack of any actioning linking verbs keeps things calmly resting in their places: the lines are equally long and the couplets are divided along the natural rhythms of speech (albeit a little less smoothly towards the end). All this contributes to the illusion that the reader is encountering each depicted thing directly and, moreover, doing so at a time at which we do not normally look at it, so it can show itself in its true form.[1]

---

1   This illusion is well thought out and very carefully built up on the tension between the subjective and objective nature of things. Williams' poem does not lack the subjective entity engaged in relating to these things. The human interest here is not given just by the topic – things of utility – but, above all, by the sequence in which the objects are presented and which could correspond to the wandering gaze of a random visitor: to one's gaze through the window, through the curtains and along the utensils standing in readiness, to the made-up bed. The visual description is soon joined by an olfactory sensation, which reinforces the idea of some perceiving subject. At the same time, this perspective is not identified in any way nor anchored in the vantage point of any particular person, the description lacks any framing, thus allowing

William Carlos Williams is one of the poets most frequently mentioned when it comes to "poems about things," and at the same time he is spoken of as one of the forerunners of concrete or visual poetry. Indeed, we would find many points of contact between the poetics of Williams' poems and the poems that fall within the realm of concrete poetry, such as the suppressing of any "lyrical subject," the minimalism of linguistic expression, or the emphasis on sensory perception. There is one very substantial difference here, however. Visual poetry is usually composed of a limited number of words, but the text itself is brought to the fore, emphasized by its visual and material qualities. At first glance, it might seem that such a redistribution of driving forces may be more likely to contribute to a "direct treatment of things" or even illusiveness. However, the aim of visual poetry is not to create the illusion of an unmediated presentation. As we shall attempt to show further on, it rather tries to bring things closer in a different way, through the mutual *reflection* of the textual and visual components.

There are three basic tendencies in the use of visual images to depict things in visual poetry:

1. The visual component consists of the typography/font and spatial distribution of words on the page (e.g., Lettrism, spatial poetry).
2. The visual component is again the lettering, but the emphasis on typography is reduced and the spatial distribution is arranged in a separate visual figure (e.g., calligrams).
3. The poem is purely visual, the text is present only in the form of a commentary or the title of the poem (e.g., object poetry).

In the first of these, the poem uses the visual quality of the letters; in the second, there are two strands to the representation – the verbal and visual – each capable of depicting the thing in their own right. In the third case, the poem is free of text as such, but the visual composition refers, for example, to a versifying scheme. The categorization offered above serves not only to

the reader to identify with it without much trouble and to fall for the notion that they are encountering these Things personally, "directly." From this perspective, the things, which seem to be apparent from an "objective" point of view, stand open to inspection by the observer, and it is precisely this readiness that brings the illusion of their objective presence (cf., for example, descriptions by Allain Robbe-Grillet).

sort visual poems into the suggested categories, but indicates the formative transformations of the visual component of the poem – from the shape of the letters, through the shape of the displayed thing, to a three-dimensional object. This progression, which has nothing to do with the "historical development" of visual poetry as a genre, shows that the visual component does not come into the poem from outside, from the world of objects or from fine art, but, on the contrary, emanates from the text and progressively gains its own independence. It is this progression, in addition to the reflection, that forms the second pillar of the relationship between the text and the visual component, as we will observe in the examples that follow.

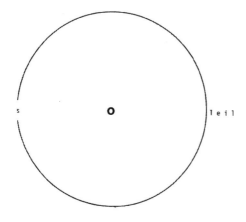

o = r o u g e   (corps glorieux)

(Garnier 1986)

Ilse Garnier's poem from her *Album à colorier* (Album to Colour In; 1986) belongs with the first of these types – poems founded on the visual aspects of the lettering. The entire collection consists of one-word poems, supplemented both by a legend assigning a colour to each of the letters, and by a short motto. The poem depicts the Sun, and to evoke its spherical appearance, it uses the shape of the letter *O*. The crux of the matter lies in how the effect of making manifest the form of the depicted thing could not be achieved using any letter other than *O*. Enlarging some other letter would lead the Sun to appear either deformed in some way, or would bring in other meanings, unrelated to the perception of the visual qualities of this particular "thing." The huge circle of the letter *O* also corresponds with the motto highlighting the "radiant corpus" or "body" (*corps glorieux*) as the most significant aspect of the depicted shape and the key to its understanding. The enlarged letter *O* offers the reader this "radiant body" not just as an idea, but as a real visual quality, such as would not be possible in a traditionally written text. However, the dynamics of the relationship between the textual and visual components do not stop at visualizing one aspect of the thing depicted. If we relate the resulting visual form of the poem back to the text – the word "soleil" – it turns out that this circular shape can form many other meanings. The circle divides the word "soleil" into three parts: the *s* interrupting the circle, the *o* situated at its centre, and *leil* beaming out of it. The first and second parts together create the expression "so," connecting the surface of the circle with its centre. If we add the first letter of the second half (which the visual arrangement does not prohibit, but on the contrary, allows us to perceive the whole circle as an extension of the shape of the letter *l*), we get the word "sol" – French for soil or the Earth's surface. The circle can then refer directly to Earth or to the orbit the Earth follows around the Sun. The last part – *leil* – can be read as a simplified phonetic notation of the French term for "eye": "l'œil." Here, the text refers to the Sun's ray as the Sun's observing eye. Yet the eye is also evoked by the dominant feature of the poem's visual arrangement, a large circle with a small one in the middle, giving a layering of meanings – eye, Sun, Earth, orbit – the universe meeting life on Earth.

Ian Hamilton Finlay's poem "The Horizon of Holland Is All Ears" (1967) is one of the first spatialist-lettrist types, already verging on a calligram. The poem is based on wordplay, on the idiom "to be all ears," which it transforms into a literal visual arrangement. From the horizontal line representing – at least, according to the content of the words that go to make it – the horizon of Holland, three pairs of alert rabbit ears perk up, formed from the repeated words of the second half of the statement. However, if we now look at the poem as a schematic visual representation of, say, the Dutch landscape that we know from postcards, we see that we are most likely not looking at any ears, but at a flat landscape dominated by the blades of three windmills. The purely verbal statement that "the horizon of Holland is all ears" would be based on a metaphor directly connecting two elements – the landscape and listening. But a visual arrangement triggers a whole series of images: the Dutch horizon is a flat land, dominated by windmills, whose blades remind one of animal ears, ears listen, and so the Dutch landscape acquires this ability from them. In this case, the depiction points to other analogies that are present in the metaphor, but would remain hidden without its agency. Nevertheless, this visual arrangement would not work without the text, since the meaning of the image is driven by language: if something else were written in the poem, we would have no reason to identify just such a layout of text with a landscape, let alone with Holland in particular. The correspondence between the text and the image is underlined here by the fact that the diagonal text connects to the horizontal at the points of occurrence of the letters *e*, *i*, and *a*, which are also the initial letters of the words "ears," "is," and "all." Thus, the arrangement of the second half of the statement, in the shape of windmill blades or ears, does not represent "added value" that would "enrich" the text by some additional dimension, but organically sprouts forth from its initial half with a logic equally visual and linguistic.

The basic difference between the visual poems falling into the first (Lettrism/Spatialism) and the second (calligrams) category depends on whether or not the visual arrangement of the text alone is capable of bearing meaning. Let us compare Finlay's poem to Salette Tavares' "Aranha." The form here is made up of words created from the Portuguese term "aranha" (spider), but we would no doubt identify the spider's body without the help of the text. In calligrams, the meaning we attach to the visual component, as the representation of a thing, may be quite independent of the specific word content. However, this does not mean that the visual and textual components are separate from each other; on the contrary, they form numerous relationships, in which the meaning expressed by one invariably directs the meaning expressed by the other. In the poem "Aranha," the meaning expressed in words and the meaning expressed by the visual arrangement complement each other. The legs of the spider are formed by a repeating command, "arre," namely "get going" or "get up." The term "arre" also corresponds to "giddy-up," the expression we use to encourage a horse to move. The meaning of the textual and visual components therefore refers to walking; yet

(Tavares 1968, 190)

to see a term typically used to prompt horses in connection with a small spider produces an ironic effect, by being all out of proportion. The rest of the poem is made up of derivatives of the term "aranha": "aranhiço" (small spider) and "aranhaço" (big spider). The second expression is divided between the letters h and a, so that its horizontal part can be read as another separate word – "aço" (steel). The visual arrangement of the top half of the poem is no longer so iconic and thus unambiguous in meaning. "Aço" can represent both a steel rod from which a solid spider-web filament is lowered down – in the visual representation domain – and could refer to the threat felt when encountering a large spider – in the play-on-words domain. The horizontal inscription "aranhisso," with no trace of steel in how it is written, can be read as the title of the poem, pointing out the subject of its depiction – a small spider. As already mentioned, the visual arrangement in the poem "Aranha" creates meaning independently, but at the same time it raises the profile of its associated properties or other subordinate meanings indicated implicitly by the word expressions; vice versa, words label properties or sub-meanings already latently contained in the visual representation.

In John Hollander's "Swan and Shadow" calligram (1969),[2] the meaning of the visual component (the swan and its shadow) and the meaning of the textual component (a description of a swan appearing and disappearing on a lake) also match. Unlike Salette Tavares' poem, however, we are not faced with two ways of referring to the same thing, but with a more complex structure of references where the motifs of the poem are referred to by formal effects induced by the arrangement of verses that at the same time create a distinct visual figure. This is true, for example, of lines grouped around the longest central line, which visually represents the water surface. The four lines that precede and the four lines that follow it together make up the swan's torso and its reflection, while at the same corresponding both in form and content. The formal correspondence consists of the equivalent lengths of the lines and end rhymes ("light" / "sight"; "awakening" / "darkening"). As for content, the corresponding verses refer instead to opposing phenomena, events, or characteristics – most notably in the verses "this object bears its image awakening" / "this image bears its object darkening." This interplay of language and visual effects contributes to the dynamics of the representation of the main motif of the poem – the mirroring of a swan. From the point of view of the poem's arrangement, however, it is even more interesting to see how the text works in the part where, due to the realistic visual representation of the swan, it has to deal with the gap that arises within the verses, between the visual surface of the neck and the wings. In the upper part, which represents the floating, living swan, the gap is used to make the text clearly structured: the neck consists of question pronouns, the wings then carry the answers to the questions they pose. Conversely, in the lower part, which represents the reflection of the swan on the water, the verse "begins" in the part forming the wing, and its last word flows into the section forming the neck. By contrast with the solid structure representing a living creature, we have here a fluid structure evocative of its reflection, stirred by ripples on the water surface. On the one hand, the visual component that forms the symmetrical figure of mirroring through the horizontal axis is more illustrative than the text itself could be; while on the other hand, the text reveals the static nature of that depiction, while bringing the dynamic of how the words separate into verses.

---

2   *Poetry* 109/3 (December 1966), p. 177. Available online at the *Poetry Foundation* website.

We have seen in the aforementioned calligrams, that the whole field of meanings referenced by the words becomes more expansive, as compared to a classical poem lacking any figural arrangement. For example, the word "swan" in Hollander's poem no longer refers just to the idea of a thing "the poem speaks of,"
but also to its visual representation on the page. At the same time, from the other
aspect, before the reader even starts to read the poem, they are provided with
a picture (in this case, the shape of a swan), and the meanings of the words is
then linked specifically to this image. If they read "water" as one of the first words,
they will think of a water surface, rather than, say, water coming out of a faucet.
In this way, the meanings of the textual and visual components *reflect*, but do not
always necessarily support, one another. A more radical approach to this principle can be found in the poem "Taube" (Dove; 1968) by Claus Bremmer. In the
text of the poem, the word "dove" does not appear at all – it is only present in the
visual component, which is not even thematized by the textual one: the visual
here is a simple but clearly identifiable image of a dove; the textual is a war cry
with extreme demands (tear down all the bridges behind you; risk everything;
cut off all roads to retreat) and a rather inhumane conclusion (victory lies in the
realization that life is not the highest good). The meaning of the text (the proclamation of war) and the meaning of the image (the dove as a symbol of peace)
are therefore in contradiction here. The poem can then be read either as a critique of the hypocrisy of peace messages or, more generally, as an expression of
the dialectical relationship of two contradictory values. History also enters into
this mutual reflection of the visual and textual components; however, not only
by way of a historical context, the events of 1968, but also in the form of artistic
tradition. The dove has a very long tradition of representing peace, especially in
Christian art; but in the mid-twentieth century this gave way to its more profane
depiction, the rallying banner of left-wing and pro-communist groups in the
West, such as in the case of Picasso's "Dove of Peace" (beginning with his litho-
graph *La Colombe* of 1949). We can interpret Bremer's ironic play politically, as
his mockery of an ageing artist who failed to take a critical look at the situation in
the Soviet Union. But it can also be seen as a way of coming to terms with artistic
tradition through an ironic treatment of a classical symbol, having nothing to do
with expressing a particular political opinion.

In the visual poems of the third category, the visual component no longer consists in the arrangement of words and lines, but in that of real physical objects.
The first example we will consider in this context falls more into the field of
conceptual art. The installation "Space Behind the Wall" (2004) by Slovak

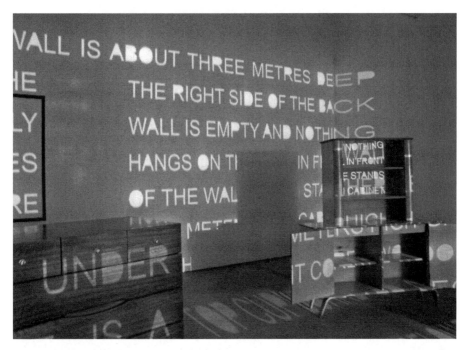

Ján Mančuška: The Space Behind The Wall..., 2004 Laser-cut particle board, furniture, light, dimensions variable. Installation view Andrew Kreps Gallery, New York, 2004. Private Collection Courtesy the Ján Mančuška Estate; hunt kastner, Prague; Andrew Kreps Gallery New York; Meyer Riegger Karlsruhe/Berlin.

artist Ján Mančuška consists of an inscription carved into chipboard, describing a simple interior, and furniture spread out in an enclosed space behind the board, exactly in keeping with this inscription. The light penetrating the holes made by the letters projects the text to the back wall of the room and covers the objects present with lucent lettering. The text reads:

The installation can be understood as a decontructed calligram, which is also spread out into three-dimensional space. Unlike the classical calligram, which consists of two components – the text and the image – here three components interact: a tangible linear text carved into chipboard; its to-some-extent dematerialized reproduction in light; and the actual objects that the words indicate. The text here does not attempt to create any illusion or other effect; it is an austere description, accurately communicating what is hidden behind it, and one completely indifferent to the reader (this is one of the main differences between Williams' description of the hotel interior and Mančuška's text as used in the installation). Words are not being granted any creative power here; quite on the contrary, they are reduced to the merely descriptive tool of a given reality. The viewer has the opportunity to look into the space that lies "behind the words," where they encounter this reality and can easily verify that the words mean what they say. In addition to real objects, however, there is also the middle component of the decomposed calligram – the lucent text. The real objects that are present, hiding behind the text and the wall, are not standing here on their own, but continue to be accompanied by words, a trail of language superimposed on them by light. The visual component emerging out of the text has formed into the shape of a three-dimensional object, but it is still accessible only through words. The mutual reflection of the visual and textual components here takes on a philosophical dimension: on the one hand, the light inscription points out that it is not possible to completely separate the objects on display from the words that refer to them; on the other, this light inscription is deformed and shaped by the very objects upon which it appears.

The last poem that concludes our exploration of the trajectory of the growing independence of the visual component is Jiří Kolář's object poem "Černý cukr" (Black Sugar; 1963). The poem is composed of small, ordinary objects, which are sometimes barely recognizable or broken. Text is notable for its complete absence here: the visual component – in the form of a specific three-dimensional object – has now fledged to full independence. Yet the arrangement of these objects hints at the regular structure of verses grouped into stanzas. The selection of objects and the way they are arranged within this structure is also

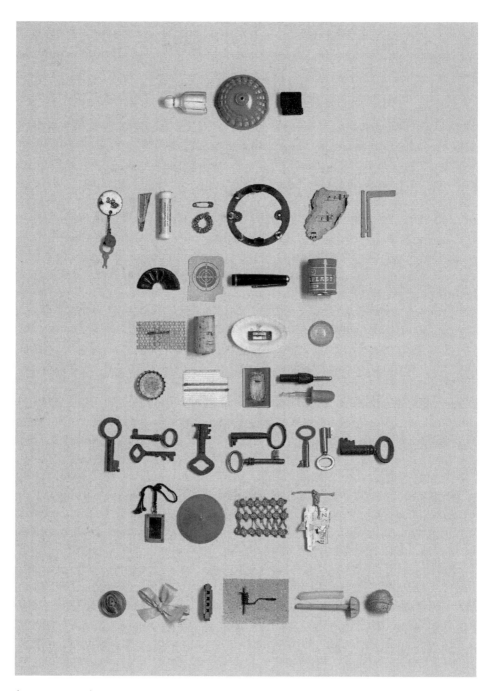

(Kolář 1999, 142)

not random. All the objects share the same nature of being useless, discarded, or broken things, and, more importantly, there are several shapes that formally structure the poem here: a circle, a cylinder, a rectangle, a "double line," and, towards the end, some kinds of ribbons. At first glance, the reader's attention will be drawn to the "line" composed entirely of keys – among the few objects that are instantly easily recognizable and at the same time composed of most of the aforementioned shapes: a circle or oval, a cylinder, and a rectangle. The key thus represents the real "key" to understanding the shape-based relationships between the individual elements of the poem. The visual, aesthetic qualities of objects here are more important than, for example, their purpose or the words that denote them (in fact, it is difficult to identify and therefore to name most of the objects that appear in the poem). In "Black Sugar," the visual component of the poem – which, as we've gone from spatialist poems through calligrams, has become more and more clearly outlined and semantically independent – is now set completely free and rid of verbal expression, and becomes the dominant structural principle of the whole poetic work. The mutual reflection of the textual and visual components here acquires a meta-poetic dimension. The visual component consists of small, useless objects arranged in the formal principle of a poem: this regular rhythmic structure makes visible such relationships between objects as would not be obvious at first sight, and which are usually reserved for words. By becoming elements of the poem, these objects conversely draw attention to what is not typically emphasized: that one of the facets of a poem is its ordered structure, entirely regardless of the content of the words that make it up.

We have examined all the aforementioned poems with two aims in mind: noticing both the gradual self-assertion of the visual component in relation to the textual component, and the different ways the two components can mutually reflect. The separation of the visual and textual components, and the *reflexive structure* as a principle that keeps the two components together, are not two distinct and independent phenomena: the degree of the former is in direct proportion to that of the latter. This would be a good place to compare Williams' poem "Nantucket" and Kolář's "Black Sugar." The basic compositional principle of both poems, which each works with in its own specific way, is that of a list. That being said, "Nantucket" describes a hotel room and the things within it, creating the illusion that the reader is encountering these items directly, without an intermediary. The poem does, of course, also have its visual shape; but, unlike visual poems, this shape does not relate in any way to the subject

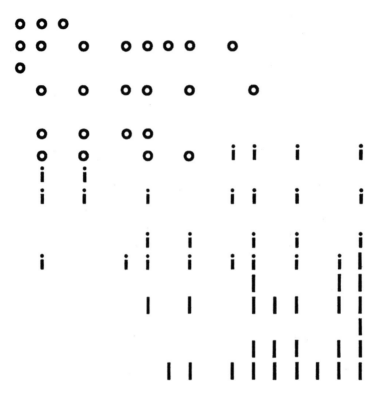

(Mayer 1968: 124)

depicted. While the sequence of individual words and the relationships between them can be significant, there is no other "component" that influences their meaning. As we have seen the visual component progressively gaining independence from the textual component and, accordingly, its ability to produce meanings in its own right – from the shape of a letter, through a visual representation of the displayed thing, to a three-dimensional object – the space inside the poem begins to open up, allowing the two components, now separated, to enter into a reflective relationship. And it is this reflection that makes the objects displayed in "Black Sugar" still refer to language, even though the textual component is completely missing here. As we have shown, these three-dimensional objects have not made an appearance in the poem as some alien element from outside, from the world of objects or from the visual arts; but they represent one of the poles of the strained relationship between the textual and the visual component striving to detach from it. Thus, "Nantucket" and "Black Sugar" can be read as two poems built on completely contradictory approaches: while Williams' intention is to talk about things by means of a poem, Kolář's intention is to talk about poetry by means of things.

Kolář's "object poems" are not the only ones that examine different aspects of poetic language, rather than the things the poem depicts. Many lettrist poems deal exclusively with the visual quality of the typography, while some calligrams treat the visual representation purely rhetorically (as we can partially observe in the case of Bremer's poem "Dove"). In none of the examples cited can we see a firm line drawn between attention to the subject displayed and attention to the display method. The visual component of the poem provokes questions about the relationship between language and the world, the relationship between the word and the thing that the word refers to. Does language put up an obscuring barrier between us and the world that needs to be overcome so that we can get closer to things and know them for what they really are; or is language a natural part of the world, and knowledge of its possible representations a part of the knowing of things? Let us leave these questions in the realm of the philosophy of language, which is better equipped to deal with them. However, we can pay attention to them in connection with the mutual reflection of the textual and visual components at the level of a particular text.

Hansjörg Mayer's composition (1965) from the *typoems* cycle can be classified as the first spatialist-lettrist type of visual poems. The textual component consists of the single word "oil," the visual component of numerous *o*, *i*, and *l* letters spread across the page. Like Ilse Garnier's poem "Soleil," Mayer's visual composition references a feature of the thing it depicts, in a way that a purely linguistic expression could not exude on its own: namely, the viscosity of oil. This time, however, it does so not through a static reference to the mimetic quality of one of the letters, but through a gradual, dynamic transformation of the shapes, where the letter *o* is oozing into the dot that is part of the letter *i*, and this in turn is oozing into the upright of the letter *l*. The visual arrangement here, as in other cases, highlights how a purely verbal expression would not suffice to cover all the aspects of the thing depicted. Yet, by transforming the shapes of all the letters involved in labelling the thing, while maintaining their standard linear notation – the visual arrangement once again "emerges" directly out of the text, rather than being superimposed upon it – it also reveals the close relationship between the worldly thing to which the word refers and the visual representation of that thing in the language domain. With his composition, Mayer creates something like a visual equivalent to the onomatopoeic quality of language sounds.

It now remains to describe in a little more detail the principle of the reflexive structure and to explain what relation it has to the thing the poem describes. That being said, the reflection occurs between two components – the textual and the visual. Unlike a classical poem, which is homogeneous in terms of its media, in a visual poem these two components face off, each presenting the thing the poem depicts from a different perspective. The nature of this reflection stands out better when compared to the theory of description in narrative texts, as formulated by the Israeli literary scholar Meir Sternberg. In his study "Ordering the Unordered: Time, Space, and Descriptive Coherence" (1981), he explores the ways in which the description of an object occupying space, rather than time, becomes part of a linear, time-unfolding sequence of text, how this sequence is arranged, and how it holds together. Sternberg distinguishes three kinds of coherence, to which the textual arrangement is also subordinated: chronological, hierarchical, and perspectival. And it is the description arranged in a narrative text from a given perspective that can be compared with the description in a visual poem, where each of its components arranges the text in a different way. Perspectival coherence differs from chronological and hierarchical coherence mainly in that it is *mediated*. In a novel, where events, characters, or things are described from the "objective" perspective of the author, there may be sudden changes in the way they are described. The reader understands this discontinuity (and can derive some sense from it) because they identify the description with the "voice" of a particular character: "It all goes back to the fact that such mediation entails the described object's leading a double life: within the mediated world and within the mediating mind" – one interposed between the author and the reader (Sternberg 1981, 85). If we wanted to demonstrate the difference between an unmediated and mediated description in the examples above, we could now say that Williams' "Nantucket" makes use of the first option, by presenting the reader with a reality described as seen by the "author" of the poem (whose rhetorical strategy is to create the illusion that he lets the reader take his place); while, on the other hand, the reading of Hollander's "Swan and Shadow" is *mediated* by a third element – the visual arrangement of the text. Yet there is one significant difference between narrative texts, as

discussed by Sternberg, and visual poems – and essential to the reflexive structure we are examining.

As an example of a description making sense to the reader thanks to perspectival coherence, Sternberg cites the irony of Jane Austen. The author organ-
izes her description in line with her own, and generally accepted, hierarchy of
values. Once this order is overturned in the description (e.g., when the characterization of the wife precedes that of her husband), the reader is forced to seek
some explanation, another agent who has aligned the description according to
their own values (e.g., the more significant position of women within a particular family). But the dual perspective – of the author and the character – is recognizable and understandable here only because the first forms a stable "backdrop" for the brief transitions of the second. And here lies the very substantial
difference. Although the visual component *mediates* the text to the reader, represents one of the principles of its coherence, and gives it meaning (e.g., Bremer's "Dove"), this does not happen on a "backdrop" of the textual component:
the textual component does not prevail over the visual component spatially
or temporally. The space occupied by the text coincides with the space occupied by the image, and neither of them is "foremost." Both components have
the same standing in the poem, neither takes priority, and so neither depicts
"objective" reality. If the visual component draws attention to how language
itself was not able to describe all aspects of the "thing", and so failed to portray
it to the full (the glow of the sun disc, the mirroring of the swan and its shadow,
the existence of a poem without words), it does not do so just to prove the language inadequate or to supplement what is lacking in language to make the representation complete. The visual component is similarly proven inadequate by
the textual component, which in turn points out the deficiency and incomplete-
ness of the meaning mediated by the image (linguistic analogies, the dynamics
of verse structure, new relationships between objects). The textual component
of the poem therefore has the same *mediating* and perspective-based character
as the visual component. The reflexive structure is based on confronting the
two partial representations – the textual and the visual. Being the poem's fundamental structural principle, it will not allow any "illusion of direct presentation" or "direct treatment of the thing." In the end, the reflexive structure reveals
that the "thing" cannot be fully grasped by any single means of expression, but
at the same time it opens up a different path to its comprehension: the path of
gradual, indirect approaching, which is constantly aware of the fact that its end
is forever beyond reach.

Things on an Island

JOSEF HRDLIČKA

> *Poznat květinu tu rostlinu s jinými cévami*
> *snad proto že předměty jsou často tak na místě*
> *že se člověk neubrání aby je nemiloval*
> *když už je vytvořil*

> To get to know the flower the plant with other blood vessels
> perhaps because objects are often so spot-on
> that one can't help but love them
> having created them

> Vladimíra Čerepková (2001)

I.

Things can, *in a sense,* exist without any relationship to humans. In saying this, I do note that the concept of a thing comes from the human mind. Thinking can undoubtedly rise above the horizons of the human world and consider things without humans. But it can only do so *in a sense,* because we are still referring to the act of thinking. Similarly, when I talk about the "life" of things, this is in the first place a projection of human life into things; but there may be another underlining temporal progression involved and a distinction between a tangible *object* and an intangible *thing,* as noted by Bill Brown (Brown 2015, 17ff.), following on from Heidegger, that prevents us from settling the notion of "what things are" once and for all. Such a treatment of things without the human can be approached through poetic imagination. Roger Caillois, for example, contemplated the life of stones on Earth before any sign of humanity even appeared, and arrived at the imaginary idea of an archaeological layer of life of stones, by negating the anthropomorphisms that inevitably set off such a reverie. Likewise, we can dream of things as they are when quite by themselves, and perhaps, as Caillois writes, take on some of their essence.[1] Arising from these not-so-simple relationships, which show up only when we think about things rather than just making use of them, we reach a certain imbuing or exchange through which things actually do have a life. It cannot be unequivocally argued that this is merely a projection of life, a *pathetic fallacy* that can be easily dispelled to allow us to see things as they really are. We are constantly being drawn into that kind of interplay with things around us. Our social life is never isolated from things (cf. ibid., 6). To assume that we perceive and utilize all Things around us as mere objects and tools would be as one-sided as to claim that all Things are alive in the same sense as ourselves.

Poetry can throw some of these circumstances into sharper focus, and when it comes to an intimate coexistence with things, an island offers an almost laboratory environment for such a poetic exploration. It should be noted that the *island* in this case is not merely a geographical phenomenon, a piece of land bounded by the sea; but in its literary image, the literary scene – introduced into literature by Daniel Defoe and those who came after him – it is a particular kind of constrained *horizon* that allows one to study man in a relatively enclosed and limited space – in our case, having only a limited number of things at their disposal. The island makes palpable one particular type of horizon, and it is worth at least recalling a number of other horizons within which things reveal to man.[2] When the poet Jiří Wolker writes "I love things, silent comrades" (Wolker 1953, 44), he is seeing things as his counterparts – touchable, graspable. Wolker's anthropomorphizing is preceded by another, tacit action: namely, picking out things that are appropriately close to man, having due dimensions and shaping one's intimate surroundings. Yet there are objects that are too close for me to grasp routinely (by hand or sight), which do not conform to what we usually consider when speaking of things – a bracelet, the earrings one is wearing, but also a dental filling, a pacemaker, or artificial limb. On another scale, there are microscopic objects or objects too far distant or too large, scattered hyperobjects that transcend the normal scale of our perception.[3]

---

1   Caillois is quoted in Hrdlička 2014, 189.
2   The "horizon" in modern poetry is a topic dealt with by Michel Collot (2005).
3   Cf. Justin Quinn's chapter on the topic.

When we think about things, we usually give pride of place to those nearby that match our scale, which is then the foundation of their "life story." I will try to show this by reference to several poems.

II.

But first, let us look at the island. The story of Robinson Crusoe is one of the touchstone works and formative fables of Western literature. It inspired a number of follow-up stories that, in various ways, develop the basic theme – a castaway on a desert island. For such a castaway or castaways, things are of great importance. Although we cannot claim that things are not important for someone still living in the civilized world, on a castaway's island things gain extra importance for the role they play in coping with the extreme situation, as is well-illustrated by the ever-recurring episode in many of these stories – that of rescuing things from a shipwreck. Defoe's Robinson Crusoe needs tools to enable him to live as closely as possible to how he did back home. The colonial spirit of such stories is quite openly presented in Jules Verne's *Mysterious Island*, whose protagonists even call themselves "colonists." The original Robinson Crusoe struggled to mimic civilization, and the things he made were often very clumsy and makeshift – such as his goatskin parasol. His things are quite distinctive in that respect. The colonists on *Mysterious Island*, on the other hand, manage to replicate industrial society almost perfectly, and their things are products of great utility, first and foremost. In one chapter, Captain Nemo secretly sends them a crate of things, complete with a precise list amounting to a kind of practical colonist's encyclopaedia of things, or Verne's idea of it, typical of the nineteenth century in many ways. By contrast, in the much later take on Robinson by Michel Tournier, the hero distances himself from civilization and tries to live in harmony with the island, along the lines of Man Friday. His transformation is completed by an explosion that destroys all the remnants of civilization that Robinson had assembled. After this turn of events, the things on the island become significantly different: more akin to living beings or per-sonified natural elements.

The tale of Robinson Crusoe has also inspired several poems divergent from prose, quite differing and diverse in many respects, such as in their take on things. All things, or more precisely, all man-made products, are precious to a "Crusoe." And here comes the question that stories usually leave aside: what is Crusoe's relationship to things when he is not working or thinking about work? Does he perceive their presence? It is arguably problematic to claim that there is some natural intimate experience of "living together with things" and what exactly that entails. We can say that, even in conditions of existing in proximity to a large number of readily available items and serially produced artefacts, we do tend to form our own inner circles from those items to which we feel more or less close. The pen I have been writing with for several years is closer to me than, for example, a disposable recyclable plastic bottle – although island conditions can redefine the boundaries of such circles and change how we relate to things. Is it possible to live without making such circles – to be either completely without things, or to treat all things as equal? Apparently not, because of the make-up of the human body, which itself has a certain "thing-like" aspect and which governs these relationships in a signicant way. Martin Heidegger's *Der Ursprung des Kunstwerkes* (The Origin of the Work of Art) postulates something like a natural order when listing examples of things: "The stone in the road is a thing, as is the clod in the field. A jug is a thing, as is the well beside the road" (Heidegger 1993, 146). John Frow takes his list to illustrate "nostalgia for a world of simple objects" and the supposed "authentic experience" of the Greeks, which has progressively been lost to Western history (Frow 2001, 270–71). Examples of the encircling distribution of things in several poems put the question of natural relation to things on another level; they show how strongly the relationship to things depends on the given horizon and, incidentally, also indicates an uncertainty as to the natural extent or horizon of human life.

III.

I will start with two poems pertinent to Czech poetry. The Czech poet Richard Weiner (1884–1937) wrote a poem in 1913[4] called "Jean Baptiste Chardin." It is a gently ironic portrait of the well-known French painter of genre pictures, Jean Baptiste Siméon Chardin (1699–1779). The poem begins with the lines:

---

4   The poem is dated 11 September 1913 in the manuscript and was published in the collection *Usmĕvavé odříkání* (Smiling Renunciation) in 1914 (cf. Weiner 1997, 406–7).

To je můj stůl,
to jsou mé papuče,
to je má sklenice,
to je můj čajník.

To je můj etažér,
to je moje dýmka,
to je má cukřenka,
rodinný odkaz.

That is my desk,
These are my slippers,
That is my glass,
That is my teapot.

That is my étagère,
That is my pipe,
That is my sugar-shaker,
a family heirloom.

The poem continues with similar anaphoric enumeration in its subsequent stanzas and ends as follows:

Doma je dobře.
Doma je nejlíp.
To je můj koutek,
to jsou mé papuče.

Po smaltech zařinul –
zlatistý odraz.
To je má žena.
To je můj obraz.

(Weiner 1997, 83–84)

At home feels good.
At home is best.

This is my nook,
These are my slippers.

Along the enamels effulgent –
a golden gleam.
This is my wife.
This is my picture.

All the things in the poem, comprising a list of objects in a bourgeois interior, evoke the mood of thoughtfully commensurate luxury. Everything here is
determined by the relationship of being owned: "This is my...." It culminates in
the penultimate line, where the painter's wife is also added to the list. In ordinary conversation, the phrase "this is my wife" or "this is my husband" is not
loaded with other meaning; but in Weiner's poem, in the context of possessive
relationships, its literal meaning is brought to the fore. The last line thus brings
great ambiguity to what otherwise seems a straightforward poem. "This is my
picture" could mean a painting on the wall (as mentioned already in the fourth
stanza: "To je můj obraz / dal mi jej Frago" ["This is my picture. / Frago gave
it to me."]).⁵ The word "picture" can also refer to the poem as a portrait of
Chardin, as a man defined by his possessions, in the manner of Arcimboldo's
compositions. Or, in a third interpretation, the picture may refer to the image
created by a poem, whose authorship is claimed by its speaker (with "I painted
it" implied by the possessive pronoun), as if the poem was describing a real or
imagined painting. In this last case, the poem itself also becomes the subject of
ownership. Weiner thus managed by means of a relatively simple technique to
describe an intimacy with things based solely on the relationships of ownership, expressing the comfort of a secluded bourgeois household, in which
everything comes down to objects.

---

5   "Frago" refers to Jean-Honoré Fragonard (1732–1806), a painter and younger contemporary of
     Chardin. The section "Zastávky na procházkách" (Stops along Walks) in the *Smiling Renuncia-
     tion* collection contains several poems dedicated to painters, Fragonard among them. The col-
     lection was put together at a time when Weiner wrote intensively about French fine art– among
     others, in the Czech magazine *Volné směry*. Here, in 1912, he published an article under the title
     "Měšťák mezi básníky" (A Burgher among Poets), also devoted to Fragonard and Boucher.

Weiner's poem was not often mentioned or quoted in the Czech context, but has led an interesting second life in German poetry. In 1916, it was published in German translation in the anthology *Jüngste Tschechische Lyrik* (Youngest Czech Lyric). The first stanza of the poem in German reads as follows:

Dies ist mein Tisch,
Dies ist mein Hausschuh,
Dies ist mein Glas,
Dies ist mein Kännechen.

(Weiner 1916, 113)

A few decades later, the German poet Günter Eich (1907–1972) wrote his well-known poem "Inventur" (Inventory), quite probably inspired by the form of Weiner's poem.[6]

Dies ist meine Mütze,
dies ist mein Mantel,
hier mein Rasierzeug
im Beutel aus Leinen.

Konservenbüchse:
Mein Teller, mein Becher,
ich hab in das Weißblech
den Namen geritzt.

Geritzt hier mit diesem
kostbaren Nagel,
den vor begehrlichen
Augen ich berge.

---

6   In German literature, the possible inspiration from Weiner has been mentioned several times, most likely first in Suzanne Müller-Hanpft's dissertation (1972). Here I am drawing mainly on the study by Gerhard Kaiser (2003), who gives further references. Eich, as Kaiser writes, denied knowing Weiner's poem at the time of writing his "Inventory," but his assertion cannot be taken for granted (cf. Kaiser 2003, 283).

Im Brotbeutel sind
ein Paar wollene Socken
und einiges, was ich
niemand verrate,

so dient es als Kissen
nachts meinem Kopf.
Die Pappe hier liegt
zwischen mir und der Erde.

Die Bleistiftmine
lieb ich am meisten:
Tags schreibt sie mir Verse,
die nachts ich erdacht.

Dies ist mein Notizbuch,
dies meine Zeltbahn,
dies ist mein Handtuch,
dies ist mein Zwirn.

(Eich 1991, 35–36)

This is my hat,
this is my coat,
here are my shaving things
in a canvas bag.

A tin can:
My plate, my mug,
where into white enamel
I have scraped my name.

Scraped with this
priceless nail,
that I keep hidden
from avaricious eyes.

In a sandwich box
a pair of woollen socks
and something, that I
won't reveal to anyone,

serving as a pillow
at night for my head.
This piece of cardboard
lies between me and the ground.

The pencil lead
I like best of all:
By day it writes verses for me,
that I made up by night.

This is my notebook,
this is my groundsheet,
This is my towel,
This is my thread.

The poem, referencing Eich's stay in an American prisoner-of-war camp at the end of the Second World War, was written at that time or shortly thereafter.[7] Eich is close to Weiner's paradigm particularly in his use of repetitive possessive constructs; and, as Gerhard Kaiser points out, the speaker of the poem is also a creative artist, a poet (Kaiser 2003, 282–83). But there are also subtler parallels that stem from the logic of the adopted form: the several lines in which Chardin names his favourite dishes correspond to the stanza where Eich speaks of his pencil lead; and where Weiner's word "obraz" ("painting/image/picture/depiction") can stand for the entire poem – for Eich the poem and the process of writing are thematicized by a notebook. Yet the differences between the two poems are also worth noting, as Eich puts the adopted form in a different horizon – in a POW camp, in dire conditions – and his speaker is not some other persona, but an I,

---

7   Eich was in the camp near Sinzig am Rhein from April 1945 until the summer months. It is not
      certain whether the poem originated there or came about a little later, being first published in
      1947 (cf. Kaiser 2003, 269–70).

with autobiographical traits. In Eich's "Inventory" we are constantly reminded of the conventions of a bourgeois household, with the need to own things even in a POW camp; but it is all in ironic contrast with the circumstances of scarcity and improvisation. Eich's things carry no attributes of comfort, nor the remotest hint of luxury; they are everyday necessities. And while Weiner's Chardin is almost shaped by his possessions, the speaker of Eich's poem is not defined by his things, but needs them, living alongside them and with their help. This aspect culminates precisely in the motif of the pencil lead, which Eich characteristically personifies, as if he were collaborating with it on a joint artistic work.

The world-space of both poems is enclosed, yet their horizons differ: an intentional, cosseted isolation in the ample comfort of a bourgeois salon contrasts with the forced isolation of the POW camp. Kaiser emphasizes the seclusion and withdrawal of the speaker (hiding the nail "from avaricious eyes") and recalls that there is no "you" in the poem (ibid., 271), the second person, which is also missing from Weiner's poem, because everything there, including the wife, is a possession. Eich enables this closed-off world to expand the horizon of captivity in a romantic way: the solitary self keeps its freedom in the world thanks to the things and fragments of things that refer to life beyond the POW camp fence. Unlike Weiner's poem, the seclusion from the camp's immediate surroundings also means openness to the world beyond the imposed boundaries of captivity. Likewise, there are differences as regards time: Weiner's Chardin is stuck in a frozen and immobile present moment, without events, something we might liken to a "still life" image – what the French call *la nature morte*.[8] The possessive relationship is mortifying, deadening, turning things into mere inert objects. Eich's "Inventory", on the other hand, is characterized by a kind of personification that spreads to the whole world: when "this piece of cardboard / lies between me and the ground," the delicate agency of words transfers human life onto the earth by the image of touching: cardboard does not protect or separate, but rather lies together with the speaker and the earth in their places. All this is happening in some uncertain present moment, connected with creating and writing, open to the future – where both man and things are contributing as participants.

---

8   Kaiser (ibid., 283) aptly links Weiner's character, the artist Chardin, with *fin de siècle* poetics: a similar motif of a secluded interior also appears in the title poem of Weiner's collection *Smiling Renunciation* (Weiner 1997, 142–44), in which the speaker voluntarily shuts himself inside, seeking isolation from the outside world.

IV.

Eich's personifying relationship could be described as a subjective projection; but the differences between the two poems also point to the scale in which this type of relationship has its place, circumscribed by the entire situation's encircling horizon. The following two poems about Robinson Crusoe show very well how a similar type of relationship can suddenly alter along with the whole situation's horizon, although the man and the things remain the same.[9] Personification thus takes on not so much an anthropomorphizing aspect, purporting that a thing has a life story comparable to man's own, but instead portrays the particular way that thing was at some time, when it evoked a human response. Both poems mention an older Robinson Crusoe, following his return to England, and things have an important role to play in both cases. The cycle of poems in the prose *Images à Crusoe* (Pictures for Crusoe) of the French poet Saint-John Perse dates back to 1904.[10] This date is typically also cited in publications of a later version of the text, which Saint-John Perse adapted in 1925, notably doing so to tone down its Symbolism-associated elements (cf. Gardes-Tamine 2002, 132).[11] The collection, made up of a total of nine poems in prose, depicts old Crusoe as a man who has lost his life's purpose upon his return from the island. Apart from the poems "Le perroquet" (The Parrot) and "Vendredi" (Friday), all feature some object in the title; but in only three of them is the particular thing cardinal. I will focus here on these three poems, representing short and lapidary portraits of things familiar from Defoe's novel – the parasol, the bow, and the seed.

Le parasol de chèvre

Il est dans l'odeur grise de poussière, dans la soupente du grenier. Il est sous une table à trois pieds ; c'est entre la caisse où il y a du sable pour la chatte et le fût décerclé où s'entasse la plume.

(Saint-John Perse 1967, 66)

---

9   The Crusoe poems of Saint-John Perse and Elizabeth Bishop are compared by Joseph Acquisto (2005), who also drew attention to the role of the lyrical poem and the motif of things.

10 An overview of the early work of Saint-John Perse with a detailed description of *Pictures for Crusoe* is provided by Záviš Šuman (2012).

11 An earlier text version of the *Pictures for Crusoe* is cited by Mireille Sacotte (1991, 199–209).

The Goatskin Parasol

It is in the grey smell of dust under the attic closet. It is under a three-legged table; between a cat's sandbox and a keg without hoops filled with feathers.

L'Arc

Devant les sifflements de l'âtre, transi sous ta houppelande à fleurs, tu regardes onduler les nageoires douces de la flamme. – Mais un craquement fissure l'ombre chantante: c'est ton arc, à son clou, qui éclate. Et il s'ouvre tout au long de sa fibre secrète, comme la gousse morte aux mains de l'arbre guerrier.

(Ibid., 67)

The Bow

In front of the crackling fireplace, chilly in your flowery jacket, you watch the blazing supple fins of flame. But a sharp snap breaks the shadowy dance: your bow, hanging from a nail, has cracked. It has snapped along the entire length of its secret fibre like a dry husk in the grip of a battling tree.

La graine

Dans un pot tu l'as enfouie, la graine pourpre demeurée à ton habit de chèvre.
Elle n'a point germé.

(Ibid., 68)

The Seed

You buried it in a pot, the purple seed that got stuck in the goat hairs of your coat.
It didn't germinate.

These three things are back in England with Robinson Crusoe, and with the change of location all have lost something of their significance, they are now unnecessary: the bow has cracked, the seed has failed to germinate, the parasol lies thrown aside. Yet this does not fully do justice to the situation described by the poems. The things are still at hand, their relationship with Crusoe has loosened, and their status as necessities has turned into their mere presence in the same location. The things exist alongside Crusoe, but theirs is no longer the intimacy of a life in need, as with Eich, nor luxuriating ownership. The objects are now stuck within their own timeline and storyline. In fact, each of them tells a slightly different story about the change: the parasol lies discarded in dust and darkness; the seed fails to germinate in non-native soil; and the bow is cracked by being too near to the fire. The change of horizon reveals the otherness of the lives of things, which had only briefly crossed paths with one human life. This stands out clearly by comparison with the poems "Friday" and "The Parrot," which provide a certain parallel to the three poems about things. For both of these beings, civilization means depravity and sickliness: Friday turns into a conniving and gluttonous servant; the parrot is ailing. Both their fates are those of the living, whereas the three objects take us out of the realms of human stories.

Elizabeth Bishop wrote the poem "Crusoe in England" in 1971. Her long poem takes the form of a dramatic monologue, in which the protagonist first recalls and thinks about his island. In the final part, her motifs are close to Saint-John Perse's *Pictures for Crusoe*: the transformation of things after their relocation to England and Friday's death from the measles. Bishop's personification of things is more explicit and far more blatant than that of Saint-John Perse, who achieves it by, for instance, discreetly placing a bow in Robinson's new vicinity. The difference allows for a different way of speaking: the second-person form of address by Saint-John Perse creates the effect of a certain epic distance and allows us to view Crusoe and his things from an external perspective; while the first-person form by Bishop is much more subjective – Crusoe speaks of his separation from his knife as if it were a living being.

> Now I live here, another island,
> surrounded by uninteresting lumber.
> [...]
> The knife there on the shelf –
> it reeked of meaning, like a crucifix.

It lived. How many years did I
beg it, implore it, not to break?
I knew each nick and scratch by heart,
the bluish blade, the broken tip,
the lines of wood-grain on the handle...
Now it won't look at me at all.
The living soul has dribbled away.
My eyes rest on it and pass on.

The local museum's asked me to
leave everything to them:
the flute, the knife, the shrivelled shoes,
my shedding goatskin trousers
(moths have got in the fur),
the parasol that took me such a time
remembering the way the ribs should go.
It still will work but, folded up,
looks like a plucked and skinny fowl.
How can anyone want such things?
– And Friday, my dear Friday, died of measles
seventeen years ago come March.

(Bishop 1983, 166)

V.

Hannah Arendt in her book *The Human Condition* ascribes to things the role of providing stability in human life:

> [...] the things of the world have the function of stabilizing human life, and their objectivity lies in the fact that – in contradiction to the Heraclitean saying that the same man can never enter the same stream – men, their ever-changing nature notwithstanding, can retrieve their sameness, that is, their identity, by being related to the same chair and the same table.

(Arendt 1998, 137; see Brown 2015, 155ff.)

Covertly underlying her take on things is the assumption that the world's horizon is to some extent unchanging. We could indeed read Weiner's or Eich's poem through the eyes of Hannah Arendt, but the island poems of Saint-John Perse and Elizabeth Bishop point out how the entire relationship between man and things is determined by the given horizon; how a change in that contextual setting fundamentally alters the relationship, so that things provide stability only at first glance – and are in fact only a counterparty, as dependent on the setting or situation as man. It is precisely when the horizon changes and becomes apparent that we can say more about our relationship to things.

In the case of Weiner, we can speak of a voluntary horizon that cuts off the rest of the world; with Eich, a horizon imposed by the extreme situation of being deprived; and as for Saint-John Perse and Elizabeth Bishop, a horizon of recent change, which has subverted the relationship with things. The lyrical perspective of the poems rather takes the things out of the domain of practical relationships: Eich, for example, does not say that he is obliged to sleep on cardboard, but that there is cardboard between him and the ground; Crusoe's bow in Saint-John Perse's poem cracks, as though it were embarking on another life story; and in Bishop's poem, the knife turns away from Crusoe as if offended. In their lyrical departure from the plot, things seem to have something in common with man. The exception is Weiner's poem, in which, on the contrary, things are reduced to mere human property as much as they can be. The difference lies in how the poem manages (or at least tries) to keep out the wider horizon of the world, which in other cases remains hidden, but is present within the things: in Eich's case, in their fragmentary glimpses of a world beyond the camp boundary; in the Crusoe poems, harking back to another place, where things seemed different. While the characters in the poems are largely trapped within their given horizon, their reader may, by contrast, see both the perspective of the characters and how the situation is set in the wider scheme of the world and the inner horizon's boundaries. Weiner's poem is a good counterexample here: for Chardin, the whole world comes down to one particular interior. In contrast with the wider horizon and compared to Weiner's other poems of the time, this situation seems desirous of blocking out the exterior world, which is a source of unforeseen events prone to upset the self-chosen image of the speaking character. The horizon of the secluded space is supposed to merge with the horizon of the outside world: while Weiner's "Chardin" postulates such merging, the reader of the poem has the opportunity to see it as wishful thinking, not a reality. The purely proprietary relationship to things does not then seem objective or realistic compared to those of the other four poets, but, indeed, as lacking the very aspect that makes things exist in their own right.

Bill Brown in his landmark work *Other Things* follows on from Heidegger and develops the distinction between an object and a thing into a complex dynamic relationship (Brown 2015, 17–43). The island poems can serve as a good example of how a familiar and graspable *object* suddenly reveals its *thingness*, once it enters a new situation. While in one unchanging setting or horizon things may seem subservient to human consideration, complete with providing support and stability, a change of horizon brings the ungraspability and intangibility of a thing to the fore. The anthropomorphizing of things in an enclosed space is not merely a projection of human qualities into them, but is given by the simultaneous presence of the man and the things, set by their bounded horizon. It could be said that the life of things is inherently about their moving from one horizon to another: from a human standpoint, their life is fragmentary and inconspicuous, at times also unexpected and unpredictable. [12]

12   This work was supported by the European Regional Development Fund project "Creativity and Adaptability as Conditions of the Success of Europe in an Interrelated World" (reg. no.: C Z.02.1.01/0.0/0.0/16_019/0000734).

The Brazenness of Things in Czech Surrealism of the 1960s

JAROMÍR TYPLT

Is it not in the nature of every thing that it eventually gets out of hand? Isn't that its very definition, after all? A thing is what gets out of hand?

> Teprve naposledy, někde na konci parku, spíš u rozvalin než u zdi, kam odváželi shrabané listí, byla nepopsatelná hromada (*kompost, slatina, nakupenina...*), překonávající veškerá má očekávání, zejména mou jedinou zkušenost s železnými hráběmi...: rozpadly se, jakmile jsem je vzal do rukou, takže jsem vzápětí byl nucen vzít nové hrábě a staré jimi shrabat.
>
> (Dvorský 2006, 94)

> Only at long last, somewhere at the end of the park, by what was more a ruin than a wall, where they take the raked-up leaves, was an indescribable pile (*compost, mire, heap...*), beyond all my expectations, especially beyond my sole acquaintance with an iron rake...: which fell apart as soon as I took hold of it, so I then had to grab a new rake and with it scrape up the old one.

It seems like there is no time for a longer pause, to look or wonder at what actually happened. The speaker of this disclosure in the poetic prose of Stanislav Dvorský, the "ventriloquist" – although the name "Zpěv břichomluvce" (The Song of the Ventriloquist; 1963–1964), which is a text included in the larger cycle *Hra na Ohradu* (The Corral Game), should of course not be taken quite literally – perfectly fulfils his sadly comic role. It would seem he just shrugged his shoulders at the rust-crumbled rake, and then stoically dealt with how the whole situation had conspired against him: he "then had to grab a new rake and with it scrape up the old one." Quite clearly, this was no showcase for his ingenuity or wit. The new rake was inevitably to hand, he only had to reach for it and grab it. And we can really suspect some intent in this, a "forced move," a pre-prepared connection between the two events, as if the two things had long made a deal, contrived together to set him up.

While on the one hand we see something akin to resignation in the face of futility, on the other we see a hint of a conspiracy of sorts. The rake continues to serve, seemingly, but its service is very ambivalent, suspicious, and unpredictable. Maybe it is just a game, one of thinly veiled ridicule. Everything supports the impression that the man is being led along like a puppet, through his habitual tasks, an artifice to prolong his obliviousness, so it takes him a little while longer to grasp his true situation: that he is only being kept under the impression that he controls things and has the upper hand over them.

Yet even he cannot escape the fact that things are becoming increasingly brazen towards him. Likewise, as is the case with the kind of psychological displays we usually associate with a teenager's growing independence, we find things brazenly defiant, in an unexpected burgeoning of self-assertion. This surprises us most when it comes to, say, work tools that have long been overlooked and meekly subordinate.

> Věc se dá složit. Věc se dá sestavit, věc se dá zpřítomnit, věc se dá znevěcnit, znevlastnit, zmnožit. Všechno buď stojí, či leží, či strojí se.
>
> (Nápravník 1995, 121)

> A thing can be put together. A thing can be assembled, a thing can be made present, a thing can be deobjectified, disowned, multiplied. Everything is either standing or lying, or posturing.

The speaker in Milan Nápravník's poetic prose "Příšeří" (Owl Light; 1965) – from his cycle *Obestín*, whose title speaks of "encircling shadow" – seems to be hammering the thoughts into his own head through short, rhythmic sentences. Taking on board the entirety of his declamation, it dawns on us that he is only trying to reassure himself in his own wishful thinking – for we observe him literally buried under the clutter of countless things, which he is ceaselessly

dragging from place to place for no quite fathomable reason, cluelessly strug-
gling even to name them correctly:

> Co jsem měl na mysli? Plaze se chodbami, stále se setkávám s novými
> nesmysly. Na co ta zrcadla? Cvoky a žebříky? Na co ta vajíčka, sklíčka
> a knedlíky? Na co ty odnože? Na co ti mravenci? Na co ty zástupy
> krémových kredencí? Chápu, že tápu. Tápání, myslím, je podmínkou
> chápání: tápu-li, chápu.
>
> (Ibid., 119)

> What was I thinking of? Crawling through the hallways, I keep
> coming across fresh nonsense. Why the mirrors? Tacks and ladders?
> What's with the eggs, the glass slides and the dumplings? What's
> with the offshoots? What's with the ants? What's with the legions of
> cream-coloured cupboards? I grasp that I am fumbling. Fumbling is,
> I think, a precondition of grasping: if I fumble, I grasp.

In the first half of the 1960s, when both Stanislav Dvorský and Milan Nápravník
were writing the cited texts, they were members of a freewheeling grouping
around the poet and theorist Vratislav Effenberger. Very simplistically, this artistic circle is often written about as the Czech Surrealist group, although between
1957 and 1967 the connection of most of the members to Surrealism was rather
loose and the circle defined itself at that time only as an open "opinion plat-
form," deliberately cryptically naming itself with the letters UDS. In addition
to the poets already mentioned, it included figures as well-known and diverse
as Mikuláš Medek, Emila Medková, Věra Linhartová, Zbyněk Havlíček, Petr
Král, Karel Šebek, and others.

But there is no denying that, in many ways, these artists kept up a nodding
acquaintance with original Surrealism as they knew it from the 1930s to the
1950s. It certainly wouldn't have occurred to them to reject "*surrealism*, which
by contrast sought to rehabilitate all kinds of junk and monstrosities [...] and
thus, fundamentally undermined people's rational attitude to things" (Brouk
1947, 121). This is, incidentally, a truly landmark denouncement, being the surprising statement of a former Surrealist, who back in March 1934 even had his
place among the founding members of the Surrealist Group in Czechoslovakia – the psychoanalyst Bohuslav Brouk. In 1947, when Brouk tried to establish
a whole new scientific field of the study of Things, or "Chrematology," in the

book *Lidé a věci* (People and Things), he regarded the views he had once personally identified with only as examples to avoid:

> There is not, and never has been, any other world teaching so encouraging of a foolish and pathological relationship to things, as with surrealism, whose proponents would become ecstatic when faced with, e.g., a house that one could not get into in any way, for its oddball builder had not provided it with an entrance.
>
> (Brouk 1947, 121)

According to Brouk, behind this undesirable rehabilitation of "junk and monstrosities" can readily be discerned the "surrealist objects," which the Surrealists, especially of the 1930s, liked to such an extent that they even sorted them meticulously into a range of categories: objects that were dreamy, moving, mute; spectral objects, found objects, even hypnotic objects, and so on. And Brouk's Prague friends did not lag far behind their French paradigms. The poet Vítězslav Nezval said it was his "interest in attractive, intrusive random objects, called surrealist objects" (Nezval 1937, 199) that brought him to the poetic images of his first Surrealist collection, *Žena v množném čísle* (Woman in the Plural; 1936). After all, it was indeed as though André Breton himself had symbolically drawn the attention of his Czech friends in this direction when in Prague during his much-commemorated visit of 1935 he gave a talk on "The Surreal Situation of the Object – The Situation of the Surrealist Object."

The "junk and monstrosities" that were to fill the texts of writers from the UDS circle in the 1960s were no longer to bring any sense of "surreal" unusualness or of being astounding: these things were to be predominantly unattractive rather than appealing, obdurately insistent rather than inspiringly random, altogether obstructive rather than enthralling. Instead of wondrously grouped items, there were to be only "bundles of dried laundry," "mutually indistinguishable logs," "blemished potatoes," "long-since weathered mortar," and countless other similar things, mentioned here just for example and more or less at random from the poems of Vratislav Effenberger (2007, 487, 456, 471, 516).

> The perceived crisis of life's core values had seemingly turned creative work into a new examination of the most elementary certainties: texts, images, photographs and scenic projects were invaded by everyday life at its most overwhelmingly banal and drastic, more

disturbing than the anarchistically angry metamorphosis that had lost its subversive function in a world without order.

(Král 1969, 115)

Thus wrote Petr Král aptly in one of the accompanying texts in the anthology *Surrealistické východisko* (Surrealist Stance). Instead of a far-sighted view into the distance, the entire aspiration of poetry had suddenly become just – once again citing Effenberger – "vidět až za hrnec a zase zpátky" ("to see past the cooking pot and back again", Effenberger 2007, 515).

But why were everyday, ordinary things to play such a vital role?

In one of his theoretical texts, published also in *Surrealist Stance* and entitled "Na pozadí světa, který nevoní" (Against the Backdrop of an Unfragrant World) – itself a clear allusion to Karel Teige's poetistic manifesto – the poet Stanislav Dvorský made his point. After analysing classical Surrealist found objects (*l'objet trouvé*), he wrote about the "current found and captured fragments of true absurdity," in which "consciousness recognizes its epoch-conditioned limit state, the range and extent of its not only likely, but in certain areas of life already present degeneracy" (Dvorský 1969b, 133).

Jindřich Heisler, Rake, 1943, object only extant in the photograph

For such an object, not only is "the fact of its discovery itself no longer deci-sive," but "there is also very little to marvel at" in it. Dvorský certainly did not make this comment as a mere marginal remark in his text.

> It would be fitting to speak only in terms of some choice examples of a characteristic failure of judgement, of the sense of reality and an ele-mentary, pathos-free level of human dignity; yet there are countless many of them these days.
>
> (Ibid., 134)

Thus, Czech poets inspired by Surrealism stopped setting store by poetically exceptional manifestations of "marvellous," only to keep up their attacks on the main enemy against which André Breton had directed Surrealism from the very first manifestos – the "civilized" levelling and circumscribing of the mysterious unpredictability of our lives, in favour of simple predictability, reliability, and usability.

Things continue to have their reason to "fail" and break out of the confines of their original purpose and the regimentation of practical purpose itself. But the strategy is different now.

By way of a good example, we can compare the ventriloquist's "sole acquaint-ance with an iron rake," as described in Dvorský's poetic prose of 1963–1964, with the principle on which the poet Jindřich Heisler based his creation of the surreal object *Hrábě* (Rake) in 1943. Instead of the original six wooden pegs, Heisler placed six lit candles on the rake. In this, we immediately recognize that sudden, immedi-ately obvious, and henceforth unforgettable imaginative "leap" with which Surre-alism is most often associated in the public mind, thanks to the works of Man Ray, Salvador Dalí, and others. Although the poet has reached for a tool so ordinary and inconspicuous, his transformation of the rake undoubtedly belongs to the world of the surrealist "marvellous." Here we have an object intended to enlighten us in a special way, undeniably created for a moment of wonder or fascination.

At the same time, such a transformation irretrievably strips things of their former trustworthiness. The very element of their change tends to be the most telling warning against any attempt to reuse them as would have been custom-ary. Picking up the crustaceous earpiece of Salvador Dalí's *Téléphone-Homard* (Lobster Telephone; 1936), one must be constantly, at least subconsciously, wary of the residual risk that the creature might suddenly begin to move. If we were to deploy Man Ray's iron (*Cadeau* [Gift]; 1921) to laundry, we would be tearing it up with a row of sharp nails. Heisler's rake, with its six silently blazing candles, is "injudiciously" surrounded by dry hay, as seen in the notorious photograph of the object. So there is a lurking threat here – the foreshadowing of a rebellion, and necessarily so, since, after all, according to the Surrealists, "marvellousness" should always act to subvert and undermine the established order.

And where else but in this hidden threat should we see the seed of that unexpected obdurate defiance of things we noted at the beginning of these thoughts? That brazenness, whose main weapon is the more or less open scorn for someone until recently in charge, but now taken aback by their own helplessness?

But the transition to brazenness also brings another way to subvert and disturb: defiance need not be particularly conspicuous – often the way things are, as we know them, will suffice. Dvorský's iron rake is just an ordinary iron rake. Compared to Heisler's rake, it also seems to have a much more modest, pedestrian role to play. It is there to make the ventriloquist try "matter-of-factly" to deal with its disintegration, and then to go on to do something that seems both reasonable and utterly absurd. He is there to experience "failure of judgement, of the sense of reality," to cite Dvorský's theoretical tenet.

More importantly – and this aspect of these motifs is one we have been thus far quietly avoiding – is the fact that in the whole paragraph of "The Song of the Ventriloquist," the rake only plays a subsidiary role, as a tool to reveal to the full the staggering scale of the "indescribable pile" found by the ruins at the far end of the park. If we were to try to put the ventriloquist's thought process into simple words, we might ask: how and with what did someone manage to heap up such a huge pile, when here one can barely manage to scrape up a broken rake?

Thus, Dvorský's particular object draws attention only transiently: the thing is merely there to point us to the trail of something we cannot essentially see as far as, or give a name to, but which is at the same time all around us and uncomfortably physically close:

> mezitím už sem také vnikly různé předměty dosud jen
>   obtékané vědomím ale pro něž neexistují žádná
>   nezaměnitelná jména
> začínají páchnout nadýmat se hranatět a připomínat
>   otevřenou konzervu přeplněný popelník kořen stéblo
>   a podobně
> je to totéž jako se vzpomínkami
>
> (Dvorský 2006, 8)

in the meantime, various objects have come in here hitherto only
        passed by by consciousness for which no
        incommutable names exist
they are starting to smell bloat become rough-edged and remind
        of an open food can a brimming ashtray a root a reed
        and the like
the same as with memories

These few lines come from the poem "Několik minut ticha" (A Few Minutes of
Silence), which Stanislav Dvorský wrote in 1962 and later included at the beginning of the entire cycle *The Corral Game*. That collection not only comprises
"The Song of the Ventriloquist," but also several other texts explicitly attributed to this same character – his diaries or his dream. As a whole, *The Corral
Game* is a focused poetic exploration of an infinitely variable space, in which
not only are there "no uninterchangeable names" for individual objects, but also
no uninterchangeable shapes. Also missing here is a clear transition between
names and shapes: indeed, things seem to dissolve into words, and conversely
the text becomes a dense, seemingly substantial mass. Dvorský's words themselves often appear more substantive than that which they are to name:

hranatější a snadněji pojmenovatelné věci se stávaly pouhými
        vyvřelinami slov
netknuty prožitkem… rozpadávaly se mezi hadrové výplně
stále v plném měsíčním osvětlení
nechtělo se mi zahrávat si bezdůvodně s tím vším
        v obvyklém prostředí ani rozběhnout se znovu
        k průzorům ze tmy do peří a z peří zase do tmy
ani se mi nechtělo dotýkat čerstvé zavařeniny vyrážet proti
        poškozeným plotům vyřazovat povadlé věnce stáhnout se
        zpět do studeného „sklepa" kde bych mohl beze strachu
        zvukomalebně mlátit do tmy
stále rychlejší tlak na všechny strany se soustředěným
        dlouhodobým vymrštěním v jediném směru…

(Dvorský 2006, 11; from the poem *Vzpomínka na realitu* [Remembering Reality])

[...]
more sharp-edged and easier-to-name things were becoming mere
            porphyric outcrops of words
untouched by experience... crumbling between rag infills
still in full moonlight
I didn't want to mess with all this for no reason.
            in the ordinary setting nor to take a fresh run
            to the visors of darkness into the feathers and from the
                                    feathers again into darkness
nor did I want to touch the freshly made preserves nor rail against
            damaged fences to discard withered wreaths to withdraw
            back to the cold "cellar" where I could without fear
            onomatopoeically thrash at the darkness
an ever-growing pressure in all directions with a focused
            prolonged out-fling in one direction...

Dvorský in *The Corral Game* quite deliberately exaggerates the attempt to describe as precisely as possible a range of relationships and characteristics, such as "palpability," "stratification," "trellising," and the like, as well as the greatest diversity of smells and odours, sounds, motions, and processes. The result of all this "phenomenological" thoroughness, all the constant naming and renaming, regrouping, repetition, and refinement, is naturally that the reader very quickly loses track and begins to get lost in the text. Yet, in this way and with extraordinary persuasiveness, Dvorský evokes the feeling he seeks most: that of a confused fumbling, a groping around.

We saw this already with Milan Nápravník: "I grasp that I am fumbling. Fumbling is, I think, a precondition of grasping: if I fumble, I grasp." And it seems apt to add: every now and then I hit upon something, I grapple with something, I have to constantly touch, relocate, or look for something. Hitting upon things gives such fumbling a rhythm, it represents a fundamental event that – typically only for a moment – promises some kind of a break point in the plot, or at least some minor change. This has been true for the poetics of Milan Nápravník since his first texts in *Kniha Moták* (The Reel Book), which are dated to 1957. Here, the reader becomes a participant in a kind of laboratory observation, in which the "experimental subject" compulsively performs what seem to be completely self-serving activities, and pointlessly wanders about either in a closed circle, or to and from nowhere in particular. Going round in circles – "reeling" – lends itself as one way to understanding the title of *The Reel Book*, including other derivative meanings of "moták": such as the derogatory term for a confused bungler who constantly just "tangles things up," complicating matters; or the rebuke that someone is just needlessly "getting in the way" of others, reeling along, obstructing and delaying.

Of course, this "tangle" is also reflected in the treatment of things and very far removed from any truly expedient utilization or arrangement of them.

> Příkladně: zuji si botu a zatloukám, zatloukám hřebík. Zatloukám kladivem. Jsem se svým pohybem vedoucím kladivo, zatloukám, odbíhám, peru se s předivem. Vlastnost, která mě před jistým časem a před jistým otřesem, škubání masem. [...] Třeba se zakuklím. Třeba se zadusím. Není to nemožné. Během let (snad bych to neměl tak říkat) v některých dnech dýchat už ani nemusím. Nevadí. Bota mě vrací k mým věcem. Hřebík mě mučí a den je tak pestřejší, stává se členitý zrnitý, teplejší. Zuji si, například, zuji si botu a zatloukám hřebík.
>
> (Nápravník 1995, 112–13)

> For instance: I take off my shoe and I hammer, I hammer a nail. I beat with a hammer. I lead with my motion the hammer, I beat, I digress, I take issue with tissue. A trait, that had me some while back and before that once shock, the meat jerking [...]. Maybe I'm due to pupate. Maybe I will suffocate. It can't be ruled out. Over the years (perhaps I shouldn't say it that way) some days I don't even care to breathe anymore. Never mind. The shoe brings me back to my things. The nail tortures me, and so makes the day chequered, more jagged, grained rugged, and warmer. I take off, for example, I take off my shoe and I hammer a nail.

This is just a short excerpt from the text "Přítmí" (Gloom),[1] and the reader is at once on the receiving end of all that insistent, agonizing intractability that

---

1   Translator's note: his *Obestín* cycle has three near-synonymous sections – *Přítmí*, *Příšeří*, and *Přísvit* – which are different expressions for and moods of twilight or half-light: such as gloom, owl light, and pallid light.

Nápravník so hews out of his texts. Whatever direction the speaker's thoughts take, wherever they are headed, it always comes back to a shoe and a nail, or even a hammer. The words themselves are digging in, stabbing: the urgency of things here is not derived from their detailed description, but rather from their being named, simply and repeatedly. The rhythm of short, mostly dactylic phrases produces a sort of jerky effect, a straitjacket constricting all the options, what to think about and what to do. It reaffirms an inability to act and a clue-lessness. Things keep on growing to increasingly monstrous proportions and we cannot be rid of them, nor can they be dealt with.

Both Nápravník and Dvorský focus in different ways on states of conscious-ness which seems to be bogged down and blinded by precisely what it had so excessively focused on. This may, rightly, remind us of the soliloquies of char-acters written by Samuel Beckett, incidentally an author avidly translated and followed in 1960s' Czechoslovakia.

We can find another analogy to these poets' way of writing in the fine art of the time, especially in the Informel movement that influenced the painters of the UDS circle, Mikuláš Medek and Josef Istler, as well as the photographer Alois Nožička. "Unbelievable remnants of reality: indescribable hills of paper bags, tangled wires, straw-glazed windows, flowers out of snow-soaked news-papers, mud-covered branches" (Dvorský 1969a, 87): when Stanislav Dvorský in *Surrealist Stance* picked out seemingly at random some of the things that a viewer might notice in Nožička's photographs, it was as though he were reflect-ing those "various objects hitherto only passed by by consciousness" from his own *Corral Game*. But also from the texts of Milan Nápravník: "Jakési krámy a hadry a plechovky, jakési pružiny ze staré pohovky" ("All sorts of junk and rags and cans, some kind of springs from an old sofa"; Nápravník 1995, 120). It is with these words that the speaker of "Owl Light" pores over the junk clut-tering up everything around him: "Cupance provázků, otoky, svraskliny, nez-bednost bedny, retnaté sousto, vrtkavá cívečka, oprasky, jedny" ("Lint clumps of strings, bloats, scabs, a crate's uncratefulness, a lippy gobbet, a fickle bobbin, sloughings, singulariness"; ibid., 120–21).

Although Dvorský and Nápravník never clearly specified the stage on which their texts are set, for good reasons, and instead tried to beguile their readers about its precise nature, we undoubtedly find them leading us into overgrown gardens, the remote corners of rubbish dumps, landfills, or weedpiles. This is precisely where Alois Nožička went for his photo shoots, "that leave us lost

Alois Nožička, from the series Complementary Testimonies, 1960s.

for words and feeling as though we are about to let loose a guffaw of cathartic laughter" (Dvorský 1969a, 87).

Pretty much in no other instance are things so brazenly in defiance of us as when they are demonstrating their demise or the undesirability of further life – there, when they are just lying around, obstructing, falling apart, rusting, rotting away, and turning to dust. Perhaps that is when they are fulfilling their main purpose – by being so earthy, material, "ignoble" as to keep a person "rooted" and almost mischievously prevented from easy elation or feeling aloof.

So should we agree with the theorist Jindřich Chalupecký that this is why art should take an interest in things – for being "unquestionably, defiantly unbeknown, for their irreducible immediacy, so capable of confirming and reaffirming the tangible reality of the subject's own life" (Chalupecký 2000, 85)?

It may seem strange that, at the end of reflections on Czech Surrealism of the 1960s, we suddenly voice sentences from the early 1940s which had been formative for a completely different circle – Group 42. There is certainly no room for us here to focus in more detail on the role of things in the poetry of Jiří Kolář, Josef Kainar, Jiřina Hauková, Ivan Blatný or Jan Hanč, not to mention the paintings of František Hudeček, František Gross and other members of this group. Nor does it make sense to collate literary-historical arguments proving that poets from the UDS circle were sensitive to a certain trait in the poetry of those from Group 42 – as indeed Petr Král or Stanislav Dvorský have expressly confirmed more than once.

However, let us recall some fundamental characteristics of things, namely the definition of things that, according to Chalupecký's essay *Svět, v němž žijeme* (The World in Which We Live), deserve the attention of modern art: "things hard, evil, mysterious, relentlessly assertive with their impenetrable firmness unyielding to the painful skin of a living organism, all the 'air, rocks, coal, iron' hungered after in Rimbaud's famed line" (ibid. 85). Only in this way, claims Chalupecký, can art grasp the stuff of objects – "things. *These* things" (his italics) – "things living, evident, extant, singular," and not merely "deadened, standardized, the typecast products of an abstracting memory." Let us not overlook that this increased attention to things was for Group 42 inherently connected with their previous take on things as Surrealist objects. Chalupecký refers explicitly in the cited text to how a dream works, "*situating* precisely those things of our everyday experience, heedless of whatever rational and aesthetic qualities we may have chosen to attribute to them or deny them." He seems to be just continuing his reflections from the 1930s, when, as a theorist, he tried to create his form of "Superrealism," as an independent alternative to the theory and practice of the Surrealist Group around Vítězslav Nezval.

Bohuslav Brouk accused Surrealism of clinging to "junk and monstrosities." Thus, would it not be appropriate to follow the whole intricate story of Czech Surrealism from this point of view, with an emphasis on how the role of things underwent change? The story of all these attempts for its revival or, on the contrary, for it to be surpassed or quietly developed into a completely different form? After all, there is some indication of a shift in the atmosphere between the 1940s and 1960s, when "things hard, evil, mysterious" started to become blatantly brazen to boot.

The Thing in Modern Lithuanian Poetry: From Social Imprint to Metaphor of Subjectivity

DALIA SATKAUSKYTĖ

Introductory Remarks: The Historical Context

In the Grand Duchy of Lithuania, material or visual poems – known as *poesis artificiosa* or *curiosa* – were already being published as early as in the sixteenth and seventeenth centuries (Patiejūnienė 1992, 72–103; Patiejūnienė 1998). However, the Renaissance and baroque poetry that was written mainly in Latin, and played with the poem's graphical form and language (including texts that closely resemble the modern graphical experiments), has been long forgotten and did not influence later Lithuanian poetry. The modern Lithuanian state (1918–1940) took the heritage of the Great Duchy of Lithuania selectively, using the idea of it as a large and powerful state to justify its sovereignty, but remaining silent about its multinational character. Lithuanian literature created in other languages was hardly known (except for the works of those who identified themselves with the historical Lithuania, such as Adam Mickiewicz[1]). For

---

1   The idea of unity between the nation, the state, and language was common for national revival of the late nineteenth century, and in this case Lithuania was no exception. There is, however, another reason why this type of baroque literature was forgotten in more than just Lithuanian poetry: ever since the times of Romanticism, Western poetry was directed at freedom of

this and many other reasons,[2] two types of poetry were established in Lithuania. The first type was the romantic poetry, with the subject's feelings or
so-called inner world serving as the structural dominant. The second type was
poetry of the mythological avant-garde, which proposed a new model of the
world as a multidimensional space and time, while using modern, experimental
forms. This type of avant-garde poetry flourished in the times of Soviet occupation and was used as the strategy of the so-called Aesopian language – an
indirect critique of the communist regime.

The thing already appeared as an important part of poetic space in the poetry
of the group Keturi vėjai (The Four Winds[3]) – the first Lithuanian avant-garde
movement. Kazys Binkis (1893–1942), the leader of the group, expressed the
need to reject the conception of romantic poetry and treat a word as a thing –
"Imame žodį ir koja, kaip futbolą, / Sviedžiame kur į dangaus pašalį" ("We
take the word and with a kick, like football / Toss it somewhere at sky's edge";
Binkis, 79). In spite of this aim, in the poems of Binkis and his comrades, the
thing still functions not so much as an object, but as a means of polemics with
romanticism, or an indicator of technical progress, dynamism of life or rude
non-romantic countryside. It represents the tension between the heritage of an
agrarian mentality and a longing for modernization in the interwar Lithuanian
Republic. Nevertheless, the keturvėjininkai, or at least some poets of this avant-
garde group[4], could be considered as the very beginners of the "thing poetics,"
which, from time to time, intervened in the two main paradigms of poetry. The
aim of this essay is to discuss these "interventions" and to analyse in more detail
the means of representing things in Lithuanian poetry.

---

creativity and originality, while *poesis artificiosa* was created according to specific rules, even if
it was based on the principles of play and concept representation (Patiejūnienė 1992, 73–74).

2   I can only mention a few of them: poorly developed city culture, poetry of national romanticism – first of all, that of Maironis (1862–1932) – late development of the high style in poetry,
and the following fifty-year-long Soviet occupation that forced literature to take on also the
function of political discourse.

3   This grouping of avant-garde writers was named after the literary almanac it was publishing
(*Keturi vėjai*, 1924–1928).

4   The poem "Plakatas" (The Poster) by one of The Four Winds, Antanas Rimvydis – published
in the collection of poems *Knyga be vardo* (Book Without a Name) in 1926 – can be considered
one of the first examples of concrete or visual poetry in Lithuanian literature. The poem was
written as an announcement for the cinema of that time (Rimvydis 1926, 29).

The Thing in Poetry: Testifying

A discussion about things or materiality in Lithuanian poetry requires distinguishing between several groups of "thing poetry" authors. The first group did not aim for a revolution in poetic language as radical as the one sought by the so-called creators of objective or visual poetry. However, the poets in this group still broke away from the romantic and neo-romantic lyricism tradition that prevailed in the Lithuanian literature of the twentieth century. Conditionally, they can be called "realists" – poets that refused to turn the environment and its objects into the equivalents of the human inner world, but instead sought to testify to reality, with objects as its main element, refreshing the language by making it more specific. One of the first such reformers of Lithuanian poetry was a famous documentary filmmaker and a member of the Fluxus movement, Jonas Mekas (1922–2019). "I wanted to write about Semeniškiai[5]. Not poetically – materially. I was thinking about materiality, material poetry," writes Mekas, in one of his poetry editions titled *Post scriptum* (Mekas 1997, 9).

Czesław Miłosz, who sees the origins of the avant-garde filmmaker Mekas in *Semeniškių idilės* (The Idylls of Semeniškiai), written in 1948, also calls him a poet of things:

> His sensitivity to unrepeatable light, color, scents of his native region, in the north of Lithuania, as shown in Idylls, is that of a visionary who lifts his most earthly details of reality to a higher level of intensity: this explains why he is both a poet and a poet of things observed and preserved on the *film reel*.
>
> (Mekas 1996, iv)

Instead of talking about nostalgia, as many Lithuanian expatriate poets did, Mekas talks about lost things, as if a film camera monitored the functioning of those things in a peasant's life rituals in the rhythm of the seasons (*Metai* [The Seasons], by the eighteenth-century Lithuanian poet Kristijonas Donelaitis (1714–1780) functions as a structural model for Mekas' *Idylls*). Mekas does not consider the organic and the material world as opposites, as postulated by

---

5   Semeniškiai in northern Lithuania was Mekas' birthplace.

objective poetry *stricto sensu*: these dimensions of the world are inseparable in his poetry as much as in the life of a peasant. Things act themselves, and they are being watched by the speaking subject and the participants of this material-organic universe, the inhabitants of Semeniškės:

> Nuo kalnelių girdite jūs girgždant svirtis
> botagų pliauškesį ir kibirų skambėjimą,
> jūs girdit mūsų vežimus nutrinksint
> pirmuoju pašalu,
> palydite vestuvininkų skambančius važius,
> svirduliuojančias į turgų uores,
> burokų vežimus ar sunkias rąstų driungas,
> bliaunančius galvijų katukus.
> Ir kai šiltais vidurvasariais
> po jūsų kvepiančiais kamienais,
> ant žaliai įsamanojusių, minkštų kalvų
> sklinda linksmas gegužinių klyksmas,
> mirguliuoja moterų kasnykai
> ir ritmiškai ūbuoja būgnas –
> jūs ošiat, lieknos moterys.
>
> (Mekas 1997, 24, "Ketvirtoji idilė")

> From the hillocks you can hear creaking sweep wells,
> whip-flails and swinging pails.
> You'll hear our wagons clatter
> across the first ground frost,
> follow bridal buggies ringing in the distance,
> tall, reeling market-bound rigs,
> beetloads, solid timber hauls,
> the heifers in drove, bawling.
> Maytimes, once summer turns the moss-soft swells
> warm among your fragrant pinetrunks
> to set off some happy partying screeches,
> flashing ribbons and braids
> to the stunning beat from a drum,
> you'll whoosh, slender women of the sand hills.
>
> (Mekas 1996, 13–14; "Fourth Idyll", trans. Vytautas Bakaitis)

This triple structure creates a document-like effect – the poet stops the things and people in motion, tearing them out of oblivion. The poem says transcendence is here, in the farmer's world, and a part of it is the thing.

Nearly a decade after the first publication of *The Idylls of Semeniškiai*, Mekas himself proposed the following interpretation of materiality and realism:

> These are my brothers that sing sadly in the horizon of the fields, these, my sisters, are my brothers singing sadly.
> And I – the smallest of them, am bowing before them, bowing before Semeniškiai. Although, with my words, my small and simple book, I would like to recall them, celebrate them, so that I would never forget them.
> Because to me, they are as saints.
>
> (Mekas 1997, 12; *Post scriptum*)

In *Jono Meko žodis* [*The Word of Jonas Mekas*], published in 1957, the poet states that his poetry of reality has nothing to do with the optimistic Socialist Realism that Soviet functionaries were at that time actively spreading in the occupied Lithuania. According to him, realism is a testament to the common peasant's hard everyday life, in nature and among things:

> And my literate friends from Lithuania write me: "Your idylls lack socialist realism. [...] [A]nd it is all the same for my Semeniškiai [...]. Their blood is what socialist realism is, their simple foods, simple doings, and simple speech, and simple works. It is not socialist realism to sing about a plough or a tractor, in the same rhymes, and then to heat up in Palanga. The life of Semeniškės is a rough kolkhoz life, and their songs are rough and inelegant. You cannot remove them from the land, nor the wind, nor the manure trucks.[6]
>
> (Mekas 1997, 11–12; *Post scriptum*)

6   In this speech, Mekas is not only discussing Socialist Realism, but also the cultural heritage of interwar Lithuania (known as "Smetona's" Lithuania – after the president of the era).

Remembering that Socialist Realism was a utopian romanticism or sentimentalism, as Mekas ironically puts it, disguised as a realistic image, we can consider that such a poetry of things acquires a political significance.

Material concreteness acquires a similar political significance in the works of some Soviet Lithuanian poets. I would like to mention two of them: Albinas Žukauskas (1912–1987) and Vladas Šimkus (1936–2004).

Albinas Žukauskas started his career in pre-war Vilnius and had connections with Czesław Miłosz and the Polish avant-garde group *Žagary*. In the 1970s and 1980s, he was developing a narrative, "prosaic" poetry as a counterweight to the pathos of Socialist Realism and the "spirituality" of romantic poetics. Archaic names of things instead of feelings (similarly to Mekas, the poetic imagination of Žukauskas comes from the peasant's everyday life), the syntax of spoken language instead of the nature–human parallelism, intense eroticism instead of shy lyrics of love – this is Žukauskas' version of material poetry that impressed the young non-Soviet modernists in the Soviet era.

One of them was Vladas Šimkus, who described his poetry as "so close to land," though this land is no longer that of peasants. There are posters with portraits of superior workers, a Soviet-era woollen work jacket (*vatinka*), a carbonated water dispenser (the so-called *gazirovka* machine), electricity wires, and railroad tracks – all of them resemble the industrial setting of a Socialist Realist novel. For Šimkus, however, these are simply objects of the Soviet everyday life in which he lived, devoid of ideological content or implicitly deconstructing that content. Soviet topography sometimes turns into a critique of Soviet ideology (also with rather open satire in the poetry collection *Bitės pabėgėlės* [Refugee Bees; 1973]) because of the lyrical subject's concern with completely non-Soviet problems, such as the relationship between a man and a thing, and the possibility of the thing to represent history. All of these issues are encountered in the poem *Senienos* (Antiquities):

> Mano senienos
> kartais be sistemos:
>> keletas lapų „Iliados",
>> neaiškaus senumo saga,
>> Teisybės akiniai,
>> gilzė
> ir kiti daiktai.

(Šimkus 2009, 95)

My antiquities
do not have a system:
        a few pages of "Iliad",
        a button of undefined age,
        the eyeglasses of Truth,
        a cartridge case
and the other things.

"Protėvių gyventa gerokai padrikai" ("The ancestors lived rather sporadically"; ibid.), Šimkus concludes, and provides an interpretation of an intimate relationship with history that was quite untypical for Lithuanian poetry, which would usually take either a romantic-heroic or a mythological attitude. Considered typologically, Šimkus' poetry may be seen as intermediate between materiality as a testifier of reality and the establishment of the thing as an object in poetry or for making poetry itself more materialistic.

A Poetry of Things: Being

The second type of intervention things have made in the lyrical tradition is concrete or visual poetry. This trend became more prominent in the late 1960s, first in the literature of emigrants and soon in Soviet Lithuania. "Eilėraštis banano formoje" (Banana Form Poem; 1969) by the US-based poet Rimas Vėžys can be considered the first manifestation of the poetry of things in Lithuanian literature. He openly declared the utopian aspiration of the so-called objective literature – not expressing, but being." "[j]ei iš manęs / norite prasmės / gerai / pasiųsiu ryt / jums telegramą!" ("[I]f you want / sense from me, / all right, / I'll send you / a telegram tomorrow!") – this is how the poem ends.

    The anthology of Lithuanian material poetry *Raidžių paveikslai* (Pictures of Letters), published in 2018, presents the full spectrum of Lithuanian poetry of this kind. It contains poems with noticeable conflicts between the iconic meaning and meaning created by language, but we also find poems of utopian attempts to become a picture or a thing, an experiment with typography, a drawing, a picture of real things, collages of poems. All these experiments testify more or less to the struggle against the meaning generated by language, the effort described by Roland Barthes – to represent a thing or object as a pure

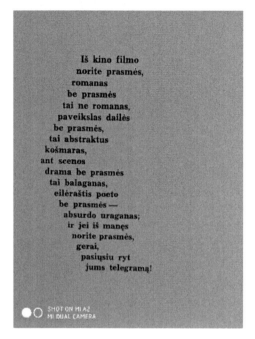

Januševičius and
Skudžinskas 2018, 20–21

phenomenon beyond which it has no substance, either psychological or social (Barthes 1964, 66). In this respect, Lithuanian poetry does not differ from the context of global objective poetry – it attempts to transform the signifier into the only one signified, or, in other words, to radicalize Roman Jakobson's principle of the "form richness" for poetry and literature in general, to reduce the usual second degree[7] signification process to a pure denotation.[8]

However, paradoxically, the most radical examples of such poetry confirm the utopian nature of the effort. Benediktas Januševičius (born 1973) – the editor of *Pictures of Letters*, author of its introductory article, and creator of Lithuanian visual poetry – considers the most radical case to be the poem "Vienatvės piešinys per Jonines" (Drawing of Loneliness at the Midsummer Night) by one of the most famous Lithuanian poets, Sigitas Geda (1943–2008):

---

7   Based on Juri Lotman's secondary modelling systems conception (Lotman 2011, 249–70).
8   Of course, some literary theorists consider such a view of the semantic mechanism in concrete poetry as a simplification, but that is a topic for a broader theoretical discussion (see Vos 1987).

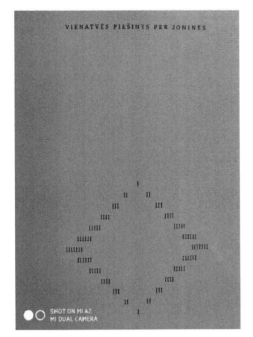

Januševičius and
Skudžinskas 2018, 73

According to Januševičius, Geda's poem marks the transition from manifests and word drawings to a poetry without text, to a visual abstraction. However, the author of the article implicitly admits that the poem is still multifaceted even if it eludes a linguistic meaning –signs that create a geometric shape rather than a thing can be considered as both vertical dashes and letters (Januševičius and Skudžinskas 2018, 18). Linguistic signification intervenes with the visual one in the title as well. On the one hand, the title opposes the abstractness of the "text" itself, since it refers to the particular state of the subject (loneliness) at a particular time (the summer solstice, or Feast of St. John). On the other hand, visual and linguistic expressions are isomorphic in at least two respects: named in the title, loneliness echoes the emptiness of the "drawing" (the geometric figure is hollow); and the drawing itself, as the name suggests, is an expression of loneliness. Thus, the poem aspiring to be an object abstraction is not only *being*, but also *meaning* that it is speaking of loneliness.[9]

---

9 Lithuanian visual poetry, of course, has some poems without titles (as well as those named "Be pavadinimo" ["Untitled"]), or with titles that indicate their graphical object – e.g., such

The other way of establishing signification beyond the object is contextual. It is prominent in Januševičius' "poems-things" ("žodžiai-daiktai"; the way the author himself defines the genre). Things are graphical representations of real paper objects that existed or exist in a certain historical context: a Vilnius public transport ticket, a Soviet design calendar leaf, a pack of Ukrainian salt, or a lottery ticket. The reader-spectator who knows the function and time of existence of those things immediately identifies them as things themselves (the author retains the font when changing the text that was on the thing), as well as a reference to a historical-social context – mostly the Soviet era and first post-Soviet decade. That is a new text, which changes the inscription on the original at least partly or completely and becomes the interpretation of context. One of the most prominent examples of such triple signification is the poem "Pasakaitė" (Fairy Tale), written on the note of a Soviet ruble:

Januševičius and
Skudžinskas 2018, 107

Januševičius rarely gives a title to his poems of things; however, he adds one on this occasion. The word "pasakaitė" (fairy tale) is inscribed in the place of the note's denomination (one ruble), and in the text below (where "one ruble" was usually written in the languages of the Soviet republics) the title is expanded with a short narrative: "[pasakaitė], kurioje kasdienybė garbina šunsnukius

---

nomination tactics are applied by one of the most prominent current poets, Gytis Norvilas (born 1976), in "Paukščio skeletas" (The Bird's Skeleton), "Maniežas [arklių ištryptas kvadratu" (Arena [Trampled in Square by Horses]), etc. However, the "psychologism" of the title, a reference to the state of the subject, is common here as for lyrical poetry.

o trečias brolis nerašo eilėraščių ir karaliumi bet išeina parsinešti ugnies" ("[fairy tale], where the everyday worships bastards, and the third brother does not write poems and does not become a king, but goes out to bring back fire")[10]. This way, the text turns the thing (a ruble note) into an ironic interpretation of the mythical narrative about the bright future of communism. On the other hand, such a poem-thing also becomes a testimony of a lost epoch, even though its signification mechanism is completely different from that employed by Mekas. This interpretation is also confirmed by an exhibition that took place in MO Museum in Vilnius – "The Origin of Species: 1990s DNA" – where Januševičius' poems-things were exhibited in photographic frames.[11]

Thing, View, Word: The Coexistence and the Conflict

These pieces of more radical avant-garde poetry were created already in the post-Soviet era. In Soviet times – the 1970s and 1980s – the so-called figure poems written in Lithuania were more moderate. They were not aimed at destroying the lyrical tradition, but rather at rebuilding it, by incorporating a modernist experiment with a representation of a thing. These poems made it rather clear that the combination of a word and an image hides the possibility of conflict between two systems of meaning, and the degree or depth of an object's representation can vary greatly. I will show this by discussing two different instances of figurative poetry.

The first one is "Atminties laivas" (Ship of Memory) by Antanas A. Jonynas (born 1953):

---

10   The story continues in the lower inscription of the ruble, where a warning about counterfeit money is placed: "nebegrįžta nei namo, nei savin" ("It does not come back, either to the inside, or itself"). There is also a remark that implies performativity: "Skaityti triukšmingoje vietoje" ("Read in a noisy place") (Januševičius and Skudžinskas 2018, 107).

11   The exhibition ran from 5 October 2019 to 23 February 2020. See more at Mo museum website: https://mo.lt/en/parodos/the-orgins-of-specias-1990s-dna/?pagen=1. As I was writing this essay, a new concrete poetry book by Januševičius – Trumpiausias Benedikto Januševičiaus eilėraštis (The shortest poem by Benediktas Januševičius, 2019) – was released, in which materiality is replaced with a visual abstraction of the concept.

O dabar
tu sakei kitados
krištoliniam laive
kuris plaukia per miegančią jūrą
aš sukaustau tave su savim atminty
ir nėra išdavystės kurios atleidimo
po virš mūsų praskriejančio paukščio sparnu
negalėčiau tikėtis
uola
sekluma
neviltis
nuolankiai grąžinu tau dienų prabėgusių miglą
nuolankiai atiduodu šnabždesius savo ir tavo
krištoliniam laive bet jo nenušviečia jau
niekas ribotoj beribėje jūroj
supas mūsų figūros deja
atmintie

(Jonynas 2017, 76)

And now
You said another time
On a crystal ship
That sails over a sleeping sea
I lock you with myself in memory
And there is no betrayal, forgiveness for which
Under the wind of a bird above us
I could not expect
Rock
Shallow
Despair
I humbly return you the fog of days passed
I humbly return you whispers of mine and yours
In a crystal ship, but it is not illuminated anymore
By anything, in the endless sea
Our figures are swinging alas
Memory

The poem is a good example of both the simultaneous representation and non-representation of a thing at the same time. Indirectly referring to Stéphane Mallarmé's "Salut" and Arthur Rimbaud's "Le Bateau ivre" (The Drunken Boat), Jonynas' poem is from a book with the same title as the quoted poem, published for the first time in 1981. "Ship of Memory" graphically represents an icon of a ship, but the ship loses its materiality within the text and openly becomes a metaphor of lost love and memory. Simply speaking, rather than the ship itself, the subject of the poem is the memory process, and the graphical form of a ship as well as the all isotopy of navigation (using a concept of Greimasian semiotics) symbolizes the process of remembering. The poem represents the ship by its graphical form, but deconstructs the representation of the ship in the text itself. The tension or conflict between representation and metaphorization starts with the title, in which the figure of the ship is used to indicate an unstable memory structure.

The visual representation of the thing seems to be similar in the poem "Pavasaris" (Spring), written in 1969 by Judita Vaičiūnaitė (1937–2002):

> Ir sukasi
> sukasi
> sukasi lakūs sparnai lėktuvų
>   malūnų
>   žuvėdrų...
>
> Ir supasi
> supasi
> supasi kiemo berniūkščiai ant purvino
>   lentgalio
>
>
>   vėtroje...

(Vaičiūnaitė 1985, 196)

> And they are spinning
> spinning
> spinning the lacquered wings of planes
>   windmills
>   seagulls...

And they are swinging
swinging
swinging the courtyard boys on the dirty

in the wind...

Usually, Vaičiūnaitė is described as a poetess of the city, in a radical opposition to agrarianism or nativism in Lithuanian poetry. This characteristic could be discussed further; however, the figures of nature, architecture, city space, and things most often intertwine in Vaičiūnaitė's poem to convey an impression. Using a graphical icon of the same type as Jonynas, Vaičiūnaitė is much closer to the thing as an object. Contrary to Jonynas' "Ship of Memory," the thing is not indicated in the title of her poem, but the poem itself attempts to represent the form and function of the wing (the wings of a windmill, an airplane, and a seagull) graphically and in textual structure, and to create the dynamic atmosphere of spring. The poem could be interpreted as an open discussion with the romantic landscape of spring, which is dominant in Lithuanian poetry, assuming the role of a "mirror" of the subject's mood.

The Experience of a Thing, or the Thing in a Word

Another type of material poem may be called the poetry of the experience of a thing. The thing does not physically appear in these types of poems; instead, it becomes the structural centre of the text, and is represented as an object of a multifaceted sensual experience (the figural poems-things are, first of all, visual objects). Described in detail, the thing indicates itself and, at the same time, something more than itself – therefore, the poem returns from "being" to "meaning," or the interplay between them. The poem "Kilimėlis ant sienos" (The Carpet on the Wall) by Kornelijus Platelis and the works of Nijolė Miliauskaitė that I will discuss below are great examples of such interplay.

Kornelijus Platelis (born 1951) is a poet of the so-called neoclassic stylistics that combine ancient versification, a narrative structure that imitates ancient Greek or Roman poetry, and the use of trivial things or situations as objects of description. He is considered to be one of the greatest masters of postmodern pastiche in Lithuanian poetry, and "The Carpet on the Wall" is a very good example of it:

Ten tyras upelis, guviai iš kalnų atskubėjęs į slėnį,
Čiurlena per akmenis ir padalina pusiau
Mieguistą gamtovaizdį, briedžių šeimyną atskirdamas
Nuo balto namelio po svyrančiom eglių šakom.

Sultinga žolė ir tylūs kalnai juosia saugiai
Miškakirčio baltą sodybą, tačiau nesimato žmogaus,
Kurs ką tik pakirdęs veikiausiai žvelgia pro langą
Į murmantį tyliai upokšnį ir geriančius briedžius iš jo.

Kaip aš kad nubudęs regiu kilimėlį ant sienos,
Todėl vieną kitą akimirką dar nesugrįžti galiu
Iš sapno jaukios vienumos, iš tylos, kurią saugo net siūlai,
Išblukę nuo saulės ir žvilgsnių mieguistų manų.

Bet darbas nelaukia – girgždėdamas pakelia saulę,
Išeis tuoj į lauką žmogus, ir briedžiai pradings kalnuose,
Į žvangančią dieną panirs sąnariai mano rambūs,
Ir senas naivus kilimėlis lig ryto ilgėsis manęs.

(Platelis 1995, 6)

The Carpet on the Wall

There is a clear stream, hurrying briskly from the hill to the valley,
Curling over rocks and dividing the sleepy landscape
Into two halves, separating the family of deer from
The small white house under drooping spruce branches.

Succulent grass and quiet hills snugly surround
The woodcutter's white homestead, but there's no sign of the man
Who has just awakened and probably looks through the window
At the quietly murmuring brook and the deer drinking there.

As I am, just waking and seeing the wall and the carpet,
That's why for a moment or two I may not return from dream's
Pleasant seclusion, from the silence that even the threads protect,
Faded from the years and from my drowsy glances.

But work will not wait – creaking it raises the sun,
The man will soon go out and the deer will vanish in the hills,
My tired joints will sink into the clamour of the day,
And the old simple carpet until morning will long for me.

(trans. Jonas Zdanys)[12]

The poem is a part of Platelis' first poetry collection, "Žodžiai ir dienos" (Words and Days; 1980), the title being an explicit play on Herodotus' poem "Works and Days." Platelis' text is without doubt ambivalent, but all its interpretations consider the figure of the old carpet to be central. According to one of them, the carpet is at the centre of the poem from the first line, but not the thing itself as much as the bucolic story, narrated in elegiac couplets. The carpet is concurrently both hidden and exposed: hidden in the narrative of the first part of the poem; and exposed in the second part, which gives at least two options for the interpretation of the bucolic narrative. The latter could be interpreted as the translation of a visual into a narrative – in other words, connecting the carpet's static images and turning them into the narrative. Otherwise, it could be interpreted as the dream which functions as an opposition to the dullness of the carpet and makes no allusion to the narrative at all.[13] Either way, this structure has an ironic tonality, formed not only by the juxtaposition of the so-called high and low styles, but also by the sociocultural context. Carpet on the wall was a typical detail of Soviet interior design. It could have been proof of belonging to the Soviet middle class, or, contrary to that, it could be a detail inherited from pre-war Lithuania. Lithuanian intellectuals – the so-called "westerners" – generally considered it to be a symptom of bad taste or simply kitsch. It is worth mentioning that the distinguishing feature of Platelis' poetry is the incorporation of kitsch elements into texts of classical poetics.

Although it is also at the centre of the textual structure, the thing functions quite differently in the poetry of Nijolė Miliauskaitė. Miliauskaitė (1950–2002). She is probably the most internationally well-known of Lithuanian poetesses, with translations of her work published in *The Vintage Book of Contemporary*

---

12   Jonas Zdanys translated this poem specially for this essay.
13   In a conversation with the author of this essay, Platelis mentioned that the carpet of the poem had a "prototype" in the home of his parents-in-law. While I was finishing the essay, he sent me a photograph of the "original" of the object – the carpet that inspired the poem. The "prototype" of the carpet implies the first interpretation to be more relevant.

World Poetry in 1996 (together with Joseph Brodsky, Czeslaw Miłosz, Derek Walcott, and others), as well as other anthologies in English, French, Spanish, Swedish, and further languages. Miliauskaitė's minimalist poetry has a reputation for complicated simplicity. She often gives a snippet of a story, a portrait, some detail of everyday life, or simply describes a thing or its material. More specifically, she describes not so much the object itself, but the subject's meeting with the thing or material, the phenomenological experience. Her poem "akis užmerkus" (Eyes Closed) narrates the "story" of seeing, touching, smelling, and disclosing sensual properties of silk, as a part of the human world:

akis užmerkus, liečiu galiukais pirštų
iš lėto, tyrinėdama

tai šilkas
bet ar galėčiau pasikliauti jutimais, kai šitiek
padirbinių pridaryta, beveik tobulai
megžiojančių, kas nepadirbama

atkerpu mažulytę skiautelę, uždegu
dega – nelabai noriai (taip ir turėtų būti)
uostau – kvapas įmestos į ugnį
plaukų sruogos (tai irgi
patvirtintų mano spėjimą)
pelenus sutrinu tarp pirštų – sausi
ir birūs, nesusilydę

tikras šilkas

vėsina per vasaros karščius, šildo
per žiemos šalčius, plonytis
o toks tvirtas
panardinti
rankas į šilką, panirti
gilyn, vis gilyn, visa oda pajusti
šviesą, šilkverpių išmintį
tirpte ištirpti

visa savo siela patirti kas tikra

(Miliauskaitė 1999, 449-450)

eyes closed, I touch it with the tips of my fingers
slowly, examining

it's silk but can I depend on my sensations when so many
imitations have been made, almost perfectly
copying that which cannot be counterfeited

I cut off a tiny scrap, light it
it burns – not very willingly (that's how it should be)
I smell it – the odour is that of skein of hair
thrown to the fire (that too
affirms my presumption)

I powder the ashes between my fingers – dry
and friable, not fused together

real silk

it cools in summer heat, warms
through winter cold, so fine
but so strong

to sink
my hands into silk, to plunge
deeper, ever deeper, to feel with my entire skin
the light, the wisdom of silkworms
to melt completely

with my whole soul experience what is real

(trans. Jonas Zdanys, Miliauskaitė 2002, 5)

In the context of Lithuanian poetry, Miliauskaitė's poems look "nude," prosaic; however, the rejection of rhetorical devices functions as minus devices or minus rhetoric. According to Yuri Lotman, "'anti-rhetorical' text, consisting of elements of direct, non-figurative semantics, comes to be perceived as a *meta-trope*" (Lotman 1990, 44). Miliauskaitė's poetry is a paradigmatic example of anti-rhetoric translated into meta-trope. The short, personal comment on the description of an object or its experience (usually at the end of the text) transforms the poem into a narrative about finding something genuine, truthful,[14] into a meta-metaphor of "the transcendence in the earth" (Kavolis 1992, 148).

The same strategy is used in the poem "mano močiutės monograma" (My Grandmother's Monogram). It transforms the poem, based on a description of a tablecloth and the story of its use, into a meta-trope of longing, pain, and the effort to understand *the other*:

mano močiutės monograma
ant lininės senoviškos staltiesės
aprėmintos pinikais

išbalintos ir iškrakmkolintos – kaip ledas
taip sakydavo mano močiutė, kai per karščius
atidarydavo kuparus, iškilodavo staltieses, užvalkalus
      (languotus, dar prosenelės, ir baltus, jau jos)
plonas ir storesnes drobes, rankšluoščius, lovatieses, paklodes ir skaras

ir kai nešdavom mes abidvi ir džiaudavom ant tvorų
kai vėdindavom kuparus! kur nuo kandžių
saugojo išdžiovinti tabako lapai, traškantys ir byrantys į miltelius

o nuo ugnies –
šv. Agotos duona, įrišta į nosinaitę...

mano močiutės monograma
išsiuvinėta kryžiuku raudonais siūlais

mažutė karūnėlė
o po ja
MD

(Miliauskaitė 1999, 168)

---

14   Jonas Zdanys translates the last word of the poem, "tikra," as "real." However, a more precise translation would be "genuine," as the poem "tells" a story of experiencing silk as a raw material.

my grandmother's monogram
on the old-fashioned linen tablecloth
hemmed with a crocheted border

bleached and starched – like ice,
my grandmother used to say, when during summer's
hottest days she would open the linen chests and lift out
tablecloths, pillowcases
(my great-grandmother's

checkered ones and her own white ones)
lighter and heavier linens, towels, bedspreads,
sheets and scarves

and when the two of us carried out
and hung them on the fences

and when we aired out the linen chests, where dried
tobacco leaves, crackling, crumbling to powder,
kept away the months
and St. Agatha's bread, wrapped in a small handkerchief,
protected against fire…

my grandmother's monogram
embroidered in a cross with red thread

a small crown
and under it
MD

(Zdanys 1995, 201)

The figures of clothing and textile are exceptional in Miliauskaitė's poetry because of their semantic potential. Things touched by the enunciator of the poem retain the touch of someone else who remains further in the distance (in the cited poem, the grandmother who has embroidered the tablecloth, the Chinese woman who has woven the silk scarf, the relatives who have lent a pincushion). As they remain the things and materials the experiences of which are described by the poem, they become meta-tropes of intersubjectivity, the places of personal story.

In Lieu of a Conclusion

Understanding the poetry of things in a broader sense than just concrete or visual poetry would place it in a rather large, although not the main, trajectory of Lithuanian poetry. Although sometimes it enters the dominant paradigm of lyrical poetry, it uses a thing or materiality as an alternative to the lyrical or romantic tradition. However, even in objective poetry, objectivity should be considered only an aim or an orientation *stricto sensu*. Poems-things (in the case of Benediktas Januševičius) extend the process of signification by including the material and historic context that surrounds the represented things, and the subject that selects those things. Iconic poetry that aims to represent the thing in its graphical structure can be considered a separate branch. However, the semantics of verbal text can either move away from representation and turn the thing into a metaphor (Antanas A. Jonynas), or move towards the thing itself (Judita Vaičiūnaitė). In a less radical case, the poet may choose the naming of things or their testimony as a witnessing of reality either lost (Jonas Mekas) or lived (Vladas Šimkus).

Paradoxically, the poetry that probably reaches closest to materiality is the one concerned with the relation between the things and the subject, rather than the things *per se*. In the works of Kornelijus Platelis, the thing is an object that can be experienced through vision, but at the same time it is a place where various cultural and historical codes intersect. The works of Nijolė Miliau-skaitė use all the senses for experiencing the thing, but the most important one is touch. The touched thing (material or cloth that retains someone's touch) becomes the place of intersection between various subjects, and the subjectiv-ity and objectivity complement rather than oppose each other.

In my understanding, such a phenomenological attitude expands the limits of representing the thing the most.

Two Ekphrastic Strategies in Russian Poetry of the Latter Twentieth Century: "Emptiness" in the Works of Andrei Monastyrski and Arkadii Dragomoshchenko

KIRILL KORCHAGIN

In the Soviet period, the unofficial literature of Moscow and St. Petersburg developed, in many ways, in parallel: despite the fact that contacts between them were relatively frequent and regular, the literature of each city took heed of its specifics, and in many cases the same cultural theme gave rise to completely different outcomes. This also applies to the topic of this chapter – how the philosophy of Zen Buddhism helped Russian poetry of the 1970s and 1980s resurrect the old genre of ekphrasis. I will try to show how St. Petersburg poet Arkadii Dragomoshchenko and Moscow poet Andrei Monastyrski arrived at completely different, almost contradictory conceptions of how ekphrasis could be used in contemporary poetry, despite their shared sources and ideas.

Ekphrasis can be understood either in a narrower or a broader sense. In the narrower sense, it is the poetic description of an art object, such as a painting or a sculpture (Spitzer 1962, 72). A classic example of such ekphrasis is the description of the shield of Achilles in the *Iliad*. A separate question remains as to whether we can encompass under the term "ekphrasis" literature that depicts architectural works or recounts a film. In the broader sense, ekphrasis can be taken to mean any description that "verbally represents a visual representation" (Heffernan 1993, 2), not necessarily a description of an artwork. The narrow conception of ekphrasis focuses on its cross-media nature – in other words, its ability to convey through one art form the characteristics of another (Wandorf 2003, 4–7); whereas the broad concept focuses on how the description of one thing or another, whether it be man-made or otherwise, influences the very structure of the text. One of the consequences of this action is the "slowing" of related action – something which has been examined in the context of ekphrasis since at least Lessing's time (Geller 2013, 45).

In Russian poetry of the second half of the twentieth century, we can find examples of both types of ekphrasis, sometimes in varied combination with one another. The most radical examples, which nevertheless stick to the "narrow" view of the genre, are texts that mimic cinematic language. Some of them reference the "cinematic" poems of Osip Mandelstam (Shindin 1991) and Michail Kuzmin (Ratgauz 1992), which were under the influence of the films of the 1900s and 1920s, as well as those based on the avant-garde almanac *Говорящее кино* (Movies Speak; 1928), which attempted to reproduce in poetry the poetics of collage clips, in the spirit of Dziga Vertov (an example of how the two strategies came together being the collection *Кинематограф* [Cinematographer; 1986] by Leningrad poet Alexander Mironov). Another example of a non-traditional handling of the genre is "Описание несуществующих картин" (Description of Non-existent Paintings) by the Leningrad poet Viktor Krivulin. Ekphrasis in the broad sense is typified by various kinds of conceptual texts from the 1980s, such as "Азбуки" (Alphabets) by Dmitry Prigov or "Карточки" (Cards) by Lev Rubinstein, in which the description of objects also has an important place. These texts are closer to the type of ekphrasis presented in world literature by, say, the text of the French writer Georges Perec, *Tentative d'épuisement d'un lieu parisien* (An Attempt at Exhausting a Place in Paris; 1982), in which all objects in front of the narrator are listed in intensive detail. In literature of this type, the principles of intermediality emblematic of the "classical" definition of ekphrasis are treated very loosely indeed.

The two poets who are the focus of this chapter take up the genre of ekphrasis in its broad sense: there are no copies of paintings, sculptures, or even architectural monuments in the works at which we will be looking. Moreover, in both cases, the subject of the description is not even definitively clear: in the case of Andrei Monastyrski, it is not directly named at all; and in the case of

Arkadii Dragomoshchenko, it acts merely as the impulse for developing a multilayered image of memories and contexts. Yet both of them make use of strategies typical of ekphrasis, to outline the subject of the poetic text and show the
delineation between the subject and the observer.[1] The works of Monastyrski
and Dragomoshchenko were chosen as the subject of our analysis because their
strategies for handling ekphrasis are, in a sense, contradictory. To use theological language, the strategy of the first can be called *apophatic*, whereas the strategy of the second can be *cataphatic*.[2]

According to Lessing, ekphrasis presumes a slowdown in time: "The details,
which the eye takes in at a glance, he [the poet] enumerates slowly one by
one" (Lessing 2005, 102). Hence, the poet also uses special means to recreate the wholeness that is lost in the process of gradual description. Ekphrasis, whether in the broad or the narrow sense, is always built on the balance
between description and vision, finding a niche between instantaneous perception and a gradually developing description. Ekphrasis is potentially able to
switch the reader's attention from the subject described to the process of observation itself, and from there to the viewer, his or her subjectivity – that is, to the
one who composes the various features of the subject matter into a new whole,
and, in the process, composes themselves.

The St. Petersburg poet Arkadii Dragomoshchenko (1946–2012) belonged
to that generation of the Soviet underground that did not seek to be included
in official Soviet literature, instead creating its own literary institutions: samizdat magazines, including *Часы* (The Clock) and *Обводный канал* (literally,
The Bypass Canal); literary associations, such as Клуб-81 (Club-81); or prizes,
for instance Премия Андрея Белого (the Andrei Bely Prize). In one way or
another, Dragomoshchenko participated in the activities of all these institutions: he published in *Часы*, was active in Club-81, and was the first laureate
and, subsequently for many years, a member of the jury of the Andrei Bely
Prize. At the same time, he stood in many ways on the periphery of St. Petersburg literature, outside the mainstream, which was represented by names such
as Viktor Krivulin and Elena Shvarts. Unlike them (and many other Leningrad
poets of this period), Dragomoshchenko did not speak of himself as following

---

1   In the present chapter, the subject is taken in the sense used in the collective work *Poezia*
     (*Poezia* [Poetry] 2016, 99–123), i.e., as the speaker's image that arises in each new poem.
2   For apophasis as regards ekphrasis, see Tokarev 2013.

in the traditions of pre-revolutionary modernism; he initially preferred to seek out his poetic comrades in twentieth-century European literature, and then, starting in the mid-1980s, in American poetry from the 1960s to the 1980s, and more recent continental philosophy. Unlike many of his Soviet contemporaries, this literature was directly available to him: in 1983, Dragomoshchenko met the American poet Lyn Hejinian, who, accompanied by her husband, the musician Larry Ochs, visited Moscow and Leningrad. This meeting grew into a long-term friendship – the poets wrote letters to one another, exchanged books, translated each other's poems – which in many ways influenced Dragomosh-chenko's poetic method. As a result of this, in his mature poetry, he approached his own poetic challenges together with his philosophical ones (Edmond 2012, 44–46). As a poet, he was interested in the issues of subjectivity, bodily phenomenology, the relationship of his own word to the other's word – all concerns that he developed from reading Maurice Merleau-Ponty, Jacques Derrida, and other thinkers.

The key text that distinguishes the "early" and "mature" Dragomoshchenko is the narrative poem "Ужин с приветливыми богами" (Dinner with Friendly Gods), printed in 1985 in the first issue of the samizdat magazine *Митин журнал* (Mitya's Magazine), and reissued in the same magazine only after another thirty years. Several poems can be understood as a declaration of a new take on ekphrasis:

> Теперь по утрам поверхность вещей
> я научился трогать руками,
> бумага, скважины букв, сталь, письмо, деепричастие,
> желудь, дети, деньги, счета, позвоночник, спектакль,
> иней, пустое.
>
> (Dragomoshchenko 2015, 15)

> Now every morning the surface of things
> I learned to touch with my hands,
> paper, letter loopholes, steel, writing, a participle,
> an acorn, children, money, bills, the spine, performances,
> hoar frost, emptiness.

This short passage deals with the phenomenology of a thing – with the fact that things have a "surface," available to the touch; and also that such contact is not limited to ordinary things (like "paper"), but is also possible with things of speculative character, among which appear plural or collective nouns ("children," "money"), linguistic terms ("a participle"), and even such special constructs as "letter loopholes," ending with the adjectival noun "пустое" ("emptiness"). This list is characteristic of Dragomoshchenko's poetic programme: things available to immediate visual and/or tactile contact are considered on par with abstract quiddities and theoretical constructs – one can make some kind of "tactile" contact with them all, they are all merely the outer surfaces of an "emptiness" found within them.

The cited extract in many ways evokes Merleau-Ponty's *Phénomenologie de la perception* (Phenomenology of Perception), one of whose main themes examines the subject's contact with different types of surfaces. Dragomoshchenko was an attentive reader of this book: its English translation was in his personal library, after it was apparently sent to him by Lyn Hejinian. As a result, Dragomoshchenko's latter poems and prose fragments often contain direct borrowings and quotes from this work.

In relation to phenomenological technique, there is another characteristic poem, which Dragomoshchenko wrote two years later, in 1987, in which the ekphrastic question takes centre stage. In the introduction to this text, entitled "Настурция как реальность" (Nasturtium as Reality), the poet writes:

> Из своего окна я видел настурцию на балконе, таившую в словесном своем составе, словно в слепом стручке, новые завязи, соотношения, новые меры, коим в точности было предписано повторить бывшие... словно в сумрачном стечении согласных – в смерти – где нарастающие, смывающие друг друга, возникающие дрожат бесчисленные связи реальности.
>
> (Dragomoshchenko 1987, 26–27)

From my window I could see the nasturtium on the balcony, hiding within her verbal composition, as if in a blind pod, new germ-seeds, relationships, new measures, for which it was compulsory to precisely repeat the former ones... so to say, in a crepuscular confluence of consonants – in death – wherein tremble the growing, mutually washing, and emerging innumerable interconnections of reality.

The image of the nasturtium becomes a leitmotif here, to be associated with memories, visual images, and meditative reflections of various kinds (cf. Ioffe 2013). At the same time, it is difficult to set boundaries between these fragments, since they flow smoothly into each other, while the narrative gets underway to bind in unity only the redeveloping depiction of the nasturtium: "существуя как пришедшиеся впору вечеру листья / и в виде чаши (разбросшенные края) / ускорившего / вращенье / цветка" ("persisting as leaves that came with evening / and in the form of a goblet (with frayed edges) / accelerating / the turning / of the flower"; Dragomoshchenko 1987, 39). The poem can be perceived as a kind of circling around this image, which fits the role of an "empty core" of subjectivity – that around which it is composed, but having no content of its own, as such. This "emptiness" of the nasturtium is recounted by the poet many times over: "описывает наступцию, изведенную из описания" ("describes the nasturtium, derived from description"; ibid., 33); or where he says "наступция необыкновенно проста (пуста)" ("the nasturtium, uncommonly plain (empty)"; ibid., 35).

In this poem, Dragomoshchenko directly references the language of phenomenology, although he uses it with greater expressiveness than is customary in academic philosophy. To the poet, his own body exists as a set of momentary perceptions, each of which makes for a new turn in the screw-threading of subjectivation. We can say that Dragomoshchenko's writing is subject to the following scheme:

a confrontation with the given thing → perception → its subjectivation

Previous experience of subjectivation lays the foundation for subsequent experience, but this process could be described as recursive. Since complete subjectivity is never achieved, subjectivation can never reach its conclusion, and thus can only be interrupted (Korchagin, 2020). This process is described at the very beginning of the poem "Nasturtium as Reality," even before the mechanism of continuous subjectivation begins to come into full effect:

Опыт
описания изолированного предмета
определен предвосхищеньем итога –
    взглядом через плечо другого.

Настурция состоит
из дождливой прорвы окна
для себя самой «до»,

для меня – «за». Кому достоянье
рдеющей дрожи
спрессованного обнажения
    в проеме обоюдоострых предлогов
у
створчатой плоскости,
прозрачность
разящей
стекла?

(Dragomoshchenko 1987, 28)

Experience
of the description of the isolated object
is determined by anticipating the conclusion –
    looking over the shoulder of another.

The nasturtium consists of
the rainy chasm of the window
she sees herself "before,"

I see her – "behind." Who owns
the red shivering
of the compressed revelation
    in the portal of both-sided prepositions
at
the unfolding plane
transparency
opening
of glass?

The key concept brought up here over and over again is *emptiness*. It appears clearly behind the image of the nasturtium, spreading out in all directions, and becomes the centre of subjectivation, onto which various impressions and memories are bundled. In the tenth part of the poem, the construction principle of the text is revealed:

> Я намереваюсь сказать, что сказанное и пустота,
> втягивающая на выбор элементы высказывания,
> сополагаясь, обнаруживают источник желания:
> опять не сказать то, что сказано.
>
> (Ibid., 39–40)

> I mean to say that the stated and the emptiness,
> drawing into view elements of expression,
> juxtaposed, denude the object of desire:
>   again to leave unsaid what has been said.

In this passage, the word "emptiness" could be replaced by the word "nasturtium": the object that becomes the thing being described and the focus of observation is essentially *empty,* and the poet is able to come into contact only with its surface – in other words, with the *visible of the invisible* (to use Hegel's expression) – potentially revealing behind the surface that empty point around which he is able once again to recreate his own subjectivity. Such a take on subjectivity arising around emptiness is far from accidental as a topic in the twentieth century;[3] it occupies a particularly important place in many respects in the revisionist interpretation of Eastern thought, as part of the philosophical framework of the Kyoto School, especially in the works of Daisetsu Teitaro Suzuki on Zen Buddhism.

Suzuki found himself enveloped by interest in the occult, widespread as it was at the turn of the nineteenth and twentieth centuries, and he certainly did not reach for Zen Buddhism right away: he was initially interested in Emanuel Swedenborg and European mysticism, and, later, already in his "Buddhist" period,

---

3   Compare, for example, the positional work by Slavoj Žižek, *The Ticklish Subject: The Absent Centre of Political Ontology* (2008), in which this idea assumes a central role.

was close to the Eranos grouping, which also encompassed Carl Gustav Jung and Mircea Eliade (Bramble 2015, 111n). Scholars have noted numerous points of agreement between Suzuki's own reconstruction of Japanese Buddhism and the phenomenological concept (Mickunas 1993). It seems the alignment was also observed by practitioners – poets and artists for whom both traditions represented a source of constant reflection, and who, unlike academic scholars, could afford to compare and converge these systems while downplaying their differences.

Suzuki published his first treatise on Zen Buddhism in 1927, and afterwards, over several decades, actively promoted his own interpretation of this thought system, in many respects close to that which the philosophers of the Kyoto school had elaborated (Kitaro Nishida and others; see Heisig 2001). The most laconic form of his teachings was to be found in the frequently republished books *An Introduction to Zen Buddhism* (1934) and the *Manual of Zen Buddhism* (1953). Suzuki's teachings were followed by American avant-garde masters such as Jackson Pollock and John Cage, while young beatnik writer Jack Kerouac personally tried to secure this Eastern guru's blessing after the publication of his novel *The Dharma Bums* (Falikov 2017, 207). Suzuki's influence on the art scene peaked in the 1950s, and in the 1960s his place was taken by a more eclectic constellation of esoteric and mystical views spread with the hippie movement.

The history of how Suzuki's ideas influenced Soviet intellectuals remains rather unexplored, but it is known that at least since the early 1970s a samizdat version of *An Introduction to Zen Buddhism* was making the rounds, translated as *Основы дзэн-буддизма* (Preliminaries to Zen Buddhism), supplemented by excerpts from other works (Dzhindzholiya 2004, 6). As early as 1968, Grigory Pomerants, later a prominent human rights activist and philosopher, prepared a dissertation entitled *Некоторые течения восточного религиозного ниги-лизма* (Some Trends in of Eastern Religious Nihilism), in which he detailed the views of Suzuki and Nishida (Pomerants 2015). In addition, Suzuki's central ideas, including their influence on American and European art, were described in Evgenia Zavadskaya's book *Восток на Западе* (East in the West; 1970), which had a great influence on Soviet unofficial art (Atik 2015, 6). The *Manual of Zen Buddhism* reveals the meaning of the concept of emptiness that is central to Buddhism, and to some extent paraphrases the somewhat vague formula-tions of *An Introduction to Zen Buddhism*:

"Empty" (śunya) or "emptiness" (śunyata) is one of the most important notions in Mahayana philosophy and at the same time the most
puzzling for non-Buddhist readers to comprehend. Emptiness does
not mean "relativity", or "phenomenality", or "nothingness", but rather
means the Absolute, or something of transcendental nature [...].
When Buddhists declare all things to be empty, they are not advoca-
ting a nihilistic view [...]. When the sutra says that the five Skandhas
have the character of emptiness, or that in emptiness there is neither
creation nor destruction, neither defilement nor immaculacy, and so
on, the sense is: no limiting qualities are to be attributed to the Absolute; while it is immanent in all concrete and particular objects, it is
not in itself definable.

(Suzuki 1960, 29)

This definition is a polemic with Suzuki's predecessors: such as with the
Russian authority on Buddhism, Fyodor Stcherbatsky, who, under the influence of Einstein's theory, understood emptiness as *relativity* (Stcherbatsky 1927,
69–72); and with the founding father of the Kyoto school, Kitaro Nishida, for
whom *emptiness* and *nothingness* were close in meaning (Heisig 2001, 61–64).
Notwithstanding the fact that Suzuki himself separates the concepts of emptiness and phenomenality, in his interpretation emptiness turns out to be practi-
cally synonymous with Heidegger's "being" – that which is contained in every
thing, and yet remains inaccessible.[4] Of course, Zen and phenomenology differ
substantially; but this difference seems negligible for any poetic work creating
a new montage from both intellectual directions, taking from phenomenology
an interest in things as such and the process of their perception, and from Zen
the need to reveal in each thing an underlying, transcendental emptiness.

Another example of how phenomenology relates to Zen Buddhism comes
through a third tradition, apophatic theology, which can be found in the work
of the Moscow poet Andrei Monastyrski (born 1949) – belonging to the same
poetic generation as Dragomoshchenko, but taking a different course among
the directions that transformed into Moscow Conceptualism at the turn of the
1970s and 1980s. Monastyrski is better known as the pioneer and organizer

---

4   Cf. Heidegger's closely similar concept of being espoused, which necessarily raises the question
      of whether the German philosopher was familiar with Zen Buddhism (Watts 2011, 230–44).

of the art group Коллективные действия (Collective Actions), which in the Soviet context was one of the first to develop various kinds of performative art. The happenings series *Поездки за город* (Trips out of Town), each accompanied by a rich documentation, began in 1976, with new happenings still taking place (see Eşanu 2013; Gerber 2018; Sasse 2003). Monastyrski's poetic texts are less well-known, although many anticipate the tendencies widely applied in the 1980s and 1990s in the work of Dmitry Prigov, Lev Rubinstein, and other Conceptualist poets. Notable among these texts is the extensive poem "Поэтический мир" (Poetic World), written mostly in 1976, at the same time as the first events of the Collective Actions group, and published almost thirty years later.

This poem is divided into five books, each of which makes use of characteristics of the visible world. Each stanza of the block is built on syntactically equivalent structures, formulas akin to the long enumerations of concepts in other Conceptualist texts. The multitudinous repetition of the same, minimally altered formulas creates the specific notion that all objects of the observed world can be listed in this way – when this is not, in fact, the case.

"Poetic World" is not inwardly monolithic: its parts, comprising formulaic mantras, can vary – some formulas are replaced by others (as in its third part), or, conversely, the inclination towards the formulaic is suppressed (as in the second and fourth parts). However, the parts that come closest to ekphrasis are those composed of the most monotonous formulas – especially the first and fifth parts, all built on the variation of a single formula:

было красно
все было красным
красное было везде
краснее не было никогда
всюду красное
все стало красным

(Monastyrski 2007, 65)

there was redness
everything was red
redness was everywhere
redder it had never been
everywhere redness

everything turned red
в тебе нет ничего
ни от черного, ни от белого
в тебе нет ничего
возвышенного или униженного
в тебе нет ничего
придуманного мной

(Ibid., 225)

there's nothing in you
neither black nor white
there's nothing in you
elevated or debased
there's nothing in you
made up by me

In the second and fourth parts, on the other hand, the formulaic structure is abandoned (or used only in a few lines and then replaced by a new one); coming to the fore is *what* is shown in the process of ekphrastic activity:

нет, ничего
ничего здесь нет
здесь одни невидимости
легкие поползновения
какие-то скоропалительные
чувства о пустоте
в беспредметности желаний

(Ibid., 83)

no, nothing
there's nothing here
here are only invisible things
light temptations
kind of hasty
feelings of emptiness
in the pointlessness of desires

то, что было
полным, становится
пустым,
пустое же – полным,
но не осознанным
и потому не существующим
для всего остального

(Ibid., 221)

that, which was
full, becomes
empty
empty again – complete,
but not knowingly,
and therefore nonexistent
to everything else

A somewhat confused author's afterword to the 2007 edition comments on the structure of these parts as follows:

> In Levi-Strauss terminology, the overall structure of the "Poetic World" as regards the sequentiality of its parts can be described as alternating: "bricolage – composition – bricolage – composition – bricolage." In the bricolage, ritualized parts, what exists is experienced as a universe: dynamic (1), grammatical (3) and apophatic (5). In the compositional, "historical" parts, what exists is perceived (2) or meant (4) as the experience or idea of emptiness, *sunyata*. The predicate of the compositional parts is intended to be "one and the same" (*sunya*), the analogy of this in bricolages being repeated predicative formulas, which take on indicative functions within the structural context of all five books.

(Ibid., 329)

We can say that we are dealing here with ekphrasis "dismembered": one ekphrastic strategy is brought to the fore in one part of the poem, and others in other parts, but characteristic of all of them is the attempt to capture the hidden emptiness that underlies the world. This global apophatic motion captures the entire visible world, with both specific things and abstract categories drawn into its vortex – as in Dragomoshchenko's poem. As mentioned above, the ekphrasis always turns to the "visible of the invisible," to the surface of a thing. Intellectual currents in the twentieth century force us to look deeper, trying to penetrate into a thing's interior, to reveal its inner emptiness, and thus focus on the very process of perception. This is how Dragomoshchenko's poem works, where the nasturtium progressively disembodies as the text develops, thereby turning into the empty core on which the poetic subject is focused.

In Monastyrski's poem, the following step is put to use: the object of the description is progressively eliminated completely from the ekphrasis, in order to concentrate on the subjectivation process, removing from it all incidental aspects. In the end, the poem does not answer the question of what is at the core of the apophasis; with each new turn of the screw-thread, it comes closer towards some point, but it remains unclear what point that is. It can be assumed, of course, that it is God or – if we are to express ourselves in more secular language – the transcendental; but neither the poem itself nor the text that accompanies it make direct reference:

здесь нет никаких звуков
здесь нечему звучать
я сам не умею звучать
кроме меня,
здесь нет никаких звуков
я не понимаю, что значит
звучать

(Ibid., 95)

here there are no sounds
here nothing resounds
I too don't know how to resound
apart from me
here there are no sounds
I do not understand what it means
to resound

The intellectual context of the text becomes clearer if we take into account Monastyrski's novel *Каширское шоссе* (Kashira Highway), whose events relate to a somewhat later period, to 1982. This journal-based prose presents a detailed account of a psychotic state, reminiscent of the documentation of the events organized by the Collective Actions group (Glanc 2001). The hero of the novel gradually falls into such a state, and this becomes a real test of the strength of his subjectivity. The author attributes the growing psychotic state to his being deeply affected by the mystical treatises of the Byzantine theologian Dionysius the Areopagite: *On Divine Names*, *On Mystical Theology*, and *On Heavenly Hierarchy*. As a result of reading these texts, Monastyrski's hero begins to see beyond the commonplace Soviet realities the phantasmal reality of celestial essences – the reality of angels, of royal thrones. It turns out that all these essences guide the hero, who tries to make direct contact with the transcendental, but is always thwarted in that endeavour. His failure is due precisely to the structure of the subject. As the historian of medieval philosophy Alain de Libera writes: "Man suffers from a certain hypersensitivity to angels, due to lacking his own place, so to speak" (de Libera 2015, 34). Such inability to take his place in the "celestial hierarchy" leads the hero of *Kashira Highway* to experience a painful duality of the world, a never-ending disintegration of subjectivity, which – as it turns out – is deprived of its own place. The only way out of this painful situation for the protagonist is Zen Buddhism, which offers emptiness as a kind of medical treatment for an overdose of the transcendental. If every thing is empty inside, if "there is nothing to it," this means that no thing in the world has any certain place, so there is no need to seek a psychotic way out of the commonplace order.

The text of *Kashira Highway* does not speak of any works of Zen Buddhism that Monastyrski and his protagonist would have studied. However, the way in which Buddhism is presented, as well as the fact that the concept of emptiness is brought to the fore, raises the prospect of their being influenced by Suzuki's works – either directly (through the samizdat translations of his works) or indirectly (e.g., through Evgenia Zavadskaya's book). This is how the intellectual path taken by the protagonist of *Kashira Highway* is made possible – by the fact that there is a point at which the mystical theology of Dionysius the Areopagite and Suzuki's Zen Buddhism meet.

As we know, there are two types of theological discourse – the cataphatic and the apophatic. While cataphasis attributes some particular quality to an object, apophasis conversely names the qualities which the object does not manifestly possess. As Maxim the Confessor argues in his commentary on the relevant and rather obscure passage of Dionysios the Areopagite's treatise *On Mystical*

Theology: "For God is no longer conceived in the form of an image arousing sensations, thoughts or feelings; God is now known as One who can neither be sensed, thought nor felt; He is a mystery, a divine darkness" (Areopagita Dionysius 1944, 18). Monastyrski follows Zen Buddhism as it comes to its own kind of secularization of apophasis, thereby also eliminating the hierarchy of celestial and earthly essences, which become homogeneous, differing externally, but intrinsically alike. Arising out of this transformation is the ekphrastic apophasis of the "Poetic World."

In my view, in the case of Dragomoshchenko and Monastyrski, we are dealing with two opposing ekphrastic strategies. In the first case, a potentially infinite promulgation of details that can be far removed from the subject described; in the second, an equally potentially infinite list of qualities that the object *does not possess*. Dragomoshchenko's strategy can be called cataphatic, whereas that of Monastyrski apophatic, and this theological metaphor can be elaborated: the goal of both cataphasis and apophasis is in equal measure to get close to the transcendental, but in both cases the place of this transcendental (God or His representative) is taken up by Zen *emptiness*. In other words, any object described in ekphrasis refers to the divine, but divinity is not possible in this extremely secular world, its place always remains unoccupied. This emptiness in turn shows itself to be the centre around which subjectivity is composed. Such ekphrastic strategies move the poet's and the reader's attention not only from the described thing to the mechanisms of its description and the way it is seen, but go further – to the figure of the one who completes that vision, while examining how each particular thing is woven into poetic subjectivity, transmuting it.[5]

---

5   This work was supported by a Russian Science Fund grant (no. 19-18-00429) at the Institute of Linguistics of the Russian Academy of Sciences.

Paul Muldoon's Hyperobjects

JUSTIN QUINN

- All our grid models are worthless.
- I don't think grid models are gonna be a lot of help here.
- Canadians report tremendous circulation moving down from the Arctic. In Siberia there's a low-pressure system unlike anything we've seen. And Australia just saw the strongest typhoon ever recorded.
- Hang on. Are you saying these things are interconnected?
- We have to consider the possibility.

The Day After Tomorrow (2004)

1

The Day After Tomorrow is a disastrous disaster film. The disaster in question – the event that comes after tomorrow – is planetary cataclysm precipitated by global warming. Most of the USA – and, in the background, large tracts of the globe – freezes over, and the Americans find that they have to emigrate *en masse* to Mexico. The scriptwriters are clearly tempted by the irony of that, but restrain themselves. It turns out that the Mexicans don't mind their one-time imperial neighbours moving in, and help them as much as they can. The Mexicans don't build a wall, don't close the borders, don't have Alsatians barking in children's faces.

The quotation above comes from the exposition, the point at which the science people, huddled over monitors, start to realize that the disparate, erratic weather phenomena around the world might be "interconnected." These may not be separate *things* but one big *thing*. The film spends a lot of time showing how this awareness spreads through selected characters of the population. It's humanity's (or at least US citizens') "oh no!" moment.

That's the disaster. And what's disastrous about it is the Homeric father-son plot. Mostly, European culture has agreed that this is a good plot – useful in different situations, languages, and cultures. But in a film like this, it is absurd, as it pitches a small human drama against a much larger one (planetary ecological disaster). The dimensions of this latter drama immediately and starkly render ridiculous the efforts of a father to find his son in New York City, which is underneath about ten metres of snow. It's a poor attempt to mitigate the awfulness of a disaster of these proportions.

But the curious thing is that a lot of movies that deal with this subject – this *one big thing* – are ridiculous in the same manner. *Snowpiercer* (2013) is; *Melancholia* (2011) is; while *Take Shelter* (2011) is just boring. It's hard to make a human story (and we don't really have any other type of story) meaningful in the face of a phenomenon that not only dwarfs its characters, but also makes it impossible to conceive of any further reader or viewer of such a story. There will be no one left with whom to argue about plot twists or casting after you've left the cinema and you're in the café. Because there will be no cinema, no café, no other person, no you. It's as though the scriptwriters of such films are so baffled by a prospect of this kind that they fall back on family drama. Relax, they tell you; *The Day After Tomorrow* might really just be about a father's strained relationship with his son. Global ecological disaster is possibly just the background to ongoing human dramas. The Indian novelist Amitav Ghosh discusses this difficulty in relation to literary fiction. He says that it's not due to the failings or shortcomings of particular writers – rather "it arises out of the peculiar forms of resistance that climate change presents" (Ghosh 2016, 16). The subject itself seems to counter representation in this genre (though Ghosh quickly admits that sci-fi has done much better in this respect). Here, though, I'm concerned with another genre – poetry – and one of the ways in which it represents this *one big thing* that's made up of many seemingly disparate *smaller things*. First, I'm going to take a look at those various *things* and the way that one philosopher in particular has characterized them.

2

That *one big thing* has been called by Timothy Morton a "hyperobject." It is nigh impossible, he says, for us to comprehend the planetary ecological disaster of global warming. To do so would require us to think on a timescale that we're unused to, of tens of thousands of years ("Hyperobjects are time-stretched to such a vast extent that they become almost impossible to hold in mind" [Morton 2013, 58]). It is not an object in the sense in which a table or a continent or a cloud is an object; rather, it is a set of relations between objects, or phenomena. He says it has several features. First, it is viscous. This means that it cannot be studied at arm's length or beneath a microscope (that would mean it was merely an object):

> The mirror of science melts and sticks to our hand. The very tools we were using to objectify things, to cover Earth's surface with shrink wrap, become a blowtorch that burns away the glass screen separating humans from Earth, since every measurement is now known as an alteration, as quantum-scale measurements make clear.
>
> (Ibid., 36)

Second, the hyperobject is non-local, or massively distributed in space. We only see bits of it here and there, and have to learn to see the connections. Another aspect is phasing. If it non-locality refers mainly to geographical dispersion, then phasing is about distribution over time.

> Hyperobjects seem to phase in and out of the human world. [...] [T]hey occupy a high-dimensional phase space that makes them impossible to see as a whole on a regular three-dimensional human-scale basis. We can only see pieces of hyperobjects at a time.
>
> (Ibid., 70)

We look at events in different parts of the world, but fail to join the dots.

The final one I'll mention here is interobjectivity, which means that we can only intuit the presence of hyperobjects by the marks that they leave on objects. This is connected with the aforementioned idea of non-locality. And it also connects with the first idea of viscosity, insofar as it decentralizes human agency and consciousness, locating it instead along a spectrum of consciousness, conceivably stretching even as far as mycorrhizal webs of communication in old forests (though Morton doesn't mention these). Rather than living in a world that we can control and direct, "we have discovered that we are already falling inside the abyss, which is not pure empty space, but instead the fiery interior of a hyperobject" (ibid., 160).

> If an apple were to invade a two-dimensional world, first the stick people would see some dots as the bottom of the apple touched their universe, then a rapid succession of shapes that would appear like an expanding and contracting circular blob, diminishing to a tiny circle, possibly a point, and disappearing. What we experience as a lava-lamp fluidity – flowing and oozing metaphors abound in the new materialism – is precisely a symptom of our less than adequate perception of higher dimensions of structure, which is where the hyperobjects live. That's why you can't see global warming. You would have to occupy some high-dimensional space to see it unfolding explicitly.
>
> (Ibid., 70)

On a phenomenological level – on the level of, say, everyday conversation – we do indeed catch (and give out) hints of this larger pattern, these "indexical signs" (ibid., 78); but we can't ever *see* the hyperobject in its entirety. We can grasp lots of *small things*, but we can never fully comprehend the *one big thing* – that is, global warming. There are further aspects to Morton's loose definition of the hyperobject of global warming, but now I want to turn to its relation to culture.

Morton argues that certain types of music and literature can apprehend, or at least offer glimpses of, such a hyperobject. Mainly this is done through the modes of late modernism. To take music first: composers such as La Monte Young and Robert Ashley, he believes, "attempt both to bring hyperobjects into human aesthetic-causal (social, psychic, philosophical) space, and to open that space to the wider world, or rather to the charnel ground after the end of the world" (ibid., 170–71). They do so by attuning listeners to objects. They set aside traditional arrangements of materials in order to, as it were, allow the material itself to sing. One way they do this is through compositions that exceed the normal evening performance times for contemporary music; Morton says they "create a musical-social space for a while (hours and days) in which the project of attunement to the non-human is performed" (ibid., 171).

An inspiration for La Monte Young's *Trio for Strings* (1958) was the droning sound coming from a power plant that he heard as a child (Duckworth 1999, 222). So the work is an attempt not only to catch that sound, but – and herein lies the innovation – also its duration. *Trio for Strings* is only an hour long, but it refuses to provide any drama of development, even of the kind that earlier modernist works did. It is simultaneously an attempt to let the non-human into the artwork, and also necessarily to demote human artistic agency. It seems, listening to a work like this, that the artist is doing nothing. In this respect, Young's music resembles John Cage's *4'33"* (1952). Integral to such an approach is irritation. The listeners who arrive in the concert hall to find relief from reality are frustrated to find themselves confronted by it:

> Young decided that the only way to evoke a truly new music was to stop the narrative flow that is normative in Western music, to pull the emergency break and bring to a shuddering halt the predictable journeys around the world of diatonic harmony and equal temperament. His *Trio for Strings* of 1958 is probably the first minimalist musical composition. Hanging like monoliths in huge, gorgeous swathes of silence, the trio's lapidary chords evoke something more threatening, more intimate and vast, than the repetitive riffing of the later minimalists Steve Reich and Philip Glass. It is significant that Reich and Glass have been far more successful in the bourgeois world of luxury products than Young, whose work demands a level of passion and commitment – and free time – that would probably embarrass and irritate, not to mention disturb, the average middle-class concertgoer.
>
> (Morton 2013, 170)

Now, this late modernist narrative is familiar, down to the dismissal of Reich and Glass for their commodification of the rebarbative protocols of Minimalist music. People *like* these last two composers, ergo those composers must be bad. If this were Morton's point, then he would be yet another critic who dislikes culture that the middle-classes enjoy. Rather, something else is at stake: Young's music is a mantra that attunes us to the non-human. It is a protocol and practice that helps us to break up the organizing intelligence of our ego; it slows down our thought to such a degree that we can begin to glimpse patterns that are massively distributed over time, in the first instance, and possibly over space. That is, we can begin to apprehend the hyperobject.

One can find this kind of protocol elsewhere at present. Consider the "800% slower" videos on *YouTube*. I particularly like the one entitled "Radiohead – Pyramid Song 800% slower."[1] The drowsy melancholia of the original is slowed down even further and, as one listens, one starts to recognize familiar chord progressions or drops. The video makes you wait, makes you uncertain. This is exciting, even though it's drawn-out. A further aspect that's important is the very idea of "800% slower" itself. This almost sounds like 800 times slower; but it's only 8 times slower. The formatting of the numbers themselves in this case also alert us to the limits of our own listening abilities. I would like to know, not so much what the song would sound like 800 times slower, but, rather, what it would be like to *be* a person who could listen to things at that slowed-down rate. Comparing lifespans, through the 8 times slower version we glimpse what it might be like to be a tree. At 800 times slower, we're approaching what it would be like to be a piece of rock.

This same idea informs the Clock of the Long Now – a project to build a clock that will keep time for 10,000 years. In his book about this clock, Stewart Brand writes:

> Might humanity pay consistent attention through one complete pre-cession of the equinoxes, as the Earth's axis pirouettes around a point in the sky near the Pole Star? This 25,784-year cycle is known as the Great Year. How about keeping track through one rotation of our galaxy – 220 million years? The Earth has existed for nearly twenty-five of those galactic rotations, life on Earth for nineteen rotations. Humans may well eventually affect the periodicity of ice ages – we have been frozen by one every one hundred thousand years for a million years and are now enjoying an "interglacial" period – but it seems unlikely that we will have much influence on the rotation of our galaxy or anyone else's, nor will we tally their spin. The human time frame is narrower than that of life, of the planet, and of galaxies.

---

1   "Radiohead – Pyramid Song 800% slower." YouTube video, 38:35. Posted by "dumaramutsi," 13 April 2014. https://youtu.be/XiKWfcy-Z7o.

[Brian] Eno's Long Now places us where we belong, neither at the end of history nor at the beginning, but in the thick of it. We are not the culmination of history, and we are not start-over revolutionaries; we are in the middle of civilization's story.
The trick is learning how to treat the last ten thousand years as if it were last week, and the next ten thousand as if it were next week. Such tricks confer advantage.

(Brand 1999, 31)

The Clock of the Long Now, as described by Brand, wants to remind human beings of a chronology beyond our drastically truncated ideas of the present, or "the now." This is not done out of disdain for the faster cycles (fashion, news, commerce, government), but rather out of a desire to *complement* these. He believes that civilization must move at several paces simultaneously (he calls these "pace layers"), remarking that:

The division of powers among the layers of civilization allows us to relax about a few of our worries. We should not deplore rapidly changing technology and business while government controls, cultural mores, and so-called wisdom change slowly; that's their job. Also, we should not fear destabilizing positive-feedback loops (such as the Singularity) crashing the whole system. Such disruption usually can be isolated and absorbed. The total effect of the pace layers is that they provide many-leveled corrective, stabilizing negative feedback throughout the system. It is precisely in the apparent contradictions of pace that civilization finds its surest health.

(Ibid., 39)

This is art as spiritual exercise. Mircea Eliade would figure such a movement between time frames as the interface of the sacred and the profane. Perhaps that's all that hierophany is: the revelation of a different timescale within our chronology of seconds, minutes, days, and so on.

From the most elementary hierophany – e.g., manifestation of the sacred in some ordinary object, a stone or a tree – to the supreme hierophany (which, for a Christian, is the incarnation of God in Jesus Christ) there is no solution of continuity. In each case we are confronted by the same mysterious act – the manifestation of something of a wholly different order, a reality that does not belong to our world, in objects that are an integral part of our natural "profane" world.

(Eliade 1961, 11)

The word "sacred" is helpful, as it reminds us of the way that institutional religious practices are embedded in chronological time, or more particularly, that of works and days. One partakes in a religious ceremony, one is reminded of a different time frame, and then one returns to one's works and days.

So too with Young's *Trio for Strings* or his *Well-Tuned Piano* or one of the 800% songs. After listening to them, one returns to the life one left a few hours before. Now processes, conversations, movements seem ridiculously frenetic, much as the buzzing of flies might seem to a tree, if a tree had ears. One comment on YouTube, below "Radiohead - Pyramid Song 800% slower," quips: "This is Radiohead's original, and *Pyramid Song* is just 800% faster." In mathematical terms, there is a huge difference between listening to a piece of music 8 times slower and starting to consider one's actions and the actions of one's society against a horizon of 25,000 years. Morton would, I imagine, argue that such works of art, and the work that they demand of their listeners, are simulations of the larger civilizational work that must be done.

Still, we should not forget, as I think Morton does, that the compositions of La Monte Young and Robert Ashley *are* composed. They are arranged no less than the arrangements of the collisions of horsehair and catgut, and the streams of air travelling through windpipes of wood, human flesh, and metal that we encounter in, say, Bach's cantatas. This is the lie of such late modernism: its works try to pass themselves off as non-artifice, or an approximation thereto. In the same way, Theodor Adorno analysed twentieth-century Europe and the United States, and concluded that, if one were serious, one could only endorse the art of Alberto Giacometti, Samuel Beckett, and a handful of others. Adorno thus displayed a crudity of perception incongruous with the subtle discrimination in the majority of his writing. His position is also based on erroneous analogies between political and aesthetic structures. That is, it presumes that merely because, say, Beckett's work breaks certain theatrical conventions, it is fundamentally different in kind from all theatre. Likewise, in comparing Young to Reich and Glass, Morton assumes that the kind of time-consuming, meditative dedication required for, say, the six hours of *The Well-Tuned Piano* is incompatible with the temporal rhythms of late capitalism. But capitalism is more wily than Morton will admit. In any case, the more important point here is to emphasize that although Young's music provides a good way to think about Morton's hyperobjects, it is not the only way. There is a wider repertoire of possible cultural responses to such a hyperobject than Morton acknowledges. But what are they?

3

It's impossible to say that Paul Muldoon's poetry is *about* hyperobjects. More generally, it's impossible to say if Muldoon's poetry is about *any* subject; and on a deep level, and for all their bravura technique, the poems don't seem to have been written *by* anybody. Here I don't wish to rehearse the older New Critical aesthetic, that a poem should not *mean*, but *be*. This is a more particular issue. From the start of his career, Muldoon wrote poems about particular things, people, animals, or events, only to make them turn out to be about something else entirely. For instance, in the poem "Truce," the first four quatrains describe the Christmas truce that spontaneously took place in the trenches during the First World War. The men walk uncertainly across No Man's Land, sing some Christmas songs from their respective countries, and "draw on their last cigarettes" (Muldoon 2002, 86). Immediately after that, however, in the final quatrain, the poem takes a surprising swerve:

> They draw on their last cigarettes
>
> As Friday-night lovers, when it's over,
> Might get up from their mattresses
> To congratulate each other
> And exchange names and addresses.

(Ibid., 87)

The last quatrain would seem to reveal that the preceding four quatrains were merely the vehicle and not the tenor. That is, the poem was in fact *about* the lovers all along – they were the true tenor – and this was only revealed at the poem's conclusion. Syntactically, the lovers are the vehicle, but the imaginative thrust of the poem suggests the opposite. The more I read this poem, however, the harder it is to distinguish tenor and vehicle; that is, the harder it is to say whether it's *about* the lovers or the military truce. Such uncertainty seems to be the great thing about the poem. In this respect, more than the work of other poets, it's difficult to say what Muldoon's poems are about.

Here it helps to compare him with his fellow Irish poet, Seamus Heaney. In "Sandstone Keepsake," from the collection *Station Island* (1984), the poet picks up a stone and turns that experience of prehension into apprehension of further contexts; or, as Maria Zirra remarks, it is one of a series of "philosophical lyrics where experiential contact with objects and their textures triggers reflections about the creative and formative impact of matter and intertext on the formation of cultural memory" (Zirra 2017, 465). It begins with a granular description of sense experience, of the kind that Heaney excelled at throughout his career. In this he seems the quintessential "thing" poet. That phenomenological intensity, however, leads him immediately away, into the story of how he found it near an internment camp in Northern Ireland. That precipitates a brief meditation on the place of the artist in difficult political times, as well as an extended allusion to Dante's *Inferno*, with which Heaney was preoccupied in this period. *Pace* Zirra, the end of the poem doesn't quite bring Heaney back to the phenomenological thingness of the poem; rather it ends with an assessment of Heaney's own social and political position – he is a votary of a cultural guild, and not someone who will intervene, effectively or ineffectively, in political events. Magdalena Kay is surely correct when she discusses this poem:

> His metaphors sometimes announce their awkward modesty [...] but once the scene is set, they also allow the poem to lift off from the actual into the virtual, as we contemplate his "free state of image and illusion" [*sic*, allusion]. Although the poem may have been inspired by a trip to Lough Foyle, its significance reaches beyond this. This figure is neither Herbert's moralist nor Yeats's emblematic fisherman. He absolves himself of responsibility by means of his insignificance, and even while the last phrase reaches a high note of lyricism, it also rings oddly: the "watch-tower" and "trained binoculars" are almost casual details, and the grandly Latinate "venerator" raises more questions than it answers (what is venerated? is one free to venerate? can veneration redress – or even address – the wrongs committed

elsewhere?). The poem finds resolution to its lyrical journey but not
its intellectual journey.

(Kay 2013, 278)

The thing dissolves in these proliferating social, political, and cultural ques-
tions. Indeed, self-interrogation is a staple rhetorical device of Heaney's poetry
throughout his career. It is complemented by a counter-motion, in which
Heaney tries to correct himself with self-directed imperatives. For instance, in
"Squarings," concerned that he has drifted off into, literally, airy abstractions of
"Unroofed scope. Knowledge-freshening wind" (Heaney 2010, 354), the poet
begins the next section with a fusillade of orders to himself: "Roof it again.
Batten down. Dig in. / Drink out of tin. Know the scullery cold [...]" (ibid.,
354). There is, of course, a residual, penitential Catholic cast to these com-
mands, but here I want to emphasize how that is in the service of an anxiety
about losing touch with objects. It is as though, for Heaney, poetry, or, ethically,
a life, will lose its validity if not underwritten by the prehensile contact with
things. Bill Brown's gloss illuminates this kind of dynamic:

> As they circulate through our lives, we look *through* objects (to see
> what they disclose about history, society, nature, or culture – above
> all, what they disclose about *us*), but we only catch a glimpse of
> things. We look through objects because there are codes by which
> our interpretive attention makes them meaningful, because there is
> a discourse of objectivity that allows us to use them as facts. A *thing*,
> in contrast, can hardly function as a window. We begin to confront
> the thingness of objects when they stop working for us.
>
> (Brown 2001, 4)

This can help us to read imaginative swerves of some Heaney poems. He is
anxious when he wanders into codes and signs, hankering for a return to *things*
as guarantors of thought, and more particularly his own poetry. In this sense,
things are like transcendent spiritual values; but rather than religious relics as
vectors towards godhead, we have instead physical objects, ones we can grasp
and throw from hand to hand, like this sandstone keepsake. Brown continues: "things [do not] reside in some balmy elsewhere beyond theory"; rather
they are "both at hand and somewhere outside the theoretical field, beyond
a certain limit, as a recognizable yet illegible remainder or as the entifiable that

is unspecifiable" (ibid., 5). Heaney grasps things in his poetry with the same
force that, at other times, he absconds from them, and these alternating actions
produce some of his finest passages.

Heaney is a useful foil for a discussion of Muldoon, whose poetic has no prehensile impulse: whereas Heaney, midway on flights of abstraction, allusion,
and political meditation, hauls himself back to the physical thing, Muldoon
pushes harder on the throttle, propelling himself faster over more terrains and
through more time zones. It is through such flitting lines that we catch glimpses
of other, stranger objects, unlike the keepsake Heaney chucks from one hand
to another. The kind of uncertainty that we encountered earlier in Muldoon's
"Truce" is exponentially complicated in his later work, as things, events, people,
animals become indeterminate in his poems. The lines fly between what seem to
be disparate dramatic situations, historical references, geographical locations,
and languages, metamorphosing with such fluency that it is often difficult to
say where one ends and another begins. This may sound familiar to readers of
John Ashbery, but the essential difference is that Muldoon's poems are patently
and frequently *about* certain themes, even as they point in other directions. For
instance, while the six parts of the poem entitled "François Boucher: Arion
on the Dolphin" are unambiguously *about* the eponymous painting, they are
also *about* President John F. Kennedy; and it is, probably, about some other
things (one of which I'll deal with later). It is unclear, however, to me at least,
what the connection is between that US president and the eighteenth-century
Rococo French painter. In "Truce" we had a relatively straightforward metaphor: even though we might not have been able to identify which was the tenor
and which was the vehicle, we understood that the two scenes stood in metamorphic relation to each other. In "François Boucher: Arion on the Dolphin,"
there are many connections made: for instance, between the patrol boat that
Kennedy commanded in the Pacific during the Second World War, and the
dolphin that saved the poet Arion from drowning. But the abundance of such
filaments only obscures the apparent illogic of the connection in the first place:
it simply seems random. And this is one of the great things about Muldoon's art:
the way that it lets such randomness into the rhyme and repetition, as they turn
like turbines in his poetry.

In interviews, Muldoon has frequently stated that, despite the obvious orga-
nization of his vast, intricate rhyme patterns (sometimes spanning from one
collection to another), he is not fully in control of his material. We can't adju-
dicate on this, but can only say that the frenetic, rhizomic randomness of his

poems' surfaces lends itself well to such an interpretation. In the spirit of such an approach, I want to follow the thread of one reference in this poem that is not ostensibly connected to either Boucher or Kennedy:

What's not to love about the Teflon,

its nonstick
complete with the dead giveaway of a three-day stubble
on the cheek of a dolphin?

(Muldoon 2010, 37)

In 2007, the magazine *Mother Jones* published an article entitled "Teflon is Forever," in which it reported that:

Teflon, it turns out, gets its nonstick properties from a toxic, nearly indestructible chemical called pfoa, or perfluorooctanoic acid. Used in thousands of products from cookware to kids' pajamas to takeout coffee cups, pfoa is a likely human carcinogen, according to a science panel commissioned by the Environmental Protection Agency. It shows up in dolphins off the Florida coast and polar bears in the Arctic; it is present, according to a range of studies, in the bloodstream of almost every American – and even in newborns (where it may be associated with decreased birth weight and head circumference).

(Savan 2007)

It's hard to confirm whether this was Muldoon's source for the image. There's no mention of "a three-day stubble" in the *Mother Jones* article, but the juxtaposition of the mammal, the chemical compound, and the likelihood that "François Boucher: Arion on the Dolphin" was written around the time of the article's publication, make it a strong contender. (The poem appeared two years after the *Mother Jones* article, in the chapbook *Plan B*.) There is no other flicker of this ecological theme in the poem, so the dolphins that have been poisoned by modern industry seem to be merely part of the background scenery. The lines are like an aside, marking how nature has changed from Boucher's time. (Earlier, Muldoon remarks how Arion fingers his lyre "across the span / of twenty-five centuries" [Muldoon 2010, 36].) In the work of most other poets, the introduction of such an outsized contemporary debate would throw a poem out of kilter. Two factors mitigate against this: first, the majority of readers won't automatically connect the lines to the way that Teflon is, according to this article, poisoning part of the marine ecosystem; second, in pursuit of a thread that runs through the poem's disjunctions, the reader is likely to discount those bearded dolphins as herrings, red ones.

But if we stay with the bearded dolphins for a while, the theme of ecological imbalance is picked up elsewhere in Muldoon's poetry. The poem "Some Pitfalls and How to Avoid Them," from the collection *One Thousand Things Worth Knowing* (2015), is dedicated to Muldoon's son, Asher, and the title at least seems to promise paternal guidance. Several sentences begin with the imperative to "Bear in mind," but the proffered advice doesn't amount to the usual bromides; it almost seems irrelevant to the situation, for instance, when he recommends that one should not eat too much buffalo ragout. The two seem to be making a road trip in the US, which is shadowed by the earlier expedition of Lewis and Clark. Eschewing buffalo, they pull "into the Samurai / Sushi Bar and order two Godzilla rolls." Subsequent lines riff on imagery already established in the poem, and it concludes thus:

> Bear in mind how our fireside banter
> may be lost to the generations to come
>
> but their native scouts
> will still be able to follow our route across America
> by the traces of mercury
> in our scats.

(Muldoon 2015, 70)

In the early 2010s, there were many reports about the high levels of mercury in sushi,[2] and most of this was released by industrial processes over the preceding

---

2   For instance, "What Kind of Sushi is Highest in Mercury?" *CNN*, 8 Apr. 2011, www.thechart. blogs.cnn.com/2011/04/08/what-the-yuck-mercury-poisoning-from-sushi/ (accessed Oct. 15, 2018); "What the Yuck: Mercury poisoning from sushi?" (Apr. 8, 2011); Ana Garcia and Fred Mamoun, "How Much Mercury Is in Your Sushi? (Part 1)," *NBC Los Angeles*, 12 May 2010. www.nbclosangeles.com/news/local/How-Much-Mercury-is-in-Your-Sushi-Part-1-93635804 .html (accessed 15 Oct. 2018); A. R. Williams, "Tuna Lover's Dilemma: To Eat or Not to

two centuries.[3] Fish, especially tuna used in sushi, bioaccumulates mercury in harmful amounts. The talk between father and son will vanish, but they will leave a chemical trace in the landscape that will possibly persist for many years to come. The passage also hints that the future generations might be technically backward ("their native scouts"; Muldoon has adroitly blurred such binaries – civilization and savagery, primitive and sophisticated – for most of his career). This may well gesture towards the future dystopian visions that frequently occur in ecological science fiction.

As the poem takes place in the US, those Godzilla rolls are unlikely to contain dolphin meat, but it is sometimes used for sashimi elsewhere, presenting the same mercury risk as other fish. If some people are reluctant to eat dolphins, it is perhaps because they feel that this mammal is closer to humans than, say, tuna or yellowtail. The poem "Lateral" carries an epigraph from Pliny the Elder, which relates a particular episode in that relationship: "In the province of Gallia Narbonensis and the region of Nemausus there is a marsh called Latera where dolphins and men co-operate to catch fish" (Muldoon 2010, 25). Ecology as theme in poetry often leads to lament, and in this poem Muldoon intimates the human betrayal of dolphins, and, synecdochically, of nature more generally. Humans are referred to as the dolphin's affiliates in their shared work, but latterly a "spill of venom" runs through the dolphin's veins. Nevertheless, the dolphin "won't hear of how his affiliates outsource / their dirty work to another ring of the plenum" (ibid.). The logical conjunctive adverb, "nevertheless," as so often in Muldoon, doesn't reliably conjoin; also, it's not clear what that other "ring of the plenum" is. But "outsourcing" comes from business, and hints that desire for profit has skewed an earlier transmammal cooperation. Furthermore, that "won't hear" means that the dolphin literally won't find out about this betrayal, and also that it would naively refuse to believe it of humans even if it did hear of this change. In conclusion, the poem swerves in another direction entirely:

Eat?" *National Geographic*, 21 Feb. 2014, www.news.nationalgeographic.com/news/2014/02/140220-tuna-guide-skipjack-yellowfin-albacore-bluefin-bigeye-sushi/ (accessed Oct. 15, 2018).

3   *Global Mercury Assessment 2013: Sources, Emissions, Releases and Environmental Transport* (United Nations Environment Program, 2013), www.web.archive.org/web/20140401110408/http://www.unep.org/PDF/PressReleases/GlobalMercuryAssessment2013.pdf (accessed Oct. 15, 2018), i–ii.

[...] a dolphin won't rethink his having left it to men
to send mixed signals to the mullahs they processed in some holding pen.

(Ibid.)

The mullahs emerge from the earlier mention of "mullets" (the fish, not the hairstyle). Some putative group of "men" sends mixed signals to both dolphins and "mullahs." The binaries of men and marine animals is shifted to the relationship of men and mullahs, and there is an undertow of orientalism to this (are mullahs not also men?). In any case, like "Truce" earlier, Muldoon tables a theme (humanity's betrayal of nature) only to move surprisingly to another by way of conclusion. Has he ever written *about* ecology? Has he, for that matter, ever written *about* human rights abuses, like that of the use of torture by the US?

It may well be that we have misconstrued the dolphins completely (and Muldoon's louche use of conjunctions opens possibilities for misconstrual), for they surface repeatedly in the long sonnet sequence, "Dirty Data." Yet here they accompany themes unconnected with ecology. It would seem that the ecological issue comes in and out of focus. While another poem in *Maggot*, "Charles Baudelaire: 'The Albatross,'" also has an epigraph that announces the devastation of fauna by modern industry (ibid., 62), perhaps Muldoon is just leading us astray, much as a detective writer distracts us with red herrings. (It's also noteworthy that the cover of the British edition of *Maggot* has a picture of a decomposing bird whose stomach is full of bleached plastic objects.) Perhaps we were wrong in the first place. Perhaps the dolphins with Teflon stubble in the Boucher poem were red herrings after all. "Hang on," as they said in *The Day After Tomorrow*. "Are you saying these things are interconnected?" To which the answer was: "We have to consider the possibility." And its obverse: that these things are *not* connected.

Rather than get to the bottom of it all, it may be better to think of Muldoon's approach as both a new-ish way of dealing with themes and, in the process, of dealing with a new-ish theme. This brings us back to the earlier discussion of Heaney. I figured the older poet as prehensile in his approach to the sandstone keepsake, and this holds for much of his work: his poems propose themes and turn them through different angles, seeking resolutions – whether, in Kay's terms, intellectual or imaginative. Muldoon, in contrast, seems never to deal directly with a subject: rather it flits in and out of poems, and from one poem to another. Muldoon stress-tests poems, seeking to discover how much centrifugal thematics they can take. The epigraph from Pliny the Elder is repeated as epigraph to a later poem in *Maggot*, "Loss of Separation: A Companion," a text that seems to have failed such a stress-test, as it is pulled apart in multiple directions at once (ibid., 90). It exists only in relation to the other poems in the book, as instructive example along a spectrum, which is marked by a poem near the beginning dedicated to Richard Wilbur and, near the end, another poem dedicated to John Ashbery. Of these two US poets, the former is closest to Heaney, in the terms of our argument, and the latter slightly more disjunctive than Muldoon himself. Muldoon thus wonders how far his material may stray.

Because straying is the point. Back in 1913, Ezra Pound declared that direct treatment of the thing was one of the main desiderata of Imagism. *Pace* Pound, Muldoon's idea is at all costs to *avoid* direct treatment of the thing, even as the thing, the theme, comes glancing in and out of his poems. Here I've focused on ecological disaster, but it could equally be human rights in conflict situations ("Lateral," "Dirty Data"), imperialism (*passim*), victims of road accidents ("Wayside Shrines"), the Irish language (*Rising to the Rising*, "Dirty Data"), Latin American labour rights in the US ("To Market, to Market"), to name a few of the themes that occur in his recent work, and which he carefully avoids writing about, even as they appear in his poems.

Maureen N. McLane has argued for what she calls a "compositionist poetics" through the example of the ballad. Authorless but crafted, this poetic form "offer[s] an archive for thinking across an anthropocentric poetics and horizon of pathos" (McLane 2017, 110). Like many poets since the late eighteenth century, Muldoon has used the ballad form, simulating and sampling it at multiple stages in his career. But Muldoon's poetry may be "compositionist" beyond those instances in his poems: insofar as he tends to avoid writing *about* themes in the manner I've outlined above, this nudges him away from narratives of pathos, and this helps to avoid anthropocentrism. He does not fix the symbolic meaning of his animals – those dolphins can't be constantly viewed as augurs of the Anthropocene – and that is complemented by an avoidance of the usual emotional manoeuvres that we find in representation of the nuclear family in the twentieth century (autobiographical narratives including memories of parents, relationships with partners and children – the kind of material that provides the backbone of Heaney's work). Helen Vendler remarked that his poems "too often had a hole in the middle where the feeling should be" (Vendler 1997, 58). It is not that Muldoon avoids these subjects, but rather that they are reconfigured in a new continuum, consonant with McLane's statement "that poems, like people, thoughts, plants, and ballads themselves, are cocomposed, are made and unmade together in a contingent networking of the animate and inanimate" (McLane 2017, 112).

This is where we return to the argument about Morton's hyperobjects with which I began this essay. Morton assumed that certain modes of culture were better than others for representing the hyperobject of global warming. He advocates a late modernist aesthetic in which the listener/reader/viewer is given an idea of the outsized dimensions of hyperobjects by seeing a new artwork exceed the conventional dimensions of art – thus Young's *Well-Tuned Piano* lasts six hours, for instance. Although I haven't, and probably won't ever, listen to all of Young's piece, I can understand how this works, at least on the smaller scale of the 800% slower songs. Those latter pieces provoke me to think about the scales of perception that I bring to my experience. One then understands the larger and longer horizon that, say, the Clock of the Long Now wishes to represent. Similarly, one activist has said that holding her newborn grandchild in her arms created a physical sense of these ideas: "In that moment, my sense of time altered and I began to think in a time span of a hundred years" (Carroll 2018).

Moreover, Morton writes that hyperobject art, as he conceives it, has to decentre the human. The works that he favours seem to erase human agency, and let the objects themselves sing through the medium. Such art is consonant with a broader contour of his thought:

> [W]hat has happened so far during the epoch of the Anthropocene has been the gradual realization by humans that they are not running the show, at the very moment of their most powerful technical mastery on a planetary scale. Humans are not the conductors of meaning, not the pianists of the real.
>
> (Morton 2013, 164)

If his chosen late modernist works simulate this, then so do Muldoon's poems, although in a different manner. Obviously, Muldoon's poems are highly constructed objects, as I've remarked above, drawing on the resources of conventional poetic form with a rare concentration. But equally this technique does not serve to display mastery, since his treatment of theme demonstrates none of the argumentative coherence of a single speaker, as Heaney's poem does. By weakening the logical conjunctions of his argument, he loosens such coherence, as though allowing the material of the poem to find its own paths, without being governed by an argument.

This indeterminacy affords us a glimpse of hyperobjects in Morton's idea of them. The phenomena that dart in and out of Muldoon's poems *may* be connected, and this hermeneutic drama simulates the larger drama of hyperobjects that Morton describes. They are "hyper" because they are missable in the same way that themes are in Muldoon's poetry. They phase in and out of our perception. They are distributed over long swathes of time (namely, "across the span / of twenty-five thousand years," in "François Boucher: Arion on the Dolphin") and radically sundry contexts (Kennedy, Greek myth, dolphins injured by industrial methylmercury). They are also non-local: while Muldoon returns throughout his career to Ulster, where he grew up, the province becomes like origami paper, folded into different locations, times, and mythologies. Even when returning home, Muldoon's imagination avoids old narratives of pathos. Perhaps, indeed, they don't even appear to him as options.

Twentieth-century culture is replete with artworks that simulate lack of human agency. Perhaps the orchestra is just playing itself in Pierre Boulez's *Le marteau sans maître* (The Hammer without a Master; 1956). Perhaps those Abstract Expressionist canvases were created by Jackson Pollock leaving the door open during a line storm. But Muldoon's particular combination of bravura formal technique with the poems' weird aura of authorlessness is unique. They make us question our divisions of art (modernism and the rest), and also broaden the repertoire of Anthropocene culture.

Contributors

Michel Collot, Universite Sorbonne Nouvelle, Paris
Jakub Hankiewicz, Charles University, Prague
Josef Hrdlička, Charles University, Prague
Anne Hultsch, Universitat Wien
Zornica Kirkova, Staatsbibliothek zu Berlin – Preusischer Kulturbesitz
Kirill Korchagin, V. V. Vinogradov Russian Language Institute of the Russian Academy of Sciences, Moscow
Olga Lomová, Charles University, Prague
Mariana Machová, University of South Bohemia, České Budějovice
Pavel Novotný, Technical University of Liberec
Justin Quinn, University of West Bohemia
Dalia Satkauskytė, Institute of Lithuanian Literature and Folklore
Michael Squire, King's College London
Alice Stašková, Friedrich-Schiller-Universität Jena
Karel Thein, Charles University, Prague
Jaromír Typlt, Charles University, Prague
Josef Vojvodík, Charles University, Prague
Julie Wittlichová, Charles University, Prague

Bibliography

Acquisto, Joseph. 2005. "The Lyric of Narrative: Exile, Poetry, and Story in Saint-John Perse and Elizabeth Bishop." *Orbis Litterarum* 60, no. 5: 344–56.

Adelung, Johann Christoph. 1811. *Grammatisch-kritisches Wörterbuch der hochdeutschen Mundart.* Vienna: Bauer. Accessed 20 May 2019. Münchener Digitalisierungszentrum.

Adelung, Johann Christoph. 1974. *Ueber den deutschen Styl* [1785]. Hildesheim: Olms.

Arendt, Hannah. 1998. *The Human Condition.* Chicago: University of Chicago Press.

Areopagita Dionysius. 1944. *Theologia mystica.* Translated by Alan W. Watts. New York: Holy Cross Press.

Artmann, Hans Carl. 1970. *The Best of H. C. Artmann.* Frankfurt a. M.: Suhrkamp.

Artmann, Hans Carl. 1985. "tom du tümmel." In *Wiener Gruppe,* edited by Gerhard Rühm, 102. Hamburg: Rowohlt.

Atik, Arina. 2015. *Proizvodstvo opyta osvobozhdeniya v religii i vne religii: Vliyanie dzen-buddizma na rannii moskovskii Kontseptualizm.* Moskva.

Bachelard, Gaston. 2002. *Earth and Reveries of Will: An Essay on the Imagination of Matter.* Translated by Kenneth Haltman. Dallas: Dallas Institute of Humanities and Culture.

Badt, Kurt. 1969. *Die Kunst des Nicolas Poussin.* Cologne: DuMont Schauberg.

Barańczak, Stanisław. 1994. *Uciekinier z Utopii: O poezji Zbigniewa Herberta.* Wrocław: Towarzystwo Przyjaciół Polonistyki Wrocławskiej.

Bardon, Henri. 1975. "Publilii Optatiani Porfyrii Carmina, recensuit Ioannes Polara." *Revue Belge de Philologie et d'Histoire* 53: 453.

Barnes, Timothy David. 1975. "Publilius Optatianus Porfyrius." *American Journal of Philology* 96: 173–86.

Barthes, Roland. 1964. "Littérature objective." In *Essais critiques*, 62–84. Paris: Seuil.

Batyushkov, Konstantin. 1964. *Polnoe sobranie stikhotvorenii.* Moscow: Sovetskii spisovatel'.

Baudelaire, Charles. 1976. *Œuvres complètes.* Vol. 2. Paris: Gallimard.

Bažil, Martin. 2009. *Centones Christiani: Métamorphoses d'une forme intertextuelle dans la poésie latine chrétienne de l'antiquité tardive.* Paris: Institut d'études augustiniennes.

Bažil, Martin. 2017. "Elementorum varius textus: Atomistisches und Anagrammatisches in Optatians Textbegriff." In *Morphogrammata / The Lettered Art of Optatian: Figuring Cultural Transformations in the Age of Constantine,* edited by M. Squire and J. Wienand, 341–68. Paderborn: Wilhelm Fink.

Beck, Philippe. 2007. *Chants populaires.* Paris: Flammarion.

Beck, Philippe. 2009. *Lyre dure.* Caen: Nous.

Becker, Andrew Sprague. 1995. *The Shield of Achilles and the Poetics of Ekphrasis.* Lanham: Rowman and Littlefield.

Białoszewski, Miron. 2016. *Obroty rzeczy. Rachunek zachciankowy. Mylne wzruszenia. Było i było.* Warsaw: Państwowy Instytut Wydawniczy.

Bienkowski, Piotr. 1891. "Lo scudo di Achille." *Mitteilungen des Deutschen Archäologischen Instituts, Römische Abteilung* 6:183–207.

Binkis, Kazys. 1972. *Lyrika.* Vilnius: Vaga.

Bishop, Elizabeth. 1983. *The Complete Poems: 1927–1979.* New York: Farrar, Strauss and Giroux.

Blitstein, Pablo A. 2015. *Les fleurs du royaume: Savoirs lettrés et pouvoir impérial en Chine, (Ve-VIe siècles).* Paris: Les Belles lettres.

Blumenberg, Hans. 2001. *Lebenszeit und Weltzeit.* Frankfurt a. M.: Suhrkamp.

Boeder, Maria. 1996. *Visa est Vox: Sprache und Bild in der spätantiken Literatur.* Frankfurt a. M.: Peter Lang.

Böhme, Gernot. 2001. *Aisthetik: Vorlesungen über Ästhetik als allgemeine Wahrnehmungslehre.* Munich: Wilhelm Fink.

The Book of Songs: The Ancient Chinese Classics of Poetry. 1996. Translated by A. Waley, edited by Joseph R. Allen 1996. New York: Grove Press.

Bramble, John. 2015. *Modernism and the Occult.* London: Palgrave Macmillan.

Brand, Stewart. 1999. *The Clock of the Long Now: Time and Responsibility.* New York: Basic Books.

Bremer, Claus. 1983. *Farbe bekennen: Mein Weg durch die konkrete Poesie.* Zürich: Orte-Verlag.

Brockes, Barthold Heinrich. 2016. *Irdisches Vergnügen in Gott: Fünfter und Sechster Theil* [1739]. Edited by Jürgen Rathje. Göttingen: Wallstein.

Brouk, Bohuslav. 1947. *Lidé a věci*. Prague: Václav Petr.

Brown, Bill. 2001. "Thing Theory." *Critical Inquiry* 28, no. 1:1–22.

Brown, Bill. 2015. *Other Things*. Chicago: University of Chicago Press.

Bruhat, Marie-Odile. 1999. *Les carmina figurata de Publilius Optatianus Porfyrius: La métamorphose d'un genre et l'invention d'une poésie liturgique impériale sous Constantin*. Unpublished PhD dissertation, Université Paris-Sorbonne, Paris IV.

Bruhat, Marie-Odile. 2008. "Une poétique du vœu: Inspiration poétique et mystique impérial dans le poème XIX (et quelques autres) d'Optatianus Porfyrius." *Dictynna* 5:57–108.

Bruhat, Marie-Odile. 2017. "The Treatment of Space in Optatian's Poetry." In *Morphogrammata / The Lettered Art of Optatian: Figuring Cultural Transformations in the Age of Constantine*, edited by M. Squire and J. Wienand, 257–81. Paderborn: Wilhelm Fink.

Bruun, Patrick M. 1963. "Symboles, signes et monogrammes." In *Sylloge inscriptionum Christianarum veterum Musei Vaticani*, edited by He. Zilliacus, 2:73–166. Helsinki.

Březina, Otokar. 1958. *Básně*. Prague: Československý spisovatel.

Bubner, Rüdiger. 1993. "Die Gesetzlichkeit der Natur und die Willkür der Menschheitsgeschichte. Goethe vor dem Historismus." *Goethe-Jahrbuch* 110:135–45.

Buddeus, Ondřej, and Markéta Magidová, eds. 2015. *Třídit slova: Literatura a konceptuální tendence 1949–2015*. Prague: tranzit.cz.

Cadiot, Olivier, and Pierre Alferi. 1995a. "La mécanique lyrique." *Revue de Littérature générale* 1:5–6.

Cadiot, Olivier, and Pierre Alferi. 1995b. "Digest." *Revue de Littérature générale* 2: not paginated (text no 49).

Carroll, Rory. 2018. "Mary Robinson on Climate Change." *Guardian*, 12 October 2018. https://www.theguardian.com/science/2018/oct/12/mary-robinson-climate-change-former-president-ireland-ipcc-report.

Čerepková, Vladimíra. 2001. *Básně*. Prague: Torst.

Chalupecký, Jindřich. 2000. "Svět v němž žijeme" [1939–1940]. In *Skupina 42: Antologie*, edited by Z. Pešat and E. Petrová, 81–86. Brno: Atlantis.

Cheng, Anne. 1997. *Histoire de la pensée chinoise*. Paris: Points.

Chinn, Christopher. 2005. "Statius *Silv.* 4.6 and the Epigrammatic Origins of *Ekphrasis.*" *Classical Journal* 100, no. 4 (February–March): 247–63.

Chong kan Songben Zhouyi zhushu 重栞宋本周易注疏. In *Chong kan Songben shisan jing zhushu*重刊宋本十三經注疏. Scripta Sinica electronic edition based on the 1815 Nanchang fuxue 南昌府學woodblock edition (http://hanchi.ihp.sinica.edu.tw/ihp/hanji.htm).

Cirio, Amalia Margherita. 1980–1981. "Prodigio e tecnica nello scudo di Achille." *Annali dell'Istituto Universitario Orientale di Napoli* 2–3:47–58.

Collot, Michel. 1991. *Francis Ponge entre mots et choses.* Seyssel: Champ Vallon.

Collot, Michel. 1995. *La Matière-émotion.* Paris: PUF.

Collot, Michel. 2005. *La poésie moderne et la structure d'horizon* [1989]. Paris: PUF.

Collot, Michel. 2018. *Le Parti pris des lieux.* Brussels: La Lettre volée.

Conrad-Martius, Hedwig. 1957. *Sein.* Munich: Kösel.

Conrad-Martius, Hedwig. 1939. "Schöpfung und Zeugung." *Tijdschrift voor Philosophie* 1:801–26.

Corbier, Mireille. 2006. *Donner à voir, donner à lire: Mémoire et communication dans la Rome ancienne.* Paris: CNRS.

Courtney, Edward. 1990. "Greek and Latin acrostics." *Philologus* 134:1–13.

Courtney, Edward. 1993. *The Fragmentary Latin Poets.* Oxford: Oxford University Press.

Cullhed, Eric. 2014. "Movement and Sound on the Shield of Achilles in Ancient Exegesis." *Greek, Roman, and Byzantine Studies* 54, no. 2:192–219.

David, Milan. 2001. "Dopisy Jindřicha Chalupeckého Miladě Součkové." In *Neznámý člověk Milada Součková,* edited by M. Bauer, 109–11. Prague: Ústav pro českou literaturu AV ČR.

Dencker, Klaus Peter. 2011. *Optische Poesie: Von den prähistorischen Schriftzeichen bis zu den digitalen Experimenten der Gegenwart.* Berlin: De Gruyter.

Derham, William. 1723. *Physico-Theology or, A Demonstration of the Being and Attributes of God, from his Works of Creation.* London: Innys.

Derham, William. 1728. *Astrotheologie, oder Himmlisches Vergnügen in Gott.* Hamburg: Felginer.

Derrida, Jacques. 1976. *Of Grammatology.* Translated by G. Chakravorty. Baltimore: John Hopkins University Press.

Derrida, Jacques. 1978. *La Verité en peinture.* Paris: Flammarion.

Dragomoshchenko, Arkadij. 1987. "Nasturtsiya kak real'nost'." *Chasy* 68:25–42.

Dragomoshchenko, Arkadij. 2015. "Uzhin s privetlivymi bogami." *Mitin zhurnal* 68:14–39.

Droit, Roger-Pol. 2005. *How Are Things? A Philosophical Experiment.* Translated by Theo Cuffe. London: Faber and Faber.

Dubel, Sandrine. 2006. "Quand la matière est couleur: Du bouclier d'Achille aux 'tableaux de bronze' de Taxila." In *Couleurs et matières dans l'Antiquité : Textes, techniques et pratiques,* edited by S. Dubel and V. Naas, 161–81. Paris: Rue d'Ulm.

Duckworth, William. 1999. *Talking Music: Conversations with John Cage, Philip Glass, Laurie Anderson and 5 Generations of American Experimental Composers.* Cambridge, MA: Da Capo Press.

Dutli, Ralph. 2004. "Notizen." In Ossip Mandelstam, *Der Stein: Frühe Gedichte 1908–1915,* translated by R. Dutli, 201–237. Zürich: Ammann.

Dutli, Ralph. 1986. "Nachwort." In Ossip Mandelstam, *Mitternacht in Moskau. Die Moskauer Hefte: Gedichte 1930–1934,* translated by R. Dutli, 247–266. Zürich: Ammann.

Dvořák, Max. 1936. "Kostel Il Gesù v Římě. In Max Dvořák." In *Umění jako projev ducha,* 117–40. Prague: Jan Laichter.

Dvorský, Stanislav. 1969a. "Symbol a realita." In *Surrealistické východisko,* edited by S. Dvorský, V. Effenberger, and P. Král, 83–90. Prague: Československý spisovatel.

Dvorský, Stanislav. 1969b. "Na pozadí světa, který nevoní." In *Surrealistické východisko,* edited by S. Dvorský, V. Effenberger, and P. Král, 131–36. Prague: Československý spisovatel.

Dvorský, Stanislav. 2006. *Hra na ohradu.* Prague: Torst.

Dzhindzholiya, Beslan. 2004. *Kontseptsiya prosvetleniya v uchenii D. T. Sudzuki: Teoriya i praktika voproshaniya.* Yekaterinburg: Izdatelstvo Uralskogo Universiteta.

Edmond, Jacob. 2012. *A Common Strangeness: Contemporary Poetry, Cross-cultural Encounter, Comparative Literature.* New York: Fordham University Press.

Edwards, John Stephan. 2005. "The *Carmina* of Publilius Optatianus Porphyrius and the Creative Process." In *Studies in Latin Literature and Roman History* (= Collections Latomus 287), edited by C. Deroux, 12:447–66. Brussels: Latomus.

Edwards, Mark W. 1991. *The* Iliad: *A Commentary.* Vol. 5, *Books 17–20.* Cambridge: Cambridge University Press.

Effenberger, Vratislav. 2007. *Básně.* Vol. 2. Prague: Torst.

Eich, Günter. 1991. *Gesammelte Werke.* Vol. 1, *Die Gedichte: Die Malwürfe.* Edited by Axel Vieregg. Frankfurt a. M.: Suhrkamp.

Eliade, Mircea. 1961. *The Sacred and the Profane: The Nature of Religion: The Significance of Religious Myth, Symbolism, and Ritual within Life and Culture.* Translated by Willard R. Trask. New York: Harcourt Brace.

Eliot, T. S. 1998. *The Sacred Wood: Major Early Essays.* Mineola, N.Y.: Dover.

Elsner, Jaś. 2000. "From the Culture of *spolia* to the Cult of Relics: The Arch of Constantine and the Genesis of Late Antique Forms." *Papers of the British School at Rome* 68:149–84.

Elsner, Jaś. 2002. "Introduction: The Genres of Ekphrasis." *Ramus* 31 (1–2): 1–18.

Elsner, Jaś. 2010. "Art History as *Ekphrasis*." *Art History* 33, no. 1 (February): 10–27.

Elsner, Jaś. 2017. "Late Narcissus: Classicism and Culture in a Late Roman Cento." In *The Poetics of Late Latin Literature,* edited by J. Elsner and J. Hernández Lobato, 176–205. Oxford: Oxford University Press.

Elsner, Jaś, and J. Hernández Lobato, eds. 2017. *The Poetics of Late Latin Literature.* Oxford: Oxford University Press.

Engels, Lodewijk Jozef, and Heinz Hofmann. 1997. "Literatur und Gesellschaft in der Spätantike: Texte, Kommunikation und Überlieferung. " In *Spätantike, mit einem Panorama der byzantinischen Literatur: Neues Handbuch der Literaturwissenschaft,* edited by L. J. Engels and H. Hofmann, 4:29–99. Wiesbaden: Aula-Verlag.

Enzensberger, Hans Magnus. 1962. *Die Aporien der Avantgarde.* Frankfurt a. M.: Suhrkamp.

Enzensberger, Hans Magnus. 1986. *Gedichte 1950–1985.* Frankfurt a. M.: Suhrkamp.

Ernst, Ulrich. 1991. *Carmen figuratum: Geschichte des Figurengedichts von den antiken Ursprüngen bis zum Ausgang des Mittelalters.* Cologne: Bohlau.

Ernst, Ulrich. 2012. *Visuelle Poesie: Historische Dokumentation theoretischer Zeugnisse.* Vol. 1, *Von der Antike bis zum Barock.* Berlin: de Gruyter.

Ernst, Ulrich. 2016. *Visuelle Poesie: Historische Dokumentation theoretischer Zeugnisse.* Vol. 2, *Vom Spätbarock bis zur Gegenwart.* Berlin: de Gruyter.

Ernesti, Johann August. 1761. *Institutio interpretis Novi Testamenti ad usum lectionum*. Leipzig: Weidmann.

Eşanu, Octavian. 2016. *Transition in Post-Soviet Art: The Collective Actions Group Before and After 1989*. Budapest: CEU Press.

Espitallier, Jean-Michel. 2000. *Pièces détachées: Une anthologie de la poésie française aujourd'hui*. Paris: Pocket.

Falikov, Boris. 2017. *Velichina kachestva: Okkul'tizm, religii Vostoka i iskusstvo XX veka*. Moscow: Novoe literaturnoe obozrenie.

Fei Zhengang 費振剛 et al., eds. 1993. *Quan Han fu* 全漢賦. Beijing: Beijing daxue chubanshe.

Felten, Josephus, ed. 1913. *Nicolaus, Progymnasmata*. Leipzig: Teubner.

Finlay, Ian Hamilton. 1967. "The Horizon of Holland." In *An Anthology of Concrete Poetry*, edited by E. Williams, not paginated. New York: Something Else Press.

Fletcher, Angus. 2012. *Allegory: The Theory of a Symbolic Mode*. Princeton: Princeton University Press.

Franaszek, Andrzej. 2018. *Herbert: Biografia*, Vol. 1, *Niepokój*. Kraków: Znak.

Francis, James A. 2009. "Metal Maidens, Achilles' Shield, and Pandora: The Beginnings of *Ekphrasis*." *American Journal of Philology* 130, no. 1 (Spring): 1–23.

Fredrick, David. 1999. "Haptic Poetics." *Arethusa* 32, no. 1 (Winter): 49–83.

Fridman, Nikolai. 1964. "Primechaniya." In Konstantin Batyushkov, *Polnoe sobranie stikhotvorenii*, 257–333. Moscow – Leningrad: Sovetskii spisovatel'.

Frontisi-Ducroux, Françoise. 2002. "Avec son diaphragme visionnaire: ἰδυίῃσι πραπίδεσσι, *Iliade* XVIII, 481. À propos du bouclier d'Achille." *Revue des Études Grecques* 115 (July–Decembre): 463–84.

Frow, John. 2001. "A Pebble, a Camera, a Man Who Turns into a Telegraph Pole." *Critical Inquiry* 28 (1): 270–85.

Früchtl, Joseph. 2005. "Der Begriff der Vollkommenheit als Grundlage der Ästhetik? Das 18. Jahrhundert bis Kant." In *Ästhetische Grundbegriffe*, edited by K. Barck et al., 6:378–86. Stuttgart – Weimar: Metzler.

Garcia, Ana, and Fred Mamoun. 2010. "How Much Mercury Is in Your Sushi? (Part 1)." *NBC Los Angeles*, 12 May 2010. www.nbclosangeles.com/news/local/How-Much-Mercury-is-in-Your-Sushi-Part-1-93635804.html.

Gardes-Tamine, Jöelle, ed. 2002. *Saint-John Perse sans masque: Lecture philologique de l'œuvre*. Rennes: La Licorne.

Garnier, Ilse. 1986. Soleil. In Ilse Garnier, *Album à colorier*, not paginated. Paris: Éditions André Silvaire.

Geller, Leonid. 2002. "Voskreshenie ponyatiya, ili Slovo ob ekfrasise." In *Ekfrasis v russkoi literature: Trudy lozannskogo simpoziuma*, edited by L. Geller, 5–22. Moskva: MIK.

Geller, Leonid. 2013. "Ekfrasis, ili Obnazhenie priema: Neskol'ko voprosov i tezis." In *"Nevyrazimo vyrazimoe": Ekfrasis i problemy reprezentatsii vizual'nogo v khudozhestvennom tekste*, edited by D. Tokarev, 44–60. Moscow: Novoye literaturnoye obozrenie.

Genette, Gérard. 1976. *Mimologiques*. Paris: Éditions du Seuil.

Genette, Gérard. 1997. *Paratexts: Thresholds of Interpretation*. Translated by J. E. Lewin. Cambridge: Cambridge University Press.

Gerber, Marina. 2018. *Empty Action: Labour and Free Time in the Art of* Collective Actions. Bielefeld: Transcript.

Ghosh, Amitav. 2016. *The Great Derangement: Climate Change and the Unthinkable* [e-book]. Chicago: University of Chicago Press.

Giovannelli, Alessandro. 2008. "In and Out: The Dynamics of Imagination in the Engagement with Narratives." *Journal of Aesthetics and Art Criticism* 66, no. 1 (Winter): 11–24.

Glanc, Tomáš. 2001. "Психоделический реализм. Поиск канона." Новое литературное обозрение 51:263–79.

Gleize, Jean-Marie. 1983. *Poésie et figuration*. Paris: Éditions du Seuil.

Global Mercury Assessment 2013: Sources, Emissions, Releases and Environmental Transport. United Nations Environment Program, 2013. web.archive.org/web/20140401110408/http:/www.unep.org/PDF/PressReleases/GlobalMercuryAssessment2013.pdf.

Goethe, Johann Wolfgang von. 2002. *Werke: Hamburger Ausgabe*. Vol. 11, *Autobiographische Schriften III: Italienische Reise*. Munich: C. H. Beck.

Goethe, Johann Wolfgang von. 2007. "Römische Elegien." In J. W. v. Goethe, *Gedichte, Jubiläumsausgabe*, herausgegeben und kommentiert von Erich Trunz, 157–173. Munich: C. H. Beck.

Goethe, Johann Wolfgang von. 2013. *Goethes Briefe: Hamburger Ausgabe*. Vol. 2, *Goethes Briefe 1786–1805: Briefe, Kommentare und Register*. Edited by Karl Robert Mandelkow and Bodo Morawe. Munich: C. H. Beck.

Goldhill, Simon. 2007. "What is *Ekphrasis* for?" *Classical Philology* 102:1–19.

Goldhill, Simon. 2012. Forms of Attention: Time and Narrative in Ecphrasis. *Cambridge Classical Journal* 58 (December): 88–114.

Gomringer, Eugen, ed. 1992. *Konkrete Poesie* [1972]. Stuttgart: Reclam.

Gorodetsky, Sergei. 1913. "Nekotorye techeniya v sovremennoi russkoi poezii." *Apollon* 1:46–50.

Graubner, Hans. 1990. "Physikotheologie und Kinderphysik: Kants und Hamanns gemeinsamer Plan einer Physik fur Kinder in der physikotheologischen Tradition des 18. Jahrhundert." In *Johann Georg Hamann und die Krise der Aufklarung*, edited by B. Gajek and A. Meier, 117–145. Frankfurt a. M.: Peter Lang.

Green, Roger P. H. 2010. "Constantine as Patron of Christian Latin Poetry." *Studia Patristica* 46:65–76.

Grögerová, Bohumila, and Josef Hiršal. 2007. *Let let*. Prague: Torst.

Grondin, Jean. 1996. "Hermeneutik." In *Historisches Wörterbuch der Rhetorik*, edited by Gert Ueding, 1350–74. Tübingen: Mohr Siebeck.

Guichard, Luis Arturo. 2006. "Simias' Pattern Poems." In *Beyond the Canon*, edited by M. A. Harder, R. F. Regtuit, and G. C. Wakker, 83–103. Leuven: Peeters.

Gumilyov, Nikolai. 1913. "Nasledie simvolizma i akmeizm." *Apollon* 1:42–45.

Günther, Friederike Felicitas. 2016. "Barthold Heinrich Brockes' irdisches Vergnügen am Überleben." In: *Der Tod und die Künste*, edited by F. F. Günther and W. Riedel, 133–55. Würzburg: Königshausen & Neumann.

Habinek, Thomas. 2009. "Situating Literacy in Rome." In *Ancient Literacies: The Culture of Reading in Greece and Rome*, edited by W. A. Johnson and H. N. Parker, 114–41. Oxford: Oxford University Press.

Habinek, Thomas. 2017. "Optatian and his Oeuvre: Explorations in Ontology." In *Morphogrammata / The Lettered Art of Optatian: Figuring Cultural Transformations in the Age of Constantine*, edited by M. Squire and J. Wienand, 391–425. Paderborn: Wilhelm Fink.

Haman, Aleš. 2001. "Dopisy Milady Součkové Jindřichu Chalupeckému." In *Neznámý člověk Milada Součková*, edited by M. Bauer, 104–108. Prague: Ústav pro českou literaturu AV ČR.

Hamburger, Käte. 1986. *Logique des genres littéraires*. Translated by P. Cadiot. Paris: Éditions du Seuil.

Hansen-Löve, Aage A. 1999. "Entfaltungen der Gewebe-Metapher. Mandelstam-Texturen." *Der Prokurist* 16–17:71–151.

Hansen-Löve, Aage A. 2008. "Wir sind alle aus ,Pljuškins Haufen' hervorgekrochen …": Ding – Gegenstand – Ungegenständlichkeit – Unding. In *Der dementierte Gegenstand: Artefaktskepsis der russischen Avantgarde zwischen*

Abstraktion und Dinglichkeit, edited by A. Henning and G. Witte, 251–346. Vienna – Munich: s. n.

Harder, Annette. 2007. "Epigram and the Heritage of Epic." In *Brill's Companion to Hellenistic Epigram*, edited by P. Bing and J. S. Bruss, 409–28. Leiden: Brill.

Hardie, Philip. 1985. "*Imago Mundi*: Cosmological and Ideological Aspects of the Shield of Achilles." *Journal of Hellenic Studies* 105:11–31.

Hardie, Philip. 1986. *Virgil's* Aeneid: *Cosmos and Imperium*. Oxford: Clarendon Press.

Harries, Karsten. 1998. *The Ethical Function of Architecture*. Cambridge, MA: MIT Press.

Havelock, Eric A. 1977. "The Preliteracy of the Greeks." *New Literary History* 8 (3): 369–91.

Heaney, Seamus. 2010. *Opened Ground: Poems 1966–1996* [e-book]. London: Faber and Faber.

Heath, Malcolm. 2002/3. "Theon and the History of the *Progymnasmata*." *Greek, Roman, and Byzantine Studies* 43, no. 2:129–60.

Heffernan, James A. W. 1993. *Museum of Words: The Poetics of Ekphrasis from Homer to Ashbery*. Chicago – London: The University of Chicago Press.

Hegel, Georg Wilhelm Friedrich. 1979. *Esthétique*. Vol. 4. Translated by Samuel Jankélévitch. Paris: Flammarion.

Heisig, James. 2001. *Philosophers of Nothingness: An Essay on the Kyoto School*. Honolulu: University of Hawaii Press.

Helm, Rudolf, ed. 1956. *Eusebius Werke*. Vol. 7, *Die Chronik des Hieronymus (Hieronymi Chronicon)*. Berlin: de Gruyter.

Helm, Rudolf. 1959. 29: Publilius Optatianus Porfyrius. *Paulys Realencyklopädie der classischen Altertumswissenschaft* 23.2: 1928–1936.

Heidegger, Martin. 1993. "The Origin of the Work of Art." In M. Heidegger, *Basic Writings*, 143–212. San Francisco: Harper.

Herbert, Zbigniew. 2011. *Wiersze zebrane*. Kraków: Wydawnictwo a5.

Hernández Lobato, Jesús. 2012. *Vel Apolline muto. Estética y poética de la antigüedad tardía*. Bern: Peter Lang.

Hernández Lobato, Jesús. 2017. "Conceptual Poetry: Rethinking Optatian from Contemporary Art." In *Morphogrammata / The Lettered Art of Optatian: Figuring Cultural Transformations in the Age of Constantine*, edited by M. Squire and J. Wienand, 461–93. Paderborn: Wilhelm Fink.

Heselhaus, Clemens. 1951. "Wiederherstellung. Restauratio-Restitutio-Rege-neratio." *Deutsche Vierteljahrsschrift für Literaturwissenschaft und Geistes-geschichte* 25:54–81.

Hetzer, Theodor. 1990. *Italienische Architektur*. Stuttgart: Urachhaus.

Hetzer, Theodor. 1947. *Claude Lorrain*. Frankfurt a. M.: Vittorio Klostermann.

Higgins, Dick. 1987. *Pattern Poetry: Guide to an Unknown Literature*. Albany, NY: State University of New York Press.

Hiršal, Josef, and Bohumila Grögerová, ed. 1967. *Slovo, písmo, akce, hlas.* Prague: Československý spisovatel.

Hollander, John (1969): *Swan and Shadow*, accessible from: [https://www.poetryfoundation.org/poetrymagazine/browse?contentId=30477] (25. 10. 2019)

Hrdlička, Josef. 2014. "Cruelty and Melancholy: The Stones of Roger Caillois." In *The Yearbook on History and Interpretation of Phenomenology 2013*, edited by A. Vydra, 185–203. Frankfurt a. M.: Peter Lang.

Hrdlička, Josef. 2017. "Paměť a exil v *Sešitech Josefíny Rykrové*." In Josef Hrdlička, *Poezie a kosmos: Studie o poezii a poetice*. Prague: Malvern.

Hultberg, Teddy. 1993. *Literally Speaking: Sound Poetry & Text-sound Composi-tions*. Göteborg: Bo Ejeby.

Husserl, Edmund. 1966. *Analysen zur passiven Synthesis: Aus Vorlesungs- und Forschungsmanuskripten, 1918–1926*, edited by M. Fleischer. Den Haag: Martinus Nijhoff.

Husserl, Edmund. 1973. *Ding und Raum: Vorlesungen 1907*, ed. U. Claesges. Den Haag: Martinus Nijhoff.

Ioffe, Denis. 2013. "K voprosu o tekstual'nosti i reprezentatsii khudozhes-tvennoi aktsii. Postsemiozis Andreya Monastyrskogo v traditsiyakh moskovskogo kontseptualizma ot «ottsa» Kabakova k «pasynku» Pepper-shteynu." In*"Nevyrazimo vyrazimoe": Ekfrasis i problemy reprezentatsii vizual'nogo v khudozhestvennom tekste*, edited by D. Tokarev, 210–30. Moskva: Novoye literaturnoye obozrenie.

Jakobson, Roman. 1993. "Doslov." In Milada Součková, *Sešity Josefíny Rykrové*, 214–15. Prague: Prostor.

Januševičius, Benediktas. 2018. "Vizualioji poezija lietuvių kalba." In *Raidžių paveikslai*, edited by B. Januševičius and G. Skudžinskas, 17–19. Vilnius: Nerutina.

Januševičius, Benediktas, and Gytis Skudžinskas, eds. 2018. *Raidžių paveikslai*. Vilnius: Nerutina.

Januševičius, Benediktas. 2019. *Trumpiausias Benedikto Januševičiaus eilėraštis.* Vilnius: Žiemos žodžiai.

Jeziorkowski, Klaus. 2002. "Die Grammatik der Architektur: Zum Rhythmus bei Palladio und Goethe." In *Überschreitungen: Dialoge zwischen Literatur- und Theaterwissenschaft, Architektur und bildender Kunst: Festschrift für Leonhard M. Fiedler zum 60. Geburtstag,* edited by J. Sader and A. Wörner, 29–37. Würzburg: Königshausen & Neumann.

Jonynas, Antanas A. 2017. *Šermukšnis, Pylimo gatvė.* Vilnius: Lietuvių literatūros ir tautosakos institutas.

Jünger, Ernst. 1926. *Der Kampf als inneres Erlebnis.* Berlin: Mittler & Sohn.

Kaiser, Gerhard. 2003. "Günter Eich: Inventur. Poetologie am Nullpunkt." In *Poetologische Lyrik von Klopstock bis Grünbein: Gedichte und Interpretationen,* edited by O. Hildebrand, 268–285. Cologne: Böhlau.

Kaschnitz, Marie Louise. 1989. *Gesammelte Werke.* Vol. 7, *Die Essayistische Prosa.* Frankfurt a. M.: Insel – Suhrkamp.

Kay, Magdalena. 2013. "Seamus Heaney, Zbigniew Herbert, and the Moral Imperative." *Comparative Literature Studies* 50, no. 2:262–287.

Kavolis, Vytautas. 1992. *Moterys ir vyrai lietuvių kultūroje.* Vilnius: Lietuvos kultūros institutas.

Keil, Heinrich, ed. 1855–1880. *Grammatici Latini.* 8 vols. Leipzig: Teubner.

Knechtges, David R. translator 2014. *Wen xuan or Selections of Refined Literature.* Vol. 3. Princeton: Princeton University Press.

Knoblock, John 1994. *Xunzi: A Translation and Study of the Complete Works.* Books 17–32. Stanford: Stanford University Press.

Kolář, Jiří. 1999. "Černý cukr." In *Příběhy Jiřího Koláře: Básníkovy výtvarné proměny,* edited by Vladimír Karfík, 142. Prague: Gallery.

Korchagin, Kirill. 2020. "Telesnosť i jesť gorizont ožidanija…" Arkadij Dragomoshchenko kak čitatěl Morisa Merlo-Ponty, *Izvěstija UrFU.* Seria 2, Gumanitarnyje nauki, 22/2 (198): 242–257.

Körfer, Anna-Lena. 2020. *Kaiser Konstantin als Leser: Panegyrik, performance und Poetologie in den carmina Optatians.* Berlin: De Gruyter.

Král, Petr. 1969. K dynamismu živého myšlení. In *Surrealistické východisko,* edited by S. Dvorský, V. Effenberger, and Petr Král, 111–115. Prague: Československý spisovatel.

Kratochvíl, Zdeněk. 2006. *Délský potápěč k Hérakleitově řeči.* Prague: Herrmann & synové.

Kristeva, Julia. 1989. *Language – The Unknown: An Initiation into Linguistics.* Translated by A. M. Menke. New York: Columbia University Press.

Kriwet, Ferdinand. 2011. *Yester 'n' Today.* Cologne: DuMont.

Kwapisz, Jan. 2013. *The Greek Figure Poems.* Leuven: Peeters.

Kwapisz, Jan. 2017. "Optatian and the Order of Court Riddlers." In *Morphogrammata / The Lettered Art of Optatian: Figuring Cultural Transformations in the Age of Constantine,* edited by M. Squire and J. Wienand, 165–90. Paderborn: Wilhelm Fink.

Kwapisz, Jan. 2019. *The Paradigm of Simias: Essays on Poetic Eccentricity.* Berlin: de Gruyter.

Kwiatkowski, Jerzy. 1964. *Klucze do wyobraźni: Szkice o poetach współczesnych.* Warszawa: Państwowy instytut wydawniczy.

Lachmann, Renate. 1990. *Gedächtnis und Literatur: Intertextualität in der Moderne.* Frankfurt a. M.: Suhrkamp.

Lamping, Dieter D. 2000. *Das lyrische Gedicht. Definitionen zu Theorie und Geschichte der Gattung.* Göttingen: Vandenhoeck und Ruprecht.

Landsberg, Paul Ludwig. 1922. *Die Welt des Mittelalters und wir. Ein geschichtsphilosophischer Versuch über den Sinn eines Zeitalters.* Bonn: Friedrich Cohen.

Lausberg, Heinrich. 1998. *Handbook of Literary Rhetoric: A Foundation for Literary Study,* edited by D. E. Orton, and D. Anderson, translated by M. T. Bliss, A. Jansen, and D. E. Orton. Leiden: Brill.

Legge, James 1960. *The Shoo King, or the Book of Historical Documents: The Chinese Classics.* Vol. 3. Hong Kong: Hong Kong University Press.

Legge, James 1963. *The I Ching: The Sacred Books of the East.* Vol. 16. 2nd edition. Mineola, N. Y.: Dover Publications.

Legge, James 1964. *The Li Ki: The Sacred Books of the East.* Vol. 27–28. Delhi: Motilal Banarsidass.

Lessing, Gotthold Ephraim. 2005. *Laocoon: An Essay upon the Limits of Painting and Poetry.* Translated by Ellen Frothingham. Mineola, N. Y.: Dover Publications.

Levitan, William. 1985. "Dancing at the End of the Rope: Optatian Porfyry and the Field of Roman Verse." *Transactions of the American Philological Association* 115:245–69.

De Libera, Alain. 2015. *L'invention du sujet modern: Cours du Collège de France 2013–2014.* Paris: Vrin.

Lobsien, Eckhard. 2012. *Schematisierte Ansichten: Literaturtheorie mit Husserl, Ingarden.* Munich: Wilhelm Fink.

Lomová, Olga. 2004. "The Motif of the Orange Tree in Early Chinese Poetry: From 'Deep-Rooted, Firm and Hard to Move' to 'Lacking Vigour'." *Archiv Orientální* 72:285–97.

Lotman, Yuri M. 1990. *Universe of the Mind*. Translated by Ann Shukman. London – New York: Tauris.

Lotman, Jurij M. 1990a. "Über die Semiosphäre." *Zeitschrift für Semiotik* 12, 4:287–305.

Lotman, Juri. 2011. "The Place of Art Among Other Modelling Systems." *Sign System Studies* 39, no 2/4:249–70. http://www.sss.ut.ee/index.php/sss/article/view/SSS.2011.39.2-4.10.

Lovatt, Helen. 2013. *The Epic Gaze: Vision, Gender and Narrative in Ancient Epic*. Cambridge: Cambridge University Press.

Lunn-Rockliffe, Sophie. 2017. "The Power of the Jewelled Style: Chrisitian Signs and Names in Optatian's *versus intexti* and on Gems." In *Morphogrammata / The Lettered Art of Optatian: Figuring Cultural Transformations in the Age of Constantine*, edited by M. Squire and J. Wienand, 427–59. Paderborn: Wilhelm Fink.

Luz, Christine. 2010. *Technopaignia: Formspiele in der griechischen Dichtung*. Leiden – Boston: Brill.

MacMullen, Ramsay. 1982. "The Epigraphic Habit in the Roman Empire." *American Journal of Philology* 103: 233–46.

Mallarmé, Stéphane. 1959. *Correspondance*. Vol. 1. Paris: Gallimard.

Mallarmé, Stéphane. 1998. *Œuvres complètes*. Vol. 1. Paris: Gallimard.

Mallarmé, Stéphane. 2003. *Œuvres complètes*. Vol. 2. Paris: Gallimard.

Mandelstam, Nadezhda. 1972. *Vtoraya kniga*. Paris: YMCA-Press.

Mandelstam, Nadezhda. 2014. *Sobranie sochinenii v 2 tomakh*. Vol. 1. Yekaterinburg: Gonzo.

Mandelstam, Osip. 1925. *Primus*. Leningrad: Vremya.

Mandelstam, Osip. 1925. *Kukhnya*. Moscow – Leningrad: Raduga.

Mandelstam, Osip. 2010. "Utro akmeizma." In Osip Mandelstam, *Polnoe sobranie sochinenii i pisem v trekh tomakh*. Vol. 2, *Proza*, 22–26. Moscow: Progress-Plejada.

Mandelstam, Osip. 2011. *Polnoe sobranie sochinenii i pisem v trekh tomakh*. Vol. 3, *Proza. Pis'ma*. Moskva: Progress-Plejada.

Mandelstam, Osip. 2017a. *Polnoe sobranie sochinenii i pisem v trekh tomakh*. Vol. 1, *Stikhotvoreniya*. 2nd, expanded edition. Sankt-Peterburg: Giperion.

Mandelstam, Osip. 2017b. *Polnoe sobranie sochinenii i pisem v trekh tomakh.* Vol. 2, *Proza.* 2nd, expanded edition. Sankt-Peterburg: Giperion.

Manieri, Alessandra. 1998. *L'immagine poetica nella teoria degli antichi.* Pisa: Istituti editoriali e poligrafici internazionali.

Männlein-Robert, Irmgard. 2007. *Stimme, Schrift und Bild: Zum Verhältnis der Künste in der hellenistischen Dichtung.* Heidelberg: Winter.

Manno, Yves di, and Isabelle Garron. 2017. *Un Nouveau monde: Poésies en France: 1960–2010.* Paris : Flammarion.

Marquard, Odo. 1998. "Entlastung vom Absoluten. In memoriam Hans Blumenberg." In *Kontingenz. Poetik und Hermeneutik*, edited by G. von Graevenitz, 17:XVII–XXV. Munich: Wilhelm Fink.

Marinetti, Filippo Tommaso. 1987. *Les mots en liberté futuristes.* Introduction Giovanni Lista. Lausanne: L'Âge d'homme.

Mather, Richard B. 1969. "The Controversy over Conformity and Naturalness during the Six Dynasties." *History of Religions* 9:160–80.

Matuschek, Stefan. 1991. *Über das Staunen: Eine ideengeschichtliche Analyse.* Tübingen: Niemeyer.

Maulpoix, Jean-Michel. 2000. *Du lyrisme.* Paris: Corti.

Mayer, Hansjörg. 1968. Without title. In *Concrete Poetry. A World View*, edited by M. E. Solt, 124. Bloomington: Indiana University Press.

Mayor, Adrienne. 2018. *Gods and Robots: Myths, Machines, and Ancient Dreams of Technology.* Princeton: Princeton University Press.

Mazal, Otto. 1999. *Geschichte der Buchkultur.* Vol. 1, *Griechisch-römische Antike.* Graz: Austria Akademische Druck-und-Verlagsanstalt.

McGill, Scott. 2005. *Virgil Recomposed: The Mythological and Secular Centos in Antiquity.* Oxford: Oxford University Press.

McLane, Maureen N. 2017. "Compositionism: Plants, Poetics, Possibilities; or, Two Cheers for Fallacies, Especially Pathetic Ones!" *Representations* 140, (Fall): 101–20.

Meijering, Roos. 1987. *Literary and Rhetorical Theories in Greek Scholia.* Groningen: Forsten.

Mekas, Jonas. 1996. *There is no Ithaca: Idylls of Semeniškiai and Reminiscences.* Translated by Vytautas Bakaitis, foreword by Czesław Miłosz. New York: Black Thistle Pres.

Mekas, Jonas. 1997. *Semeniškių idilės: Reminiscensijos.*Vilnius: Baltos lankos.

Mickunas, Algis. 1993. "Phenomenology of Zen." *Japanese and Western Phenomenology: Contributions to Phenomenology*, 12:263–73. Dordrecht: Springer.

Miliauskaitė, Nijolė. 2002. *Silk*. Translated by Jonas Zdanys. Klaipėda: Vario burnos.

Monastyrski, Andrei. 2007. *Poeticheskii mir*. Moscow: Novoye literaturnoye obozrenie.

Moses, Stéphane. 2006. "Goethes Entdeckung der französischen Landschafts-malerei." In *Rom – Europa: Treffpunkt der Kulturen 1780–1820*, edited by P. Chiarini and W. Hinderer, 29–42. Würzburg: Königshausen & Neumann.

Morales, Helen. 2011. "Fantasising Phryne: The Psychology and Ethics of Ekphrasis." *Cambridge Classical Journal* 57, no. 1 (December): 71–104.

Moreschini, Claudio. 2013. *Storia del pensiero cristiano tardo-antico*. Milan: Bompiani.

Morton, Timothy. 2013. *Hyperobjects: Philosophy and Ecology after the End of the World*. Minneapolis: University of Minnesota Press.

Muldoon, Paul. 2002. *Poems 1968–1998*. New York: Farrar, Straus, Giroux.

Muldoon, Paul. 2010. *Maggot*. London: Faber and Faber.

Muldoon, Paul. 2015. *One Thousand Things Worth Knowing* [e-book]. New York: Farrar, Straus, Giroux.

Müller, Wolfgang G. 1974. "Der Weg vom Symbolismus zum deutschen und angloamerikanischen Dinggedicht des beginnenden zwanzigsten Jahrhun-derts." *Neophilologus* 58 (2): 157–79.

Müller, Wolfgang G. 2007. "Dinggedicht." In *Reallexikon der deutschen Litera-turwissenschaft*, edited by K. Weimar et al., 1:366–68. Berlin – New York: de Gruyter.

Nápravník, Milan. 1995. *Kniha Moták*. Prague: Mladá fronta.

Needham, Joseph, and Wang Ling. 1956. *Science and Civilisation in China*. Vol. 2, *History of Scientific Thought*. Cambridge: Cambridge University Press.

Neumann, Birgit. 2015. "Präsenz und Evidenz fremder Dinge im Europa des 18. Jahrhunderts: Zur Einleitung." In *Präsenz und Evidenz fremder Dinge im Europa des 18. Jahrhunderts*, edited by B. Neumann, 9–36. Göttingen: Wallstein.

Neumann, Gerhard. 2001. "Rilkes Dinggedicht." In *Poesie als Auftrag. Fest-schrift für Alexander von Bormann*, edited by D. Ottmann and M. Symmank, 143–62. Würzburg: Königshausen & Neumann.

Nezval, Vítězslav. 1937. *Absolutní hrobař.* Prague: Fr. Borový.

Novotný, Pavel 2016a. "Artmannova explozivní báseň." *Souvislosti* 4:4–9.

Novotný, Pavel. 2016b. "Eine der vielen Übersetzungsmöglichkeiten. Zur Übersetzung des Gedichts tom du tümmel H. C. Artmanns." In *Poesie in Bewegung,* edited by W. Krätschmar and P. Novotný, 87–94. Dresden: Thelem.

Okáčová, Marie. 2006. "The Aural-Visual "Symbiosis" in the Poetry of Publilius Optatianus Porfyrius (Towards the Disentanglement of the Mystery of Late-Ancient Expansive Grid-Verse)." In *Laetae segeste: Griechische und lateinische Studien an der Masaryk Universität und Universität Wien,* edited by J. Nechutová and I. Radová, 41–50. Brno: Masarykova univerzita.

Okáčová, Marie. 2007. "Publilius Optatianus Porfyrius: Characteristic Features of Late Ancient Figurative Poetics." *Sborník prací Filozofické fakulty brněnské univerzity* 12:57–71. Brno: Masarykova univerzita.

Oppert, Kurt. 1926. "Das Dinggedicht. Eine Kunstform bei Mörike, Meyer und Rilke." *Deutsche Vierteljahrsschrift für Literaturwissenschaft und Geistesgeschichte* 4:747–83.

Otto, Walter Friedrich. 1934. *Die Götter Griechenlands. Das Bild des Göttlichen im Spiegel der griechischen Geistes.* Frankfurt a. M.: Schulte-Bulmke.

Padel, Ruth. 1992. *In and Out of the Mind: Greek Images of the Tragic Self.* Princeton: Princeton University Press.

Panfilov, Aleksei. 2009. "Izlechenie primusa. Bulgakov i Mandelstam," [on-line] https://www.proza.ru/2009/08/31/809.

Panofsky, Erwin. 1959. "Style and Medium in the Motion Pictures." In *Film: An Anthology,* edited by D. Talbot, 15–32. Berkeley: University of California Press.

Pappas, Alexandra. 2013. "The Treachery of Verbal Images: Viewing the Greek *Technopaegnia.*" In *The Muse at Play: Riddles and Wordplay in Greek and Latin Poetry,* edited by J. Kwapisz, D. Petrain, and M. Szymański, 199–224. Berlin: de Gruyter.

Patiejūnienė, Eglė. 1992. „Įmantrioji" poezija" XVI–XVII a. Lietuvos spaudiniuose, *Senoji Lietuvos literatūra,* 1, Vilnius: Mokslo ir enciklopedijų leidykla.

Patiejūnienė, Eglė. 1998. *Brevitas Ornata: Mažosios literatūros formos XVI–XVII amžiaus Lietuvos Didžiosios Kunigaikštystės spaudiniuose.* Vilnius: Lietuvių literatūros ir tautosakos institutas.

Platelis, Kornelijus. 1995. *Prakalbos upei.* Vilnius: Vaga.

Patillon, Michel, and Giancarlo Bolognesi, eds. 1997. *Aelius Théon, Progymnasmata*. Paris: Les Belles Lettres.

Paulhan, Jean, and Francis Ponge. 1986. *Correspondance*. Vol. 1. Edited by C. Boaretto. Paris: Gallimard.

Pelttari, Aaron. 2014. *The Space that Remains: Reading Latin Poetry in Late Antiquity*. Ithaca, NY: Cornell University Press.

Perrin, Michel J.-L., ed. 1997. *Rabani Mauri In honorem Sanctae Crucis: Corpus Christianorum: Continuatio mediaevalis*, Vol. 100. Turnhout: Brepols.

Perrin, Michel J.-L. 2009. *L'iconographie de la „Gloire à la sainte croix" de Raban Maur*. Turnhout: Brepols.

Petříček, Miroslav. 1997. *Úvod do současné filosofie*. Prague: Herrmann & synové.

Petrovic, Andrej, Petrovic, Ivana, and Edmund Thomas, eds. 2018. *The Materiality of Text – Placement, Perception, and Presence of Inscribed Texts in Classical Antiquity*. Leiden: Brill.

Petrus, Klaus. 1997. *Genese und Analyse: Logik, Rhetorik und Hermeneutik im 17. und 18. Jahrhundert*. Berlin – New York: de Gruyter.

Pipitone, Giuseppe. 2012. *Dalla figura all'interpretazione. Scoli a Optaziano Porfirio: Testo italiano e latino*. Naples: Lofredo.

Plato. 1921. *Theaetetus. Sophist*. Translated by H. N. Fowler. London: William Heinemann.

Platt, Verity. 2011. *Facing the Gods: Epiphany and Representation in Graeco-Roman Art, Literature and Religion*. Cambridge: Cambridge University Press.

Platt, Verity, and Michael Squire. 2018. "Getting to Grips with Classical Art: Rethinking the Haptics of Graeco-Roman Visual Culture." In *Touch and the Ancient Senses*, edited by A. Purves, 75–104. New York – London: Routledge.

Poezia: učebnik. 2016. Edited by N. Azarova, K. Korchagin, D. Kuzmin. Moscow: s. n.

Polara, Giovanni. 1973. *Publilii Optatiani Porfyrii Carmina*. 2 vols. Turin: Paravia.

Polara, Giovanni. 2004. *Optaziano Porfirio: Carmi*. Turin: Unione Tipografico-Editrice Torinese.

Pomerants, Grigory. 2015. *Nekotorye techeniya vostochnogo religioznogo nigilizma*. Khar'kov: Prava čeloveka.

Ponge, Francis. 1988. "Entretien avec Marcel Spada (1979)." *Le Magazine littéraire*, no. 260, (Decembre): 26–33.

Ponge, Francis. 1994. *Selected Poems*. Edited by Margaret Guiton, translated by C. K. Williams, John Montague, Margaret Guiton. Winston-Salem, NC: Wake Fores University Press.

Ponge, Francis. 1997. *Comment une figue de paroles et pourquoi* [1977]. Paris: Garnier-Flammarion.

Ponge, Francis. 1999. *Œuvres complètes* I. Edited by Bernard Beugnot. Paris: Gallimard.

Ponge, Francis. 2002. *Œuvres complètes* II. Edited by Bernard Beugnot. Paris: Gallimard.

Ponge, Francis, and Philippe Sollers. 1970. *Entretiens de Francis Ponge avec Philippe Sollers*. Paris: Éditions du Seuil – Gallimard.

Prioux, Évelyne. 2007. *Regards alexandrins: Histoire et théorie des arts dans l'épigramme hellénistique*. Leuven: Peeters.

Pound, Ezra. 1968. "A Retrospect [1918]." In *Modern Poetry: Essays on Criticism*, edited by J. Hollander, 3–14. London: Oxford University Press.

Preu, Johann Samuel. 1772. *Versuch einer Sismotheologie oder physikalisch-theologische Betrachtung über die Erdbeben*. Nördlingen: Karl Gottlob Becken.

Quan Hou Han wen 全後漢文 1958. In *Quan Shanggu Sandai Qin Han Sanguo Liuchao wen* 全上古三代秦漢三國六朝文. Vol. 1. Edited by Yan Kejun. Beijing: Zhonghua shuju.

Quan Sanguo wen 全三國文. In *Quan Shanggu Sandai Qin Han Sanguo Liuchao wen* 全上古三代秦漢三國六朝文. Vol. 2. Edited by Yan Kejun. Beijing: Zhonghua shuju.

Rabe, Hugo, ed. 1913. *Hermogenis Opera*. Leipzig: Teubner.

Rabe, Hugo, ed. 1926. *Aphthonius Progymnasmata*. Leipzig: Teubner.

Rabe, Hugo, ed. 1928. *Ioannis Sardiani Commentarium in Aphthonii Progymnasmata*. Leipzig: Teubner.

Raby, F. J. E. 1957. *A History of Secular Latin Poetry in the Middle Ages*. 2 vols. 2nd edition. Oxford: Clarendon Press.

Radiohead – Pyramid Song 800% slower. *YouTube*, uploaded by dumaramutsi, 12 Apr. 2014. www.youtube.com/watch?v=XiKWfcy-Z70&t=1325s. Accessed 25 Feb. 2019.

Ratgauz, Mikhail. 1992. "Kuzmin – kinozritel'." *Kinovedcheskiye zapiski* 13:52–86.

Rathlefs, Ernst Ludewig. 1748. *Akridotheologie*. Hannover: Johann Christoph Richter.

Rey, William H. 1978. *Poesie der Antipoesie*. Heidelberg: Lothar Stiehm.

Riegl, Alois. 1923. *Die Entstehung der Barockkunst in Rom*. Edited by A. Burda and M. Dvořák. Vienna: Kunstverlag Anton Schroll.

Rilke, Rainer Maria. 1965. "Rodin." In Rainer Maria Rilke, *Sämtliche Werke*, 5:203–16. Frankfurt a. M.: Insel.

Rilke, Rainer Maria. 1996. *Werke*. Vol. 4, *Schriften*. Frankfurt a. M.: Insel.

Rimbaud, Jean Arthur. 2003. *Rimbaud Complete*. Vol. 1, *Poetry and Prose*. Translated by Wyatt Mason. New York: Modern Library.

Rimbaud, Jean Arthur. 2009. *Œuvres complètes*. Paris: Gallimard.

Rimvydis, Antanas. 1926. *Knyga be vardo*. Kaunas.

Rispoli, Giola M. 1984. "φαντασία ed ἐνάργεια negli scolî all'*Iliade*." *Vichiana* 13:311–39.

Robbe-Grillet, Alain. 1963. *Pour un nouveau roman*. Paris: Éditions de Minuit.

Roberts, Martin. 1989. *The Jeweled Style: Poetry and Poetics in Late Antiquity*. Ithaca, NY: Cornell University Press.

Rocca, Julius. 2003. *Galen On the Brain*. Leiden: Brill.

Romains, Jules. 1983. *La Vie unanime: Poèmes 1904–1907*. Paris: Gallimard.

Ronen, Omry. 1983. *An Approach to Mandel'štam*. Jerusalem: Magnes Press.

Rühl, Meike. 2006. "Panegyrik im Quadrat: Optatian und die intermedialen Tendenzen des spätantiken Herrscherbildes." *Millennium* 3: 75–102.

Rühm, Gerhard, ed. 1985. *Wiener Gruppe*. Hamburg: Rowohlt.

Rühm, Gerhard. 2008. *Aspekte einer erweiterten Poetik*, Berlin: Mathes und Seitz.

Rühmkorf, Peter. 1959. *Irdisches Vergüngen in g*. Hamburg: Rowohlt.

Russell, Donald A., and David Konstan. 2005. *Heraclitus: Homeric Problems*. Atlanta: Society of Biblical Literature.

Ruszar, Józef Maria. 2012. "Apollo i Dionizos: Źródła mądrości poezji i filozofii." In *Między nami a światłem: Bóg i świat w twórczości Zbigniewa Herberta*, edited by G. Halkiewicz-Sojak, J. Ruszar, R. Sioma, 159–81. Toruń – Kraków: JMR Trans-Atlantyk.

Rymkiewicz, Jarosław Materk. "Krzesło." *Twórczość* 1: 50–88.

Sacotte, Mireille, 1991. *Mireille Sacotte présente „Éloges" et „La gloire des rois" de Saint-John Perse*. Paris: Gallimard.

Saint-John Perse. 1967. *Eloges suivi de La Gloire des Rois, Anabase, Exil*. Paris: Gallimard.

Sasse, Sylvia. 2003. *Texte in Aktion: Sprech- und Sprachakte im Moskauer Konzeptualismus.* Munich: Fink.

Savan, Leslie. 2007. "Teflon Is Forever," *Mother Jones,* May/June 2007 [www.motherjones.com/environment/2007/05/teflon-forever/] (25. 2. 2019).

Schapp, Wilhelm. 1925. *Beiträge zur Phänomenologie der Wahrnehmung.* Erlangen: Verlag der Philosophischen Akademie.

Schapp, Wilhelm. 1976. *In Geschichten verstrickt: Zum Sein von Mensch und Ding.* Wiesbaden: B. Heymann.

Schmarsow, August. 1914. "Raumgestaltung als Wesen der architektonischen Schöpfung." *Zeitschrift für Ästhetik und allgemeine Kunstwissenschaft* 9, 1:66–95.

Scheidegger Lämmle, Cédric. 2015. "Einige Pendenzen: Weben und Text in der antiken Literatur." In *Weben und Gewebe in der Antike: Materialität – Repräsentation – Episteme,* edited by H. Harich-Schwarzbauer, 167–208. Oxford: Oxbow Books.

Schierl, Petra, and Cédric Scheidegger Lämmle. 2017. "Herrscherrbilder: Optatian und die Strukturen des Panegyrischen." In *Morphogrammata / The Lettered Art of Optatian: Figuring Cultural Transformations in the Age of Constantine,* edited by M. Squire and J. Wienand, 283–318. Paderborn: Wilhelm Fink.

Schipke, Renate. 2013. *Das Buch in der Spätantik. Herstellung, Form, Ausstattung und Verbreitung in der westlichen Reichshälfte des Imperium Romanum.* Wiesbaden: Reichert.

Schmidt, Arno, and Barthold Heinrich Brockes. 2015. *Irdisches Vergnügen* (CDRom). Hamburg: Hoffmann und Campe.

Schneider, Manfred. 1999. "Das Grauen der Beobachter: Schriften und Bilder des Wahnsinns." In Gerhard Neumann, Günter Oesterle, and Helmut Pfotenhauer, *Bild und Schrift in der Romantik,* 237–249. Würzburg: Königshausen & Neumann.

Scully, Stephen. 2003. "Reading the Shield of Achilles: Terror, Anger, Delight." *Harvard Studies in Classical Philology* 101:29–47.

Segal, Dimitri. 1993. "Istoriya i poetika u Mandelstama. A. Stanovlenie poeticheskogo mira." *Cahiers du monde russe et soviétique* 34, 3:369–413.

Segalen, Victor. 2007. *Stèles.* Trans. Timothy Billings and Christopher Bush. Middletown, CT: Wesleyan University Press.

Sheppard, Anne. 2014. *The Poetics of Phantasia: Imagination in Ancient Aesthetics*. London: Bloomsbury.

Shih, Hsiang-lin 2013. *Jian'an Literature Revisited: Poetic Dialogues in the Last Three Decades of the Han Dynasty*. PhD thesis. University of Washington.

Shindin, Sergei. 1991. "K probleme «Mandelstam i kinematograf»." *Kinovedcheskie zapiski*, no. 10:150–61.

Shteyner, Evgenii. 2002. *Avangard i postroenie novogo cheloveka: Iskusstvo sovetskoi detskoi knigi 1920 godov*. Moscow: NLO.

Silverman, Kaja. 1988. *The Acoustic Mirror: The Female Voice in Psychoanalysis and Cinema*. Bloomington: Indiana University Press.

Šimkus, Vladas. 2009. *Po žeme ir dangum*. Vilnius: Lietuvių literatūros ir tautosakos institutas.

Simmel, Georg. 2001. Brücke und Tür. In Georg Simmel, *Aufsätze und Abhandlungen 1909–1918*, 1:55–61. Frankfurt a. M.: Suhrkamp.

Simonek, Stefan. 1992. *Osip Mandelštam und die ukrainischen Neoklassiker: Zur Wechselbeziehung von Kunst und Zeit*. Munich: Otto Sagner.

Simonini, Laura, and Flaminio Gualdoni. 1978. *Carmi figurati greci e latini*. Pollenza: La Nuova Foglio.

Smolak, Kurt. 1989. "Publilius Optatianus Porfyrius." In *Handbuch der lateinischen Literatur der Antike*. Vol. 5, *Restauration und Erneuerung 284–374*, edited by R. Herzog, 237–43. Munich: C. H. Beck.

Sommer, Manfred. 1996. Abschattung. *Zeitschrift für philosophische Forschung* 50:271–85.

Součková, Milada. 1980. *Baroque in Bohemia*. Ann Arbor: University of Michigan.

Součková, Milada. 1993. *Sešity Josefíny Rykrové*. 2nd edition. Prague: Prostor.

Součková, Milada. 1998. *Dílo Milady Součkové*. Vol. 3, *Kaladý. Svědectví. Mluvící pásmo: (1938–1940)*. Prague: Prostor.

Součková, Milada. 1999. *Dílo Milady Součkové*. Vol. 10, *Případ poezie: Básnické sbírky 1942–1971*. Prague: Prostor.

Součková, Milada. 2009. *Sešity Josefíny Rykrové*. 3rd edition. Prague: Prostor.

Součková, Milada. 2018. *Élenty: Dopisy přátelům 1942–1982 Jindřichu Chalupeckému, Ladislavu a Olze Radimským, Romanu Jakobsonovi, Otakaru Odložilíkovi, Gertrudě Gruberové-Goepfertové, Oldřichu Leškovi, Karlu Milotovi*. Prague: Prostor.

Spier, Jeffrey. 2007. *Late Antique and Early Medieval Gems*. Wiesbaden: Reichert.

Spitzer, Leo. 1962. *Essays on English and American Literature*. Edited by Anna Hatcher. Princeton: Princeton University Press.

Sprigath, Gabriele K. 2004. "Das Dictum des Simonides: Der Vergleich von Dichtung und Malerei." *Poetica* 36:243–80.

Squire, Michael. 2009. *Image and Text in Graeco-Roman Antiquity*. Cambridge: Cambridge University Press.

Squire, Michael. 2010. "Making Myron's Cow Moo? Ecphrastic Epigram and the Poetics of Simulation." *American Journal of Philology* 131, no. 4 (Winter): 589–634.

Squire, Michael. 2011. *The Iliad in a Nutshell: Visualizing Epic on the* Tabulae Iliacae. Oxford: Oxford University Press.

Squire, Michael. 2013a. "Ekphrasis at the Forge and the Forging of Ekphrasis: The Shield of Achilles in Graeco-Roman Word and Image." *Word & Image* 29:157–91.

Squire, Michael. 2013b. "Invertire l'*ekphrasis*: L'epigramma ellenistico e la traslazione di parola e immagine," *Estetica: Studi e ricerche* 1:109–36.

Squire, Michael. 2015a. Patterns of significance: Publilius Optatianus Porfyrius and the Figurations of Meaning. In *Images and Texts: Papers in Honour of Professor E. W. Handley, CBE, FBA*, edited by R. Green, M. Edwards, 87–120. London: University of London Institute of Classical Studies.

Squire, Michael. 2015b. Ecphrasis: "Visual and Verbal Interactions in Ancient Greek and Latin Literature." *Oxford Handbooks Online* [DOI:10.1093/oxfordhb/9780199935390.013.58].

Squire, Michael. 2016a. 'How to Read a Roman Portrait'? Optatian Porfyry, Constantine and the *uultus Augusti*." *Papers of the British School at Rome* 84:179–240.

Squire, Michael. 2016b. "Sémantique de l'échelle dans l'art et la poésie hellénistiques." In *D'Alexandre à Auguste: Dynamiques de la création dans les arts visuels et la poésie*, edited by P. Linant de Bellefonds, É. Prioux, and A. Rouveret, 183–200. Rennes: Presses Universitaires de Rennes.

Squire, Michael. 2017a. "POP art: The Optical Poetics of Publilius Optatianus Porfyrius." In *The Poetics of Late Latin Literature*, edited by J. Elsner and J. Hernández Lobato, 25–99. Oxford: Oxford University Press.

Squire, Michael. 2017b. "Optatian and His Lettered Art: A Kaleidoscopic Lens on Late Antiquity." In *Morphogrammata / The Lettered Art of Optatian: Figuring Cultural Transformations in the Age of Constantine*, edited by M. Squire and J. Wienand, 55–120. Paderborn: Wilhelm Fink.

Squire, Michael. 2017c. "Framing Texts: Introduction." In *The Frame in Classical Art: A Cultural History*, edited by V. J. Platt and M. Squire, 502–517. Cambridge: Cambridge University Press.

Squire, Michael. 2018. "A Picture of Ecphrasis? Re-Viewing the Homeric Shield of Achilles in the Younger Philostratus (*Imagines* 10)." In *Gaze, Vision, and Visuality in Ancient Greek Literature*, edited by A. Kampakoglou and A. Novokhatko, 357–417. Berlin: de Gruyter.

Squire, Michael, and Jaś Elsner. 2016. "Homer and the Ekphrasists: Text and Picture in the Elder Philostratus' "Scamander" (*Imagines* I.1)." In *The Archaeology of Greece and Rome: Studies in Honour of Anthony Snodgrass*, edited by J. Bintliff and K. Rutter, 57–100. Edinburgh: Edinburgh University Press.

Squire, Michael, and Christopher L. Whitton. 2016. "*Machina sacra*: Optatian and the lettered art of the Christogram." In *Graphic Signs of Identity, Faith, and Power in Late Antiquity and the Early Middle Ages*, edited by I. Garipzanov, C. Goodson, and H. Maguire, 45–108. Turnhout: Brepols Publishers.

Squire, Michael, and Johannes Wienand, eds. 2017. *Morphogrammata / The Lettered Art of Optatian: Figuring Cultural Transformations in the Age of Constantine*. Paderborn: Wilhelm Fink.

Staiger, Emil. 1990. *Les Concepts fondamentaux de la poétique*. Translated by R. Célis and M. Gennart. Bruxelles: Lebeer-Hossmann 1990.

Stanton, Graham N. 2004. "The Early Christian Preference for the Codex." In *The Earliest Gospels: The Origins and Transmission of the Earliest Christian Gospels: The Contribution of the Chester Beatty Gospel Codex P45*, edited by C. Horton, 40–49. London: Continuum International Publishing Group.

Stcherbatsky, Theodor. 1927. *The Conception of Buddhist Nirvana*. Leningrad: The USSR Academy of Sciences.

Sternberg, Meir. 1981. Ordering the Unordered. Time, Space, and Descriptive Coherence. *Yale French Studies* 61:60–88.

Stewart, Susan. 1978. *Nonsense: Aspects of Intertextuality in Folklore and Literature*. Baltimore: Johns Hopkins University Press.

Stolz-Hladká, Zuzana. 2001. "Tvořivá slova Milady Součkové." In *Neznámý člověk Milada Součková*, edited by M. Bauer, 22–33. Praha: Ústav pro českou literaturu AV ČR.

Stout, John C. 2018. *Objects Observed: The Poetry of Things in Twentieth-Century France and America*. Toronto: University of Toronto Press.

Štrpka, Ivan. 2016. *Fragment (rytierskeho) lesa.* Levoča: Modrý Peter.

Strodel, Silvia. 2002. *Zur Überlieferung und zum Verständnis der hellenistischen Technopaegnien.* Frankfurt a. M.: Peter Lang.

Sullivan, Shirley D. 1988. *Psychological Activity in Homer: A Study of Phren.* Ottawa: Carleton University Press.

Šuman, Záviš. 2012. "Energie v raném básnickém díle Saint-Johna Perse." *Svět literatury* 22 (45): 148–72.

Sun Chang, Kang-I 1986. "Symbolic and Allegorical Meanings in the Yüeh-fu pu-t'i Poem Series." *Harvard Journal of Asiatic Studies* 46 (2): 353–85.

Sun Xidan and He Xiguang, eds. 2011. *Liji jijie.* Peking: Beijing da xue chubanshe.

Suzuki, Daisetz. 1960. *Manual of Zen Buddhism.* New York: Grove Press.

Taplin, Oliver. 1980. "The Shield of Achilles within the *Iliad.*" *Greece and Rome* 27, no. 1 (April): 1–21.

Tavares, Salette. 1968. "Aranha." In *Concrete Poetry: A World View,* edited by M. E. Solt, 190. Bloomington: Indiana University Press.

Teige, Karel. 1966. "Nové umění proletářské [1922]." In Karel Teige, *Výbor z díla.* Vol. 1, *Svět stavby a básně: Studie z dvacátých let,* 33–72. Prague: Československý spisovatel.

Thein, Karel. 2022. *Ecphrastic Shields in Graeco-Roman Literature: The World's Forge.* Abingdon – New York: Routledge.

Tieleman, Teun. 1996. *Galen and Chrysippus On the Soul. Argument and Refutation in the De Placitis Books II–III.* Leiden: Brill.

Tieleman, Teun. 2002. "Galen on the Seat of the Intellect: Anatomical Experiment and Philosophical Tradition." In *Science and Mathematics in Ancient Greek Culture,* edited by C. J. Tuplin and T. E. Rihll, 254–73. Oxford: Oxford University Press.

Todorov, Tzvetan. 1985. *Théories du symbole.* Paris: Éditions du Seuil.

Tokarev, Dmitry. 2013. "Deskriptivnyi i narrativnyi aspekty ekfrasisa («Mertvyi Khristos» Gol'beyna—Dostoyevskogo i «Sikstinskaya madonna» Rafaelya—Zhukovskogo)." In *"Nevyrazimo vyrazimoe": Ekfrasis i problemy reprezentatsii vizual'nogo v khudozhestvennom tekste,* edited by D. Tokarev, 61–110. Moscow: Novoye literaturnoye obozrenie.

Troll, Wilhelm. 1956. "Die Urbildlichkeit der organischen Gestaltung und Goethes Prinzip der „variablen Proportionen"." *Neue Hefte zur Morphologie* 2:64–76.

Vaičiūnaitė, Judita. 1985. *Nemigos aitvaras.* Vilnius: Vaga.

Valéry, Paul. 1960. Œuvres. Vol. 2. Paris: Gallimard.

Vendler, Helen. 1997. "Anglo-Celtic Attitudes." New York Review of Books 44, 6. November, no. 17:57–58.

Vietta, Sylvio. 1992. Die literarische Moderne. Stuttgart: Metzler.

The Vintage Book of Contemporary World Poetry. 1996. Edited by J. D. McClatchy. [New York]: Vintage Books.

Vitry, Paul. 1894. "Étude sur les épigrammes de l'Anthologie Palatine qui contiennent la description d'une œuvre d'art." Revue Archéologique 24 (January–June): 315–67.

Vos, Eric. 1987. "The Visual Turn in Poetry: Nominalistic Contributions to Literary Semiotics, Exemplified by the Case of Concrete Poetry." New Literary History 18, no. 3, (Spring): 559–81.

Waters, William. 2010. "The Elusiveness of Things in Rilke's Dinggedichte." In Das lyrische Bild, edited by R. Simon, N. Herres, and C. Lorincz, 321–36. Basel: Wilhelm Fink.

Wandorf, Haiko. 2003. Ekphrasis: Kunstbeschreibungen und virtuelle Räume in der Literatur des Mittelalters. Berlin: de Gruyter.

Watts, Michael. 2011. The Philosophy of Heidegger. Cambridge: Cambridge University Press.

Webb, Ruth. 1999. Ekphrasis Ancient and Modern: The Invention of a Genre. Word & Image 15, 1:7–18.

Webb, Ruth. 2009. Ekphrasis, Imagination and Persuasion in Ancient Rhetorical Practice and Theory. Farnham: Ashgate.

Webb, Ruth. 2016. "Sight and Insight: Theorizing Vision, Emotion and Imagination in Ancient Rhetoric." In Sight and the Ancient Senses, edited by M. Squire, 205–219. London: Routledge.

Weiner, Richard. 1916. "Jean Baptiste Chardin." Translated by J. V. Löwenbach. In Jüngste Tschechische Lyrik: Eine Anthologie, edited by F. Pfemfert, 113–114. Berlin: Verlag der Wochenschrift Die Aktion.

Weiner, Richard. 1912. Měšťák mezi básníky, Volné směry 16 (12–13): 305–307.

Weiner, Richard. 1997. Básně. Praha: Torst.

Welser, Paul. 1595. Publilii Optatiani Porphyrii Panegyricus dictus Constantino Augusto. Augsburg: Ad insigne Pinus.

Werberger, Annette. 2005. Postsymbolistisches Schreiben: Studien zur Poetik des Akmeismus und Osip Mandelštams. Munich: Sagner.

"What Kind of Sushi is Highest in Mercury?" Huffpost, 26 Nov. 2013. www .huffpost.com/entry/sushi-mercury_n_4339401. Accessed 15. Oct. 2018.

"What the Yuck: Mercury poisoning from sushi?" *CNN*, 8 Apr. 2011. thechart
.blogs.cnn.com/2011/04/08/what-the-yuck-mercury-poisoning-from-sushi/.
Accessed Oct. 15, 2018.

Wienand, Johannes. 2012. *Der Kaiser als Sieger: Metamorphosen triumphaler
Herrschaft unter Constantin I.* Berlin: Akademie Verlag.

Wienand, Johannes. 2017. "Publilius Optatianus Porfyrius: The Man and his
Book." In *Morphogrammata / The Lettered Art of Optatian: Figuring Cultural
Transformations in the Age of Constantine*, edited by M. Squire and
J. Wienand, 121–63. Paderborn: Wilhelm Fink.

Williams, A. R. 2014. "Tuna Lover's Dilemma: To Eat or Not to Eat?" *National
Geographic*, 21 Feb. news.nationalgeographic.com/news/2014/02/140220
-tuna-guide-skipjack-yellowfin-albacore-bluefin-bigeye-sushi/. Accessed
Oct. 15, 2018.

Williams, William Carlos. 1986. *The Collected Poems of William Carlos
Williams.* Vol. 1, *1909–1939*, edited by A. Walton Litz and C. MacGowan.
New York: A New Directions Book.

Wollheim, Richard. 1986. "Imagination and Pictorial Understanding." *Proceed-
ings of the Aristotelian Society* suppl. vol. 60:45–60.

Wolker, Jiří. 1953. *Básně.* Prague: SNKLHU.

Woolf, Greg. 1996. "Monumental Writing and the Expansion of Roman
Society in the Early Empire." *Journal of Roman Studies* 86:22–39.

Yan Kejun 嚴可均, ed. 1958. *Quan Shanggu Sandai Qin Han Sanguo Liuchao
wen* 全上古三代秦漢三國六朝文. 4 vols. Beijing: Zhonghua shuju.

Yu Shaochu 俞紹初, ed. 1989. *Jian'an qizi ji* 建安七子集. Beijing: Zhonghua
shuju.

Translated by Jonas Zdanys. 1995. *Four Poets of Lithuania.* Vilnius: Vaga.

Zeitlin, Froma I. 2013. Figure: Ekphrasis. *Greece and Rome* 60.1: 17–31.

Zheng, Yuyu 鄭毓瑜 2012. *Yin pi lian lei: Wenxue yanjiu de guanjianci* 引譬連
類 ： 文學研究的關鍵詞. Taibei: Lianjing chuban gongsi.

Zirra, Maria. 2017. "Shelf Lives: Nonhuman Agency and Seamus
Heaney's Vibrant Memory Objects." *Parallax* 23, no. 4: 458–73.

Zumthor, Peter. 2006. *Atmosphären. Architektonische Umgebungen: Die Dinge
um mich herum.* Basel: Birkhäuser.

Žižek, Slavoj. 2008. *The Ticklish Subject: The Absent Centre of Political Ontology.*
London: Verso.

.

Index